RIGHTS, CULTURE, AND THE LAW
THEMES FROM THE LEGAL AND POLITICAL PHILOSOPHY
OF JOSEPH RAZ

Rights, Culture, and the Law

Themes from the Legal and Political Philosophy of Joseph Raz

Edited by

LUKAS H. MEYER
STANLEY L. PAULSON
and
THOMAS W. POGGE

OXFORD
UNIVERSITY PRESS

OXFORD
UNIVERSITY PRESS

Great Clarendon Street, Oxford OX2 6DP

Oxford University Press is a department of the University of Oxford.
It furthers the University's objective of excellence in research, scholarship,
and education by publishing worldwide in

Oxford New York

Auckland Cape Town Dar es Salaam Hong Kong Karachi
Kuala Lumpur Madrid Melbourne Mexico City Nairobi
New Delhi Shanghai Taipei Toronto
With offices in
Argentina Austria Brazil Chile Czech Republic France Greece
Guatemala Hungary Italy Japan South Korea Poland Portugal
Singapore Switzerland Thailand Turkey Ukraine Vietnam

Oxford is a registered trade mark of Oxford University Press
in the UK and in certain other countries

Published in the United States
by Oxford University Press Inc., New York

© L. H. Meyer, S. L. Paulson, and T. W. Pogge 2003

The moral rights of the author have been asserted

Database right Oxford University Press (maker)

Reprinted 2006

ISBN 0-19-924825-7

Preface

Drafts of most of the chapters of this book were first presented and discussed at the 'Colloquium on the Work of Joseph Raz' in Bielefeld, held in July 1999.

The editors would like to thank the Center for Interdisciplinary Studies (ZiF) at the University of Bielefeld for hosting the Colloquium, Profs. Ralf Dreier and Gerhard Sprenger for their advice, and, last but not least, Ms Marina Hoffmann of the Center for all that she did in organizing the event.

L. H. MEYER, S. L. PAULSON, T. W. POGGE

Contents

COMMENTS AND RESPONSES

List of Contributors

Robert Alexy is Professor of Constitutional Law and Jurisprudence, Christian-Albrecht-University of Kiel, Germany.

Rüdiger Bittner is Professor of Philosophy, University of Bielefeld, Germany.

Bruno Celano is Professor of Legal Philosophy, University of Palermo, Italy.

Timothy A.O. Endicott is Tutor in Law and a Fellow of Balliol College, Oxford.

James Griffin is White Professor of Moral Philosophy, University of Oxford.

Will Kymlicka is Queen's National Scholar in the Philosophy Department of Queen's University, Canada.

Andrei Marmor is Professor of Law, University of Southern California Law School and Associate Professor, Interdisciplinary Center, Hertzlyia, Israel.

Lukas H. Meyer is 'Wissenschaftlicher Assistent' for Political Theory, University of Bremen, Germany.

J. E. Penner is Senior Lecturer in Law, London School of Economics.

Bernhard Peters is Professor of Political Theory, University of Bremen, Germany.

Joseph Raz is Professor of the Philosophy of Law, University of Oxford, and Visiting Professor, Law School, Columbia University, New York.

Hillel Steiner is Professor of Political Philosophy, Centre of Philosophy, University of Manchester.

Yael (Yuli) Tamir is Professor of Political Philosophy, Tel Aviv University.

Jeremy Waldron is Maurice and Hilda Friedman Professor of Law and Director of the Center for Law and Philosophy, School of Law, Columbia University, New York.

Editors

Lukas H. Meyer (see above)

Stanley L. Paulson is Professor of Law and of Philosophy, Washington University in St. Louis.

Thomas W. Pogge is Associate Professor of Philosophy, Columbia University, New York.

ISSUES IN JURISPRUDENCE AND LEGAL PHILOSOPHY: THE NATURE OF LAW, PRACTICAL REASON, AUTHORITY, SOURCES OF AND GAPS IN THE LAW

1

The Nature of Arguments about the Nature of Law

ROBERT ALEXY*

I. Three dimensions and two levels of reflexivity

To know what one is doing in doing something seems—at least *prima facie*—to be an intrinsic value. Knowing what one is doing in doing something is cognitive reflexivity. The intrinsic value of cognitive reflexivity is one of the main reasons for engaging in legal philosophy. It is, so to speak, the purely philosophical value of legal philosophy. This intrinsic or purely philosophical reason for legal philosophy does not, however, exhaust its value. In addition to this philosophical dimension, legal philosophy has both a technical and a critical dimension. The technical value of legal philosophy consists in the clarification of legal concepts, the architecture of the legal system, and the structure of legal argumentation. This clarification is achieved by means of conceptual and logical analysis. Just as with any analysis, this analysis, too, has the intrinsic value just mentioned. In addition, it has an extrinsic value. Legal systems are always in danger of becoming over-complex, and of acquiring incompatible elements. Legal philosophy can help here, at least to a certain degree, by means of analysis that contributes to precision, transparency, and coherence. This may have consequences not only in traditional areas of jurisprudence but also in modern fields—such as, for instance, in the application of artificial intelligence in law. Legal philosophy has not only a purely philosophical and a technical value, but also a critical value. The latter concerns the improvement of positive law by means of philosophical criticism. Legal philosophy has a great tradition in this respect. For example, human rights would not have been institutionalized without the contribution of legal philosophy. This critical responsibility will last for as long as the law lasts. Although these three values are closely connected, we can nevertheless say that legal philosophy is valuable owing to its reflexivity in three different dimensions: the philosophical, the technical, and the critical dimension.

Now not only is the object of legal philosophy, the law, an activity, but legal philosophy is itself an activity. If reflexivity is an intrinsic value, this must also be true of legal philosophy. Reflexivity is always in danger of infinite reiteration. This danger, however, seems not to be real if we move just one level further and

*I should like to thank Stanley L. Paulson for advice on matters of English style.

ask what we are doing when we engage in legal philosophy. This question, again, is of interest for three reasons. Its philosophical value is obvious. Its technical effects are easily demonstrated, too. Reflection about what we are doing when we think about law may enhance our reflection about law by making it more precise, transparent, and coherent. Enhancing in this way one's reflection about law may contribute to an enhancement of law itself. Finally, the role of the critical dimension on the meta-meta-level is defined by the question why and how we ought to be active at the meta-level, that is, in legal philosophy. So it is that critical or normative reflexivity joins the cognitive at the meta-meta-level, too. We not only ask what we are doing when we engage in legal philosophy, but also why and how we ought to engage in legal philosophy.

Legal philosophy is argumentation about the nature of law. The reflection on legal philosophy is, therefore, a reflection on the nature of arguments about the nature of law. Law is a highly complex entity. This is the reason why, as Joseph Raz puts it, 'the list of the essential properties of law is indefinite'.[1] All, or at least nearly all, essential properties of law are topics of a seemingly never-ending dispute. The number of arguments put forward in this dispute are, as always, even greater than the number of problems that they deal with. It is, therefore, impossible to consider all the arguments found in legal philosophy. For this reason, I will begin with an attempt to identify the main problems concerning the nature of law and thereafter concentrate on certain aspects of these problems. Proceeding in this fashion, it may, I hope, become clear not only what I am dealing with when I attempt to discuss the nature of arguments about the nature of law, but also which essential properties I leave out of consideration.

II. THE THREE MAIN PROBLEMS CONCERNING THE NATURE OF LAW

If law as a whole is a single entity, then it is not possible that the main problems of the nature of law lend themselves to examination in complete separation, one from another. The fact, however, that the problems are connected does not mean that they cannot be distinguished.

With this proviso, three problems can be identified. Taken together, they define the problem of the nature of law. The first problem addresses the question: In what kind of entities does the law consist, and how are these entities connected such that they form the overarching entity we call 'law'? The second problem concerns the social reality of law, that is, the real or factual dimension of law. This problem has three centres. The first is the relationship between law and coercion or force; the second, the relationship between law and the institutionalization of norm-creating and norm-applying procedures; and the third, the relationship between law and actual acceptance or approval. The subjects of law are persons with the capacity

---

[1] Joseph Raz, 'On the Nature of Law', *Archives for Philosophy of Law and Social Philosophy*, 82 (1996), 1–25, 6.

to act on reasons and, often, an interest in doing so. The acceptance of law's authority as an essential part of law's social reality is, therefore, closely connected with the third problem, which concerns the correctness or legitimacy of law. Here the main question is the relationship between law and morality. To take up this question is to take up the ideal or critical dimension of law. It is this triad of problems that, taken together, defines the nucleus of the problem of the nature of law. Our subject matter is not the nature of law as such, but the nature of arguments about the nature of law. In what follows I will draw out certain aspects of these three problems as objects of my analysis.

III. THE NATURE OF THE ELEMENTS OF LAW

The first part of the first question, that is, the question of what kind of entities does the law consist, is the most fundamental issue. A classical answer to this question is to be found in Hans Kelsen, who, in the first edition of his Pure Theory of Law (*Reine Rechtslehre*) defines 'law as norm',[2] and norms as meaning,[3] and the 'unique sense' of this meaning as 'ought', and 'ought' as a 'category'.[4] This is the language in which abstract entities are described. Kelsen insists that norms—and thus, law—can be reduced neither to physical events nor to psychical processes. They belong to an ideal reality, not to natural reality.[5] The question, however, whether there exists, in addition to the physical and the psychical world, such a world of abstract semantic or ideal entities, that is, a 'third realm' in the sense of Frege,[6] is one of the main problems of philosophy. It concerns philosophy as *metaphysica generalis sive ontologia*. This shows us that one class of arguments about the nature of law is genuinely philosophical in nature. This applies not only to authors like Kelsen, who attempt to employ transcendental arguments in order to show that the 'ought' as a 'relative *a priori* category'[7] constitutes law as an ideal reality. It also applies to sceptical authors, who try to reduce law to psychical or even to physical facts. One such example of reductionism is to be found in Karl Olivecrona, who, with an eye to Kelsen, maintains that '[t]he rules of law are a natural cause—among others—of the actions of the judges in cases of ligitation as well as of the behaviour in general of people in relation to each other',[8] and that the 'ought' is not more than 'a verbal expression in conjunction with certain emotions'.[9] The problem

---

[2] Hans Kelsen, *Introduction to the Problems of Legal Theory*, a translation, by B. Litschewski Paulson and S.L. Paulson, of the first edition of the *Reine Rechtslehre* (1934), (Oxford: Clarendon Press, 1992), 13.

[3] Ibid., 11, 14.   [4] Ibid., 24.   [5] Ibid., 15.

[6] Gottlob Frege, 'The Thought: A Logical Inquiry', trans. A.M. Quinton and M. Quinton, in *Philosophical Logic*, ed. P.F. Strawson (Oxford: Oxford University Press, 1967), 17–38, 29.

[7] Kelsen (n. 2), 24.

[8] Karl Olivecrona, *Law as Fact* (Copenhagen: Einar Munksgaard, and London: Humphrey Milford, 1939), 16. Olivecrona explicitly declares his enterprise as reductionistic: 'My purpose is to reduce our picture of the law in order to make it tally with existing objective reality', ibid., 27.

[9] Ibid., 21.

of reductionism, too, is a genuine philosophical problem. Not only the non-sceptic, who pleads for idealistic solutions in metaphysics or epistemology, argues philosophically. A sceptic who endorses some species of naturalism does so as well.

Thus far, we have arrived at a first answer to our question concerning the nature of arguments about the nature of law: one class of arguments is genuinely philosophical in nature, for these arguments are applied to solve metaphysical (or ontological) and epistemological problems. But what are metaphysical and epistemological arguments? At this point I will stop, lest I should move too far away from the law. I must rest content with the observation that metaphysical (or ontological) arguments, which concern the question of what there is, and epistemological arguments, which concern the question of how we can know something, cannot be avoided in legal philosophy—not, at any rate, if legal philosophy is going to inform us about the nature of law.

IV. LAW AND COERCION

The second problem about the nature of law, the problem of the social reality of law, can, as we have seen, be broken down into three sub-problems. I will concentrate on the first of these; namely, the problem of the relationship between law and coercion or force. It seems to be an empirical fact that law generally includes the application of coercion based on the decisions of officials who represent the legal community. But is this necessarily so? Does coercion belong to the nature of law? This will be the case if the concept of law includes the concept of coercion. The answer to this question is contested. A positive answer is to be found in an author already mentioned, namely Kelsen. According to Kelsen, the concept of norm or the category designated by 'ought' is the *genus proximum*, and the concept of coercion, the *differentia specifica* of the law.[10] This counts as a clear case of including the concept of coercion within the concept of law. The opposite view is held by Hermann Kantorowicz who states that the value of different definitions of law 'must be judged by their comparative usefulness'.[11] To include the concept of coercion—Kantorowicz uses the expression 'enforceability'[12]—within the concept of law would rule out Grotius's *Ius belli ac pacis* (1625) in a history of legal science, for this work concerns international law in the form of natural law, which, in turn, is not 'enforced by law courts'.[13]

What kinds of arguments are available to settle this dispute concerning the question whether coercion belongs to the nature of law? It seems useful to distinguish two classes of arguments: conceptual arguments based on the use of

---

[10] Kelsen (n. 2), 26.
[11] Hermann Kantorowicz, *The Definition of Law*, ed. A.H. Campbell (Cambridge: Cambridge University Press, 1958), 6.   [12] Ibid., 59.
[13] Ibid., 14.

language, and practical or normative arguments based on the idea of making the best of a social practice in the light of its functions or tasks. I shall take up the conceptual argument first.

The analysis of the use of language is, as J. L. Austin aptly remarked, certainly '*not* the last word', but it provides a starting point for the analysis or—as Austin put it—a '*first* word'.[14] I shall attempt to confirm this by presenting a conceptual argument as the first word and a practical or normative argument as the last word. The conceptual argument proceeds by confronting, with the way we use the expression 'law', two theses about the relationship between law and coercion: the extreme coercion thesis and the extreme non-coercion thesis. The extreme coercion thesis maintains that all norms of any legal system are norms enforceable by legally issued sanctions[15] and that coercion is the only motivation for all participants to comply with the law. This is the closest conceivable connection between law and coercion. The extreme coercion thesis raises serious logical and empirical problems that need not be taken up here. It must suffice to say that a thesis of this extreme character is not presupposed by the ordinary use of the expression 'law'. It is, to give just one example, possible to designate non-enforceable norms of the constitution as 'law' without violating any rules of language. Legal as well as ordinary language is less rigid than the extreme coercion thesis. Far more interesting than this thesis is its opposite: the extreme non-coercion thesis. The extreme non-coercion thesis says that something can be a legal system in spite of the fact that it includes no norm that may, or indeed must, be enforced either by officials or by individuals or states in defence of their rights, so that coercion can never be a motivation for any participant of the legal system to comply with the law. The meaning presently inherent in the expression 'law' makes it impossible to apply this expression to a system of norms as described by the extreme non-coercion thesis. Such a system would be a system of morality in the Kantian sense, but not a legal system. It is required by the meaning of the concept of law, as presently used, that at least some norms of the legal system are enforceable and that coercion, at least sometimes and for some persons, can be a motivation to comply with the law. In this sense it is analytically true that law is connected with coercion.[16]

---

[14] J.L. Austin, 'A Plea for Excuses', in Austin, *Philosophical Papers*, ed. J.O. Urmson and G.J. Warnock, 2nd edn. (Oxford: Clarendon Press, 1970), 175–204, 185.

[15] Rudolf von Jhering comes quite close to this part of the extreme coercion thesis when he reproaches Georg Puchta with having not 'recoiled in horror from this monstrous idea of a legal norm without legal coercion'. A legal norm which is not enforceable by legally issued sanctions is said to be a 'contradiction in itself, a fire that is not burning, a light that is not shining'. Rudolf von Jhering, *Law as a Means to an End*, a translation, by I. Husik, of the second edition of *Der Zweck im Recht*, vol. 1 (1884) (Boston Book Co., 1913), 241 (trans. altered).

[16] The sentence that the concept of law necessarily includes the concept of coercion, does not imply that the concept of a legal norm also includes this concept. That a system of norms is a legal system only presupposes that a certain number of norms belonging to this system are enforceable; it is not presupposed that all norms belonging to it have this property.

The use of language can change. It is for this reason that I referred to the concept of law 'as presently used'. The necessity of a connection between law and coercion based on the use of language is, therefore, a relative necessity.[17] It is a necessity relative to the present structure of the concept of law.

An absolute necessity of the connection between law and coercion would presuppose that the present structure of the concept of law is necessary, too. Here the second class of arguments mentioned above, the practical or normative arguments, comes into play. These arguments show that the present structure of the concept of law exhibits a practical or normative necessity. Practical or normative arguments are applied when it is argued that law itself or some features of law are necessary in order to fulfil certain functions or tasks or to comply with certain norms or values. It is useful to distinguish three arguments in which an effort to establish the practical necessity of law is carried out. Each of these three arguments consists of a reason why morality as such is insufficient to resolve the problems of social co-ordination and co-operation. The first reason concerns the problem of practical knowledge. There are a great many practical questions about which never-ending debate is possible. Kant therefore demands that the rights of the citizens be determined by law. This is a central aspect of the authoritative nature of law.[18] The second reason is that a solution to the cognitive problem is not enough. In order to secure the rights of citizens, the determination of these rights by legislation and adjudication must be completed, as Kant puts it, by 'public lawful external coercion'. Determination and enforcement can never produce perfect legal certainty but they can produce legal certainty that is adequate. Through these means, law surmounts the state of nature, in which we 'can never be secure against violence from one another'.[19] Determination and enforcement not only avoid the atrocities of civil war. They are also necessary in order to avoid the erosion of law that will occur if it can be violated without cost. Only in this way can the 'assurance' be achieved which is the basis of a 'decent life in society and [the] successful pursuit of ends and projects'.[20] Determination and enforcement are completed by means of a third reason for the necessity of law: organization. Numerous moral demands and desirable aims such as unemployment benefits or support of countries in need cannot be achieved through spontaneous moral action. Organization is necessary, and organization presupposes law. Determination, enforcement, and organization, taken together, promote not only the value of

---

[17] The counterpart to relative necessity is absolute necessity. Absolute necessity implies the immunity of a conceptual scheme from revision. Relative necessity is not necessity *of* the conceptual scheme, but necessity *within* the conceptual scheme. See on this H.P. Grice and P.F. Strawson, 'In Defence of a Dogma', *The Philosophical Review*, 65 (1956), 141–58, 157–8.

[18] See Raz (n. 1), 17–18.

[19] Immanuel Kant, *The Metaphysics of Morals*, trans. M. Gregor (Cambridge: Cambridge University Press, 1991), 124.

[20] Gerald J. Postema, 'Law's Autonomy and Public Practical Reason', in *The Autonomy of Law*, ed. R.P. George (Oxford: Clarendon Press, 1996), 79–118, 89–90.

legal certainty but also the value of efficiency. Legal certainty and efficiency are the two formal and minimal values of law. Whoever adheres to these values must endorse the law, including, when necessary, its enforcement by coercion.

This is the point at which the conceptual and the practical or normative argument are connected. It is not by chance that the present structure of the concept of law includes the concept of coercion. Coercion is necessary if law is to be a social practice that fulfils its basic formal functions as defined by the values of legal certainty and efficiency. Understanding a social practice presupposes understanding its underlying values and conceiving it as an attempt to make the best of these values in view of actual obstacles and colliding values external to it. This hermeneutic principle explains why the present meaning of the expression 'law' includes the concept of coercion. The social practice to which we refer when we use the concept of law must have the use of coercion at its disposal if it is to be as good as it can be. As long as the world and its human inhabitants are as they are, the practical necessity of norms backed by the threat of coercion exists. This practical necessity is mirrored in the conceptual necessity of the present structure of the concept of law.

With Kantorowicz in mind, one might object that all of this applies only to law as created and administered by officials of a centrally organized system, but not to international law as found in Hugo Grotius's *Ius belli ac pacis*. This, however, is not the case, notwithstanding the fact that today's international law is not the same as that of Grotius. Specifically, it is not the case for two reasons: the first is that there exists the possibility of lawful coercion in international law even if centrally organized sanctions are lacking. The plainest example is the 'inherent'[21] right of a state to counter an armed attack by force of arms. In this case, Kant's famous dictum 'Right and authorization to use coercion therefore mean one and the same thing'[22] applies without modification. This is the reason why the extreme non-coercion thesis presented above contains the clause 'or by individuals or states in defence of their rights'. So far, my concern has been with the conceptual argument. The second point stems from the practical argument and the hermeneutic perspective. A system of legal norms lacking centrally organized adjudication and enforcement is an imperfect system of law. To be something in an imperfect way does not mean, however, not to be that thing.

V. LAW AND MORALITY

The third main problem of the nature of law is the problem of the relationship between law and morality. This problem comprises many questions. The most fundamental one is whether there exists any kind of necessary connection between law and morality. The two most elementary and general answers are the separability and the connection thesis. The separability thesis says that there

---

[21] Compare, on this expression, Art. 51 of the UN Charter.   [22] Kant (n. 19), 58.

is no necessary connection between law and morality. The separability thesis, surely, does not exhaust legal positivism. But it is found at its core. It is impossible to be a positivist without adhering to the separability thesis. The separability thesis is, therefore, necessarily presupposed by legal positivism. This means that the negation of the separability thesis necessarily leads to non-positivism. The negation of the separability thesis is the connection thesis. The connection thesis says that there exists at least one kind of necessary connection between law and morality. Jules Coleman calls a version of legal positivism which consists of nothing more than the separability thesis 'negative positivism' and declares negative positivism to be 'true, but uninteresting'.[23] I will defend the thesis that the separability thesis and, with it, negative positivism is false. This has consequences for the question whether the separability thesis is interesting. Negative positivism, as an exclusively negative thesis, may not be very interesting as a thesis about the nature of law from the point of view of positivism. But this does not mean that the separability thesis is uninteresting. Should its opposite, the connection thesis, be true, the nature of law would appear in a completely different light. If the nature of law is of any interest, then the opposite of a thesis that casts the nature of law in a completely different light is itself of interest.

The connection thesis is true if there exists at least one kind of necessary connection between law and morality. Very different kinds of necessary connection are conceivable. Here the primary question is not whether there exist necessary connections between law and morality. Our main topic is the nature of arguments for and against the connection or separability thesis. I will concentrate on two arguments for the connection thesis and against the separability thesis that are quite different in nature from each other: the argument from correctness and the argument from extreme injustice. The first is a paradigm case of a conceptual argument, the second, a paradigm case of a normative argument.

1. The argument from correctness

The argument from correctness proceeds in two steps. In a first step, the attempt is made to show that law necessarily raises a claim to correctness. The second step consists in explaining that this claim implies a necessary connection between law and morality.[24]

How is it possible to show that law necessarily raises a claim to correctness? Philip Soper has argued that the question of which kinds of claims are raised by

---

[23] Jules Coleman, 'Authority and Reason', in *The Autonomy of Law* (n. 20), 287–319, 316.

[24] The claim to correctness—together with its bad twin brother, the power claim, which is still to be introduced—is the most abstract claim which can be raised by law. A more concrete claim is the claim to 'legitimate moral authority', which according to Raz is raised by law; see Raz (n. 1), 16. Beginning with the most abstract claim has the advantage of covering the most fundamental questions.

the law is an empirical question.[25] If this should prove to be correct, the law could then decide whether or not to raise the claim to correctness. The argument from correctness, which attempts to prove not merely a contingent connection between law and morality, but rather a necessary connection, would collapse at the very outset.

Before any attempt is made to show that a certain claim, the claim to correctness, is necessarily raised, it seems useful to ask what the raising of a claim means. Claims can only be raised by subjects capable of speaking and acting. That 'law' raises a claim means that persons working in one legal capacity or another do so. This is most obvious in the case of institutional acts such as acts of legislation or of judication. The core of the argument from correctness is that such institutional acts are always connected with the—normally implicit—non-institutional act of asserting that the legal act is substantially and procedurally correct. This assertion of correctness is further connected with a guarantee—normally implicit—of justifiability, and an expectation—again normally implicit—of acceptance.[26]

The crucial question is whether it is true that legal acts are necessarily connected with an assertion—normally implicit—of correctness. This question is a question of legal philosophy *qua* a theory about the nature of law. At our meta-meta-level we have to add the question: How is it possible to prove the truth of the thesis that legal acts are necessarily connected with a claim to correctness comprising an assertion of correctness? What kind of argument can be adduced in order to show this?

I will try to answer this question with the help of an example. Consider a judge who hands down the following judgment: 'The defendant is hereby sentenced to life imprisonment, albeit wrongly, because valid law was interpreted incorrectly.'

This judgment is somehow defective. The question is how the peculiar character of the defect is to be explained. One might think that the defect is merely conventional. The judge has surely violated conventions or social rules that define the role of the judge. But social rules would also be violated if he were to announce his judgment with a cigarette hanging out of his mouth. This might be seen as inappropriate or even outrageous, but it would lack the absurd character of our judgment. Violation of convention, therefore, is not enough to explain the peculiar character of the defect. Another explanation might be the assumption of a legal mistake. In perhaps all legal systems our judge will be violating legal norms that demand correct interpretations of valid law. But these norms would also be violated where the judge interprets valid law incorrectly, while believing and claiming that his interpretation is correct. In this case he would commit a legal mistake, but nothing absurd has transpired. This shows

---

[25] Philip Soper, 'Law's Normative Claims', in *The Autonomy of Law* (n. 20), 215–47, 217, 230–1.
[26] See Robert Alexy, 'Law and Correctness', in *Current Legal Problems* (Legal Theory at the End of the Millennium, ed. M.D.A. Freeman), 51 (1998), 205–21, 208.

that a legal defect does not by itself explain the absurdity of the verdict. That the absurdity has to be understood apart from the violation of legal rules becomes even more clear if we imagine a legal system that demands correct interpretation but contains no positive norm that forbids judges to declare their judgments incorrect. A judge erroneously declaring his judgment incorrect, under this condition, would not have committed a legal mistake. The absurdity, however, remains. A third possibility arises in classifying the defect as a moral mistake. Let us assume that the incorrect interpretation leads to the conviction of an innocent person. This is a serious moral mistake. But the moral mistake would be the same if the judge were to convict the innocent person without declaring his judgment incorrect. The moral defect might even be greater for reasons of dishonesty. Nevertheless, the two judgments differ greatly with respect to the issue of absurdity. The judgment without the incorrectness clause would only be morally outrageous; the judgment with this clause is also absurd.

Neither the conventional, nor the legal, nor the moral defect explains the absurd and somehow crazy character of the incorrectness clause. This stems, as is often the case when something absurd is at issue, from a contradiction. Such a contradiction emerges because the claim to a correct application of law is always raised in a judicial decision, however badly the upshot of this claim may turn out to be, and whatever the actor's thoughts and wishes may be. Claims comprise—as mentioned—assertions. In the case of our judgment it is the assertion that the judgment is correct. This assertion, being implicit in the act of judging, contradicts the explicit assertion connected with the judgment that it is wrong. This contradiction between the implicit and the explicit is what explains the absurdity.

What kind of argument is this? Is it an argument at all? The argument consists of a 'what-else' conclusion leading to a performative contradiction. A performative contradiction is a contradiction of an explicit assertion and an implicit assertion, where the latter is assumed to be necessarily presupposed by performing the act that contains the explicit assertion. If one uses the term 'conceptual' in a broad sense that comprises the necessary structure of speech acts, one may conclude that the judge in our example commits a conceptual mistake and that this conceptual mistake reveals the conceptual necessity of the claim to correctness in law.

It might be argued that this machinery is not enough to prove the necessity of the claim to correctness in law. The conceptual mistake and, with it, the absurdity were avoidable. One needs only to give up the claim to correctness. To be sure, this would mark a radical change in the present practice and in what the law stands for at present, but such a change is possible. One has only to understand law in all its ramifications as an expression of power, will, and decision. In this way, the claim to correctness would be replaced by something like a power claim.

This alternative clarifies the sense in which the claim to correctness is necessary. Giving up the claim to correctness is to abandon a practice that is defined by the distinctions of correct and wrong, true and false, objective and subject-ive, and just and unjust. Even the category of the 'ought' would disappear, for to say that someone has a legal obligation, following the criteria of the legal system in question, means that it is correct that something is to be done. An 'ought' that is more than an expression of will can only be defined by means of the concept of correctness. This shows that the third problem of the nature of law, the problem of law and morality, is internally connected, through the concept of correctness, with the first problem, i.e. the question concerning what kind of entities the law consists of. Indeed, we could attempt to dismiss alto-gether the present practice constituted by the categories of truth, correctness, objectivity, and 'ought' and substitute for it a practice constituted by nothing other than power, emotion, subjectivity, and will. But this would be to abandon law. A social practice constituted by nothing other than power, emotion, subject-ivity, and will would not be a legal system.[27] It would be a system of brute force, manipulation, and emotional response. The price of abandoning law would be high. We would not only lose the advantages of social co-ordination and co-operation regulated by law. Once the claim to correctness were given up, our acting and speaking would be essentially different from what they are now. The changes would concern not only the character of our community. They would also concern ourselves. We would not remain the same persons. The practice defined by correctness and its related concepts of objectivity, truth, and 'ought' is, therefore, not just one practice among others, as Scrabble is one game among others. The decision between it and its alternative is an existential decision.

All of this means that the claim to correctness is necessary in a two-fold sense. It is, first, necessary if our community is to be constituted by law. There cannot be law without the claim to correctness. This is a conceptual connection. But, as the possibility of the substitution of the claim to correctness by a power claim shows, there can be human interaction without law. The claim to correctness is, therefore, only necessary within a specific practice; thus, the necessity in ques-tion is only a relative necessity. I have maintained above that an 'ought' that is more than an expression of will can only be defined by means of the concept of correctness. Should this be true, the relative necessity of the claim to correctness would come close to Kelsen's thesis that '[t]he "ought" designates a relative *a priori* category'.[28] The second sense in which the claim to correctness is necessary stems from the existential impact of the claim to correctness. This implies a practical necessity that is stronger than that of coercion, which I discussed above. The necessity of coercion is rooted in the values of legal certainty and efficiency. The necessity stemming from this is at least primarily an instrumental or extrinsic, practical necessity. The existential impact of the claim to correctness creates an intrinsic, practical necessity.

---

[27] See Robert Alexy, *The Argument from Injustice. A Reply to Legal Positivism*, trans. B. Litschewski Paulson and S.L. Paulson (Oxford: Clarendon Press, 2002), 32–4.
[28] Kelsen (n. 2), 24.

A positivist could agree with all of this and still maintain that it does not imply that there exists a necessary connection between law and morality. All he/she needs to say is that the claim to correctness has a purely legal content and that this legal content does not have any moral implications. The question therefore is whether the claim to correctness raised in law has any moral content.

Here this question shall only be examined with respect to adjudication. Two things will be taken as given. First, that law necessarily has, as Hart put it, an open texture[29], and, second, that cases falling thereunder, which are commonly termed 'hard cases', cannot be decided solely on reasons taken exclusively from positive law. In this situation, two possibilities exist. The first is that the decision is made without any reasons. This, however, is excluded by the claim to correctness. The second is that the decision is made on the basis of reasons that are not reasons of positive law.[30] There are very different kinds of reasons outside the class of the reasons of positive law. The spectrum comprises considerations of utility, tradition, and common ideas of what is good and bad, as well as principles of justice. One can take up the question of where among all these non-legal reasons the line is to be drawn between moral and non-moral considerations. What cannot be doubted, however, is that considerations of justice belong to moral reasoning. When the reasons of positive law run out, the claim to correctness allows for all kinds of reasons, where they are good reasons for a judicial decision, provided that priority is given to considerations of justice over other considerations that are also not based on positive law.[31] This is enough to establish that the claim to correctness necessarily refers to moral reasoning where the decision cannot be made solely on grounds of positive law. The claim to correctness implies not only the legal power of the judge to apply moral reasons in hard cases, it implies also the legal obligation to do so, where possible. From the point of view of legal positivism, this is a necessary connection of positive law and morality. This necessary connection has the consequence that morally defective decisions are also legally defective. From the point of view of a broader non-positivist conception of law, this amounts to an inclusion of moral reasons within the law.[32] A great deal more could be said about the role of moral arguments in legal reasoning,[33] but what has been shown is enough to demonstrate that the claim to correctness implies a necessary connection between moral and positive legal arguments in legal reasoning.

The claim to correctness is necessarily raised in all legal systems. If it is not raised, the system is not a legal system. Thus, it is superfluous to base the incorporation of moral principles by virtue of their correctness into the law by

---

[29] H.L.A. Hart, *The Concept of Law*, 2nd edn. (Oxford: Clarendon Press, 1996), 128.

[30] See Joseph Raz, 'The Problem about the Nature of Law', in Raz, *Ethics in the Public Domain*, rev. edn. (Oxford: Clarendon Press, 1995), 195–209, 207.

[31] See Robert Alexy, 'The Special Case Thesis', *Ratio Juris*, 12 (1999), 374–84, 378–9.

[32] See Alexy (n. 26), 217–18.

[33] See Robert Alexy, *A Theory of Legal Argumentation*, trans. R. Adler and N. MacCormick (Oxford: Clarendon Press, 1989), 211–20.

means of a rule of recognition *qua* 'conventional normative practice',[34] as Coleman does. The incorporation of moral principles is not a matter of convention. If this were the case, there would then exist the alternatives of either incorporating or electing not to incorporate. This, however, as the claim to correctness shows, is not the case. The incorporation is necessary. If it makes sense to construct a rule of recognition, an issue that I shall not take up here, then it is not a matter of positive law whether this rule of recognition incorporates moral principles by virtue of their correctness but a matter of the concept of law. This point is obscured by Coleman's concept of 'inclusive positivism'.[35]

The argument from correctness is a conceptual argument—in the broad sense sketched above—for a necessary connection between law and morality. The connection stemming from the claim to correctness is, however, notwithstanding its conceptual necessity, a weak one. It is only a qualifying and not a classifying connection. One is defending a classifying connection when one maintains that norms or systems of norms that fail to meet a particular moral criterion do not count as legal norms or legal systems. A qualifying connection demands much less. One defends such a connection when one maintains that norms or systems of norms that fail to meet a particular moral criterion might well nevertheless count as legal norms or legal systems, albeit as legally defective legal norms or legally defective legal systems. The claim to correctness only leads to a qualifying connection. This point, however, is not without interest. The qualifying connection means that morally mistaken legal decisions are necessarily legally mistaken. In this way, an ideal dimension is incorporated into the law. This affects the picture of law fundamentally.

2. The argument from extreme injustice

The question remains whether there exists a classifying connection, too. Such a classifying connection is expressed by Gustav Radbruch's formula, which was applied by German courts after the defeat of National Socialism in 1945 and after the collapse of the German Democratic Republic in 1989. Kent Greenawalt maintains that '[t]he "unjust-law" issue has largely receded in significance'.[36] On the contrary, application of Radbruch's formula by the German courts shows that this issue has by no means receded in significance: indeed, it will remain significant for as long as the possibility of unjust or wicked legal systems exists. The shortest conceivable formulation of Radbruch's formula runs as follows:

Extreme injustice is not law.

This formula does not require any sort of complete fit as between law and morality. It allows that appropriately issued and socially effective norms are valid law even when they are severely unjust. It is in cases of extreme injustice

---

[34] See Coleman (n. 23), 316.   [35] Ibid., 287.
[36] Kent Greenawalt, 'Too Thin and Too Rich: Distinguishing Features of Legal Positivism', in *The Autonomy of Law* (n. 20), 1–29, 9.

that it gives preference to material justice over legal certainty. In this way, it builds into law an outermost limit.

I do not wish to discuss the correctness of Radbruch's formula here. This I have done elsewhere.[37] I will confine myself to the question of the nature of arguments adduced in connection with the dispute concerning the problem whether even extreme injustice can be valid law. My thesis is that although all kinds of arguments that have been considered thus far are applicable, the decisive role is played by a mixture of normative and philosophical arguments.

Semantic arguments are of no importance. The meaning of the expression 'law' neither excludes Radbruch's formula nor its negation. The argument from correctness, which is another kind of a conceptual argument, offers a reason for not conceiving of extreme injustice as law, but it does not decide how to deal with the problem of retroactivity after the breakdown of an unjust system. The problem of *nulla poena sine lege* is the main problem. This problem is a practical or normative problem. It concerns the weighing of the principle of *nulla poena sine lege* against material justice. The trust in legal immunity from prosecution on the part of those who have been or will become active in an unjust state is protected by the principle of *nulla poena sine lege*, whereas the rights of past and future victims of legally imposed extreme injustice are protected by the principle of material justice. It is characteristic of the nature of arguments about the nature of law that the solution of this normative problem depends not only on normative arguments but also on genuinely philosophical arguments concerning the possibility of moral knowledge or moral justification. Hart has argued that nothing follows for the concept of law from the fact alone that moral principles are 'rationally defensible' or 'discoverable'.[38] It may be left an open question whether this is correct. In any case, the converse is correct. If all judgments about justice were nothing more than mere expressions of emotions, decisions, preferences, interest, or ideologies, in short, if the metaethical thesis of radical relativism and subjectivism were correct, little could be said in favour of the non-positivist concept of law expressed by Radbruch's formula.[39] Thus, at the end of our journey through the realm of arguments about the nature of law, we arrive at that type of argument with which we began: the genuinely philosophical argument.

---

[37] See Alexy (n. 27), 28–31, 40–62.

[38] H.L.A. Hart, 'Positivism and the Separation of Law and Morals', in Hart, *Essays in Jurisprudence and Philosophy* (Oxford: Clarendon Press, 1983), 49–87, 84.

[39] In 1932, Radbruch formulated this in the following way: 'relativism, up to now only our method, is at this juncture received into the system as one of its essential components', Gustav Radbruch, *Legal Philosophy*, trans. Kurt Wilk, in *The Legal Philosophies of Lask, Radbruch, and Dabin*, intro. by Edwin W. Patterson (Cambridge, Mass.: Harvard University Press, 1950), 43–224, 116 (§10) (trans. altered).

2

Stronger Reasons

RÜDIGER BITTNER

It is widely held that reasons are normative. Whatever this assertion means precisely, it would seem that it entails something on the lines of:

(1) What you have reason to do, you ought to do.

Something on the lines of (1), but it had better not entail (1), since that is false. After all, you certainly have reason to keep the fat wallet you found in the park, and yet you ought not to do so. Yes, it will be replied, but that is because there are stronger reasons for trying to return the wallet to its owner, and no other reasons even stronger against doing so. The amendment proposed, then, is this:

(2) What you have strongest reason to do, you ought to do.

Note: strongest reason, not *the* strongest reason. *The* strongest reason may come into conflict with an alliance of reasons all individually weaker, but jointly stronger. In that case you have the strongest reason (among all the reasons you have) for doing one thing, but you have strongest reason to do another; and the idea is that in this case the latter course of action is what you ought to take.

The trouble with (2) is that it is not clear what it means. We would need to know what it is for one reason to be stronger than another. The literature is generous with using, and stingy about explaining, this predicate. Explaining it needs, however. We know what strong and weak people are, and we know what strong and weak winds, currents, pressures and the like are. What strong and weak reasons are we do not know, even if we handle the predicate effectively and consistently. The exception to the rule of general reticence on the subject is Joseph Raz, who some twenty-five years ago proposed an explication.[1] In the following I am going first to discuss this explication, arguing that it is not satisfactory. I shall then offer the outline of what I consider to be a better one and discuss, finally, its implications for the question of whether reasons are normative.

---

[1] Joseph Raz, *Practical Reason and Norms* (London: Hutchinson, 1975), sect. 1.1. See also his 'Reasons for Action, Decisions and Norms', Mind (1975), reprinted in an abridged version in *Practical Reasoning*, ed. Raz (Oxford: Oxford University Press, 1978).

I.

To discard first of all some unsatisfactory suggestions: a stronger reason, as Raz emphasizes,[2] need not be a reason looming larger in the agent's consciousness. (Raz, perhaps not altogether happily, distinguishes these as the logical and the phenomenological notion of strength). People can worry deeply about trifling things, and treat casually what is all-important.

Secondly, a stronger reason should not be explained as a reason more likely to be acted upon. People quite regularly do things which they have strongest reason not to do. The strength of reasons cannot be identified with effectivity.

Nor should a stronger reason be explained as a reason that ought to be acted upon, whereas a weaker reason ought not. We distinguish stronger and weaker reasons even among reasons that should all be acted upon. Indeed we distinguish stronger and weaker reasons among reasons that should all not be acted upon. After all, there is stronger reason for you to steal a thousand marks from your neighbour on the right than a hundred marks from your neighbour on the left. Moreover, if a reason's strength is just its 'ought-to-be-acted-upon-ness', it is bad news for the friends of the normativity of reasons, since it turns (2) into a tautology. To be sure, it would be interesting news to be told that our ordinary notion of a stronger reason is just that of a reason that ought to be acted upon. It would be news, though, about what our words mean or what our concepts are, not about the question whether reasons are normative. Under that heading we would only learn that reasons are normative to the extent they are.

Raz's proposal is that a reason is stronger than another by virtue of overriding it in cases of conflict. Reasons are in conflict if the one is a reason for doing, and the other is a reason for not doing, the same thing. And one conflicting reason overrides the other if the conjunct of the two is a reason to do what the overriding one by itself is a reason to do; whereas the conjunct is not a reason to do what the overridden one by itself is a reason to do. Think of it as a see-saw for reasons: either reason makes the plank go down on its side when sitting on it alone, but only the stronger one pushes the plank down its side when both are sitting on it at opposite ends.

As Raz points out,[3] this allows for ties and incommensurability between reasons: reasons may conflict, in the sense explained, and yet their conjunct may not be a reason for either course of action—again, as with people on a see-saw.

The problem is that Raz's criterion may produce too many ties, or indeed only ties. Consider one of Raz's examples of one reason overriding another:

'The fact that my son has been injured is a reason for me to drive him to the hospital at 45 mph. It overrides the only conflicting reason present: the legally imposed 30 mph speed limit.'

---

[2] Raz, *Practical Reason and Norms* (n. 1 above), 25.
[3] Raz, *Practical Reason and Norms* (n. 1 above), 26, n.

On Raz's proposal, the former reason is overriding, the latter overridden thanks to this: the joint fact of his son's having been injured and of there being a legal speed limit of 30 mph is a reason for driving to the hospital at 45 mph, but this joint fact is not a reason for driving to the hospital at 30 mph at most. However, it is hard to see the joint fact of his son's injury and the legal speed limit of 30 mph as indeed providing a reason for driving to the hospital at 45 mph. On being told that the legal speed limit of 30 mph is part of a reason he has for driving his son at 45 mph to the hospital, an ordinary speaker will be baffled, or else will suspect him of an unusually rebellious temperament. Or consider the situation in which he drives his son to the hospital, not because of an injury, but for a routine check-up: we do not want to say that some of the reason persists that he had in the previous case for driving at 45 mph. We rather want to say that the injury alone gave him reason to drive faster than permitted. Thus we want to say that it is false that the joint fact of injury and speed limit is a reason for driving fast. Nor, to be sure, is the joint fact a reason for driving more slowly. The joint fact, it would seem, is not a reason for anything. Hence on Raz's criterion the two reasons, injury and speed limit, come out tied, which they should not.

In defence of Raz's proposal it might be suggested that the situation should rather be described as follows. While it is both true that he has reason to drive his son to the hospital at 45 mph and to do so in violation of the legal speed limit, it is only true that he has reason to stick to the speed limit, but not true that he has reason to endanger the life of his son by doing so; and this difference accounts for the former reason's overriding the latter. This may not in fact be a friendly amendment, since Raz's proposal was about a conjunction of reasons, whereas here we are talking about a conjunction of actions or action descriptions. In any case, the main problem with the suggestion is that this account of the situation is not even correct. Only the first half is: he has reason to drive his son to the hospital at 45 mph, and he has reason to do so in violation of the speed limit. The second half is not correct. It is not only true that he has reason to observe the speed limit, it is also true that he has reason to endanger his son's life by doing so. The existence of the speed limit counts against violating it, however narrowly or broadly the violation may be described. Thus no difference emerges here which could be used for an account of reasons overriding and overridden.

II.

We have not made any progress so far in understanding the comparative strength of reasons. For a fresh start it may help to think of other, more or less metaphorical uses of comparisons of strength. What makes a wind strong? Not the fact that it neutralizes or gets the better of another wind, for ordinarily winds do not meet. Not even the fact that it moves trees rather than leaves: that only demonstrates, but is not, its strength. Rather, winds being movements, they come with an in-built comparability to speed, so that a strong wind is just more of a wind. Appropriately, therefore, when the wind is fairly strong, we also just say: 'It is windy'.

Analogously, then, a strong reason should be more of a reason. In fact, we use 'reason' quite often like a mass term, as I did earlier when I insisted on putting (2) in terms of one's having strongest reason, rather than the strongest reason, for doing something. Indeed, instead of your having stronger or strongest reason, we can speak, equivalently, of your having more or most reason for doing something, which shows that we take strong reasons to be more of a reason. Yet on what dimension do reasons as such compare? Winds blow, and the more they do, the stronger they are. What, in lieu of blowing, do reasons do?

They weigh. Reasons are things to which you may respond by action, initial parts of histories which you may continue; the world's serve, as it were, for you to return. (Raz too takes reasons to be, not mental states, as in the current orthodoxy, but states of the world.) Unlike tennis, however, the world offers you many serves at the same time. For instance, let me suppose your son is injured: you are apt to respond to that by driving him to the hospital at 45 mph; but then there is also the legal speed limit, and to that you are apt to respond by driving no more than 30 mph. However, the available continuations offering themselves to you come with different weights. Your practical field is not flat, with one thing to which you may respond merely standing beside the other. It has depth: some things stand out, others recede. So in the case of your son, the injury at this time is the first thing to take care of. The legal speed limit remains a reason for you to drive no more than 30 mph. It just comes up against a reason that counts for more; and saying 'First things first', you rush him to the hospital.

This importance of a reason, its prominence within an agent's practical field, is its relative strength. Stronger reasons are the ones mattering more to an agent. They do not matter more thanks to their strength, otherwise defined. Their strength is their mattering.

This is not to explain the relative strength of reasons in terms of the relative strength of the agents' desires. That a reason matters more to you is one thing; that you are more eager to act on this reason, or more eager to reap the benefits of doing so, is another. Sometimes we find ourselves wanting to do something very much, but we may admit, perhaps later, perhaps even at the time, that the reason for doing it is not especially weighty. And conversely: a reason for action can be very significant, without inspiring a particularly heated desire. What is important and what is not is a matter of what your life is like: what you did and went through, what you became and what you are, and what you may be going to be in the future. It is not a matter of just that part of your life that consists of your wanting things.

Nor is a reason's importance manifested in its effectivity. People can fail to act on reasons which are extremely important for them. They can go astray from what is nonetheless their centre of gravity. Augustine, for instance, describes his earlier life in such terms.[4] We may disagree with him on whether he correctly identifies what for his younger self actually was important. We should not disagree with him on the grounds that in principle people cannot go wrong the way he takes his younger self to have done.

Finally, Raz distinguished between a reason's strength and its dominating the agent's consciousness. Am I still with Raz on that point? Yes, I am. What is important for a person, and what that person considers important may be different things. You may worry yourself out of your wits over things of no significance, and neglect what is truly important. And this is no less true for having been used as a tenet in Christian homily, often to deceptive effect.

What sort of knowledge, it will be asked, allows us to overrule people on how important some of their reasons are, and indeed to overrule them on what reasons they have in the first place? Broadly speaking, historical knowledge does: we watch people's ways, and the ways of humans in general, and thus we gather what counts for them and what counts more than something else. Here is Linda, for example, dropping out of college to live with Nicolas: Linda underestimates the importance of getting a good education. That is to say, she has reason to finish college, and that reason has more weight than the reason she has for joining Nicolas, her own judgement to the contrary notwithstanding. No doubt I may be mistaken in saying so. The costs, both financial and intellectual, of an incomplete education may in fact be negligible compared to what life with Nicolas is like. Still, knowing something about Linda, about Nicolas, about the wear of affection, I may disagree; and I may be right. I may *be* right; which is not just to say that events may prove me right, or that Linda will come round to share my view. These things may happen or not; it may still be true that now Linda has stronger reasons to continue college. Agents do not hold a privileged position in determining what is more and what is less important for them.

This is after all why people sometimes ask others to help them work out the weight of reasons. That practice only makes sense if there is a difference between being important and being considered important, for otherwise people could stay with whatever opinions and feelings they happen to have on the question. The practice only makes sense if there is a fact of the matter determining whether some reason outweighs another or not.

I have suggested that 'stronger reasons' can be explained as 'reasons that matter more to the person in question'. With this notion of things that matter I take myself to be roughly following Harry Frankfurt's ideas about caring. Frankfurt, intent on bringing out 'the importance of what we care about' (the title of the first of his papers on the topic), drew attention chiefly to cases of caring deeply about persons or causes, cases of love, for example, or cases of devoting oneself to the pursuit of an ideal. That restriction does not seem to be essential, though. In fact, Frankfurt's remark that there are 'wide variations in

---

[4] See *Confessiones*, I, 1, 1; II, 4, 9; II, 10, 18; XIII, 9, 10.

how strongly and how persistently people care about things'[5] can be read as allowing one person to care about a large number of things with different degrees of intensity; so that for each person we get a landscape of things cared about, with a few peaks perhaps, a range of middling hills, and a large area of very low elevation. Now reasons could be understood to be stronger or weaker depending on where they are located in this field. Thus, in the first example cited, you do care about the legal speed limit, and so the reason you have for observing it has some strength. Still, you care a great deal more about your son's health or perhaps life, and this is what makes the reason stronger for driving him to the hospital faster than permitted.

Note that on Frankfurt's view, contrary perhaps to what the word 'caring' suggests, we need to be prepared to overrule people on whether they do or do not care about a certain thing.[6] That makes the order of caring compatible with the order of reasons in the way I proposed, since in Raz's opinion, which I followed, people's testimony on the strength of their reasons is not decisive, either.

Admittedly, I am diverging from Frankfurt's original line of thought in using the landscape of what one cares about to account for the strength and weakness of reasons. For Frankfurt, acting for reasons as strong as to be incontrovertible is different from acting under 'volitional necessity', i.e. acting because one cares about something in such a way and to such a degree that one cannot forbear from doing it.[7] It may well be doubted, however, whether this difference is borne out by our experience. People who do what they do because they care so much and in such a way about something, are quite likely to explain themselves by saying that they have insuperable reasons for this course of action. True, it may seem that the converse does not always hold: there are those who take themselves to be following the strongest reasons, but not to be acting under any sort of volitional necessity. This, however, may be due to the fact that in such cases the strongest reason only wins by a small distance, so that it is felt that, as in an auction, the defeated reason would have had to pay only a bit more to win the contest; or the strongest reason may be quite weak, as in a minor purchasing decision. In such cases, understandably, a feeling of necessity is not likely to arise, whereas it may well do so when the winning reason is exceptionally strong, compared either to its competitors or to the common run of reasons. In fact, it may be an advantage of the present line of thought that it does away with the difference between the order of reasons and the order of caring, for otherwise we would find ourselves subject to two sorts of guidance, the relation between which is unclear and indeed problematic.

[5] Harry Frankfurt, *The Importance of What We Care About* (Cambridge: Cambridge University Press, 1988), 85.

[6] Harry Frankfurt, *Necessity, Volition, and Love* (Cambridge: Cambridge University Press, 1999), 162.

[7] Frankfurt, *The Importance of What We Care About* (n. 5 above), 86–7; see also *Necessity, Volition, and Love* (n. 6 above), 80. For a critique of the notion of 'volitional necessity' see my 'Ich kann nicht anders', *Autonomes Handeln. Beiträge zur Philosophie von Harry G. Frankfurt*, ed. Monika Betzler and Barbara Guckes (Berlin: Akademie Verlag, 2000), 179–191.

III.

To return now to the beginning, to the alleged normativity of reasons: is it true that

(2) What you have strongest reason to do, you ought to do?

In Raz' view, this is true, for in his view even the statement

(1) What you have reason to do, you ought to do

is true. I rejected that claim out of hand at the beginning, arguing that there are cases where one ought not to do what one has nevertheless some reason to do. Raz admits that his view appears to entail a paradox. He explains it away by pleading pragmatic implicature: those who say that somebody ought to do a certain thing are only suggesting, but not in fact saying, that there are no other reasons overriding those in favour of doing it; they are only suggesting, that is, that it is not true also that the person rather ought not to do it. And in fact it may be true that the person both ought and ought not to do something.

This line of argument does not appear convincing. Take an ordinary case of pragmatic implicature, like "She swam nine tenths of the way to Calais": this indeed suggests, but does not strictly say, that she did not make the last tenth. However, "He ought to return the wallet he found in the park", seems to be different. This seems, not just to suggest, but indeed to say that returning the wallet is what the agent, everything considered, should do. And then it is definitely false to say that he ought to keep it.

If (1) is false, that leaves us with (2), and thus with the question as to what makes a reason stronger than another. In the foregoing I have sketched an explanation: one reason is stronger than another if it matters more for you. On such an explanation, there does not seem to be sufficient ground for supposing that, generally, you ought to do what you have strongest reason to do. Perhaps with some people, perhaps with all people, the range of what is important for them is laid out in such a way that what they have most reason to do is not what they ought to do. If you ought to do something you are under a requirement to do it. Your doing it is 'outstanding', the way a debt is. It does not matter here why this is so; whether the demand was placed on you by 'the eternal fitness of things', or by God, or by yourself. The point is that what you are thus asked to do may have little to do with what you are and what you have become, and so it may have little to do with what matters to you. To you, as we know you from your history, the demand may still be alien. One hopes that people have some reason to do what they ought to do, but one only hopes. It cannot be supposed that what we ought to do fits like a glove what, by nature and by history, we are and what therefore is important to us. Such confidence has had its day.

3

Are Reasons for Action Beliefs?

BRUNO CELANO

I. INTRODUCTION

Suppose John takes his umbrella because he (rightly, as it turns out) believes that it will rain. Is the reason for him to take his umbrella his belief that it will rain, or is it the fact that it will? Joseph Raz reminds us that:

> reasons are used to guide behaviour—and people are to be guided by what is the case, not by what they believe to be the case. To be sure, in order to be guided by what is the case a person must come to believe that it is the case. Nevertheless it is the fact and not his belief in it which should guide him and which is a reason. If p is the case, then the fact that I do not believe that p does not establish that p is not a reason for me to perform some action. The fact that I am not aware of any reason does not show that there is none.[1]

Their undeniable plausibility notwithstanding, Raz's claims, I shall argue, leave something out of the picture.

I shall proceed as follows. Reasons-statements (statements such as, e.g., 'There is a reason for X to φ', or 'The fact that p is a reason for X to φ') are, I take it, conceptually related to judgements of practical rationality (statements such as 'Given the circumstances, X's φ-ing was rational', 'In φ-ing, X would act reasonably', and the like). A satisfactory theory of reasons for action should account for their relationships. Raz's position, as stated in the quoted passage, may be termed an 'objectivist' one (objectivism about reasons for action). I shall build what may appear as a natural extension of it, 'pure' objectivism about reasons for action, and show that it is untenable. Pure objectivism's main weakness lies in its failure to account for the relationships existing between reasons-statements, on the one hand, and judgements of practical rationality, on the other. There is, it will be shown, an important sense in which practical rationality is to be assessed relative to the beliefs of the agent, or from within the agent's perspective. What this implies as to the nature of reasons for action is not on the whole clear. But, I shall argue, we are to some extent justified in holding our reasons for action to be what-we-believe (or, facts-believed), rather than the facts themselves, whether they are believed or not. To this extent, Raz's

---

[1] Joseph Raz, *Practical Reason and Norms* (3rd edition, Oxford: Oxford University Press, 1999), 17. See for a closely related passage Raz, 'Introduction', *Practical Reasoning*, ed. Raz (Oxford University Press, 1978), 3.

quoted claim, 'it is the fact and not his belief in it which should guide him and which is a reason' is inherently unstable. Claiming, as Raz does, that 'if p is the case, then the fact that I do not believe that p does not establish that p is not a reason for me to perform some action'—or that 'the fact that I am not aware of any reason does not show that there is none'—may be misleading.

A few preliminary remarks are in order here. First, I shall be concerned with normative (i.e. justifying, good, valid) reasons only. Explanatory (or motivating) reasons will be touched upon only in passing. Thus, unless otherwise specified, what is meant by 'a reason' is a normative reason (a good, or valid, reason). What an agent has 'reason' to do is, in this sense, what reason requires him to do, or what is rationally required of him to do. The issue I am addressing is whether our normative reasons for action are facts, or whether they are beliefs (or perhaps both, or neither of them). It is not whether what motivates us, or what may explain our actions, are our beliefs, or the facts our beliefs are about.[2]

Second, my argument will be neutral *vis-à-vis* the controversy among Humeans and anti-Humeans in the theory of reasons for action (be they motivating or normative reasons). Some—call them 'Humeans'—will hold that our reasons for action are (or, are grounded in) desires. Their opponents will deny this, by claiming, for example, that usually, and fundamentally, what we desire, we desire for (more or less good) reasons (evaluations are not desires). I shall not be concerned with this issue. Humeans, too, will happily grant that our beliefs— or, perhaps, the facts they are about—are part of our reasons for action ('Why open the fridge?' 'Because I am hungry, and there is some cheese inside'). True, they will not regard them as the 'operative', or 'active' part (they will, that is, regard beliefs as merely ancillary reasons for action, in themselves 'inert'). But, for my purposes, that doesn't matter. The issue I shall address is not whether our reasons for action necessarily are, at least in part, non-cognitive in character (whether, fundamentally, it is our desires that provide us with our reasons for acting in some way or other). It is, rather, whether, to the extent that our reasons for action are not desires, nor grounded in desires, it is our beliefs, or the facts they are about, that constitute reasons (be they merely ancillary ones).

Third, when considering what to do, usually a plurality of reasons of different strength, some of which count for, and some against, a given course of action, come into play. Some of the relevant reasons may be defeated, or

---

[2] Thus, our initial question: is the reason for John to take his umbrella his belief that it will rain, or is it the fact that it will rain? cannot be disposed of by answering that, while the fact that it will rain is a normative reason for John's taking his umbrella, John's belief that it will rain is the relevant explanatory reason. This may be true, but the issue I am addressing is different. Granted that the fact that it will rain cannot explain (so far as intentional explanation is concerned) John's taking his umbrella unless John believes that it will rain (or even allowing that John's belief that it will rain is the reason that explains his taking the umbrella; that, i.e., motivating reasons are beliefs), our question is whether normative reasons themselves are, or somehow involve, beliefs. (For Raz's own views concerning the difference between the use of '[a] reason' in explanatory contexts and its use in normative or evaluative contexts see *Practical Reason and Norms* (n. 1 above), 15–19, 39, 48, 84, 186; Raz, 'Introduction' (n. 1 above), 3–4; J. Raz, *Engaging Reason* (Oxford: Oxford University Press, 1999), 23, n. 5, 25–6, 47, n. 5.)

excluded, by others. Some of them may, perhaps, be incommensurate. I shall completely disregard these possibilities. Thus, I shall not, in this paper, touch upon the plurality of (possibly incommensurate) reasons, and issues related thereto (such as the balancing of conflicting reasons, the status of defeated reasons, moral dilemmas, etc.). My remarks will be confined to what we may label 'the minimal case' ('There is a reason for X to φ', or 'The fact that p is a reason for X to φ', period). Nothing in my argument depends—or so I hope—on this restriction.

II. PURE OBJECTIVISM ABOUT REASONS FOR ACTION

Statements of the form:

(1) The fact that p is a reason for X to φ;

(2) There is a reason for X to φ

and the like, I shall term 'reasons-statements'. Statements of the form:

(3) In the circumstances, X's φ-ing was (is, would be) rational (reasonable, sensible);

(4) In φ-ing, X acted (is acting, would act) rationally (reasonably, sensibly);

(5) φ-ing was, given the circumstances, a sensible thing for X to do

and the like, I shall term 'judgements of practical rationality'. Judgements of practical rationality may also be phrased in terms of the 'right' ('appropriate', 'proper', 'correct', etc.) thing to do, being understood that what is at issue is whether the action was right, appropriate, etc., in so far as what reason requires is concerned (i.e., from the standpoint of reason). Reasons-statements and judgements of practical rationality are, I take it, conceptually related. There has to be some conceptual link between X's having a reason to φ and X's acting rationally, reasonably or sensibly (i.e., X's doing the right thing, so far as reason is concerned). Reasons-statements may support judgements of practical rationality; they are supposed to ground answers to questions as to whether a given action, performed by a given agent, is, was, or would be, a rational, reasonable, or sensible, thing to do. This is no surprise. Reasons for action 'determine what ought to be done';[3] they ground conclusions to the effect that given agents ought to perform given actions.[4] Reasons, in short, are supposed to speak in favour of a given action (or against it): they are supposed somehow to make it rational, reasonable or sensible to act in some way or other—to make actions right or wrong.[5] Any satisfactory theory of reasons for action has to account for this connection.

---

[3] *Practical Reason and Norms* (n. 1 above), 18. See also Raz, 'Introduction' (n. 1 above), 4 (Reasons 'affect what one should do'). [4] See *Practical Reason and Norms* (n. 1 above), 186.
[5] See J. Dancy, *Practical Reality* (Oxford: Oxford University Press, 2000), 1.

How do we get from reasons-statements to judgements of practical rationality? This is a difficult question, and I shall not attempt to provide an answer (some mistaken ways of making this move will be exposed below, in sections III and IV). For our purposes, it will be enough to note that an account of reasons for action, of what they are and of how they work, should provide us with an understanding of the way reasons may ground judgements of practical rationality. This is, I submit, an adequacy condition for any satisfactory account of the nature, and import, of reasons for action. A fully-fledged theory of reasons for action will also have to be a theory of practical rationality. It will have to provide a view of the nature of reasons (i.e., what they are), *and* to specify under which conditions, relating to the relevant reasons, actions may be said to be rational, reasonable or sensible. Unless the relations existing between there being a reason for X to φ (or, the fact that p being a reason for X to φ), on the one hand, and φ-ing being the right thing for X to do (so far as what reason requires is concerned), on the other hand, are accounted for, our understanding of reasons will remain defective.

With this adequacy condition in mind, let us turn back to Raz's key passage, quoted at the beginning of section I above. In what I take to be a perfectly intelligible sense of 'objective', Raz's understanding of the nature of reasons for action, as expressed in the quoted passage (and in related ones),[6] may be termed an 'objectivist' one. Reasons for action are facts: they are features of the world, aspects of it (or, alternatively, they are properties of the actions they are reasons for). The world being as it is, there is a reason for X to act in some way or other, whether he believes the world to be like that or not (or whether he believes himself to have a reason to act that way or not). Whether the fact that p is a reason for X to φ, or whether there is a reason for X to φ, is an objective matter, independent of X's beliefs thereabout.[7] Thus, objectivism claims, agents may have mistaken beliefs about whether they have reason to act in some way or other, and about what their reasons are. X may mistakenly believe that there is a reason for him to φ (or, that the fact that p is a reason for him to φ), or that

---

[6] See *Practical Reason and Norms* (n. 1 above), 18, 22, 24, 51, 186, 198; Raz, 'Introduction' (n. 1 above), 4, 12; *Engaging Reason* (n. 2 above), 1, 22–23, 25, 31, 47, 65, 67, 70, 75, 77, 90, 219–20, 228–30.

[7] There are, indeed, cases in which the agent's belief provides a reason for her to perform a given action, in a way which, however, poses no threat to objectivist claims. Thus, for example, in special circumstances, the fact that X believes that p may be a reason for her to perform some action, which, were her belief that p true, she would have no reason to perform ('that I believe that everyone is out to get me is a reason for me to seek professional help' (Dancy, *Practical Reality* (n. 5 above), 65). Such cases do not, of course, qualify as counter-examples to objectivist claims. While its being the case that it will rain may indeed be counted as a reason for taking one's umbrella, its being the case that everyone is out to get me would not count as a reason to seek professional help ('if it were true, I would have a reason not to put myself in the hands of professionals, where I will be at my most vulnerable', ibid., 65). Those who, contrary to Raz's and other objectivist views, hold that reasons for action are beliefs, will not want the connection between the belief and the action, in ordinary cases, to be the same as in the professional help case. They will want to say that my believing that everyone is out to get me is a reason to avoid putting myself in the hands of professionals.

he has no reason to φ (or, that the fact that p is no reason for him to φ). He may have a reason to φ, while not believing he has one, or believing he has none.

Objectivism is, I think, a plausible view. It is, in fact, strongly supported by the agent's own understanding of the matter. Suppose, once again, that John takes his umbrella because he (rightly, as it turns out) believes that it will rain, and suppose, further, that we ask him whether it is the fact that it will rain, or his belief that it will, that is a reason for him to take the umbrella. He would probably choose the former answer. Special circumstances (such as the case cited in note 7 concerning professional help) aside, when acting on the belief that p, we tacitly raise the claim that our belief is true—that it is the case that p—and that the fact that p, rather than our believing it, is our reason for acting as we do. In short, were we to ask an agent whether, when he φ-s because he believes that p, it is the fact that he believes that p, or the fact that p, that, according to him, is a reason for his φ-ing, he would normally regard the former answer as correct.[8] (I shall call this the 'direct question' argument.)

The direct question argument lends strong support to an objectivist understanding of reasons for action. By itself, however, objectivism, as introduced so far, does not amount to a fully-fledged theory of reasons for action—not unless supplemented with an understanding of the way reasons may make it rational, reasonable, or sensible to act in some way or other (remember our adequacy condition). So far, nothing has been said about when, and how, reasons-statements may be held to ground judgments of practical rationality. If we now try to expand objectivism into a fully-fledged theory, meeting our adequacy condition, the following account—'pure' objectivism about reasons for action—suggests itself as a natural development.[9]

According to pure objectivism, first, reasons for action are facts (that which is a reason for acting this way or that is a fact). Being facts, second, they are independent from our beliefs. Special cases apart, it is not because we believe this or that that we have the reasons we do: what reason requires of us does not depend on what our mental states are. Specifically, there being a reason for X to φ does not depend on X's recognizing or accepting it—not even on his believing that there is one. Reasons for action are not, in short, 'sensitive to the contingencies of our psychological makeup'.[10]

Thus, third, it is not our beliefs, or what we believe, that make it rational, reasonable or sensible for us to act in some way or other. What makes an action rational (sensible, etc.) is independent of the agent's beliefs. The agent's beliefs, thus, make no difference as to whether an action is rational or not. Or, in other

---

[8] See *Practical Reason and Norms* (n. 1 above), 18; see also Raz, *The Morality of Freedom* (Oxford: Oxford University Press, 1986), 159; *Engaging Reason* (n. 2 above), 226; T. M. Scanlon, *What We Owe to Each Other* (Cambridge, Mass.: Harvard University Press, 1998), 56.

[9] I owe to discussion with Jonathan Dancy my understanding of what a purely objectivist view of (normative) reasons for action might look like. This does not mean that pure objectivism, as defined in the text, coincides with Dancy's position. For Dancy's own view of these matters see Dancy, *Practical Reality* (n. 5 above), 49, 60, 70. [10] Ibid., 48.

words, practical rationality is not to be assessed relative to the agent's beliefs—
it is not to be judged from the standpoint of the agent, relative to how he sees
things. Rather, whether a given action is reasonable or not, sensible or not, is to
be determined by looking at the facts. It is not the agent's beliefs, it is the facts,
which make it rational to act in some way or other. Practical rationality, in
short, is not to be assessed 'from within the agent's perspective'.[11]

Pure objectivism is what we get when we develop objectivist claims to their
extreme consequences—an uncompromisingly objectivist theory. It is, I shall now
argue, an untenable position. This does not mean that there is no truth in objectivist claims. Acknowledgment of the latter is, however, consistent with acknowledging a subjective dimension in our notion of practical rationality. There is,
indeed, an important sense in which practical rationality is to be assessed relative
to the beliefs of the agent, from within the agent's perspective. As a consequence,
objectivist claims about reasons for action have to be amended.

In showing that pure objectivism is untenable, I shall proceed as follows. Let
us stipulate that a statement of the form:

(6) X has a reason to φ

is true if and only if there is a reason for X to φ (this is mere stipulation about
how the phrase 'having a reason to φ' is to be understood here; no doubt it can
also be understood differently). I shall scrutinize three different hypotheses,
according to whether (i) X does or doesn't have a reason to φ, (ii) X does or
doesn't believe that he has one, and (iii) X does or doesn't actually φ. The question I shall ask about each hypothesis is whether, under those conditions, X may
be judged to have acted rationally, reasonably or sensibly (to have been
rational, as an agent, in acting as he did; or to have done the right thing, so far
as what reason requires is concerned). The three hypotheses I shall scrutinize
are the following: (i) X has no reason to φ, he believes he has one, and he φ-s
(or, alternatively, X has a reason to φ, he believes that he has none, and he
doesn't φ); (ii) X has a reason to φ, he believes he has that reason, and he φ-s;
(iii) X has a reason to φ, he doesn't believe he has one (or, he believes he has
none), and he φ-s (I shall term the latter hypothesis 'the odd case').

III. Two Hypotheses

How do we get, then, from reasons-statements to judgements of practical
rationality? At first sight, the move may appear to be an easy one; e.g., 'If X has
a reason to φ, then X's φ-ing is (would be) rational', or 'X had a reason to φ;
therefore, φ-ing was a sensible thing for him to do'. This is the answer pure
objectivism is committed to. It is, however, mistaken.[12]

---

[11] The quoted phrase is Dancy's, ibid., 60.

[12] One reason why it is mistaken shall not detain us here. An agent may have a plurality of
reasons, of different strength, some of which count for, and some against a given action. Thus, from

An objectivist account of reasons for action allows both for the possibility that a statement to the effect that X has a reason to φ be false, although X believes it to be true (that, namely, while X believes himself to have a reason to φ, in fact he has none), and for the possibility that it be true, although X does not believe it to be true—or, believes it to be false (that, namely, while there is a reason for X to φ, X doesn't believe himself to have one, or believes he has none). It allows, in short, both for the possibility that X mistakenly believes that he has a reason to φ, and for the possibility that he does not believe that he has a reason to φ (or, he believes that he has none), although he in fact has one.

Let us now suppose that X believes himself to have a reason to φ, and that he φ-s (for that reason). Did he act rationally? Did he do the right thing (in so far as what reason requires is concerned)? Pure objectivism's answer to this question is, it depends on whether X actually has a reason to φ or not. In case he has one, then her action is *pro tanto* rational. If, on the other hand, he mistakenly believes himself to have one, then his action is not rational. (This does not necessarily mean that it is irrational. It does mean, however, that, for all we know, there is no reason supporting his action—there is nothing that, so far as reason is concerned, speaks in its favour.) The same holds, *mutatis mutandis*, when X does not believe himself to have a reason to φ (or, he believes he has no reason to φ), and, accordingly, he doesn't φ. Whether, in such a case, X acted rationally depends, pure objectivism claims, on whether X actually had a reason for φ-ing or not (or whether there actually is a reason for him to φ). In case he mistakenly believes himself to have no reason to φ (or, alternatively, in case he actually has a reason to φ, though he doesn't believe he has one) his not φ-ing is unsupported by reason. It is, in fact, contrary to what reason requires (for all we know, nothing in reason speaks in its favour, and something speaks against it). X's φ-ing is, in short, irrational.

Pure objectivism's claims, however, are to be rejected, for two interrelated reasons. On the one hand, false beliefs may be rational. And, on the other hand true beliefs may be irrational. The significance of these two possibilities may be brought out by considering two hypotheses.

Suppose, first, that (i) X mistakenly believes that he has a reason to φ; (ii) he φ-s (for the reason he mistakenly takes himself to have), and (iii) his belief that he has a reason to φ, though false, is perfectly reasonable. Should we say that, in φ-ing for the reason he mistakenly believed himself to have, X acted with no reason whatever—that, normatively speaking, there is no reason

---

reasons-statements taken in isolation no judgement whatever may be inferred about what reason requires, all things considered, the agent to do. As remarked above (section I) I shall not, in this paper, address issues relating to the plurality of reasons. The argument is focused on the minimal case. We may distinguish between *pro tanto* and 'all things considered' judgements of practical rationality; and maintain that judgements of practical rationality inferred from reasons-statements taken in isolation are only *pro tanto* judgements (e.g., 'If X has a reason to φ, X's φ-ing would be, *pro tanto*, rational').

at all for what she did (that, namely, nothing in reason speaks in favour of his acting that way)? Should we say that his action was a-rational, or even irrational? Contrary to what pure objectivism suggests, the answer seems to be, no. Unless further details are added into the picture, we shall be inclined, I submit, to reject pure objectivism's answer. The same goes so far as our coordinate hypothesis is concerned—that, namely, X has a reason to φ, he reasonably believes himself to have no reason to φ and, accordingly, he doesn't φ.

And now suppose that, second, (i) X rightly believes that he has a reason to φ; (ii) he φ-s (for that reason), and (iii) his belief that he has a reason to φ, although true, is utterly unreasonable. Should we say that, in φ-ing for the reason he actually had, X acted reasonably? That, namely, the reason which (by hypothesis) he actually had, made his φ-ing a rational, reasonable or sensible thing to do? Once again, contrary to what pure objectivism suggests, the answer seems to be no—not unless further details are added into the picture.

These two hypotheses, I submit, dictate the rejection of pure objectivism. Let us consider the former (X mistakenly believes that he has a reason for φ-ing, and he φ-s for the reason he mistakenly believes himself to have; or, alternatively, X mistakenly believes that he has no reason for φ-ing, and, accordingly, he doesn't φ). The argument draws on the possibility that the agent's beliefs, though false, might be rational. One common strategy in defending objectivist claims against the challenge posed by putative counter-examples of this sort consists of allowing justifiable ignorance about the reasons one actually has as an excuse. When X, albeit mistakenly, non-culpably (relative to some presupposed standard of rationality in belief, to be specified) believes himself to have a reason for φ-ing, and he φ-s (for the reason he mistakenly takes himself to have)—or, when he non-culpably, albeit mistakenly, believes that he has no reason to φ, and he doesn't φ—then, although what he actually did was unsupported by reason (nothing in reason speaks in favour of what he did; and, in the latter case, he did, so far as the reasons for action he actually has are concerned, the wrong thing), he may be excused. Although what he did was not rational, a-rational, or even contrary to what reason required, we are not going to find fault in him. He is excused for having acted as he did—or, what he did, though at variance with what reason required, may be excused.

This is a promising strategy. By resorting to it, it seems, pure objectivism may effectively be defended against the challenge posed by our first hypothesis, at the cost of a slight qualification. Action at variance with the reasons one actually has is a-rational, or even irrational; it is, thus, to be condemned (in the court of reason), unless one non-culpably (i.e. reasonably) believes that the reasons one actually has aren't there—or, non-culpably believes himself to have some reason one doesn't actually have. In such cases, action at variance with the reasons, though unsupported by reason, or even contrary to it—i.e., wrong, so far as what reason requires is concerned—will be excused.

This strategy may be further developed by resorting to two interrelated moves. First, by adding into the picture the notion of a 'filter' through which facts are to pass, if they are to ground judgements of practical rationality.[13] Reasons for action are facts. But, so the argument runs, reasons for action are allowed to ground judgements of practical rationality only if they pass an epistemic filter (or, better, an epistemic and normative one, excluding what is epistemically inaccessible to the agent, and what, though accessible to him, he permissibly ignores). Facts that do not pass the filter (e.g., features of the situation 'that I have no chance whatever of discerning'), though reasons for acting in some way or other, do not dictate unfavourable verdicts in the court of reason. When X mistakenly believes himself to have no reason to φ, his not φ-ing is excused, if the fact that is a reason for him to φ does not pass the filter.[14]

The second move consists in exploiting the difference between the evaluative and the deontic.[15] Consider the claim that, when X reasonably, though mistakenly, believes that she has a reason to φ, and she φ-s (for the reason she reasonably believes herself to have), X acts rationally (i.e., she does the right thing). Pure objectivism may try to accommodate such remarks by claiming that they are to be understood as evaluative, rather than as deontic. True, X had no reason for φ-ing (i.e., φ-ing is not what he should have done); but 'given his (rationally permissible) beliefs', 'he acted as a sensible person would have done'[16] Our remark is one 'whose main purport lies in the evaluation of how well he acted', rather than in specifying 'how he *should* have acted'.[17]

By allowing reasonable belief as an excuse (and by bringing into the picture an epistemic filter, plus the difference between the evaluative and the deontic), it seems, pure objectivism effectively copes with the difficulty posed by our first hypothesis, at the price of what may appear as a minor adjustment. Our second hypothesis shows, however, that this is not enough. The real issue is not, in fact, whether reasonable, though mistaken, belief may work as an excuse.

In our second hypothesis—X rightly believes, albeit irrationally, that he has a reason to φ, and he φ-s (for that reason)—excuses are simply beside the point. Pure objectivism would want us to say that, on this hypothesis, X acted reasonably—and we are not willing to accept this suggestion. Does allowing for excuses dispel the difficulty? But, what is to be excused, and why? Shall we say that what X did is to be excused, although X had a reason to act that way? Or perhaps that what he did is to be excused, because he had a reason to act that way? What sense could be made of the claim that X is to be excused for having acted as he had a reason to act, because of his having acted on the basis of an irrational, true belief that he had that reason? Is the fact that he actually had that reason an excuse for his having acted on the basis of an irrational belief to that effect? Or is irrational belief that one had a reason an excuse for having done what one actually had a reason to do? The issue is not, it seems to me,

---

[13] See Dancy, *Practical Reality* (n. 5 above), 56–9, 65.

[14] 'Suppose that, unknown and unknowable to me, someone has been buried alive in my garden during the night. Could this make it wrong of me to go away for a fortnight's holiday?' (Ibid., 57)

[15] Ibid., 53, 56, 62, 64.   [16] Ibid., 62.   [17] Ibid., 53.

whether what the agent did, although wrong, should be excused. Talking of excuses is, I repeat, simply beside the point.[18] The issue is, rather, whether our reasons for action may be understood as being independent from our beliefs.

Nor do pure objectivism's further strategies—granting that judgements of practical rationality depend on the operation of an epistemic filter, and resorting to the difference between the evaluative and the deontic—fare any better. The requirement that facts should pass an epistemic filter was introduced above as a development of the idea that agents acting on the basis of reasonable false beliefs may be excused. But how would a parallel move, concerning our second hypothesis, look like? In our second hypothesis, too, conditions of rationality in belief are supposed somehow to explain why judgements of practical rationality do not directly track reasons-statements. In this case, however, conditions of rationality in belief are not supposed to account for the possibility of excusing action at variance with the reasons the agent has (talking of excuses is beside the point). It is not that failure to satisfy rationality conditions in belief may provide an excuse. (Why should it be so?) What our second hypothesis shows is, rather, that its being the case that X has a reason to φ itself depends on whether X's belief to that effect does meet suitable rationality conditions or not. When X's belief to the effect that he has a reason to φ is, though true, irrational, the fact that, by hypothesis, is a reason for X to φ cannot serve as a reason—it cannot count as a reason. (As it were, it doesn't speak in favour of the action any more.) Thus, what our second hypothesis shows is that the operation of the required epistemic filter—satisfaction of rationality conditions in belief—infects reasons themselves. It affects, namely, what it is that is a reason for action.

What about resorting to the distinction between the evaluative and the deontic? Presumably, the suggestion would have to be that, on our second hypothesis, X, while doing the right thing (i.e., while doing what he had a reason to do, or what reason required him to do), acted badly. What sense could be made of this claim? I can see no answer other than reading it as saying, 'while doing what he had a reason to do, he did it *for the wrong reason*'. 'For the wrong reason', i.e., for something that does not speak in favour of the action; for all we know, the agent had, in fact, no reason for doing what he did. (I am not equivocating on 'reason' here. In the phrase 'for the wrong reason', the word 'reason' does not mean 'explanatory reason'. What is at issue is whether something speaks in favour of the action, that is, whether the agent had a normative reason for acting as he did.) The issue raised by our second hypothesis is, thus, plainly a normative one. There is no independent role to play for evaluative considerations. Evaluation simply follows normative considerations.

---

[18] Let us turn back to our first hypothesis. In such cases, Dancy writes, 'we want to be able, not to diminish the sense that what he did was wrong, but to diminish our condemnation of him for having acted wrongly' (ibid., 64). Perhaps. (Regarding permissible ignorance as an excuse, it will be remembered, answers this need.) But, it seems to me, we also want, in such cases, to be able to express the sense that what the agent did was *right*. Reasonable (though mistaken) belief answers this need too. This is clearly brought out by our second hypothesis, where unreasonable (true) belief renders the action unsupported by reason.

What our second hypothesis shows, then, is that satisfaction of rationality conditions in belief infects reasons themselves. It affects what can count as a reason, that is, I suggest, what can *be* a reason. (I can see no difference other than a merely verbal one, here, between something 'counting as' a reason, or 'serving as' a reason, and something *being* a reason. In the present context, whatever affects something counting as a reason affects its *being* a reason.) This means, it seems to me, that facts, by themselves, are not reasons. Or, rather, that, depending on whether the agent has suitable beliefs, facts speaking in favour of a given action may stop doing so—depending on the agent's beliefs, facts being reasons for a given action may turn out to be, or not to be, such reasons. In this sense, I suggest, objectivist claims to the effect that (i) reasons are facts, and (ii) being facts, they are belief-independent, are inherently unstable.

IV. THE ODD CASE

That this is so may best be brought out by considering a third hypothesis. Let us suppose (the odd case) that (i) X has a reason to φ, (ii) he believes himself to have no reason to φ (or, he doesn't believe himself to have a reason to φ), and (iii) he φ-s. Suppose, for example, that, unknown and unknowable to me, someone has been buried alive in my garden during the night; and that, instead of going away for a fortnight's holiday, I stay at home, and spend some time digging holes in my garden. Does the fact that someone has been buried alive in the garden make it rational for me not to go on holiday, and to dig holes there?[19]

Reasons for action are, objectivism claims, independent from the psychological makeup—and, therefore, from the beliefs—of the agents concerned. Pure objectivism builds this claim into its understanding of practical rationality; into its specification, namely, of the conditions under which an agent, or an action, may be judged to be rational, reasonable, or sensible. Its core argument runs as follows: reasons for action are independent of the agent's beliefs; they are what makes an action rational; therefore, whether an action is rational or not does not depend on the agent's beliefs.

Pure objectivism is, I think, committed to holding that, in the odd case, X acted rationally. This claim is, however, highly counter-intuitive. Nobody, I think, would be willing to grant that, if X has a reason to φ, he doesn't believe he has one (or, he believes he has none), and he φ-s, then X's φ-ing is, *pro tanto*, rational (that, namely, the reason he has makes it rational for him to act that way: what he does is the right thing to do, so far as what reason requires

---

[19] This is an elaboration on one of Dancy's examples (quoted at n. 14 above). While Dancy asks whether it would be *wrong* of me, under those conditions, to go away for a fortnight's holiday (the example is, thus, intended to make the point about permissible ignorance as an excuse), my question is, whether it would be *right* of me, under those same conditions, to do what, by hypothesis, I have a reason to do—namely, digging holes in my garden. This is not, as will soon be apparent, a question about excuses. It is, rather, a question about the nature of reasons.

is concerned). For all we know, X's action may have been a piece of utterly irrational behaviour.

True, X's action may turn out to be successful (by digging holes in my garden, I may happen to find someone who, unknown to me, has been buried alive there). It may, *ex post*, appear to X himself as a good thing to do, or even as the right thing to do. Success, goodness, or rightness, however, are, so understood, a matter of sheer luck. This is not what being successful as a rational agent—doing what reason requires one to do—amounts to. Nobody, I submit, would be willing to say that what X actually did—apart from its being successful, a good thing to do, etc.—was made a rational course by the reason he had, and because of his having it. In the odd case, in short, X neither would nor, I take it, should be judged to have acted rationally (he was not, as an agent, rational), although we may perhaps judge that what he did was, though unsupported by reason, the right thing to do. While his action was not supported by reason, it was, by luck or by chance, successful.[20]

Notice that the issue is not, once again, whether we should allow for excuses. That I non-culpably believe that nobody has been buried alive in my garden may indeed count as an excuse for my not digging holes there. But, when I do actually start digging holes, excuses are beside the point. The argument drawing on permissible ignorance as an excuse amounts to claiming that reasonable ignorance prevents us from finding fault in what the agent did. The odd case shows, however, that belief is required in order to find *merit*, in the court of reason, in the agent's action.

These considerations feed back on our understanding of the nature of reasons for action. Let us consider a statement of the form:

   (1) The fact that p is a reason for X to φ

---

[20] See for a closely related point Dancy, *Practical Reality* (n. 5 above), 65, 66, 68. The notion of a rational action should be sharply contrasted with that of the successful action. Rational action may be unsuccessful; an action may be unsupported by reason, even irrational, and yet successful—it may even be the 'best' or the 'right' thing to do, in some senses of these words. The main reason why the two notions have to be kept apart is that an action may be successful by accident, or by luck. Acting rationally, however, should be sharply contrasted with merely happening to hit one's target by luck, or by accident. In this respect, the notion of rational action raises difficulties analogous to those raised, in the field of the theory of knowledge, by Gettier-style counter-examples to the standard tripartite analysis of sentences of the form 'X knows that p'. Paraphrasing what Jonathan Dancy writes about the point of such counter-examples (J. Dancy, *Introduction to Contemporary Epistemology* (Oxford: Blackwell, 1985), 23, 24, 32, 33, 36, 38, 40) it might be said that the point of contrasting rational action with action merely happening to be in accordance with the reasons for action which, according to objectivist views, one actually has, is to shape our understanding of practical rationality so as to 'prevent any lucky strike to count as rational action' (a rational agent 'does the right thing, and not just by luck'). In the odd case, X's φ-ing is 'too lucky or too luckily right to count as rational action' (there is 'too much luck around'). It should be noticed, however, that Raz may not agree with the general thrust of these remarks. See *Engaging Reason* (n. 2 above), 93, 94; and (about knowledge, and 'epistemic luck') ibid. 141, 155. See also, for a clear statement of the background view Raz endorses (though not directly related to the issues we are now discussing), Raz, *Ethics in the Public Domain* (Oxford: Oxford University Press, 1994), 16. The issue will be briefly taken up below, in section VI.

Suppose X does not believe that p is the case (or, he believes that it is not the case that p). Might p be reason for X to φ? (i.e., might (1) be true?) Suppose, once again, that, unknown and unknowable to me, someone has been buried alive in my garden. Is the fact that someone has been buried alive in my garden a reason for me not to go on holiday, and to dig holes there instead? On the one hand, we may be inclined to give an affirmative answer (Raz's reminder: 'if p is the case, then the fact that I do not believe that p does not establish that p is not a reason for me to perform some action').[21] On the other hand, however, we may feel uneasy. Should the agent refrain from going on holiday, and start digging holes in his garden? As long as he doesn't believe that somebody has been buried alive there, no. Should we say that the action (refraining from going on holiday, and digging holes instead) is made rational—that it is shown to be reasonable— by its being the case that someone has been buried alive in the agent's garden?[22] Or that reason requires of him that he doesn't go on holiday, and spend some time digging holes there? No, I think. So, might a statement of the form:

(2) There is a reason for X to φ

be true, in case X doesn't believe that there is reason for him to φ? On the one hand, yes ('the fact that I am not aware of any reason does not show that there is none').[23] But, should X φ? So long as he doesn't believe that there is a reason for him to φ, reason doesn't require him to φ.

This doesn't mean that reasons for action are beliefs. On the one hand, the direct question argument (section II above) stands unchallenged. And, on the other hand, the argument so far leads to a different conclusion. Our second and third hypotheses show that its being the case that X has a reason to φ depends on X's beliefs. Lacking belief, or suitably qualified belief, the fact that, by hypothesis, is a reason for X to φ cannot count as a reason—it doesn't speak in favour of the action any more. Thus, what these hypotheses show is that belief affects what can count as a reason, that is, what can *be* a reason. Depending on whether the agent has suitable beliefs, facts being reasons for a given action may be, or be not, such reasons.[24] In this sense, and to this extent, objectivist claims about the nature of reasons for action are inherently unstable.

---

[21] *Practical Reason and Norms* (n. 1 above), 17.

[22] See Dancy, *Practical Reality* (n. 5 above), 65.

[23] Raz, *Practical Reason and Norms* (n. 1 above), 17.

[24] The odd case, too, shows that, in explaining what it is to act rationally, an epistemic filter is required. (The agent must at least believe that someone has been buried alive in his garden.) Once again, however, the function of the filter, here, is utterly different from the one it had, according to defenders of pure objectivism, in our first hypothesis. There, the filter's point was to help us in identifying excuses. And this, in turn, allowed for the distinction between the deontic and the evaluative to play a role in the account. In the odd case, the filter is required in order to identify what may count as a reason—in short, what may held to *be* a reason. Here, so far as I can see, the distinction between the evaluative and the deontic has no bearing whatever. (Should we say that, in acting as he did, the agent, though not doing what he should have done, acted well? Or that, though acting badly—or indifferently—he actually did what he should have done?)

Reasons for action are, it might perhaps be said, what-we-believe, or facts-believed (this is only a tentative suggestion). They are not, plainly, the facts themselves, whether they are believed or not.[25]

Let us now take stock. Pure objectivism is committed to holding that, in the odd case, X's φ-ing is, *pro tanto*, rational. This claim is, I think, patently absurd. Therefore, pure objectivism must be rejected. Practical rationality *is* to be assessed relative to the beliefs of the agent, or from within the agent's perspective. As a consequence, objectivist claims about reasons for action turn out to be inherently unstable. This is, in fact, what was to be expected. If reasons are what speaks in favour of actions, or what makes them rational, reasonable, or sensible, then, if reasons are belief-independent, its being rational to φ or not will itself be belief-independent—it will depend on the facts alone. But this, as our three hypotheses show, has counter-intuitive implications. If, on the other hand—granted that reasons are what makes it rational to act in some way or other—belief (as our three hypotheses show) does indeed play a role in making it rational to act in some way or other, then reasons for action are not belief-independent.[26] Reasons are what-we-believe (or, the facts-believed).

V. RAZ'S POSITION (I): OSCILLATIONS

The upshot of our discussion so far is that (i) practical rationality has a subjective dimension (in the sense specified above), and (ii) objectivism about reasons for action has to be amended. Purely objectivist accounts of the relationships existing between reasons-statements and judgements of practical rationality lead to strongly counter-intuitive results. This is pure objectivism's main weakness. It, in turn, reflects on the objectivist's understanding of the nature of reasons. Reasons for action are not belief-independent.

Is Raz's position a version of pure objectivism? As far as I can tell, it isn't. On the one hand, Raz does not explicitly endorse pure objectivism's third claim (the agent's beliefs make no difference as to whether an action is rational or not; above, section II). On the other hand, he is well aware of the complexities surrounding 'the relations between rationality and reasons',[27] and he carefully distinguishes questions as to what reasons there are from issues concerning the

---

[25] What are facts-believed? I have no answer to this question. My argument is dialectical.

[26] Dancy, *Practical Reality* (n. 5 above) 58, 65, denies this. We may, he claims, ask 'what it would have been right to do relative to a certain body of facts' (e.g., a body of facts delimited on the basis of a suitable 'agent-relative epistemic filter'), but the relevant notion of a reason is, in all such cases, still the objectivist one (reasons themselves are not, that is, relativized to the agent's beliefs). I find this remark puzzling. The odd case shows that in asking questions as to what would be right to do, we *have* to ask them relative to those facts which are, in some suitable sense, available to the agent (unless we do that, we will have to grant that, in the odd case, the agent is acting rationally). What else could be needed in order to show that the notion of a reason has to be relativized to the agent's beliefs—namely, that reasons are not belief-independent?   [27] *Engaging Reason* (n. 2 above), 1.

evaluation of actions, or agents, as rational or irrational.[28] I think it is fair to say, however, that Raz doesn't directly address the difficulty raised by our three hypotheses, nor pays it the attention it deserves (though it is, I have attempted at showing, a genuine difficulty for objectivists, deserving careful consideration). True, he distinguishes between questions as to what reasons there are and issues about whether actions are, or would be, rational or irrational (and he also allows the agent's beliefs to play a role in answering questions of the latter sort).[29] But—quite apart from not providing a systematic treatment of the issue—there are, in his work, some oscillations, and some obscurities.

Thus, Raz claims that 'a person's action can be judged to be well grounded in reason or not according to whether there actually are reasons for performing the action. It can also be assessed as reasonable or rational according to whether the person had reasons to believe that there were reasons for his action'.[30] But what is, exactly, the difference between an action being 'well grounded in reason', on the one hand, and its being 'rational or reasonable', on the other hand? When X unreasonably, though rightly, believes that he has a reason to φ, is his φ-ing well grounded in reason? Or, when I start digging holes in my garden, is what I am doing well grounded in reason? (Luckily, someone has been buried alive there.)

Elsewhere, Raz even claims that 'we use explanatory reasons in judging the agent's rationality in doing what he did—rationality is measured in the light of the agent's own beliefs and goals'.[31] But this seems too harsh. There has to be some connection between rationality in action and what (normative) reasons the agent has. This is more so for an objectivist.[32]

At times, it seems to me, Raz comes very close to endorsing pure objectivism. He writes that 'intelligibility depends, according to the common assumption, on how things looked to the agents at the time. *Justification and evaluation depend on how things really were at the time*, though they allow for different types or dimensions of evaluation which take greater or lesser account of the agent's subjective perspective'.[33] The claim I have emphasized is, I think, vulnerable to the odd case objection (and, generally, to the criticism raised by our three hypotheses)—though no doubt what immediately follows should make our verdict uncertain. He explains: 'justifications (at least some kinds of justifications) do not depend on the agents' perspective, and do not depend on the reasons for which agents actually acted'.[34] Once again, the position looks vulnerable to the

---

[28] See *Practical Reason and Norms* (n. 1 above), 22; Raz, 'Introduction' (n. 1 above) 3; *Engaging Reason* (n. 2 above), 31, 74–5, 183, 219–20, 229–30.

[29] See *Practical Reason and Norms* (n. 1 above): 'it is the world which guides our action, but since it inevitably does so through our awareness of it, our beliefs are important for the explanation and assessment of our behaviour'.   [30] Ibid., 22.

[31] Raz, 'Introduction' (n. 1 above), 3.

[32] According to Raz, the main defect in Dancy's particularistic understanding of reasons for action is that 'it drives a wedge between reasons for action and the evaluation of those actions' (*Engaging Reason* (n. 2 above), 229; see also ibid., 219–20, 230). But, it may be argued, objectivist claims are liable to the same charge (driving a wedge between its being the case that there is a reason for X to φ, and its being rational for X to φ) unless the wedge is removed by endorsing pure objectivism.

[33] Ibid., 31 (my emphasis).   [34] Ibid., 31.

odd case objection—though the bracketed qualification makes things uncertain (*what* justifications are we talking about, exactly?).

These oscillations are, I suggest, symptoms of an unresolved tension—of what I termed the inherent instability of objectivism. Does rationality in action amount to being responsive to reasons, as Raz often suggests,[35] or does it amount to being responsive to reasons 'as we see them' ('acting [. . .] for reasons, *as one takes them to be*')?[36] Is a rational agent responsive to the reasons he has, or is he responsive to what, as he believes, are the reasons he has? The crux of the matter lies, I have argued, in the conceptual relation between reasons-statements and judgements of practical rationality (i.e., between there being a reason to φ and its being rational to φ). Raz is, of course, well aware of the difficulty. There are, in Raz's work, some hints as to the necessity of a subjective epistemic and normative filter on which facts can count as reasons.[37] I have shown, however, that full acknowledgment of this difficulty dictates both the rejection of pure objectivism, and an acknowledgement that objectivist claims about the nature of reasons are unstable. (That is, arguments leading to the abandonment of pure objectivism feed back on an objectivist understanding of the nature of reasons.) Though not endorsing pure objectivism, Raz is somehow unclear on the former. The latter is missing in his work.

VI. Raz's position (II): conformity vs. compliance

In discussing Raz's approach to the topic of this paper, however, a further element has to be taken into account. There is, in Raz's work, a strand that, to some extent, prevents his views from being liable to the criticism I have put forward, in the previous sections, against objectivist claims. Raz is strongly inclined towards understanding reasons for action as reasons for conformity, rather than as reasons for compliance. And this, perhaps, diminishes the extent to which his views may be held to be vulnerable to anti-objectivist claims. Let us see why.

The words 'conformity' and 'compliance' (with a reason) are to be understood, here, as follows.[38] Assume the fact that p is a reason for X to φ. X conforms with the reason if he φ-s; if, in addition, he φ-s because he realizes that p, and that the

---

[35] See e.g. *Engaging Reason* (n. 2 above), 11, 15.

[36] Ibid., 1 (my emphasis), 10. See also ibid., 8, 15, 76 ('. . . whether they are appropriate or intelligible given the reasons for and against them, as these reasons are, or as they are reasonably perceived by the agent'), 77 (Rationality is 'the ability to respond appropriately to (perceived) normative aspects of the world'); *The Morality of Freedom* (n. 8 above), 339.

[37] 'Whether or not an act is justified is an objective question, depending on how things were or could reasonably have been believed to be, rather than on the agent's beliefs' (ibid., 153, n. 2). (What the odd case shows, however, is that the latter, too, is somehow required.) See also *Engaging Reason* (n. 2 above), 76, 90, 151, 183. On reasonable ignorance as an excuse, see *Practical Reason and Norms* (n. 1 above), 186; and, on the possibility of rational false beliefs, see *Engaging Reason* (n.2 above), 75.

[38] These are, in a simplified form, Raz's own definitions. See *Practical Reason and Norms* (n. 1 above), 178.

fact that p is a reason for him to φ, then he (also) complies with the reason. The question Raz asks is:

Are reasons for action reasons for conformity or for compliance? That is, does one do all that one has reason to if he conforms with the reasons which apply to one, or need one comply with them, so that one is at fault if one does not? [. . .] Do they aim at action, so that if the action occurs all is as well as it should be? Or do they aim at one's reasoning as well, so that they demand, as it were, to figure in one's reasoning and/or in one's motivation?[39]

He then goes on to argue that 'reasons for action are, barring special circumstances, merely reasons to conform' ('what matters is conformity with reason').[40]

Regarding reasons for action as reasons for conformity, rather than reasons for compliance, weakens, to some extent, the strength of the anti-objectivist objections prompted by our three hypotheses. The reason is obvious. Conformity (with a reason one has) does not, by definition, require belief (that one has the reason). An agent may conform with a reason he has while remaining wholly unaware of it. Thus, if rationality in action consists, fundamentally, in conforming to the reasons for action there are, belief may, it seems, be removed from the picture, at no loss whatever. True, compliance will often be the way rational agents conform to reasons. But this is not (special cases aside) required by reason.

The issue of whether reasons for action are reasons for compliance or for conformity is a deep and difficult one. I shall confine myself to a few general remarks.

First, the conformity thesis (reasons for action are, fundamentally, not reasons to comply, but only reasons to conform) may be held to have counter-intuitive implications. Since 'in order to be guided by what is the case a person must come to believe that it is the case',[41] we would have to grant that reasons for action are not—not primarily, nor fundamentally—guides to action; that their point is not—not primarily, nor fundamentally—to guide behaviour.[42] That is, we would have to give up the view that 'reasons are there to guide action'— that 'their very nature is that they should guide'.[43] This I find implausible.[44]

---

[39] Ibid., 179.
[40] Ibid., 180, 190. See also ibid., 182, 183, and the argument in *Engaging Reason* (n. 2 above), 90–4.   [41] *Practical Reason and Norms* (n. 1 above), 17.
[42] See ibid., 179. Or, perhaps, that they are 'merely legitimate guides' (ibid., 179, 183).
[43] Ibid., 183. Contrast Raz, 'Introduction' (n. 1 above), 4: 'Reasons are those facts by which behaviour should be guided'.
[44] The implausibility of giving up the idea that reasons are, fundamentally, reasons for compliance is perhaps mitigated by a remark of Raz's: 'All reasons are reasons to take sufficient steps to conform to them, and attempting to comply is such a step' (*Practical Reason and Norms* (n. 1 above), 197). But this is puzzling. Suppose that X conforms to a reason he has, R, because he (intentionally, I assume) takes sufficient steps to conform to it; does he not also comply with R? Thus, if reasons are reasons to take sufficient steps to conform to them, they are reasons for compliance.

Specifically, second, endorsing the conformity thesis may make our understanding of reasons vulnerable to the odd case objection. In digging holes in my
garden while unaware that someone has been buried alive there, I do conform
to the reason, while not complying with it. True, Raz's position is not itself
liable to this charge. The question Raz asks is whether there is anything *wrong*
with mere conformity—whether agents who merely conform fail in any way.[45]
His claim is that, other things being equal, as long as one conforms with
reasons, though not complies with them, 'there is nothing wrong with one'.[46]
But, it might be replied, the point of the odd case is not to show that, under
those conditions, we may find fault in the agent. It is, rather, to insist that we
cannot find in him any *merit* either, in the court of reason. Granted that, from
the point of view of reason, there is, in mere conformity, 'no loss, no defect,
blemish, or any other shortcoming',[47] it should also be granted that there is, in
it, no gain, no achievement, no merit as well.

This leads us to a third and more fundamental point. Mere conformers with
reasons do not act for the reason they have. They merely happen to behave as
the reasons indicate. That is, it is generally possible, though often unlikely, 'that
one could conform with reason by chance'.[48] Thus, the conformity thesis blurs
the distinction which, I suggested (above, section IV), should be drawn
between, on the one hand, rational action, or acting for a good reason, and, on
the other hand, merely successful action. A mere conformer's action is, by luck
or by chance, successful. Reason does allow this—he is not acting irrationally.
But should we say that (special circumstances apart) this is all that it requires?
I would rather say that, while his action is lucky, this is not what being
successful as a rational agent—doing what reason requires one to do—amounts
to. Doing what reason requires should be sharply contrasted with merely
happening to hit one's target by luck, or by accident.[49]

VII. CONCLUSION

Does my argument show that reasons for action are beliefs? No. On the one
hand, the direct question argument stands unchallenged. From the agent's own
perspective, what should guide his actions are—special circumstances aside—
the facts, not his beliefs thereabout. And, on the other hand, the conclusion the
argument leads us to is, I think, a genuinely paradoxical one. What our three
hypotheses show is that, depending on whether the agent has suitable beliefs,

[45] See *Practical Reason and Norms* (n. 1 above), 178, 179.
[46] Ibid., 183.   [47] Ibid., 182.
[48] *Engaging Reason* (n. 2 above), 94. See also ibid., 93, 112.
[49] As hinted above (see n. 20), however, Raz may not agree with the general thrust of these
remarks. His understanding of whether, and how, rationality, knowledge, morality, and well-being
are to be contrasted with merely happening, by luck, to hit some target, may be different.

facts being reasons for a given action may turn out to be, or not to be, such reasons. An objectivist view of the nature of reasons for action is, though plausible, unstable. We are pulled in opposite directions at the same time.[50]

'Ultimately'—Raz writes—'reasons are facts; our beliefs matter only inasmuch as and because they aim at the facts.'[51] The argument in this paper does not challenge this claim. My aim has been to lay stress on Raz's 'ultimately', and to spell out its implications. In a metaphor, rational agents never get where reasons ultimately are; their ways move at a distance from there. When considering the nature of normative reasons for action (i.e. what it is that is a reason for acting in some way or other), it has to be granted that, be it only inasmuch as and because they aim at the facts, beliefs matter.

---

[50] Whether this is Moore's paradox in disguise is an issue I shall not take up here.
[51] *Practical Reason and Norms* (n. 1 above), 198.

4

Authority for Officials

JEREMY WALDRON

I. INTRODUCTION

In philosophical discussions of authority, we usually have in mind a confrontation between an official and a subject. Some ordinary citizen with views of his own about how to behave confronts an official directive which purports to steer him on a path he would not have chosen had he been left to his own devices. Can submission to such directives ever be justified? The best recent work on authority (the work of Joseph Raz) has consisted in elaborating the conditions that would have to be satisfied, in terms of the subject's reasons for action, before an affirmative answer could be given.[1]

But not all questions of authority are of this type. They do not all involve subjects' responses to directives from officials. I don't mean to raise issues about theoretical authority (the authority of a historian, for example, or the authority that one might cite for a proposition). I want to remain firmly in the area of practical authority. But I want to consider *authority as between officials or institutions*— the authority of a legislature over a court, for example, or the authority of a constitutional court over a legislature, or the authority of a legislature over an administrative agency. As we shall see, it is usually not possible to understand the relation between one official or institution and another without understanding the relation between officialdom in general and those over whom officialdom ultimately rules (ordinary citizens). The relations come in one package. However, I would like to examine the package afresh in a way that emphasizes inter-official or inter-institution authority. And at the end I shall consider whether or not this relation can usefully be treated as a special case of Raz's general conception.

II. THE PRINCIPLE OF INSTITUTIONAL SETTLEMENT

The model which I shall set out is inspired by something called 'the principle of institutional settlement' (PIS) expounded in the 1950s at the beginning of the

---

[1] For Joseph Raz's work on authority, see *The Authority of Law. Essays on Law and Morality* (Oxford: Clarendon Press, 1979), chs. 1–2; 'Authority and Justification', *Philosophy and Public Affairs*, 14 (1985), 3–29; *The Morality of Freedom* (Oxford: Clarendon Press, 1986), chs. 2–4; 'Introduction', *Authority*, ed. Raz (New York: New York University Press, 1990); and *Ethics in the Public Domain. Essays in the Morality of Law and Politics* (Oxford: Clarendon Press, 1994), esp. ch. 9.

well-known 'Legal Process' materials, by Henry Hart and Albert Sacks of Harvard Law School. Hart and Sacks began their account with the following platitudes:

> People who are living together under conditions of interdependence must obviously have a set of understandings or arrangements of some kind about the terms on which they are doing so. . . . [H]owever such understandings have come about—whether by the development of customary patterns of behavior, or express agreement, or both—they will necessarily be indeterminate in many respects. They will therefore require to be clarified from time to time as points of dispute or uncertainty arise, and some means of securing resolution or clarification will accordingly be needed. . . . [Also] as people gain in experience and social conditions change, existing understandings will prove from time to time to be inadequate, or at least will be thought inadequate by some members of the community. Demands will arise both for changes in the existing group understandings and for additional arrangements, and some means will be needed for dealing with these demands.[2]

Thus substantive understandings or arrangements will have to be complemented by what Hart and Sacks call '*constitutive* or *procedural* understandings or arrangements about how questions in connection with arrangements of both types are to be settled.'[3] In a complex society, these procedural arrangements are institutionalized. But institutionalization by itself is not enough. It is important that the determinations be *respected* in the society. That's where law and law's authority come in.

Implicit in every such system of procedures is the central idea of law—an idea which can be described as the principle of institutional settlement. The principle builds upon the basic and inescapable facts of social living which have been stated: namely the fact that human societies are made up of human beings striving to satisfy their respective wants under conditions of interdependence, and the fact that this common enterprise inevitably generates questions of common concern which have to be settled, one way or another, if the enterprise is to maintain itself and to continue to serve the purposes which it exists to serve. . . . The principle of institutional settlement expresses the judgement that decisions which are the duly arrived at result of duly established procedures of this kind ought to be accepted as binding upon the whole society unless and until they are duly changed.[4]

PIS

Hart and Sacks do not assume that PIS governs primarily the actions of ordinary citizens.[5] It is not presented as a straightforward principle of obedience—as

---

[2] H. M. Hart and A. M. Sacks, *The Legal Process. Basic Problems in the Making and Application of Law*, ed. W. N. Eskridge and P. P. Frickey (Westbury, NY: Foundation Press, 1994), 3.
[3] Ibid.
[4] Ibid., 4. (W. N. Eskridge and P. P. Frickey, 'The Making of the Legal Process', *Harvard Law Review*, 107 (1994), 2031–55, 2045 observe that this was the most revised passage in the *Legal Process* materials.)
[5] But see the gloss on it by Eskridge and Frickey, ibid.: 'This statement of legal obligation was succinct, elegant, and straightforward: citizens have a duty to follow 'duly arrived at' decisions by the

though its normative output were simply: '*Comply* with institutional settle-ments.' They observe that their principle is an 'ought'-statement, based on certain reasons;[6] but they do not assume that the principle's prime function is to indicate reasons for the ordinary citizen. Certainly it indicates reasons for citizens. But—at least as important—the principle indicates reasons for other *institutions* and for *officials* operating such institutions. As a matter of fact, it is best-known in legal theory as a principle governing the activity of courts. It 'forbids a court to substitute its own ideas for what the legislature has duly enacted,'[7] and against the background of a practice of *stare decisis* it also commands respect for precedent. 'Respect for the principle of institutional settlement demands . . . [that what] a legislature has duly determined ought not to be set at naught by any other agency or person. What earlier judicial decisions have duly settled ought not to come unsettled.'[8] In other words, the principle characteristically commands respect for a given settlement from other bodies whose function it might also be, in certain circumstances, to arrive at binding settlements.

III. FROM PRINCIPLE TO CONDITION

The Hart and Sacks principle of institutional settlement has been criticized by some theorists as unduly conservative, redolent of a Cold War 'end-of-ideology'

state.' See also Charles Fried, 'Moral Causation', *Harvard Law Review*, 77 (1964), 1258–70, 1268, applying the principle to civilly disobedient protestors.

[6] With quite extraordinary analytic sensitivity for Harvard law professors in the 1950s, Hart and Sacks make the following observation (*The Legal Process* (n. 2 above), 5):

> When the principle of institutional settlement is plainly applicable, we say that the law 'is' thus and so, and brush aside further discussion of what it 'ought' to be. Yet the 'is' is not really an 'is' but a special kind of 'ought'—a statement that, for the reasons just reviewed, a decision which is the duly arrived at result of duly established procedure for making decisions of that kind 'ought' to be accepted as binding upon the whole society unless and until it has been duly changed.

> Later they gloss this position as follows: 'Insistence on the distinction between law and morals can at times be understood as an expression, in substance, of PIS. That principle requires that a decision which is the due result of duly established procedures be accepted whether it is right or wrong—at least for the time being. . . . Yet it is important that this distinction—even in this situation, in which a duly made settlement is in question—is not in a just sense a distinction between law and morals. It is a distinction rather between one aspect of morals in relation to law and another. For the proposition that settled law should be respected, until it is duly changed . . . is itself an ethical concept. . . .' (Ibid., 109.)

[7] Ibid., 1194.

[8] Ibid., 147. Note that this does not mean that every piece of legislation must be regarded as duly enacted. In an American-style system with constitutional restraints on the legislature, one of the tasks of an ordinary court may be to determine, for a contested piece of legislation, whether or not it is *intra vires* the legislature, so far as its content and its form as well as its mode of enactment are concerned. Nor does it mean that legislation or past precedents are always clear or self-applying: where their implications for an instant case are unclear, what the principle explains is why the court should take it as its task to interpret *this text* rather than simply address the presented issue afresh. (See ibid., 1194–6.) Nor, finally, does PIS entail that a court should never revisit an issue, assuming it is competent to do so. (See, e.g. the House of Lords' *Practice Statement (Judicial Precedent)* [1966] 1 WLR 1234.)

proceduralism.[9] Many of these critiques are actually focused on the combination of PIS with a theory of institutional competence which (the critics believe) amounts to an attack on judicial review of legislation and civil rights litigation; and that does not interest us here. In the broader Legal Process school, PIS was complemented by theories of institutional competence (claiming, for example, that courts are better at settling certain kinds of issues than others.)[10] However, it is important not to conflate institutional settlement and institutional competence.[11] Claims of institutional competence are contributions to disputes about the allocation of institutional authority—disputes which themselves must be settled by authority. Suppose a given official believes (on institutional competence grounds) that a certain type of issue would be better settled by a legislature than by the courts. If the constitution in fact entrusts such issues to the courts, then PIS requires respect for *that* settlement; and this means that the official should respect the determination of a court on such an issue, whether or not he agrees with that determination and whether or not *he* thinks courts are in fact competent to decide such issues well. Still, even leaving institutional competence aside, PIS by itself seems to invite criticism, inasmuch as it just asserts with very little argument the importance of respecting duly arrived at settlements.[12] What argument there is seems Hobbesian in character.[13] After setting out the principle, the authors remark: 'To leave

[9] J. Auerbach, *Unequal Justice. Lawyers and Social Change in Modern America* (New York: Oxford University Press, 1976), 260. Another scholar said that it 'rested on the complacent, simplistic assumption that American society consisted of happy, private actors maximizing their valid human wants while sharing their profound belief in institutional competencies.' (E. Mensch, 'The History of Mainstream Legal Thought', *The Politics of Law. A Progressive Critique*, ed. David Kairys (New York: Pantheon Books, 1990), 18–39, 30)

[10] See, e.g., Lon Fuller, 'Forms and Limits of Adjudication,' *Harvard Law Review*, 92 (1978), 353–409.

[11] For an unhelpful example of such conflation, see D. K. Brown, 'Structure and Relationship in the Jurisprudence of Juries,' *Hastings Law Journal*, 47 (1996), 1255–1323, 1263, reading PIS as holding that '[i]n the absence of a consensus on whether a particular policy or decision is substantively correct, decision making by government bodies is legitimate when it comes from institutions that are the most competent (relative to other institutions) to make that decision.'

[12] According to G. Peller, 'The Metaphysics of American Law,' *California Law Review*, 73 (1985), 1151–1290, 1184, it appears that 'Hart and Sacks have utmost confidence that the principle is not controversial; it is either logically self-evident or a matter of universal consensus that peaceful dispute resolution is preferable to violence.' Peller continues:

The . . . principle of institutional settlement not only asks the reader to prefer peace to violence, the aspect of the principle which establishes its appeal, but further asks the reader to associate violence with disorder and peace with order. The underlying metaphoric structure groups are law, order, institutionalization, and peace on one side and non-law, disorder, non-institutionalization and violence on the other. These metaphoric connections between the dichotomies silently exclude the possibility that disorder may be peaceful and that order can be violent. In the process, the Hart and Sacks rhetoric implicitly de-legitimates insubordination as it exalts subordination.

[13] I am indebted here to A. J. Sebok, 'Reading the Legal Process,' *Michigan Law Review*, 94 (1996) 1571–95,1596.: 'The principle of institutional settlement clearly springs from Hobbes. . . . In Hart's notes to his 'Legislation' course, . . . Hart's debt to Hobbes becomes even more pronounced: 'When questions arise which in some way or other have to be settled, people find a means for settling them. The alternative to war is peace; the alternative to force is law.'

decision of these questions to the play of raw forces would defeat these purposes. The alternative to disintegrating resort to violence is the establishment of regularized and peaceable methods of decision. . . . [D]efiance of institutional settlements touches or may touch the very foundations of civil order . . . .'[14]

Now, as Raz has pointed out, this is not the way to articulate a theory of authority. One should not begin by assuming that we need authority, or that respect must be accorded to persons or institutions who currently claim authority for themselves. The point of a theory of authority is not to bolster such claims, but to provide a lucid basis for assessing them. True, a theory of authority is not just a list of the conditions under which an authority claim is justified: it must also illuminate the *justificandum*.[15] But it should not be presented in a way that claims there *is* a justification for any particular authority or even authority of any particular sort. To use the Hart and Sacks principle as the basis for a critical theory of authority, we must restate its premises as conditions. Instead of saying that the principle 'builds upon . . . *the fact* that human societies are made up of human beings striving to satisfy their respective wants under conditions of interdependence, and *the fact* that this common enterprise inevitably generates questions of common concern which have to be settled, one way or another, if the enterprise is to maintain itself,'[16] we say that duly arrived at settlements should be respected only if the following *condition* is satisfied: 'Human interdependence generates questions of common concern which have to be settled, one way or another.'

How can we tell whether this condition is satisfied? In particular, what is meant by 'question of common concern'? Well, something is a question of common concern among a group of persons if it is better for a single answer to be accepted among them than for each person to deal with the question on his own, as best he can, as far as it affects or interests him, acting unilaterally on the basis of his own answer. 'Better' here may mean 'better for each' or simply 'better.' The idea of common concern is not tied rigidly to the self-interest of the persons affected.[17] It may be better, for example, that a group of people act together to save the dolphins than that each follow unilaterally the course he thinks appropriate so far as dolphins are concerned, even though the *interests* of none of the people concerned are promoted by the common strategy. (Obviously PIS will have a somewhat different ethical basis and force depending on whether 'better' is used in this way or in a way that makes reference to the parties' self-interest. However, there is no need for this to be settled in the model, provided we are aware of the difference it might make.)

[14] Hart and Sacks, *The Legal Process* (n. 2 above), 4 and 109.
[15] See Raz, *The Authority of Law* (n. 1 above), 5.
[16] Hart and Sacks, *The Legal Process* (n. 2 above), 4 (my emphasis).
[17] The comments on this in Raz, 'Introduction,' (n. 1 above), 7–9, are very helpful.

Notice also that something being a question of common concern is relative to a given range of answers, as well as to a given group of people. Question Q may admit of answers X, Y, and Z. As between X and Y, it may be better that either answer be settled on as a common policy among the group than that each member choose between them as best he can, so far as Q affects or interests him, acting unilaterally on the basis of his own answer. But Z, though also a *possible* answer to Q, may be so bad that it would be better for each member to select and act on his own answer to Q than for Z to be adopted among them as a common policy. Strictly speaking, then, 'Q is a question of common concern in G' is an abbreviation for something like 'It is better that a single choice between X and Y as answers to Q be made for the whole group G than that the individual members of G select as between X and Y, each acting unilaterally on his own selection.'

Which questions actually *are* questions of common concern in this sense is not something which a theory of authority should try to settle. Also, something may be a question of common concern even though no member of the relevant group knows or believes this.[18] Obviously an appeal to PIS will get no grip on someone who believes that the matter in question is *not* a matter of common concern; nor, if he is *right* that this is not a matter of common concern, *should* the principle have any grip on him.[19]

To summarize: we have said that a duly arrived at settlement, X, should be respected by the members of group G, only if the following condition is satisfied:

X is chosen from a set of answers to a question arising in G such that, for each item in that set of answers, it would be better that that answer be adopted by all the individuals in G than that each individual in G select and act unilaterally on his own answer to the question.

This is not a sufficient explication of institutional settlement. We still need to analyse 'duly arrived at,' and we need also to understand the exact role and rationale of this requirement of respect in various circumstances.

IV. PUBLIC SETTLEMENT

When the condition set out at the end of section III is satisfied, there will be some cases in which everyone sees that there is but one way in which the question of common concern can be disposed of (i.e. the relevant set of answers is a singleton),

---

[18] See the comments on this in Raz, 'Introduction,' (n. 1 above), 9, are very helpful.

[19] Arguably, however, the question of which questions are questions of common concern is itself a question of common concern. It is common for constitutional systems to make arrangements for providing settled answers to that question, in which case applications of PIS become nested in a complex and interesting way.

and other cases in which there are several possible ways of disposing of it. So far as cases of the latter sort are concerned, some may involve options among which everyone is indifferent (no one has a view or preference in favour of one option or the other), while others may involve options over which people disagree.

In all three cases—i.e., (1) only one acknowledged option, (2) multiple options over which everyone is indifferent, (3) multiple options about which people disagree—the idea of institutional settlement has important work to do. The third case is the most important,[20] and I shall devote most of the rest of the paper to it: this is the case in which PIS seems most demanding. But (1) and (2) are important also. In all three cases, the principle asks officials and citizens to accept the fact that an institutional directive has been issued as a reason for putting the determination which it embodies into effect in order to settle the question of common concern that it addresses. There are various reasons that officials and citizens might hesitate to do this. They might disagree with the determination and maintain that the question should have been settled along different lines: this is case (3). Or they might hesitate to begin playing their own part in the given settlement unless they have an assurance that others will orient themselves to this particular settlement and play their part in it as well: case (2) is of this kind. (Actually case (3) will raise issues of this kind as well.)

Even when there are no such issues of disagreement or coordination along these lines—i.e., even in case (1)—there may still be work for the principle to do. A situation in which everyone sees (and agrees) what is to be done is not yet necessarily a situation in which they begin doing it. To respect a settlement in such circumstances is to register the fact that the given question of common concern *has* been answered officially and to do (or refrain from doing) whatever follows from the fact that this settlement has now officially been adopted. Here's an example: Everyone might see that a Declaration of War is the appropriate response for the United States after the attack on Pearl Harbor in 1941. But there are certain things to be done in the light of such a Declaration—rounding up enemy aliens, mobilizing troops, etc.—which are to be done only when it has actually been issued. To respect the Declaration is to accept for practical purposes that *now is the time* for those actions to be undertaken.

In cases where the implementation of a given settlement requires the action of two or more people, respecting the settlement will involve each person proceeding to his post, as it were, in readiness to act as soon as the others whose action is also required reach *their* posts. It may not require each person to literally begin the actions that he is supposed to perform along with the others—the first lifeboat man on the scene is not required to start rowing until the others are also actually there at the oars, ready to proceed. Still, at a minimum,

[20] See J. Waldron, *Law and Disagreement* (Oxford: Clarendon Press, 1999), 101–5 for the argument that, for the purposes of normative analysis, partial-conflict coordination games capture the essence of politics.

respecting a settlement means stepping out of pure readiness *in foro interno*[21] and signalling (by one's presence and preparation) to any others who turn up that their action along with one's own will not be in vain. Even pure coordination problems have this character: I should not actually begin driving on the right until I am assured that it is the practice of driving-on-the right rather than driving-on-the-left that others are about to participate in. Solutions to collective action problems like n-person Prisoner's Dilemmas have this character too, as do more simple cases involving the straightforward aggregation of effort.[22] Respecting the settlement in any case of this kind, then, involves not just getting ready to play one's part: it also involves taking the publicized fact of the settlement as the appropriate signal to take one's place in readiness for action.

Notice how important it is in all these cases that the settlement in question have a public dimension or presence. Hart and Sacks talk about a 'duly established' settlement,[23] where 'duly' refers to publicly recognized procedures, not just procedures which the person using the word 'duly' happens to like or admire. They are presumably themselves the product of institutional settlement of the question concerning public procedures. The latter question is an important one for any society to address. Members of the society should be interested not just in the quality of the procedures,[24] but in their status as *public* procedures. The specific ideal of legal settlement embodies this notion of public presence and so—I shall argue—does the notion of authority, at least in the political realm.

V. COORDINATION AND SALIENCE

In this section I want to concentrate on cases of types (2) and (3): questions of common concern which admit of several answers such that each member regards common action by the whole group on any one of the answers as a better outcome than his acting unilaterally on the option he thinks best, irrespective of what the other members do. In a case like this, though each prefers either of the coordinative outcomes to either of the non-coordinative outcomes, things can still go badly. If neither has any preference between the two coordinative outcomes, still (if they have to decide simultaneously or incognito) each may be at a loss as to which option to set forth on.[25] If they do have a preference, there is no guarantee that their preference will coincide with

---

[21] Adapting a phrase from Thomas Hobbes, *Leviathan*, ed. Richard Tuck (Cambridge: Cambridge University Press, 1988), ch. 15, 110.

[22] See Donald Regan, *Utilitarianism and Cooperation* (Oxford: Clarendon Press, 1980). See also Leslie Green, *The Authority of the State* (Oxford: Clarendon Press, 1988), ch. 4.

[23] See text accompanying footnote 2, above.

[24] Hart and Sacks, *The Legal Process* (n. 2 above), 6, argue that lawyers must pay 'attention to the constant improvement of all the procedures . . . in the effort to ensure that they yield decisions which are not merely preferable to the chaos of no decision but are calculated as well as may be affirmatively to advance the larger purposes of the society.'

[25] See Regan, *Utilitarianism and Cooperation* (n. 22 above).

the preference of the other members. If they have a strong preference for one option, and they can communicate this to the other members, they may hold out for that option, hoping that the other members (with the contrary preference) will give in. On the other hand, even if they choose to defer to the other members and refrain from holding out, there is no guarantee that at the same time the other members will not have chosen—infuriatingly!—to defer to them.[26]

In all such cases, what is needed is for one of the options to be marked for all the members to see as *the one for everyone to follow*—I mean the one that everyone can follow in the confident expectation that others will do the same.[27] Such marking can occur in many ways—for example, by custom or other modes of informal convention.[28] If these don't work, however, and if the matter is regarded as important,[29] then the group will want to develop more formal procedures for settling on one of the options as the one for everyone to follow. This may be conceived as one of the functions of law-making: to make particular options salient in pure or partial conflict coordination problems. Certainly it is an obvious ground for the application of PIS. A duly enacted determination that X (for example) is the option to be followed in a situation of the sort we are considering should be respected by anyone who cares about the settlement of questions of common concern.

Some might ask whether 'respect' is the right word for the appropriate response to what after all is a mere signal of salience. Surely all that is required is that the members of the society *take note* of anything that promises to be a signal of salience noticed by all. In recent discussions, Donald Regan, Leslie Green, and others have emphasized that there is no question of obedience or submission here, or of any of the other attitudes and postures usually associated with respect for authority. No new reason enters the picture. Each member continues to act in response to exactly the array of reasons he was acting on before: the enactment of a signal—a legislature announcing, e.g., 'Round here we all drive on the right'—simply provides new information.[30]

I am not convinced. The criticism overlooks what has to be the case in order that something like law can provide signals of the appropriate sort.[31] Green

---

[26] For an excellent analysis, see Jean Hampton, *Hobbes and the Social Contract Tradition* (Cambridge: Cambridge University Press, 1986), ch. 6.

[27] I have adapted this formulation from Raz, 'Introduction' (n. 1 above), 7.

[28] See David Hume, *A Treatise of Human Nature*, second edition, ed. P. H. Nidditch (Oxford: Clarendon Press, 1978), 490; see also Leslie Green, 'Law, Coordination and the Common Good,' *Oxford Journal of Legal Studies*, 3 (1983), 299–324, at 312 ff.

[29] See John Finnis, *Natural Law and Natural Right* (Oxford: Clarendon Press, 1980), 232, for an account of how important such cases might be: '[U]ntil a particular choice is made, nothing will in fact be done. Morever in some forms of human community, that something be done is not just a matter of optional advantage, but is a matter of right, a requirement of justice.'

[30] Donald Regan, 'Authority and Value,' *Southern California Law Review*, 62 (1989), 995–1095, 1024–31; Green, 'Law, Coordination and the Common Good' (n. 28 above), 320–1. See also Raz, 'Introduction' (n. 1 above), 7.

[31] See Raz, 'Facing Up,' *Southern California Law Review*, 62 (1989), 1153–1235, 1118 '[T]he law endows the course of action it requires with salience precisely because it is recognized as authoritative by the population.'

rightly ridicules any suggestion that the key here is law's association with the Weberian power of the state and the pretensions to supremacy that this encourages: 'To simply assume that law's self-image as comprehensive and supreme is enough to procure this is to assume that its subjects are as idolatrous as it is egotistical.'[32] For law to be the signaller of last resort (when informal conventions fail to establish themselves), people must adopt in advance a certain attitude to it. That attitude, we may say, is respect for the law as a source of signals of salience, which general respect is then related dispositionally to one's respectful response to a particular signal designating an option as salient in coordinating a response to a question of common concern.

An analogy may help. During a pitched battle, it may be desirable for the soldiers on one side to move together (into some sort of formation) at a rallying point. If such a rallying point has not been designated in advance, then in the heat of battle it may be designated by some means such as a bugle call to attract attention and the raising of the regimental flag: the soldiers then break off their particular engagements if they can and move to the site where the flag has been raised. Now in a sense it is true that the raising of the flag provides nothing but information: anyone who understands the need to rally (at this moment) will simply see from the flag-raising that *that* is the site where the rally should take place. Still, it is not inappropriate to talk of respect for the flag in relation to a case like this. To respect the flag is to be alert to its raising, and then to respond quickly and without much further question or deliberation to the site where it has been raised, confident that one is responding in this way as part of a shared practice of responding to flag-raising, against a background of some awareness of the good such a practice might do. If a regiment did not have a flag and a practice of responding to it, it would have to invent something roughly equivalent. And what that shows is that it is not a matter of there being a flag, which then *happens* to provide this information at crucial moments; rather the regiment has a flag and the practice of responding to its raising as a way of quickly and decisively settling coordination problems in circumstances where failures of coordination (or even hesitating before coordination) would be disastrous.

All this reinforces the point made at the end of the previous section. It is important that the settlement of questions of common concern have a public presence. A procedure for settling such questions must be public not only in the sense of being prominent, but also in the sense of being the focus of a shared practice among those whose common affairs are implicated in the questions that arise for settlement. The practice is that of looking to the procedure for solutions to problems of this sort, being alert to its dispositions, communicating this alertness to others, and refraining from doing anything to diminish the confidence that others may have in the appropriateness of regarding the outputs of this procedure as salient. It's a practice in the strict sense of being something in which one cannot really participate on one's own without reference to the

---

[32] Green, 'Law, Coordination and the Common Good' (n. 28 above), 320.

participation of others; the attitudes that it embodies are necessarily thought of as *shared*. For all that, however, the practice does demand things of people one by one. As we saw in the previous section, it demands of each of us that we be alert to the appropriate signals, and that in receiving them we prepare to act in the appropriate way the instant it is clear—from the readiness of others—that our participation will not be futile. And it demands of each of us, for his or her part, that he/she not undermine the practical confidence we have in one another as an aspect of this practice.

VI. RESPECT AND COMPLIANCE

What does the PIS requirement of respect for duly arrived at settlements amount to? It means more than mere *compliance*. There are several points here. First, as we have seen, the requirement of respect may be incumbent on officials or institutions whose compliance or non-compliance with the decision is not in question. A judge faced with a statute, of which he disapproves, banning nude dancing for example, may have no intention of cavorting naked himself. If PIS applies to him *qua judge* in regard to this statute,[33] it requires him to respect the statute as settling something on which he and others disagree: namely whether nude dancing is to be prohibited. Respect for the settlement means that he is not to think of himself as being either permitted or required to decide whether nude dancing is to be prohibited. He is to treat that issue as settled in his dealings with citizens and other officials.[34]

Secondly, 'compliance' is an all-or-nothing word and as such it may fail to capture what respect for a settlement requires of an individual in circumstances where it is not yet clear how others will behave. If what is required is cooperative action, then respecting a settlement (e.g. that now is the time for some such action to be performed) means standing ready to play one's part, whether that amounts to full compliance or not.

Thirdly, if we identify respect too closely with compliance, we leave out all the cases where the settlement in question does not consist of a directive.[35] There may be a dispute in a community as to whether gifts made in immediate contemplation of death (*causa mortis*) are voided by the donor's recovery: the settlement of this question does not in itself amount to a directive with which anyone is required to comply. The matter may be settled even while other

---

[33] However, the judge would not be violating the duty of respect were he to make a good faith determination, on constitutional grounds, that the statute has not been 'duly' enacted. See note 8, above.

[34] Of course, the judge may face a decision about what counts as nude dancing, i.e. how to interpret and apply the provision in a hard case (topless dancing, for example, or baby shows). In such cases, the requirement of respect may mean that he should take the statute as a starting point for his decision.

[35] See H.L.A. Hart, *The Concept of Law*, 2nd edition, ed. Raz and Penelope A. Bulloch (Oxford: Clarendon Press, 1994), ch. III.

adjacent issues about gifts, wills, and property (which, with this, *would* add up to a directive) remain unsettled; the point is that one who respects the settlement will likely approach the task of settling any outstanding matters in a distinctive way.

What is common to all these cases is not that PIS requires action in accordance with the settlement, but that it requires that a duly enacted decision be treated *as a settlement*, and not as something which is of no consequence, leaving open for us the question it purports to address. It may not be possible to specify in advance what detailed actions or omissions are involved in treating a decision as a settlement of a question of common concern. And my points about compliance mean that seldom will it be possible simply to read this off from the content of the decision. A lot will depend on circumstances, for example whether we are in a case of type (1), (2), or (3), as set out in section 4.

In addition, I believe that different conceptions of the relation between respect and compliance may be articulated in different legal theories. For example, although it is no part of PIS that decisions should never be revisited,[36] opinions may differ as to the attitude to a given decision that the principle requires of those who propose, when they can, to repeal it. In *Law and Disagreement*,[37] I considered a case where the opponents of a statute proposed not merely to repeal it at a later date but also to indemnify anyone who had been fined in the meantime for breach of its provisions. The reaction to this proposal indicated that many jurists, politicians and observers regarded this as an affront to something like PIS; but one can imagine opinions differing on this, and those opinions would amount to differing conceptions of respect, so far as PIS is concerned.

If there is an essential core to the idea of respect in the context of institutional settlement—the *concept* of respect, perhaps, as opposed to particular conceptions of respect[38]—it is this. First, one must acknowledge that what is at stake here is a question of common concern; second, one must recognize the presence of established arrangements for producing answers to such questions; third, one must ascertain whether such arrangements have actually produced a decision that answers the question; and fourth, if they have, one must play one's part in the social processes that are necessary to sustain and implement such decision as a settlement.

The fourth requirement will seem particularly burdensome in cases where a person might contemplate answering the question of common concern in some different way, especially if he is not just a private citizen but an official, whose own determination might actually have some social influence of its own.

[36] Hart and Sacks's formulation (*The Legal Process* (n. 2 above), 4) talks of decisions being accepted 'as binding upon the whole society *unless and until they are duly changed*' (my emphasis).
[37] Waldron, *Law and Disagreement* (n. 20 above), 100–1. See also J. Waldron, *The Law* (London: Methuen, 1990), 8–11.
[38] For concept/conception, see Ronald Dworkin, *Taking Rights Seriously* (London: Duckworth, 1977), 134–6 and his *Law's Empire* (Cambridge: Harvard University Press, 1986), 70 ff.

A particular official, B, might be tempted to gainsay the decision that has actually been produced (let's say, by A), substituting for it a different decision of his own. Now B hopes, presumably, that the new decision will meet with more acceptance from other officials than A's decision received from B himself. The last point is very important: if B acknowledges that what we all face here is a question of common concern, then he cannot be satisfied simply with *announcing a view of his own*, with which he feels personally comfortable (on moral or whatever other grounds). B has to take an interest in the collective action structure of the problem that he and other members of the society face: he must take an interest in whether the question gets answered effectively *as* a question of common concern. Noticing the existence of the procedural arrangements that empowered A to make a decision—the second element of respect—is therefore not without consequence: in noticing that, B is observing that the society has and sustains a practice (or might do, if he and others played their part in it) of settling questions of common concern by making certain answers salient. By choosing nevertheless to gainsay A's decision, B in effect is acting as a hold-out, reckoning that the difference between the value of his decision and the value of A's decision is so great as to make it worth running the risk (to which he contributes) of no decision at all being accepted by the whole society.

Now maybe B is right about this: maybe the risk is worth running. PIS may require him to defer to A's decision nevertheless, as a matter of inherent respect for the practice which has been set up in his society for coping with such questions of common concern. For by ignoring A's decision, by holding out for his own, and by choosing unilaterally to run the risk of society's failing to settle on and implement a common answer to the question, he is making light of efforts that have been made already to solve these problems—efforts that depend for their success on the assurance of support from him and people like him. This point is particularly important, given A's position *as an official* vis-à-vis ordinary citizens. Ordinary citizens must take their cues from the behaviour of officials as to when a settlement has been duly enacted, and it is important that these cues be available and reliable so that citizens know when it is appropriate for them to defer to a decision (which otherwise may not suit them or which they may not think appropriate) rather than make the best of one of these situations on their own.[39] If the official institutional structure is complex, then, decisions will come at the ordinary citizen from all directions—sometimes from police officers, sometimes from the IRS, sometimes from the courts, sometimes from Congress. To assure himself that his compliance with any number of these directives is not in vain, a citizen, C_1, must assume (implicitly or explicitly) that officialdom is operating coherently *as a system*, so that (for example) C_1 is not responding to Supreme Court directives on affirmative action while his fellow citizens, C_2, C_3, etc., are responding to contrary legislative directives. Which

---

[39] For the importance of an apparatus of recognition in this regard, see Waldron, *Law and Disagreement* (n. 20 above), 38–41.

cues C_1 is given, and his perceptions of the circumstances in which they are given and of the effects of responding to them, will in the long run either substantiate or undermine this assumption. That's why officials must proceed carefully.[40] Certainly there are things that C_1 can do on his own, without the complicity of officials like B, to subvert social processes for settling questions of common concern. That's why the laws said to Socrates: 'Do you imagine that a city can continue to exist and not be turned upside down, if the legal judgments which are pronounced in it have no force but are nullified and destroyed by private persons?'[41] But the amount of harm that an official can do is immeasurably greater.

Someone may complain that it is a mistake to associate official duties in this regard with something as theoretical as PIS. Surely, in a well-structured legal system, the duties associated with each official's role will indicate who he is supposed to defer to and when. In the last resort, the constitution will tell him what to do. No doubt. And if things are this well-organized, then the function of PIS is just to indicate what is at stake in rules of this kind and to encourage those to whom they apply not to take them lightly. Often, however, in complex institutional systems, the matter is indeterminate and controversial; and conflicting theories will be put forward indicating how an official (such as a judge) should behave when faced with an institutional decision he regards as wrong.[42] At that point PIS weighs in with its case for respect for decisions as settlements.

VII. FROM RESPECT TO AUTHORITY

The arguments so far have been set out in terms of a requirement of respect. Is there any reason not to rephrase them in terms of *authority*? Certainly common usage does not oppose such a characterization in inter-official contexts. We talk for example of courts deferring to legislatures, and deference is an appropriate response to an authoritative directive. We should also note the use of the language of authority in courts' respect for precedent: this should not be seen as purely theoretical authority, but as a matter of respect for institutional settlement.

Structurally, too, the account we have given seems appropriate for the language of authority. It provides an easy explanation of the relation between the uses of 'authority' and 'authoritative.' The decisions we are to respect we

---

[40] Compare Raz's apparently contrary view in *Ethics in the Public Domain* (n. 1 above), 330.

[41] Plato, *Crito* in *The Last days of Socrates*, trans. Hugh Tredennick (Harmondsworth: Penguin Books, 1959), 90. See also R. Kraut, *Socrates and the State* (Princeton: Princeton University Press, 1984), 115 ff.

[42] Often, too, these will be entangled with theories about institutional competence and also theories about how broadly we should construe constitutional requirements for designating a prior decision as appropriately or inappropriately taken. For various examples, see R. Cover, *Justice Accused* (New Haven: Yale University Press, 1973), on the judicial 'can't' and Dworkin, *Taking Rights Seriously* (n. 38 above), ch. 8.

may speak of as *authoritative*. And such decisions are to be respected (they are authoritative) not because of anything particular about *them* but because they have been produced in the right way by the appropriate person or entity: they spring from an *authority*, understood as such on the basis of the general account we have been giving. I have been at pains in this paper not to confine the appropriate response to authority to compliance. But whatever it is, respecting, responding, submitting, deferring to authority on the present account involves setting aside the reasons and reasoning one might use if there were no authority or if it had not issued any applicable decision; it means acting in a way that only makes sense because an authority has spoken in the kind of situation for which authorities are appropriate and important.

This, then, gives us a broad schema for testing authority claims. Not every claim of legal authority is justified or even appropriate. The account I have given insists first that the claims of any official or institution to authority be related to the need to settle certain questions of common concern. If a given institution does not characteristically address questions of common concern (in the sense defined in section 3), deciding among the set of answers that constitute such questions, then its claim to authority is suspect (or it will have to be assessed in some other way). Even if it does address such questions, there will be a further issue about whether the institution has the appropriate social presence. Not every entity that proposes to address questions of common concern is in fact in a position to address them. Whether it is or not will depend on whether there actually is or is emerging the appropriate social practice among those whose behaviour has to be coordinated.[43] Once we have established that we *are* dealing with an entity actually established as an authority and proposing to deal with questions of common concern, then there may be further questions about the authoritativeness of its particular edicts. Does a given decision actually address a question of common concern, and if it does not, is that a matter of controversy in regard to which a settlement procedure has been established? Has the decision been duly enacted, given the rules and other arrangements that establish the public existence and presence of the authority? What does the decision actually amount to and how is it to be interpreted? As one proceeds down this list of questions, one sees the way clear to setting up an adequate critical basis for the discernment, testing and recognition of authority claims.

VIII. Pre-emption and Dependence

Philosophical discussions of authority took an enormous step forward with the general acceptance of Raz's analysis, in particular with his so-called pre-emption

---

[43] A king in exile may issue all sorts of pronouncements for his erstwhile subjects which might in themselves helpfully answer such questions; in most cases, however, those few subjects who hear of these announcements will have no assurance that enough others will participate in implementing them to make their own participation worthwhile.

thesis, dependence thesis, and normal justification thesis.[44] How does Raz's conception relate to the account I have given of institutional settlements and authority as among officials?

Applying the pre-emption thesis to the cases we are discussing is pretty straightforward. The pre-emption thesis is the following:

the fact that an authority requires performance of an action is a reason for its perform-ance which is not to be added to all other relevant reasons when assessing what to do, but should exclude and take the place of some of them.[45]

The respect required by the PIS is a matter of setting aside reasoning that one might undertake in the absence of an authoritative directive. In the absence of a directive, one might try on one's own to figure out what is to be done and issue a directive of one's own in regard to a question of common concern. Respect for an existing settlement requires that one refrain from doing this. And the idea embodied in the pre-emption thesis is that it is not enough just to factor the existing settlement into one's own effort to settle the question. Nor is it a matter of factoring the desirability of this deference into one's own overall estimation of whether gainsaying the existing decision would be well- or ill-advised. Even doing that is disrespectful, inasmuch as it threatens to diminish the efforts *already* made by one's fellows in society to set up and sustain deter-minate procedures for settling questions of this kind. The extent to which the pre-emption thesis is common ground between the two conceptions—Raz's conception and the Hart and Sacks conception—is shown by the fact that PIS will not work unless settlements can be identified as such by subjects without their having to engage in the sort of activity that was necessary to produce them. This is very important in Raz's jurisprudence (particularly for his argu-ments against Ronald Dworkin's interpretive theory).[46] On Raz's account, it is important for law's aspiration to authority that recognizing and following something as law be an *alternative* to trying to figure out for oneself what is to be done about the matter that the law addresses.[47]

But all this has to be understood quite carefully. Suppose that a question, Q, arises in a certain community and that official A, determining that Q is a ques-tion of common concern, proceeds duly to settle it. Now Raz is right that B cannot respect A's decision in the appropriate sense if B has to go through the very process of deciding the question that A went through. But equally, B cannot respect A's decision, on the account I have given, without observing that Q *is a* question of common concern, i.e., without following A's reasoning *at least to that extent*. Maybe in real-life cases, B's grasp of this will be abbreviated or implicit. But if it is too abbreviated, it may be hard to justify describing B's posture as

---

[44] See Raz, *The Morality of Freedom* (n. 1 above), 46–53.   [45] Ibid., 46.
[46] See Raz, *Ethics in the Public Domain* (n. 1 above), 209.
[47] Ibid., 203: '[T]he subjects of any authority . . . can benefit by its decisions only if they can estab-lish their existence and content in ways which do not depend on raising the very same issues which the authority is there to settle.'

accepting A's decision as authoritative, as opposed to *simply submitting to A's decision*. Accepting A's decision as authoritative has a certain shape to it, on the account we are considering. In *central* cases of the acceptance of authority,[48] B's response will definitely be shaped by explicit awareness of what authority is and why it is important.

I suspect Raz might not accept this. He thinks the main contribution that legal authority can make in this kind of case is in the determination of when we are actually facing a coordination problem.[49] If *that* determination is to be authoritative, then it must pre-empt the subjects' own reasoning on the matter: so obviously the subject must have a way of identifying it (as authoritative) which does not involve him having to figure that we are actually facing a coordination problem. However, I imagine that Raz will accept that in these cases, authority does have to operate at two levels, and in the ideal case the levels will present themselves separately (or serially) to those contemplating them: at the first level, one accepts the authoritative determination that we face a coordination problem, and then at the second level we accept the authoritative determination of what is to be done in that situation.

These considerations also indicate some likely complications with Raz's dependence thesis. The dependence thesis goes as follows:

[A]ll authoritative directives should be based on reasons which already independently apply to the subjects of the directives and are relevant to their action in the circumstances covered by the directive.'[50]

The general picture that Raz presents is this: apart from the authority, citizen C is faced with a choice on which a set of reasons S_1 bear in fact (whether C is aware of those reasons or not); and a decision by A is authoritative for C as regards this choice only if A's decision is also based on the reasons in S_1, i.e., only if A addresses the choice situation on the very basis that it would have been appropriate for C to address it.

Now in coordination situations of the sort we have been examining, there are necessarily some complexities in the application of this schema. The choice between options X and Y as answers to Q may be understood in at least four ways: (1) a choice on the merits between X-ing and Y-ing as options for C considered on his own; (2) a choice on the merits between X and Y considered as options for the whole society; (3) a strategic choice (in the game-theoretic sense of 'strategic') for C, bearing in mind that X and Y present themselves as options in a coordination game in which C is participating along with others; and (4) a choice (probably also strategic) conceived explicitly as a way of trying to solve the coordination problem, e.g., as a way of *making* one of the options salient or riveting attention on its salience. There is no guarantee, I think, that a single set of reasons, S_1, is the set of reasons appropriate to each and all of these

---

[48] The reference here to 'central cases' alludes to the methodology of Finnis in *Natural Law and Natural Rights* (n. 29 above), ch. 1.   [49] Raz, 'Introduction' (n. 1 above), 10.

[50] Raz, *Morality of Freedom* (n. 1 above), 47.

choices, and so we should not presume any straightforward identity between the set of reasons to which it is appropriate for C to respond apart from the existence and actions of the authority, and the set of reasons which it is appropriate for the authority to use in formulating a directive for C.

For example, where C is an ordinary person, it might conceivably be appropriate for him to face up to the choice as presented in (1); but it would seldom be appropriate for A, the authority, to approach the choice in that light. It's no good saying that if A's intervention is appropriate, then the choice cannot be like (1) for C; for A's intervention may be the very thing which makes the difference between its being appropriate and its being inappropriate for people like C to think of this in some way other than (1). Let S_1 be the set of reasons appropriate for answering question (1). It seems to me very likely that A will have to address the matter with a slightly different set of reasons, perhaps S_2, oriented to question (2) above, with some help from S_4, oriented to (4), as well in cases where anticipated problems about compliance may affect what should be the course of action for the whole society. Raz's simple model—in which A and C (if C were acting alone) should be using the same set of reasons—is appropriate only to cases where (1) and (2) are in effect *the same question*, i.e., where there is no coordinative or strategic element.

On the other hand—in some complicated sense that I will not formulate here—there is clearly *some* dependence-relation between the set of reasons S_1 that would face C acting alone and the set of reasons S_2/S_4 that A should use in making his official decision. For A should certainly respond to the fact that the situation is as it is for C and people like him. If it is a coordination problem for C and his fellows, then A's response should bear that in mind, even if he cannot respond in exactly the way that C should respond when C is acting on his own. If there is nothing to choose between the options, then A should respond to them in that light; or if one option is better than another then A should respond to them in *that* light, bearing in mind of course the structure of the coordination problem (any coordinative choice being better than none, etc., even when the options are not indifferent). In other words, the spirit behind Raz's dependence thesis clearly does apply: there is no separate set of reasons for authorities to use that would not in principle be appropriate for the subjects of the authorities to use. It is just harder to formulate that point in regard to these coordination problems, where the presence or possibility of A as an authority actually changes the nature of the choices that the others face.

Now if all this is true as to the relation between official A and citizen C, it makes a difference I think to the relation between official A and official B (where B is tempted to second-guess A's directive). B's deference to A's authority may be rooted *ultimately* in the reasons for action (S_1) that would pertain to citizen C's own decision in the matter if C were figuring it out alone, just as A's exercise of his authority is rooted ultimately in those reasons. But the relation is pretty indirect. And I think that even more than in the case of A, B must orient himself primarily to a set of reasons that is in the first instance quite remote from the reasons that would face C (acting alone). B's deference to A's authority is based primarily on S_4 and some version of S_3, oriented to questions (3) and (4) respectively. What B most needs to know, as he contemplates whether to second-guess A, is that we are facing a question of common concern and that an attempt has already been made using recognized institutional arrangements to settle it *as a question of common concern*. That is the basis on which B should defer to A's decision. Now, as I said, the force of that argument does trace back ultimately to the importance of the original question and that will eventually engage some of the reasons in S_1; but in most cases the matter will be settled for B, the second official, long before we get to that stage of our reasoning.

IX. THE NORMAL JUSTIFICATION THESIS

'[T]he normal and primary way to establish that a person should be acknowledged to have authority over another person,' says Raz, 'involves showing that the alleged subject is likely better to comply with reasons which apply to him (other than the alleged authoritative directives) if he accepts the directives of the alleged authority as authoritatively binding, and tries to follow them, rather than if he tries to follow the reasons which apply to him directly.'[51]

As it stands, Raz's normal justification thesis (NJT), seems to apply best to simple relations between say, official and citizen. It is not clear how it applies to relations among officials. In fact, however, some of the difficulties surrounding the application of NJT to relations among officials stem from a fairly obvious shortcoming in NJT even for the simpler case. Here's the problem. As it stands, NJT seems to justify saying that A has authority over C simply by virtue of what would happen if C were to follow directives issued by A as opposed to following the reasons that apply to his choices as far as he himself can figure them out. But if this were accepted as a sufficient condition of A's having authority over C, it would imply that millions of people have authority over each one of us. For example: I have made a number of disastrous romantic choices, and on many of these choices I would have done better following the instructions of my closest friends than trying to figure things out for myself. Do we want to say therefore that my friends had authority over me in this regard? Or consider another example. In recent years the U.S. Congress, left to its own devices, has made disastrously unjust decisions about welfare reform, whereas the Conference of Catholic Bishops has produced several powerful and illuminating statements on the matter.[52] It is evident that the Congress would do better in

---

[51] Raz, *Ethics in the Public Domain* (n. 1 above), 198; see also Raz, *Morality of Freedom* (n. 1 above), 53.

[52] For instance, National Conference of Catholic Bishops, *Economic Justice for All: Pastoral Letter on Catholic Social Teaching and the U.S. Economy* (Washington D.C.: United States Catholic Conference, 1986). See also the discussion in Jeremy Waldron, 'Religious Contributions in Public Deliberation,' *San Diego Law Review*, 30 (1993), 817–48.

relation to the reasons that really apply to the choices it faces on this matter by submitting to directives from the bishops than by trying to figure things out for itself; but is that really a ground for saying that the bishops have authority over Congress? In both examples, the most that the conditions stated in Raz's NJT imply is that my friends and the Catholic bishops *ought* to have authority over me and the U.S. Congress respectively; and probably it doesn't even imply that. It certainly doesn't justify the inference—which Raz makes—that they already do have such authority.[53]

The broader point that concerns me here is that NJT fails to capture the *public* or *official* dimension of authority, and in particular the presence that a person or organization must have in public life before it is appropriate for the ordinary citizen to regard him or it as an authority. Though Raz distinguishes between practical and theoretical authority, the argument embodied in NJT does not seem to cast any distinctive light on what we might think of as the *institutional* aspect of practical authority in the public realm.

In a subsequent chapter of *The Morality of Freedom*, Raz does address the possibility that 'public' might define a distinct *subject matter* for authority. But he is skeptical about this as a basis:

> It is not good enough to say that an authoritative measure is justified because it serves the public interest. If it is binding on individuals it has to be justified by considerations which bind them. Public authority is ultimately based on the moral duty which individuals owe their fellow humans.[54]

Nor does he seem to think that the involvement of large numbers of people makes a difference. The NJT is stated initially as a condition for the proposition that '*a person* has authority over *another person*,'[55] and Raz asks: 'Does not the fact that political authorities govern groups of people transform the picture?'[56] He seems to suggest that the answer is 'No,' as though the justification of public authority could be built up by the simple accumulation of pair-wise applications of NJT, i.e., applying NJT to the relation between A and C_1, then A and C_2, then A and C_3, . . . etc. (In other parts of his discussion, though, he is a little more cautious than this.)[57]

Raz does say that NJT is supposed to operate wholesale, not retail, so that it is not enough on his account to show that C would be better off deferring to A on just one issue. 'Authority is based on reason and reasons are general, therefore authority is essentially general.'[58] This seems right. One of the distinguishing features of public authorities, surely, is that they are supposed to be *standing*

---

[53] There are places where Raz seems happy to run these questions together. 'A person has authority,' he writes, 'either if he is regarded by others as having authority or if he should be so regarded.' (Raz, *Practical Reason and Norms*, new edition (Princeton: Princeton University Press, 1990), 62–3)

[54] Raz, *Morality of Freedom* (n. 1 above), 72. Elsewhere—'Introduction' (n. 1 above), 16–17—Raz insists that individuals' relations with government are not different from, in fact they literally *are* still, relations with other individuals.

[55] Raz, *Morality of Freedom* (n. 1 above), 53 (my emphasis).   [56] Ibid., 71.

[57] The discussion is ibid., 71–4 and is quite tantalizingly compressed.   [58] Ibid., 73.

authorities, not just occasional sources of authoritative directives. If an institution were incapable of issuing a series of authoritative commands over an indefinite period of time, it could not plausibly be regarded as a public authority, no matter how authoritative (by the lights of NJT) its pronouncements were on particular occasions. But generality might not be enough. I suspect the U.S. Congress would do better in almost *every* case to rely on directives issued by the Conference of Catholic Bishops than to rely on its own fatuous 'deliberations.' But still that doesn't make the Conference of Catholic Bishops into a standing authority in the relevant sense.

Part of what is going on here involves Raz's insistence that a good theory of authority should not beg any questions as to which persons or entities or offices or institutions actually have authority. There should be no presupposition that we already know who is in authority, or that we can tell on the basis of some badge or official credential.[59] Raz would say, I think, that it is possible that Catholic bishops should be regarded as having authority on public affairs and it is possible that they should not be so regarded. Whether they should be is a matter of applying the test furnished by NJT to their situation. This is a fair point, as far as it goes. But we have to be careful with it. The fact that we should not defer to or connive in common presuppositions about who possesses public authority is perfectly compatible with pubic authority presenting a distinct case for critical assessment. In a given situation, it may be unclear or controversial who has authority of any sort; or it may be unclear or controversial who has *public* authority. Now the latter controversy might not be the same as the former. It may be a special case of it—in which case we do need to know the indicia of the publicness aspect of public authority. Or—worse still, for Raz's account—public authority might best be analysed *sui generis*. There might be a danger of distorting our account of public authority if we treat it as a special case of authority in general.[60] It might be better to begin with public authority and then develop our accounts of non-public (but still practical) authority by analogy with that, rather than starting from a general account that purports to embrace both public and non-public cases. We must not rule out these analytical possibilities in advance.

The closest Raz comes to acknowledging any of this is in his suggestion that *de facto* power might be regarded as a necessary condition for political authority.[61] The reason has to do with the relation between power and coordination, which

---

[59] Ibid., 74: 'Most common discussions of political authority presuppose existing political institutions and ask under what conditions do institutions of that kind have legitimate authority. This begs many questions, and precludes many possibilities.'

[60] Raz himself has argued something analogous in the case of the concept *law*: law, he says, has an institutional aspect, and it might be quite un-illuminating to regard that institutional sense of law as just a special case of *law-in-general*, analysed without regard to institutional considerations. (See Raz, *Practical Reason and Norms* (n. 53 above), 123 ff.; see also Raz, *Ethics in the Public Domain* (n. 1 above), 187 ff.)

[61] See also the excellent discussion in Finnis, *Natural Law and Natural Rights* (n. 29 above), 246–50.

on Raz's account, is one of the main functions (though not the only function) of legal authority:

> If there is any range of activities in which those who possess great power clearly can do better than most people it is in co-ordinating the activities of many people. It seems plausible to suppose that unless a person enjoys or is soon likely to enjoy effective power in a society he does not possess legitimate political authority over that society.[62]

Raz is certainly prepared to acknowledge that a person without power may deserve to have authority. But he says of such a person:

> It may be better if he acquires it. He may even have a right to have it. But he does not yet have it. One crucial condition which, in the case of political authorities governing sizeable societies, is necessary to establish their legitimacy, does not obtain.[63]

This is helpful, because it explicitly rejects the implication of NJT that we can move from saying that there is good reason to regard A as a public authority to saying that A *is* a public authority. Maybe the normal justification of *public* authority, in particular, has two levels to it: the first level might be given by something like Raz's NJT; but the second level requires in addition some sense that a large number of the people who would be governed by the putative authority if it were an authority do actually accept that it satisfies NJT (or that, in some cruder sense, they do actually regard it as an authority). It may be quite inappropriate for me to regard A as a public authority unless I am sure that many others do in fact so regard it (or are prepared to do so if they see that enough others are prepared to do so if . . . etc.)[64] I believe this second level test is not something we can just fold back into the first level, laying it out as one of the reasons on which the justification of authority is dependent. It operates as a different sort of reason.

Unless this second condition is satisfied, A has no hope of being appropriately regarded as an authority in the sense of public authority for a community on matters of common concern. Some assortment of individual citizens—say, C_1, C_7, and C_{23} may have reason, individually, to treat A in the way one would treat someone who satisfies NJT so far as one's own reasoning is concerned. But this would not at all be the same as their having collectively—let alone in common with all the other C's—a reason to regard A as an authority on the questions of common concern that they face. And one doesn't reason to the existence of a public authority as such simply by adding more C's to this list. Instead one has to reason in a different way about the relation between the whole class of C's and the putative authority A.

---

[62] Raz, *Morality of Freedom* (n. 1 above), 75–6.   [63] Ibid., 76.

[64] For a stronger statement to this effect, see Finnis, *Natural Law and Natural Rights* (n. 29 above), and 250: 'Authority (and thus the *responsibility* of governing) in a community is to be exercised by those who can in fact effectively settle co-ordination problems for that community. . . . [T]he sheer fact that virtually everyone *will* acquiesce in somebody's say-so is the presumptively necessary and defeasibly sufficient condition for the normative judgment that that person has (i.e. is justified in exercising) authority in that community.'

X. AUTHORITY AMONG OFFICIALS

Our aim is to understand authority relations as between officials A and B, in regard to a requirement that B defer to A's directive issued to C_1 (and all the other citizens), and that B not gainsay A's settlement of a question of common concern.

It is not implausible to say that in order to understand this, we first have to understand the one-on-one relation between A and C_1, and build up our account of the relation between A and B on the basis of that. After all, the relation between A and B within the official realm is, so to speak, *about* the relation between officialdom in general to C_1 and his fellow citizens. We must not lose sight of that.

However, there are various false leads we should eschew. One possibility would be to apply NJT comparatively as between A and B. We might ask whether C_1 would do better, in relation to the reasons that apply to him, by following the directives of B rather than the directives of A; and say that only if this is not so, should B defer to A. But in the cases we are envisaging, B will almost always believe that his directive is better (for C_1 to follow) than A's; otherwise he would not have produced it. It is part of our understanding of this sort of authority relation among officials that sometimes B should defer to A even though he believes this to be the case, indeed even when it *is* the case; not only that, it is part of our understanding of this sort of authority relation among officials that in some cases B should not even start off down the road of considering whether he could come up with a better directive (for C_1) to follow than A has. This is often what we say for example about the authority relation between courts and legislatures. If the legislature has spoken to an issue on which it is competent to speak, the courts should not even begin to second-guess it, not even if they are sure they could come up with a better answer. No doubt, this is largely based on questions of legitimacy that are not under discussion here: the legislature has democratic credentials that a court may lack. But as Hart and Sacks have shown, the prior basis of the courts' deference is just the principle of institutional settlement.[65] I suppose it is possible that this whole understanding of inter-official authority is misconceived and that a naive application of Raz's NJT explains why. But I don't think we should accept that unless we find that there is no other way of adequately explicating the common understanding of authority in this area.

A second possibility would be to take the second official, B, as one of the subjects (along with C_1 etc.) of A's exercise of authority. In laying down a directive for C_1, A is also perhaps implicitly telling B not to lay down any contrary directive. Of course these directives—the one to C_1 and the one to B—are not the same. So we would have to apply NJT separately to the directive issued to B. We would say: A's directive to B to refrain from countermanding A's other directive

---

[65] Hart and Sacks, *The Legal Process* (n. 2 above), 143 and 146–7.

issued to C_1 is authoritative for B, just in case B would do better following A on this than figuring out for himself whether it was a good idea to second-guess A's directive to C_1. But this will hardly do. For one thing, A may have had no intention of issuing the second directive (which is not the same as saying he intended not to issue it). For another, B might acknowledge that he is required—e.g. by the constitution—to defer to A, quite apart from anything A says or intended, and again without acknowledging that A is a better judge of these matters (of constitutional deference) than B is.

So is it the constitution—or something relevantly like the constitution, such as the Framers—that has authority over B in the case we are considering? Well, certainly the constitution may contain a rule saying that B should defer to A. But such a rule embodies a proposition about authority, and our question is: how is such a proposition to be assessed?

A third possibility—and, always with the Rule of Three, this is the one I think we should pursue—is to focus on the primary authority relation between A and C_1 and then grasp the requirement that applies to B as a requirement not to disrupt that relation. However, I don't think this will work if we understand A and C_1 as though they were private persons. If we treat A as someone whose reasoning just *happens* to be superior to C_1's and then treat B's intervention as an attempt to distract C_1's attention from that fact, then we may get a sort of 'duty of deference' incumbent on B, but it will be entirely contingent and, so to speak, external to the relation between A and C_1. In some circumstances, B should defer to A in this sense; and in others he shouldn't; and we are really back with the first false lead I rejected.

I don't think we can proceed successfully along these lines unless we already have a good understanding of A as a *public* authority, established to deal with questions of common concern arising among C_1 and all the other C's. A's position is that of someone who seems to be looked to by the bulk of the C's for guidance in cases where the C's need to coordinate—cases where they will be better off coordinating under the direction of someone like A than figuring out what to do each on his own. That's the capacity in which A has issued his directive; that's the coordination that B's intervention has the prospect of disrupting; and so that's the capacity—as a *public* authority not just as a general Raz-ian authority—in which A ought to be deferred to by B.

The gist of my argument, then, is this. We need to focus very closely on public authority, either as a distinctive special case of authority in general or as something which requires *sui generis* analysis. Public authority exercised among large numbers of people characteristically addresses what I have called questions of common concern. These questions are often urgent, and it is important that citizens be in a position quickly and readily to identify answers as salient, even when there are disagreements as to what the answers should be. An official determination in accordance with an established procedure may afford a basis for such identification, provided there is a settled practice among the citizens of responding quickly, with justified confidence, to the signals produced by such procedures. But such practice can be undermined and the citizens left confused and uncoordinated if contradictory signals come at them from a variety of official directions. Now, the temptation to produce contradictory signals stems from the structure of questions of common concern. We know the citizens may disagree about what is to be done to answer such a question; and this disagreement is likely to be echoed among the officials (who are, after all, drawn from the citizenry). If coordination is nevertheless important, then we say that each citizen must be prepared to swallow hard and submit his own sense of what the best option might be in order to join in with group coordination on *some* option even if it is not the best. That's the usual story about authority and political obligation. Well, there is also a similar duty incumbent on officials. Once an official directive has been issued that holds a fair chance of securing coordination among the citizens, other officials ought to be prepared to swallow hard and refrain from issuing contrary directives, even when they are convinced (perhaps rightly) that it would be better for the citizens to coordinate on their directive than on the basis of the one that has already been issued. That's an important aspect of authority too. The underlying issue is the same as it is with the obligations of the citizen. But it is important to understand the particular way that it plays out, as far as the obligations of citizens are concerned.

XI. RAZ'S CONCEPTION

A final word about the point of this paper. I wonder whether in the end all that I have said might not be accommodated perfectly well within the four walls of Raz's conception. I have oversimplified Raz's account a little in order to highlight the contrast between an approach to authority that stresses the public dimension and an approach to authority that regards that as at most a special case. Raz's account of authority is the richest and most fertile account we have, and it would not surprise me if it could just absorb the argument I have given, or whatever is of value in it.

Still, I think this is one of those cases where the exploration itself is worthwhile. I did not embark on this study of authority among officials as a counterexample to Raz's conception. I embarked on it because it seemed to me an interesting case that Raz's conception does not immediately illuminate, a case that would repay some further consideration. Moreover it is an important case to consider with regard to the authority of law and legal institutions. And I suspect that our understanding of the various authority claims put forward and sustained in our legal system will be the richer for seeing how to elaborate Raz's conception in relation to cases like this.

5

Legal Reasoning and the Authority of Law

J.E. PENNER[1]

I. THE AUTHORITY OF LAW

Joseph Raz's theory of law makes the notion of authority central. In so far as the law is authoritative, it mediates between the reasons that apply to the subjects of the law and those subjects themselves, by providing guidance via exclusionary reasons in the form of rights, duties, rules and so on. An important aspect, or consequence, of Raz's characterization of authority is what Coleman has dubbed the 'practical difference thesis'[2]: in so far as authorities mediate between the reasons for action[3] and the subjects of the authority to whom those reasons apply, the directives of the authority have practical importance because they tell the subject how to act so that he does not need directly to consider (at least some of) the reasons that would bear on his acting in the particular circumstance. In this way, the authoritative directive replaces those reasons for action: the subject takes the directive as the reason for acting, rather than directly assessing all the reasons (other than the directive itself) which apply to his case. Therefore, if an authority is doing what an authority does, its directives cannot 'make no difference' to the way in which its subjects decide how to act. If an authority's directives make no practical difference to the behaviour of its subjects, it is simply not an authority.

An authority is *legitimate*, that is, subjects of the authority are justified in following its guidance, and an authority is justified in issuing directives to guide the behaviour of those subject to it, when those subjects are more likely to comply with the reasons that ought to govern their behaviour if they follow the directives of the authority than if they were to try themselves to follow those reasons directly. This is Raz's famous 'normal justification thesis'.[4]

[1] I wish to thank members of the University of Alberta Faculties of Law and Philosophy, students on the London LL.M Jurisprudence and Legal Theory Course, and Hugh Collins, Ted DeCoste, Pavlos Eleftheriadis, Tony Honore, Nicola Lacey, Richard Nobles and Richard Samuels for useful comments and criticisms of earlier presentations of the ideas in this paper. For support of the research leading to this work I am grateful to the ESRC and the Nuffield Foundation.
[2] Jules, Coleman, 'Incorporationism, Conventionality, and the Practical Difference Thesis' (1998) 4 *Legal Theory*, 381–425.
[3] And/or reasons for belief, in the case of authorities that are/are also theoretical authorities.
[4] Joseph Raz, *The Morality of Freedom* (Oxford: Clarendon Press, 1986), 53.

Both the practical difference thesis and normal justification thesis requirements for a legitimate authority are met most clearly and intuitively in the case
of authorities which have expertise or superior knowledge. A doctor's advice
clearly makes a difference to how one acts, and one is more likely to comply
with the medical reasons applying to one's case and pursuing the correct treatment by following a doctor's advice than if one were to try to diagnose and treat
oneself (assuming one is not oneself a doctor).[5]

Despite the obvious intuitive resonance of legitimate authority and expertise,
it is commonly accepted that political authorities make a practical difference and
legitimately do so in the other major way Raz identifies as a ground of authority, that is, in an authority's capacity to solve coordination problems[6] by issuing
directives that institute conventions. We are in need of a convention as to which
side of the road to drive on; neither the right nor the left is more obviously the
right choice, and no general and sustained convention may have arisen in practice. By instituting a directive to drive on the left, the authority provides a
reason to act which makes a crucial practical difference, for (if the authority is
effective) the authority's directive will provide a reason for action which did not
previously exist, compliance with which will solve the coordination problem.

Furthermore, political authorities, because of their ability to operate through
various administrative agencies and bureaucracies, create conditions for the
better compliance by its subjects with reasons applying to them. For example,
individuals may be required on the balance of reasons that apply to them to
contribute money for the provision of public goods in their community, and by
providing a means (a taxing and spending agency with associated directives
governing how its subjects deal with the agency) the authority can provide a
conventional means of their doing so, which will make a practical difference in
that such a means simply did not exist previously. At first glance, at least, the
entire body of official directives can be explained as an authority's institution
of conventions, both directly, as in the case of a making an authoritative choice
that subjects should drive on the left, or indirectly, as in the case of providing a
means for its subjects to comply with reasons and then instituting specific
conventions which reflect those reasons but which also reflect the character of
the authoritative institution and its organs, such as its taxing and spending
apparatus, or its provision of criminal courts and punishment facilities.[7]

---

[5] This quick characterization of a doctor's authority hides a wrinkle. A doctor is clearly a
theoretical authority, because a doctor's diagnosis and suggested treatment counts as an authoritative reason to believe that one has a particular medical condition indicating a particular medical
treatment. A doctor is a practical authority in so far as one has other reasons (e.g. moral ones) to
maintain good health, and so should follow the doctor's advice.

[6] I follow Raz here in taking 'coordination problems' in a lay sense, i.e. as encompassing more
than the problem of settling upon one of several possible equilibria each of which would equally
serve as the solution of a coordination problem framed in game theoretical terms. See Joseph Raz,
'Facing Up: A Reply' (1989) 62 *Southern California Law Review*, 1153–1235, 1190–4.

[7] See Raz, *supra* n. 4, 48 et seq.

This analysis is cogent even in areas where the guidance of the law's directives appears to be very far from the setting of standards to solve coordination problems. Consider, for example, the criminal law and the private civil law of contract, tort, unjust enrichment, and property. These areas of law are conventionally regarded as the law's giving effect to moral norms which would exist independently of the existence of any legal system. The injunctions not to murder, to keep one's agreements, not to harm others, to respect the property of others, and so on, are not standards that solve coordination problems. They are (to the extent they are valid, of course), morally required of every individual in a society regardless of the behaviour of others, or of the individual's expectations of the behaviour of others. But the law does more than simply enforce pre-existing, independently valid moral norms of this kind. The exact extent, scope, and justification of these norms are controversial and uncertain. While the law, to be legitimate, must by and large reflect the moral considerations which underpin these moral norms, the law can and does serve as an authority which solves a coordination problem by specifying in more or less certain terms legal norms which reflect these moral ones. Further, the law specifies more or less certain remedies or punishments for their breach, and enforces compliance with these norms to deal with those subjects of the law who would otherwise disregard these moral norms. The 'coordination' problems here are not, of course, identical to that of having two available sides of the road to drive down. They are more akin to the problems of uncertainty, stasis, and inefficiency Hart identifies in his depiction of the 'pre-legal' society.[8] The present point, however, is that the authority of the law can be justified here as much as in the road traffic case by reference to the fact that by instituting a legal norm which subjects of the law are bound to follow, the law adopts a conventional standard which is justified not on the basis that the law claims any particular expertise or superior knowledge in these matters of morality, but that the choice of some standard which the subjects of the law are to follow is more likely to lead to the subjects' conformity with these moral norms than if the subjects of the law are left to determine their behaviour by their own lights. This is not to say, of course, that the law's particular choices are not subject to criticism on the basis that they deviate from what morality requires, nor that the law should not seek to adopt standards which better reflect what morality requires while still providing this coordinating function. But in determining the legitimacy of the law's authority in these areas, any such criticisms must be weighed against the greater conformity to these moral standards in the bulk of cases which is provided by the law's issuance of these more or less certain standards of behaviour and its enforcement of compliance with them.

Despite the obvious attraction of this position (Raz clearly holds a view along these lines[9]), in this paper I will explore the legitimacy of the authority of

[8] HLA Hart, *The Concept of Law* (Oxford: Clarendon Press), 1961, 89–91.
[9] See Raz, *supra* n. 4, 56; *supra* n. 6, 1164; *Practical Reason and Norms* (Oxford: Oxford University Press, 1999), 64.

judge-made law from the perspective that the authority that common law judges and lawyers legitimately possess is the authority generated by their having a kind of expertise. I will go about doing so somewhat indirectly. The reason for taking an indirect approach flows from the fact that the kind of expertise I wish to consider that common law judges and lawyers may have is *moral* expertise. Clearly lawyers and judges have legal expertise. What I am interested in considering is whether lawyers and judges, in working together in a common law system to make new common law, have a legitimate authority to make that new law because they have expertise or knowledge superior to (many, at least, of) the law's subjects, in moral matters.

The prospects may not look encouraging. Green argues:

In certain areas, for example in the sciences, some people are more knowledgeable than others. We often do better to follow their advice in the relevant matters than we would do either by acting on our own views or by trying to second-guess and correct their views . . . [T]here may be expertise in moral matters as well. Although some actions are inherently wrong, or *mala in se*, it does not follow that individuals acting on their own will always be able to comply with the dictates of morality. Even if law cannot make things right or wrong, legislators, judges, and bureaucrats may have a keener insight into morality or into what best secures compliance with it. If so, we would do better by taking their directives as binding than we would by following our own lights.

That argument, though capable of greater subtlety and elaboration, is in all forms an unattractive justification for the authority of law. First, it is unlikely that the relevant sort of expertise is available in political affairs. . . . Second, even if policy-relevant expertise is available, there is little reason to suppose that officials have uniquely rich reserves of it. Universities, research organisations, and private individuals often have greater or equal knowledge in certain matters and thus deserve a hearing as well. . . . Finally, and this is in any case conclusive, there are profound moral objections to a society run by experts, which are rooted in the values of government and political equality.[10]

I hope, in the course of what follows, to dispel these cogent doubts. I will start by looking at one strand in the thought of Dworkin, the idea that as participants in a forum of principle, lawyers and judges might be engaged in a *theoretical* enterprise, requiring expertise in matters theoretical or philosophical.

II. COMMON LAW LEGAL EXPERTISE CONSTRUED AS PHILOSOPHICAL EXPERTISE

Perhaps the most plausible and obvious candidate *type* of moral expertise that judges and lawyers might have is a kind of theoretical or philosophical expertise in matters of political morality. The most prominent advocate of this sort of view is Ronald Dworkin.[11] Being subject to a doctrine of political responsibility,

---

[10] Leslie Green, 'Law, Legitimacy, and Consent' (1989) 62 *Southern California Law Review* 795–825, 803–4.
[11] See, in particular, Ronald Dworkin, 'In Praise of Theory' [1997] *Arizona State LJ* 353–76, 357–60, in which Dworkin analogizes a hierarchy of philosophical knowledge, with foundations in

Dworkin states that judges 'must make only such political decisions as they can *justify* within a *political theory* that also justifies the other decisions they propose to make' (my italics).[12] This doctrine would seem to require that judges must be competent enough to construct or adopt and defend political theories in the course of acting responsibly. The character of the theoretical or philosophical expertise described in Dworkin's writings is one which operates at a fairly abstract level of moral political thought, an example being, perhaps, an expertise akin to Dworkin's own in his development of 'law as integrity'. Without taking this as a term either of approbation or disapproval, the expertise might be characterized as a kind of 'academic' philosophical or theoretical expertise. I am unable to state with any assurance whether Dworkin thinks judges not only should, but generally do, theorize about the abstract moral and political philosophical justifications of their decisions, for I find his writing somewhat ambiguous in this regard, in particular *Law's Empire*[13] where he employs analogies to literary criticism to describe the 'interpretive' enterprise of law, and his claim that legal discourse is characterized by 'theoretical disagreement'. Consider this passage:

Any practical legal argument, no matter how detailed and limited, assumes the kind of abstract foundation jurisprudence offers, and when rival foundations compete, a legal argument assumes one and rejects others. So any judge's opinion is itself a piece of legal philosophy, even when the philosophy is hidden and the visible argument is dominated by citation and lists of facts. Jurisprudence is the general part of adjudication, silent prologue to any decision at law.[14]

Philosophy a judge's opinion may be, but it is not clear how close in form and abstraction most, some, or any judges' opinions are understood to come to the sort of academic moral and political philosophizing which characterizes the area of inquiry that is jurisprudence. At first glance, these opinions would seem even on Dworkin's account not to resemble jurisprudence very much. That may change. Perhaps the advent of a more theoretical approach in law schools will begin to generate judges' decisions which will begin to resemble more and more the sort of argument one would expect Dworkin himself to make were he on the bench. Dworkin does seem to urge that judges, nowadays at least, must take on the burden of becoming more philosophical in their reasoning. I think there

metaphysics and epistemology and extending to ethics, morality and political morality (which is the underlying philosophical foundation of law), to a hierarchy of scientific theory, with physics at the most general and abstract level of a hierarchy of sciences, physics, chemistry, and so on.

[12] R. Dworkin, *Taking Rights Seriously* (London: Duckworth, 1977), 87. It is worth pointing out parenthetically how peculiar this doctrine of political responsibility is. The duty one would naturally ascribe to political officials is to serve only the interests of their subjects to the best of their ability (in particular not abuse their office by serving their own interests), for acting in this way justifies their holding office. While acting in contradictory ways which defeat their honest objectives would be a bad thing, it would seem novel to impose a duty on officials not only to make 'honest best efforts' but to achieve as well a rather high 'cognitive' standard in justifying their actions, i.e. to act only in ways which they can explicitly justify as part of a theoretically coherent political programme. As far as I know only certain totalitarian Marxist regimes states have ever officially set themselves this sort of goal.

[13] R. Dworkin, *Law's Empire* (Fontana Press, 1986).   [14] Ibid., 90.

is at least an implicit push in this direction from his recurrent resort to Hercules as a model for understanding legal reasoning. Dworkin would also seem to require that judges must reflect on the abstract, philosophical, academic elaboration of their justifying theories, when, for example, they decide whether to accept or reject an economic analysis approach to a legal question, for 'it is the academic elaboration that reveals the true character of a moral theory'.[15] Perhaps most explicitly, Dworkin has written,

> It is irresponsible for a lawyer to insist that the concepts of meaning and original intention should occupy the center of constitutional practice and then ignore the revolution in our understanding of those concepts in this century. He cannot pretend that Wittgenstein or Donald Davidson, for instance, had never written about mental events.
>
> I know that these remarks raise many problems for and about both legal practice and academic law. It seems irresponsible, as I just said, for lawyers to ignore philosophical discussion of the concepts they treat as central to their work. But it is also true that most lawyers and judges, and indeed most legal scholars, have no time for serious study of technical philosophy.[16]

Whether or not judges have any such expertise and apply it in practice, it is worthwhile considering it as a model of common law legal expertise that would give judges and lawyers the authority to develop the law by way of common law decision-making. At first glance at least it seems right to say that philosophical competence of this kind would count as a kind of expertise or superior knowledge in moral matters, and so worth considering here as a possible candidate for an expertise-based justification of common law judicial authority.

I think it best to begin assessing this candidate by exploring the observation that common law legal discourse, despite whatever links it may have to moral and political philosophizing, is very typically 'non-theoretical'. Lawyers' arguments and judicial decisions rarely (never?) explore in any real philosophical depth the abstract principles of moral and political philosophy—if they did, the names of philosophers whose arguments need assessing in order to do so would simply appear in the discourse of judges and practitioners, which they do not. Legal discourse, to borrow Sunstein's term, is from the perspective of academic moral and political philosophy or jurisprudence 'incompletely theorized',[17] that is, legal discourse does not, characteristically, incorporate or take advantage of the available abstract theory that seems to address the same subject matter as that which raises the questions that lawyers and judges must address in resolving conflicts before them and in creating rules to guide the behaviour of the law's subjects, theory which has been well and thoughtfully produced by clever people. Thus, our task in assessing whether 'philosophical' moral expertise might ground the authority of judges must be, for the present time, hypothetical.

---

[15] R. Dworkin, *Law's Empire* (Fontana Press, 1986), 286.

[16] R. Dworkin, *Freedom's Law* (Cambridge, Mass: Harvard University Press, 1996).

[17] Cass Sunstein, *Legal Reasoning and Political Conflict* (New York: Oxford University Press, 1996), ch. 2.

However, exploring the puzzle of why judges and lawyers do not, as yet, take advantage of moral and political philosophy, might contribute to our understanding of whether it is a possible basis for judicial expertise.

Sunstein offers what might be called a 'political' explanation for this 'incomplete theorization' of the law. (It should be pointed out that Sunstein intends to address the law in general—principally of the United States—not just the common law. However, I shall restrict my concern to his arguments with respect to the common law.) He attributes the law's reticence to engage in abstract theory to a number of factors, but to my mind the most important is the following, which is interestingly similar to a view expressed by Raz, to wit: Incomplete theorization allows lawyers, judges, and the subjects of the law to reach a consensus on particular legal outcomes, i.e. the decisions in actual cases or the implementation of certain rules, without requiring a consensus of abstract political/philosophical perspectives, such as utilitarianism or Kantianism. In this way, incomplete theorization engenders stability, for not every issue then raises the most fundamental disagreements over values or the right way to see the world. Furthermore, to the extent that there is a plurality of values, finding a consensus amongst individuals at the level of fundamental values is made doubly difficult.[18]

Thus, argues Sunstein,

[I]ncompletely theorized agreements can promote two goals of a liberal democracy and a liberal legal system: to enable people to live together and permit them to show each other a measure of reciprocity and mutual respect. The use of low-level principles or rules generally allows judges on multi-member bodies and hence citizens to find commonality and thus a common way of life without producing unnecessary antagonism. Both rules and low-level principles make it unnecessary to reach areas in which disagreements are fundamental. . . . If reciprocity and mutual respect are desirable, it follows that judges should not challenge a litigant's or another person's deepest and most defining commitments if those commitments are reasonable and there is no need to do so. . . . Institutional arguments in law—especially those involving judicial restraint—are typically designed to bracket fundamental questions about and to say that however those questions might be resolved in principle, courts should stand to one side.[19]

Sunstein is well aware that the law will sometimes take the absolutely opposite approach, that is, adopt fairly high-level abstract principles or values upon which individuals can agree, though they cannot agree on more low-level principles for implementing them, or even in how they should apply to particular concrete cases. Here, rather than adopting incompletely theorized norms, the law adopts incompletely *specified* norms. Nevertheless, this approach, when taken, is taken on the basis of essentially identical political considerations:

Much law-making becomes possible only because of this phenomenon. Consider the fact that the creation of large regulatory agencies has often been feasible only because of incompletely specified agreements. In dealing with air and water pollution, occupational safety and health, or regulation of broadcasting, legislators converge on general, incompletely

---

[18] Ibid., 39, 44.   [19] Ibid., 39–40.

specified requirements—that regulation be 'reasonable', or that it provide a 'margin of safety'. If the legislature attempted to specify these requirements—to decide what counts as reasonable regulation—there would be a predictably high level of dispute and conflict, and perhaps the relevant laws could not be enacted at all. . . . [Incompletely specified agreements] allow people to develop frameworks for decision and judgment despite large-scale disagreements. At the same time, they help produce a degree of social solidarity and shared commitment. People who are able to agree on political abstractions—freedom of speech, freedom from unreasonable searches and seizures—can also agree that they are embarking on shared projects. These forms of agreement help constitute a democratic culture. It is for this reason that they are so important to constitution-making. Incompletely specified agreements also have the advantage of allowing people to show one another a high degree of mutual respect. By refusing to settle concrete cases that raise fundamental issues of conscience, they permit citizens to announce to one another that society shall not take sides on such issues until it is required to do so.[20]

But it is worthwhile noticing the effect of this abstraction-bound approach to law-making. As Sunstein recognizes, the effect of such laws is essentially to shift the law-making power into the hands of the courts which interpret the legislation, courts which will, as a general rule, expound the legislation in the normal, untheorized, way. That is, the courts will build up a body of decisions which will give rise to a number of low-level rules and principles, which rules and principles will then, to all intents and purposes, govern the application of the statutory or constitutional provision. Thus the use of incompletely *specified* provisions is a means in certain political circumstances of obtaining incompletely *theorized* norms, which, as it turns out, serves the same basic political principles of helping to constitute democratic culture and express mutual respect. The democratic impulse and mutual respect is misunderstood if it is taken to mean an allegiance to settling disputes of fundamental principle, in whatever democratic forum—even in the case of incompletely specified provisions one presupposes an allegiance to the possibility of low-level incompletely theorized decision-making; the faith is that, given broad and abstract direction, the courts will be sufficiently constrained and sufficiently directed not to make particular decisions which are so sectarian or particular that they violate any politically acceptable interpretation of those abstractions. Each legislator knows that a risk is taken when a commitment is made to such an abstraction, but the risk is regarded as acceptable because the stakes are no more than that the court might determine disputes in concrete instances which go against one's views, not that the court will adopt an abstract theory to fill out the abstraction.

Sunstein's political explanation of incomplete theorization is both plausible and compelling but not, or so I shall argue, ultimately convincing. In the first place, we must notice that it appears to demand an artificial limit on legal

---

[20] Cass Sunstein, *Legal Reasoning and Political Conflict* (New York: Oxford University Press, 1996), 36.

reasoning and knowledge. Sunstein addresses this in the passage below:

Some people think of incomplete theorization as quite unfortunate—as embarrassing or reflective of some important problem or defect. Perhaps people have not yet thought deeply enough. When people theorize, by raising the level of abstraction, they do so to reveal bias, confusion, or inconsistency. Surely participants in a legal system should not give up this effort. . . . But this is not the whole story. On the contrary, incompletely theorized judgements are an important and valuable part of both private and public life. They help make law possible; they even help make life possible. Most of their virtues involve the constructive uses of silence, an exceedingly important social and legal phenomenon. Silence—on something that may prove false, obtuse, or excessively contentious—can help minimize conflict, allow the present to learn from the future, and save a great deal of time and expense. In law, as elsewhere, what is said is no more important that what is left unsaid. Certainly this is true for ordinary courts, which have a limited expertise and democratic accountability, and whose limits lead them to be cautious.[21]

As I said, Raz expresses a similar view in explaining the role of rules in practical reasoning (though I hasten to point out he is not addressing the issue of incomplete theorization, at least not in terms):

[Rules] mediate between deeper-level considerations and concrete decisions. They provide an intermediate level of reasons to which one appeals in normal cases where a need for a decision arises. . . . More importantly, the practice [of proceeding through the mediation of rules] allows the creation of a pluralistic culture. For it enables people to unite in support of some 'low or medium level' generalizations despite profound disagreements concerning their ultimate foundations, which some seek in religion, others in Marxism or Liberalism, etc. I am not suggesting that the differences in the foundations do not lead to differences in practice. The point is that an orderly community can exist only if it shares many practices, and that in all modern pluralistic societies a great measure of toleration of vastly different outlooks is made possible by the fact that many of them enable the vast majority of the population to accept common standards of conduct.[22]

It is certainly true that people may disagree about the correct abstract perspective to take on moral and political issues while at the same time agreeing upon the disposition of particular cases. In a similar fashion, individuals may disagree about what ought fundamentally to be valued, and whether there is a plurality of basic values, while agreeing as to the disposition of particular cases. In view of this, it does appear to make good 'political' or practical sense for lawyers and judges (both in their law-applying and law-making roles) to avoid grounding their arguments and rulings, respectively, on abstract theories of justice.[23] Their decisions will give rise to disagreements less often simply because there will not usually be a large theoretical issue to chew on, and further, the scope of disagreement will be narrower because the scope of a less abstract decision will be. If it is regarded as a value within the liberal constitution that the courts be the

---

[21] Ibid., 38–9.   [22] Raz, *supra* n. 4, 58.
[23] It may be sensible to extend the same advice to legislators, though their greater 'democratic' legitimacy may entitle them, as Sunstein apparently thinks, to broader scope for the implementation of abstract conceptions of justice.

least contentious branch, out of a concern to provide individual legal subjects with a measure of certainty as to their rights and efficiency in the application of the law, for example, or that the courts be the branch in which officials have smaller room for manoeuvre in making law, for reasons of democratic pedigree, for example, then a judicial practice that law is applied and created on the basis of low level principles may serve such a value. Such a value appears to reflect the particular nature of a pluralist and democratic state, providing one contour of the institutional competence of the judiciary. Quite clearly one can take a different view. It is certainly arguable that the judiciary ought to be institutionalized as a 'forum of principle', in which a fair amount of moral philosophy is done. As far as Dworkin is concerned, any apparent limit on judicial theorization would not be a puzzle to solve, but a deficiency of current judicial practice to be remedied.[24]

Assuming, however, that incomplete theorization is a genuine phenomenon to be explained, it is submitted that the combined forces of Raz and Sunstein in developing this practical, political point, do not do so, for the simple reason that contentious fundamental belief and abstract theoretical commitment are not to be treated as the same thing. If it were the case that deep fundamental belief, drawn from whatever source, religion, Marxism or what have you, were identical to commitment to an abstract theoretical position, then Sunstein and Raz would surely be correct. They are right to say how disastrous it would be for a pluralist society if lawyers could ground their arguments, and judges their decisions, in the fundamental tenets of one religion or another, or in political theories like Marxism or Libertarianism. But that is not the issue that needs addressing. 'Incomplete theorization' expresses exactly what it denotes: an absence of reliance on theory, not an absence of reliance on religion or contentious political allegiances. It is simply untrue to equate abstraction, as in the abstraction that the various rights protected in a bill of rights serve the value of autonomy, or in the abstraction that all elements of the law of contract can be explained in terms of a philosophically precise concept of promise, with this kind of commitment. It is not the case that people's most sincere moral commitments, commitments which if excluded from political consideration are likely to drive them to the barricades, are to be identified as allegiances to abstract theoretical positions. For example, a person's opposition to abortion or capital punishment, or another's belief that a woman has the right to choose abortion or that the state has a duty to take the lives of certain criminals, tend to express attitudes of great importance to them; having to subject themselves to the opposing position would be to renounce acting upon a fundamental commitment. But strong proponents of these views need not, and typically will not, have allied themselves to any particularly abstract theoretical positions to hold them as strongly as they do. For many, the issue is decided by a deep sense or

---

[24] Though Sunstein argues that Dworkin misinterprets the facts of judicial practice; see Sunstein, *supra.* n. 17, 48–50; For Dworkin's reply see Dworkin, *supra* n. 11, 367–74.

intuition that abortion or capital punishment is just fundamentally wrong somehow, or by contrast, that allowing abortion or capital punishment in some circumstances is justifiable or even morally required. If a judge held, in reviewing the academic contract literature that, in his opinion, Charles Fried has got contract right,[25] and therefore he decided the case before him applying the most up-to-date philosophical literature on the nature of promises, he would not be expressing an allegiance of a kind which raises any danger for a pluralist society, or at least no greater danger than he would by adopting the views of a black letter authority like Treitel.[26] All he would be saying was that he found that Fried, rather than, say, Atiyah,[27] had the better of the philosophical argument, in the same way as he might justifiably prefer the view of Treitel to Cheshire and Fifoot.[28] So it is wrong to think that the sort of practical or political considerations Sunstein and Raz raise explains incomplete theorization in the law.

III. Solving the puzzle of 'incomplete theorization' in law: common law legal expertise as expertise in dealing with thick evaluative concepts

I want now to suggest that expertise in academic or philosophical political morality is the wrong sort of moral expertise for judges to have, which goes a long way to explaining why judges do not typically reason like moral philosophers. In doing so, I hope to provide a rough sketch of the sort of moral expertise it might be more plausible to ascribe to them. Rather than offering a 'political' explanation of incomplete theorization in common law legal reasoning, I want to offer what might be called a 'cognitive' one. The central claim of this explanation is that the kind of expertise judges and lawyers have is the expertise that comes from having acquired a great deal of moral knowledge and having to make sense of that knowledge, not in terms of aiming at theories which explain the fundamental or ultimate character of morality, but in terms of attending to moral concepts and moral beliefs so as to maintain their practical ability to judge the moral implications of a situation more or less successfully.

Once again, the starting point is the work of Raz. Without doing violence to the subtlety of Raz's work on the nature of morality and moral reasoning, the following perhaps captures the essential features of his position that are relevant to my purposes here. Humans are valuing creatures, which is to say that human beings respond to features of the world so as to value or dis-value them. A well-lived life is one in which values are realized and dis-values avoided, so it

[25] Charles Fried, *Contract as Promise* (Cambridge, Mass: Harvard University Press, 1981).
[26] Gunther Treitel, *The Law of Contract*, 7th Ed. (London: Stevens & Sons, 1987).
[27] P.S. Atiyah, *Promises, Morals, and Law* (Oxford: Clarendon Press, 1981).
[28] M.P. Furmston, *Cheshire, Fifoot, and Furmston's Law of Contract*, 13th Ed. (London: Butterworths, 1996).

is in the interest of humans to realize values and avoid dis-values. There is an irreducible plurality of values. There are many distinct aspects of the world which can be valued or dis-valued by humans, and no individual human can realize all values in a single life, though a well-lived life will be one in which a variety of values has been realized. Therefore values and dis-values, or the realizing or avoiding of them, respectively, constitute reasons for action, and roughly speaking, reasoning in respect of values constitutes the core of practical reasoning, and where the values and dis-values are of primary importance, this practical reasoning can be regarded as moral reasoning. Moreover, reasoning in respect of values and dis-values in this way is rational, which is to say that we reason in terms of our understanding of the nature of these values and dis-values. It therefore follows that we can conceptualize these values and dis-values, i.e. can have concepts of them, for it is only in virtue of having a concept of something that one can think about it, reason about it, form beliefs about it, and so on. In this respect, our concepts of values and dis-values are no different than our concepts of anything else. Having a concept of dogs allows us to entertain thoughts about dogs, acquire beliefs about dogs, and so on. But in other respects, our concepts of value, or perhaps the aspects of the world that we conceive as values, may have special characteristics. It is important therefore, in understanding moral reasoning and practical reasoning in general, to appreciate any special characteristics of value concepts (also known as 'evaluative' concepts) or the aspects of the world these concepts are concepts of.

Raz has recently written about this. He examines the extent to which our moral reasoning, depends upon 'parochial' concepts and 'thick' concepts. As to the former, Raz states:

'Parochial concepts' are concepts which cannot be mastered by all, not even by everyone capable of knowledge. 'Non-parochial' concepts can be mastered by anyone capable of knowing anything at all.[29]

The acquisition of certain parochial concepts will depend upon having certain perceptual capabilities (i.e. the ability to see to acquire colour concepts),[30] but our chief concern here are parochial evaluative concepts, and the way in which access to certain evaluative concepts may depend upon one's living in cultural circumstances which create, sustain, or provide access to certain values. To the extent that one's exposure to these values is contingent in the sense that they depend upon one's being in or sufficiently related to a particular culture, the concepts of those values are parochial.

---

[29] Raz, *Engaging Reason* (Oxford, Oxford University Press, 1999), 132.

[30] In one sense, all concepts are parochial, in that access to all aspects of reality will depend upon the conceiving creature's sensory and cognitive apparatus. Thus humans, with their particular sensory and evaluating capabilities, will acquire a different array of concepts than will, for example, Martians who have different such capabilities.

Thick evaluative concepts are related, but distinct. 'Thick' evaluative concepts are concepts which cannot be analysed into descriptive and evaluative elements so as to preserve their normative sense. According to Williams:

What has happened is that the theorists have brought the fact-value distinction to language rather than finding it revealed there. What they have found are a lot of those 'thicker' or more specific ethical notions . . . such as *treachery* and *promise* and *brutality* and *courage*, which seem to express a union of fact and value. The way these notions are applied is determined by what the world is like (for instance, by how someone behaved), and yet, at the same time, their application usually involves a certain valuation of the situation, of persons or actions. Moreover, they usually (though not necessarily directly) provide reasons for action.[31]

Now the point about the thickness of these concepts[32] is not that they cannot be analysed into parts, so to speak, to give a description which differentiates factual and evaluative elements. That is easy: consider this analysis of courage: courage is personally dangerous risk-taking for worthwhile purposes (personally dangerous risk-taking which is, for the agent, 'valuable'), whereas the failure to undertake a personally dangerous risk when it is worthwhile to do so is cowardice, and undertaking of personally dangerous risks for low-value or trivial purposes is foolhardiness. The same can be done for murder: murder is killing that is evil, wicked, or otherwise 'bad'. These analyses are unacceptably vague, of course, but vagueness is always a problem and no doubt these definitions could be sharpened, yet what these thumbnail demonstrations show is that nothing in principle would appear to make such analyses impossible. And if that is right, then on what basis does Williams assert that theorists have 'brought' the fact-value distinction to these concepts, rather than its inherently being part of them? The mere existence of such 'thick' concepts in our thinking, which have both factual and evaluative criteria for their proper application, and corresponding words in our natural language to express them, cannot decide the issue. For in acquiring these concepts we may simply have acquired them on the basis of our attention being drawn to both the factual and evaluative criteria. That we now apply such concepts 'unreflectively', that is, when we identify an event as a murder we don't consciously reflect to ourselves 'killing' and 'evil' and then infer 'murder' is neither here nor there, for we apply all kinds of concepts on the basis of multiple criteria unreflectively. For example, assume that one workable set of criteria for the application of 'chair' is 'portable', 'seat' 'for one'. No one would insist that I reflect to myself on such criteria when I invite you to 'Take a chair'.

---

[31] B.Williams, *Ethics and the Limits of Philosophy* (Fontana, 1985) at 129–30. I should make it clear that by following Williams (in addition to Raz) on the nature of thick and thin ethical concepts I am not thereby subscribing to the arguments Williams goes on to make with the use of that distinction about the failures of modern moral philosophy. For a critique of Williams's use of the distinction in that regard, see Samuel Scheffler, 'Morality Through Thick and Thin' (1987) XCVI *The Philosophical Review*, 411–34.

[32] Some further examples of thick ethical concepts Williams gives are: malicious, selfish, brutal, inconsiderate, self-indulgent, lazy, greedy. Ibid., 192.

The crucial factor is the *abstract character* of the evaluative terms that are employed in the analysis. We see this when we look closely at the thumbnail analyses, or any others that people come up with: the evaluative criteria are all 'thin', that is, the most general, abstract terms of approbation or disapprobation, 'ought', 'good', 'right', 'praiseworthy', 'bad', 'wrong', 'wicked' and so on. All the thickness, the local, specific, character of the concept, is deposited in the factual criteria. 'It is essential to this account that the specific or "thick" character of these terms is given in the descriptive element. The value part is expressed, under analysis, by the all-purpose prescriptive term *ought*.'[33] So undertaking these analyses *itself* appears to 'reflect' an unspoken theoretical perspective, for these thin terms are, of course, the very sort of abstract theoretical terms which are the very essence of modern moral philosophizing. From this perspective there is no courage-specific evaluative dimension in the statement that 'Paul displayed courage', no value, specifically, in or of 'courage' *per se*. Courage is merely the instantiation of the good or the right or what one ought to do where circumstances provide for personally dangerous risk-taking. The somewhat disconcerting message of the fact-value distinction as applied here, which at first glance seems so innocuous, is that there are no particular, specific, non-abstract ethical evaluations, so no specific ethical concepts to represent them, so no such particular, specific, non-abstract ethical thoughts or reasons—when we treat of the ethical or moral, it's abstract all the way down, so to speak. The application of the fact/value analysis drains most of the significance or meaning from ethical judgements employing these terms.

Given the prevalence of thick evaluative concepts in everyday practical judgement,[34] it is worthwhile considering whether they, rather than thin concepts, are the basic foundation of normative or evaluative judgement, including moral judgement. If they are, then we might plausibly be able to construct a picture of common law lawyerly and judicial expertise which is not equivalent to expertise in abstract moral philosophical reasoning. Instead, perhaps, common law lawyers and judges may have some kind of superior knowledge of, i.e. expertise in dealing with, thick ethical concepts. Such an expertise, if it exists, would presumably be manifest or reflected in a legal discourse which is incompletely theorized from the perspective of moral and political philosophy.

IV. THICK AND PAROCHIAL CONCEPTS AND
THE TRANSPARENCY AND UNIVERSALITY, OR
UNIVERSALIZABILITY, OF MORAL REASONING

There does, however, appear to be a problem in this perspective, concerning the transparency and universality of the values which thick evaluative concepts represent. The problem can be stated in this way: according to Raz and Williams,

---

[33] Some further examples of thick ethical concepts Williams gives are: malicious, selfish, brutal, inconsiderate, self-indulgent, lazy, greedy, 130, italics original.   [34] Raz, *supra* n. 29, 146.

thick ethical concepts are parochial concepts; they are 'thick' because they represent values which are created, sustained, or accessible only because of complex cultural or social practices of particular groups. Therefore they are neither 'transparent' nor 'universal' in the way we expect moral concepts to be. Moral concepts should be transparent in the sense that if we have them, we should have a grasp of their intelligibility which explains why they apply in specific circumstances. Thin ethical concepts offer this promise, in that the generality of the evaluations they permit us to make applies across specific thick ethical judgements. Thus the concept 'right' applies to and makes intelligible any number of different ethical circumstances, as do the concepts of 'duty', or 'freedom' or 'autonomy'. Thin ethical concepts also offer, if not the established reality of an appreciation of universal moral values, at least the means to achieve that appreciation. Thin ethical concepts, so the argument goes, are not parochial. Their very function lies in the fact that they make intelligible more specific or thick moral judgements, allowing us to see contradictions in our moral reasoning.

Raz examines the basis of this sort of argument, and concludes that both thick and thin ethical concepts have a role in our moral understanding. The analysis is rich and detailed, but I can, I think, present the general outline.[35] According to Raz's account, thick ethical concepts and thin ethical concepts have different roles to play in our moral understanding. Roughly, the acquisition of thick ethical concepts by individuals goes hand in hand with the fact that the plurality of values which we are able to realize is context-dependent. In the case of some values,[36] access to them is dependent upon cultural conditions. In the case of others, they exist only where they are created and sustained by cultural or social practices. This cultural dependence is reflected in our possession of parochial, thick concepts of the values in question. The value of chess, for example, is dependent upon being familiar with the specific character of chess-playing, and the value of mastering the game so as to play it to some level of success. Roughly then, to realize the value of say, chess, is to have a concept of its value which is thick. On the other hand, our evaluative judgements are, more or less, intelligible to us. To act in response to values just is to act for reasons, and if that is right and we are rational, then we must have some appreciation of the character of all values *as* values, i.e. as possible instantiations of value. This intelligibility is provided by thin evaluative concepts. If thick evaluative concepts serve to represent the plurality of values in all their specificity, it is only by being able to subsume such thick evaluative concepts under thin evaluative ones which allows us to recognize them as intelligibly being examples of value. To quote Raz at some length:

Evolving practices give rise to new values. Commonly their emergence is recognized by subsuming them under familiar values. Thus existing values make possible the recognition

---

[35] The account I present here is drawn principally from chapters 6, 7, 9, and 10 of Raz, *supra* n. 29.

[36] The following argument applies as well to disvalues, thick disvalues, e.g. torture, or libel, or fraud, or thin, disrespect, inequality, alienation.

of new values when encountered, but they do not allow either the prescribing or design-ing them, in the sense of saying 'these are the values one should have in these cultural con-ditions', nor do existing values provide a base for predicting which new values would evolve. New values emerge with evolving social practices and cultural developments. Once new subsumed values emerge reflection on them leads to a reinterpretation and a change of understanding of the more universal value concepts under which they were subsumed, thus leading to the emergence of new abstract value concepts to cover both new and old concrete values. In this way the intelligibility and the social dependence of values are rec-onciled. They are reconciled through the fact that intelligibility does not mean a perman-ent frame of reference. . . . [I]n general it seems that the emergence of abstract value concepts merely improves the understanding of previously existing values. . . . [I]f there is a right not to be tortured that right predates the concept of a right. The emergence of the concept merely enables us to understand that the right exists. The same goes for other abstract value concepts, such as the value of self-expression or autonomy. The reason is that in these cases, the value can be enjoyed by people who do not have the abstract con-cept. They cannot enjoy it without some concepts, but it is enough for them to have more concrete concepts, which are appropriately related to the right against torture, or to the state of expressing oneself, or of being autonomous. . . . The thin and thick concepts are interdependent. Thick concepts have to be explained by reference to thinner ones in order to satisfy the requirement of intelligibility. The thin concepts, on the other hand, while explained by reference to thicker ones, also have an open-ended aspect: new thick concepts subject to them can always emerge. This makes them relatively independent of the thick concepts currently subsumed under them.'[37]

This is an attractive and plausible picture, and can be taken as one perspective on the possibility that common law judges and lawyers have a kind of moral expertise endowing them with authority. Legal development in the common law occurs on the occasion that disputes are presented to courts. In order to under-stand the moral character of these disputes, one must understand their facts, and properly appreciate what values and dis-values, in all their cultural contin-gency, are instantiated. It follows from that that lawyers and judges would have to be familiar with the culturally thick ethical concepts which represent those values and dis-values. Furthermore, lawyers and judges are, in the common law tradition, supposed to explain their appreciation of the facts and reasons for their decisions. They must show the intelligibility of their reasoning. Thus one would expect them also to make use of thin ethical concepts for this very reason, perhaps in particular to show that their instant decision is not incon-sistent with other relevant past decisions, or that no factors of importance (which possession of the more general, thin concept, prompts one to consider) have been left out of their reasoning or argument. This picture, besides being, I think, attractive, seems to represent the character of legal discourse with some fidelity. It occupies a median level of abstraction. And it also seems to permit the claim that judges and lawyers can have (not always, nor necessarily) the moral expertise which would entitle them to make law. This would lie in both

---

[37] Raz, *supra* n. 29, 208–10.

their familiarity in applying thick ethical concepts to often puzzling or complex sets of facts, and in their learned facility in giving voice to the intelligibility of these thick ethical concepts and their application in particular cases by reference to thin ethical concepts, in particular thin ethical concepts which have made their appearance in law as much as moral and political philosophy, thin ethical concepts such as 'right' and 'just'. Thus in addition to what I called his 'political' explanation for the law's being incompletely theorized from the perspective of academic moral and political philosophy, I think we can glean from Raz's recent writing a 'cognitive' explanation, i.e. one that arises from the nature of the concepts with which lawyers and judges must work. This latter explanation also provides some reason to believe that common law lawyers and judges might also be able to claim some legitimacy for their authority to make law: it lies in their ability, acquired through experience and study, to use this conceptual apparatus with greater facility than most of the subjects of the law. In short, in areas like the common law where the legal concepts at work are very closely related, if not identical to, moral concepts treating of the same factual situations, their legal expertise is, because of this facility, a kind of moral expertise.

Despite the attractiveness of this picture, it seems to me to embrace a mistaken assumption, viz. the assumption that thick evaluative concepts are parochial concepts, and that in comparison to thick evaluative concepts, thin evaluative concepts are less parochial in virtue of the fact that they, being more general and less context-dependent, can subsume thick ethical ones. What I am going to argue for (though unfortunately not nearly sufficiently to establish the truth of it) is the claim that the universality of ethical judgement is secured by the universality of certain thick ethical concepts, and that our claim to the intelligibility of these concepts and our application of them, while undoubtedly assisted by more abstract arguments making use of thin ethical concepts, lies more in acquiring true beliefs about what thick ethical concepts represent and systematizing that knowledge for use in our practical reasoning.

The general drift of the argument to follow turns on treating evaluative concepts in the same way one would treat non-evaluative concepts to examine their role in our reasoning and understanding.[38] The 'ontological' status of values may be puzzling to us, but if we accept (which is true) that we are valuing creatures, i.e. creatures which have access to and realize values, just as we are creatures with certain perceptual capacities able to access perceptual properties, there seems no reason to believe that our concepts of values should be puzzling *qua* concepts. That is, if the nature of values is mysterious to us, then that will make it difficult to form true beliefs about values. But it seems to be a necessary premise for a discussion of evaluative reasoning that there are values, and that we have enough acquaintance with them to be able to distinguish values

---

[38] This seems also to be the general drift of Raz's argument against taking the thesis that the evaluative supervenes on the non-evaluative as an important premise in our understanding of the evaluative. Ibid., 219–25.

from dis-values and one kind of value from another. If so, then we must have concepts of values and dis-values in significant working order to do for us what other concepts do, i.e. allow us to consider, form beliefs about, and otherwise deal with features of the world.

If this is roughly right, then just as it is the case that our access to different features of the world and our ability to form concepts[39] of those features of the world may be underpinned in different ways, so may our access to values and concepts of values. We have already noted the distinction Raz draws between values which are dependent upon culture in the sense that they are created by culture, and dependent upon culture in the sense that access to them is mediated by cultural practices. The question I want to pursue is whether there is reason to believe that there are any universal *thick* evaluative concepts, in particular any universal thick *ethical* concepts, and if so, what their relation is to evaluative concepts which show this sort of cultural dependency. If there are universal thick ethical concepts, then the transparency and universality we associate with (or demand from) moral concepts may be secured, not because we have thin ethical concepts under which values can be intelligibly subsumed, but because we have universal access to certain thick values more or less as a matter of being human. It seems to me that there obviously are universal thick ethical concepts.

Williams identifies his thick ethical concepts as being the most *culturally specific* ethical concepts, and as far as I can tell, Raz assumes the same thing. However, a scan back over the examples Williams gives suggests that, if anything, these concepts will have the most universal instantiation. What human culture, for example, would not have acquaintance with and formed a concept of courage, or could not think about brutality or promises or greed? As far as I can tell, Williams gives no reason for regarding these concepts as culturally specific beyond the fact that they are 'traditional', or 'hyper-traditional' as he puts it.[40] But because a battery of concepts has existed as a long-standing feature of a traditional culture does not entail that the concepts are specific to that traditional culture, but only that even members of traditional cultures can acquire them, i.e., these concepts are not restricted to moderns. Neither, however, are moderns excluded from acquiring them (which Williams seems clearly to imply, since by presenting them to modern readers in our language without quotation marks around them, he would seem to indicate he believes that we have the concepts of courage, brutality, and so on). It may well be the case that

---

[39] My views about the nature of concepts have been very much influenced by considerations about the nature of concepts that have been raised by the work of cognitive scientists and which have been discussed by philosophers of mind, in particular the views of Jerry Fodor; see, e.g., his *Concepts: Where Cognitive Science Went Wrong* (Oxford: Oxford University Press, 1998).

[40] It is interesting to note that when Williams introduces the idea of thick ethical concept, he discusses plausibly universal concepts, such as courage, but when discussing his claim concerning their cultural specificity, he uses examples such as the value of the life of a samurai warrior, *supra* n. 31 at 161, or obscenity or chastity, B. Williams, 'Truth in Ethics' (1995) VIII *Ratio (New Series)* 227 at 237, 241 respectively, all three of which are to my mind heavily theorized and complex concepts and not at all like the examples with which we began.

in a very real way having access to the values and dis-values these concepts are concepts of, and therefore having the ability to acquire these concepts, does depend in a significant way on cultural or societal practices. It is, I think, easy to imagine the circumstances of someone who might not acquire such concepts. Consider a child raised in conditions of unrelenting abuse, perhaps one raised in a gulag or concentration camp. It seems right to suggest that there is a minimum standard of cultural practice, a recognizable level of basic human cultural 'success', for want of a better term, against which the plurality of values such as courage, or generosity, or dis-values such as malice or lying would be distinguishable. However I take it that concerns about cultural relativity are not primarily concerned with these sorts of possibility. The present point is that it seems right to think that in the vast range of human societies with their specific cultures of which we have knowledge, it seems much more plausible to believe that all of them would instantiate values like courage or generosity and dis-values like malice, and that people would acquire concepts of them, than that no instantiations of these values would occur, and that no concepts of them would be acquired. This, of course, is not to deny by any means the existence of those values whose creation or access to which has been shown to depend upon cultural practices which are far from universal. But the truth of that is not incompatible with there being universally instantiated values and dis-values, and universally acquired concepts of them.

'But', you may say, 'while we are able to perceive courage, malice, and so on in every culture, and can acquire the concepts 'courage', 'malice' etc., it does not follow that the members of those cultures have the *same* concepts of 'courage' and 'malice' we do, even if they have concepts which in some way or another represent those values. Therefore what has been said in no way proves the universality of these concepts.' This objection is roughly expressed, but I put it in these rough terms so as to reproduce a possible ambiguity in the sort of objection I am describing. The objection might be simply that people in different cultures, although they have a concept of courage or whatever, have different beliefs about courage than do we, and attribute different significance to it. If that is all that is meant, the claim is true, but does not undercut the claim of universality. Something Raz says is helpful in showing why not:

Consider the sort of normative considerations advanced as universal and timeless. For example: it is always wrong to murder an innocent person. If we can judge people to have acted wrongly in having committed murder we must assume that it is possible for them to know that they should not perform the actions which are the murder of innocent people. But we need not assume that they must have been able to understand the concept 'murder', 'person', 'innocent', 'intention', and 'killing', which we use to articulate and explain this rule. Arguably, even before these concepts were available to people they had other ways of categorizing mental states, other ways of marking transgressions, other ways of marking animals we now know belong to the species *Homo sapiens*. Their concepts and generalizations may have been based on false beliefs, and we may find them inadequate in many ways. But they may have enabled them to know that the acts which in fact constitute murder of innocent people are wrong. That is enough to establish that they had the access to the norm which is a pre-condition of being able to blame them for its violation. If people at all times had access to the norms, in one form or another, then we have here an example of a consideration, to which there is universal access, though that access is culturally determined.[41]

Here Raz is directing his attention to the ability to appreciate a norm, and conceive of it, rather than appreciate a value, and have a concept of it, but I think the lesson is the same. As Raz points out, if all that this sort of objection is claiming is that the person from the other culture, though having the norm, has as well different concepts and beliefs which form part of his (to our minds, insufficient or flawed) overall understanding of the norm, that, while important, does not undercut the claim about universality. The same lesson must be applied to distinguish between having a concept and having particular beliefs about whatever the concept is a concept of. I think it plausible to say that I and Aristotle had the concept 'food', though I have beliefs about food which Aristotle did not, and indeed could not have. I, for example, believe, and indeed know, that many foods contain saturated fats. Aristotle didn't. Simply having different beliefs about the thing that a concept is a concept of does not entail that two people have a different concept of it. As a rough and ready guide, if two persons' concepts both distinguish paradigm cases of the thing a concept is a concept of, then they have the same concept.[42] The beliefs one has about the thing may, and often do, lead different persons to disagree about whether a non-paradigmatic case falls under the concept or not. But this happens between different people in the same culture. The claim about the universality of the concept of 'courage' is that it is difficult to imagine any more or less functioning human culture in which cases we would regard as paradigm examples of the value of courage would not be accessible, whether courage in battle, or in facing wild animals, or in facing other hazardous physical dangers, and equally difficult to imagine that these paradigm examples would not be paradigm examples of courage in those cultures as well. It doesn't turn on different cultures' particular beliefs about courage, for example that courage is a gift of the gods, or that one instils courage through physical privation, or anything else. Concepts are not to be individuated in terms of every belief that a person has in which that concept figures. One should not say that Aristotle and I have a

---

[41] Raz, *supra* n. 29, 152.

[42] This is a very rough and ready guide. The treatment of something of a paradigm case of a concept is an historically and culturally contingent affair, even for paradigms cases of the same concept. For the Inuit, raw seal meat may be (or have been) a paradigm case of food, not a paradigm case I share even though I would want to maintain that the Inuit and I share the concept of food. The claim about sharing paradigms must in this sense be counterfactual, the question to be asked being something like: having acquired the concept of food and then placed in the Inuit's situation (or vice versa), would we agree upon treating the same items as paradigm cases of the concept in question in that context. In other words, would I treat raw seal meat as a paradigm case of food when with the Inuit, and would he treat, say, steak and chips, as a paradigm case of food when with me. The example was suggested to me by Richard Samuels.

different concept of food only for the reason that I, unlike he, believes that my Aunt Ethel eats food. Nor should they be individuated in terms even of every belief about the nature of the thing that a concept is a concept of. One should not say that Aristotle and I have a different concept of food only for the reason that I know that some foods contain saturated fat. But one must be judicious about this. When we speak of concepts, we do sometimes wish to speak of more than people's ability to distinguish paradigm cases; rather, we wish to consider the broader constellation of beliefs which more or less make up a department of their thought. Here it is perfectly right to say that there was a different 'concept' or 'conception' of, say, 'courage' in Rome than most people have nowadays. This is a perfectly valid point to make: the point is that for some purposes, we should individuate concepts not on a belief-independent basis, but in terms of some more or less essential constellation of beliefs that a person has in respect of the feature of the world that the concept represents. But again, this does not count against the universality point. It only requires us to distinguish between different notions of a concept. For my purposes, the universality point is secured if restricted to individuating concepts on the basis that a person has a concept when able to identify paradigm cases of the value the concept represents, for the point is that the value the concept represents is a value which will be instantiated in any society and to which any individual will have access. Indeed, it would not only undercut the universality point to adopt the 'complex of beliefs' formulation of concept, it would obscure an important aspect of the universality claim.

The claim is precisely not that universal access to these values guarantees a universal set of beliefs in which the concept of the value figures, or a universal complex of beliefs about the nature of the concept. That would be a preposterous claim to make even within one's own culture in respect of the concepts people acquire and the beliefs they form. It is crucial to understand that having a concept does not make one an immediate know-it-all about whatever the concept is a concept of. Having the concept courage does not tell us everything important or significant about courage. Indeed, it may be the case that concepts (in the 'grasp of paradigms' sense) come cheap, in that one acquires concepts fairly easily either by direct exposure to the values or dis-values in question, or by being informed about those values or dis-values in various ways by others, but that knowledge of the things they are concepts of is hard-won: knowledge requires investigation and thought. Think of it this way: acquiring a concept is like opening a file on a research project. Getting the concept of 'dog' so that one can distinguish dogs may not require much more than having dogs pointed out to one a couple of times; children seem to learn to pick out dogs very easily. But getting that under one's belt does not guarantee one much in the way of knowledge. There is a lot to learn about dogs, and indeed, having the concept of dog (having opened that file) is a pre-condition of learning new things about dogs, for only by having the concept 'dog' is one able to acquire new beliefs *about* dogs, about dogs *qua* dogs, about dogs as such.

There seems no reason to believe that evaluative concepts are any different in this regard. There is a lot to learn about the actual nature of murder, about its particular dis-value (how important is the mental state attending it, how are different cases of murder worse than others), about its relation to other dis-values (whether, and in what respects, it is like and different from, worse or less bad than, say, rape or treason), and about its limits (is euthanasia murder?). Forming new, true, beliefs about the nature of murder will require investigation into actual instances of it, and thought.

If this is right, then we have a picture of ethical evaluation which looks something like this: on the basis of our grasp of universal, thick ethical concepts, *and* whatever knowledge about what those concepts represent that we've managed to assemble and remember (knowledge that will turn very largely on the conditions of one's culture, for example, whether there are institutions in which this knowledge is developed or preserved, for example), we apply those concepts to particular cases to determine what appears to us to be the morally correct response.

But how, one may ask, do universal thick ethical concepts interact with thin ones? Recall that according to Raz, thinner concepts, those more abstract and general concepts, function in part to render intelligible the evaluative nature of thick evaluative concepts. Raz also makes the point that thin evaluative concepts are parochial. He says:

But the same [parochial character] is true of our abstract normative concepts such as those designated by the terms 'duty', 'obligation', 'a right', 'valuable', 'good', 'beautiful', 'person', 'happiness', 'pleasure'. The history of these terms shows how their meaning mutated over time, and how different languages differ in their abstract normative vocabulary.[43]

This point can be strengthened. To the extent that thin evaluative concepts are theoretical or philosophical, that is, derive (much of) their meaning from their situation within explicit philosophical theories, they depend upon (not necessarily academic) social practices in which theories or philosophies are formulated, considered, and criticized; it follows that these terms must be parochial, perhaps very parochial, for these practices are far from universal, and different cultures show very different practices of this kind.

If I am right about the universal, i.e. non-parochial character of (certain) thick ethical concepts and about the parochial character of thin ethical concepts, then the general relationship of thin to thick evaluative concepts advanced by Raz and discussed above is reversed. In particular, it does not seem clear from this new perspective quite how thin ethical concepts are necessary for our appreciating the intelligibility of thick ethical concepts. It would seem that thick evaluative concepts must provide intelligible access to value, or they would not be concepts of the values they must be. On the other hand, one could have access to these values without having the abstract theoretical concept 'value'. One would, of course, be less knowledgeable about the nature of the world than one who had

---

[43] Raz, *supra* n. 29, 133.

such a concept, where, however, it is important to emphasize, that 'thin concept' was supported by an intellectual practice which ensured that this thin ethical concept was in some sort of order, i.e. answered some sensible questions or organized the realm of values in some useful way. Presumably one would appreciate a range of values, and be able to respond more or less rationally to them—what one would be incapable of would be certain more sophisticated thoughts about these values, in particular thoughts which allowed one to treat the plurality of values as being of a kind. Furthermore, without these thinner terms, one would presumably be unable to discern certain aspects about the nature of values, which higher order theories provide one access to. 'Right', as in individuals possessing rights like the right to life, is an example. This term is clearly parochial, appearing in the West only from about the beginning of the 17th century.[44] Having this concept of right allows us to organize what morality and law requires by reference to the interests of persons.[45] And to say this is not to treat 'rights' as merely an 'interpretive' term in a theoretical framework, but to acknowledge that rights may be as real as any other thing of which we may have an evaluative concept. Acquiring the concept 'proton' depends on the access provided by theories in physics, but protons are real just the same, and there is no a priori reason that the same theory-dependent access to the normative realm can not be provided. (Again, it is worthwhile stressing that any truths being made available by these concepts depend upon these concepts being in 'working order', that is underpinned by practices, scientific or intellectual or otherwise which sharpen rather than obscure our grasp of reality.)

Thus, although the parochial/non-parochial polarity between thick and thin terms is reversed on the account I have offered, the role of thin concepts, in particular thin 'theoretical' or 'philosophical' concepts appears to be much the same. But rather than framing their function as subsuming thick terms to *provide* them with intelligibility or *make* them intelligible, they rather *advance* our understanding of the evaluative realm by providing access to aspects of that realm which are not captured by thick terms. To isolate one line previously quoted from Raz:

. . . [I]n general it seems that the emergence of abstract value concepts merely improves the understanding of previously existing values.

In doing so, thin ethical concepts should also point out, or lead us to consider or examine, possible aspects of the nature of the values and dis-values that thick ethical concepts are concepts of.

V. COMMON LAW MORAL EXPERTISE

I can now outline two claims about the nature of common law legal reasoning and the possibility of common law lawyers' judges having a kind of moral

---

[44] J. Finnis, *Natural Law and Natural Rights* (Oxford: Clarendon Press, 1980), 205–10.
[45] See Raz, *supra* n. 4, ch. 7; J. E. Penner, 'The Analysis of Rights' (1997) 10 *Ratio Juris*, 300–15.

expertise. The first is that, despite a long history of the law's looking at the values and dis-values these concepts are concepts of, much of our knowledge remains in terms of a collection of relevant cases in which the facts have led us to apply one or more of our thick ethical concepts, a collection which is maintained by us through various methods of memory and recording. Not only does the past consideration and memorizing of actual cases engender a facility of applying thick ethical concepts, but continuing exposure to actual cases of moral relevance allows us to refine our beliefs about those concepts. If this is right, then a casuistic approach to moral reasoning might better reflect what we most know about the values and dis-values our concepts represent; reflect it better, by and large, that is, than more abstract theoretical statements about what morality requires. And this casuistic approach is typical of common law reasoning. The law 'exists' in the cases because it is the cases which re-trigger our thick ethical concepts, and their interactions with each other in actual cases prompt further beliefs about the nature of what those concepts represent and the ways in which they interact. The short way of putting this is that *continuing* acquaintance in different contexts with the things our concepts of which are learned by acquaintance is probably the best trigger of our more or less untheorized catalogue of knowledge about the values and dis-values our thick ethical concepts represent, *and* the best ground of new knowledge about those values and dis-values. Beliefs newly acquired in the course of this exercise are then articulated and fitted within the catalogue of pre-existing belief, but generally 'locally', i.e. in specific areas of our body of knowledge, to refine and explain only a relatively small portion of the body of knowledge, and at a suitably low level of abstraction.

The second claim is that, despite the fact that I have emphasized the universal character of certain thick ethical concepts, any set of moral norms organized into a system which is to apply to persons within a society generally will be conventional to a large extent. This contention rests upon what might be called our 'paradigmatic' or 'stereotypical' access to concepts.[46] This is simply the idea that, whilst our concepts are about more than paradigmatic or stereotypical instances of what they are concepts of—non-stereotypical dogs are still dogs—our ability to apply our concepts is more difficult where non-stereotypical instances of the thing a concept represents are instantiated. Now, one obvious thought that arises from this is that in any system of norms where our concepts have uncertain boundaries in this way it will be imperative to stipulate (reasonable) boundaries for the application of these terms in order to provide some measure of certainty. This, recall, is one way in which the authority of law-makers can be justified, as providing conventions to ensure more or less certain boundaries, to ensure a more effective compliance with moral norms. But

---

[46] See Fodor, *Concepts, supra* n. 39, chs. 6 and 7. See also Rey, G. 'Concepts and Stereotypes' (1983) 15 *Cognition*, 237.

I think a different claim about the common law's conventionality can be made, having to do with what Raz calls the path-dependence of epistemic justification, and therefore of knowledge. If our understanding of the different values our thick concepts represent depends upon our experience in dealing with actual cases to which they apply, then it is obvious that different cultures or societies might come to more knowledge about, and therefore rely more upon, certain of these thick ethical concepts than others, simply because for various reasons they have acquired greater knowledge of some of the values and dis-values these concepts represent than others. Having the paradigmatic instances under one's belt is one thing; having a sophisticated knowledge of the value a concept represents so that one can identify the value's instantiation in atypical circumstances is quite another. Furthermore, here is a point where the influence of thin, parochial concepts, may have a great influence. A society's success in developing thin abstract concepts that illuminate and advance the intelligibility of the battery of universal thick ethical concepts will vary from one concept to another. Its appreciation of certain values and dis-values, and hence its interest in acquiring greater knowledge of these values and dis-values, will also be influenced by other factors, such as religion, economic conditions, and so forth. In consequence of these different cultural factors, different societies will have differing levels of interest and differing levels of knowledge about the values and dis-values represented by universal thick ethical concepts, and so will tend to rely upon some more than others in making sense of what is morally good, morally required, morally prohibited, and so on. Our thick ethical concepts interact, and different concepts may be instantiated in the same circumstances. An act may be courageous, generous, but also disloyal. A sale of goods reflects concepts both of agreement and property. In making sense of the moral significance of particular cases, different ethical concepts may be emphasized over others. As a result of this, different cultures will give rise to different moral systems of norms, even if they all begin with an identical battery of thick ethical concepts.

By making these remarks, I do not mean to suggest that all systems of norms represent morality in an equally sophisticated or equally valid way. But I do think that we must allow for the possibility that there is more than one way to skin a cat, morally speaking. It may be the case that given the plurality of even universally accessible values, success in generating a basic system of norms for the governing of behaviour may depend upon emphasizing certain values over others—which is not to say that any value may be denied outright. The particular emphases of a culture in this respect will reflect something of its character. And it follows that the particular emphases a culture places on certain values must be preserved in its moral reasoning if basic desiderata such as certainty in norms, treating like cases alike, and so on, are to be achieved. In this way a culture of moral discourse, in particular an institutionalized culture of moral discourse, might make what appear from the outside to be purely arbitrary 'selections' of values to emphasize. My point is that given the state of knowledge, it might be not only perfectly sensible but morally praiseworthy to do so.[47]

Much more needs to be said to flesh out this very rough sketch. But to give an indication of the kind of 'selection' I am talking about, consider the institution of the trust in English law. The norms governing the law of trusts reflect a number of thick ethical concepts, of which I would cite 'property', 'agreement', and 'loyalty' as being three examples. But this particular combination of norms is absent in civilian jurisdictions, though there are similar sorts of legal devices. Having made the selection to analyse cases in these terms, that is, as cases of trusts, will direct common law judges and lawyers to appreciate aspects of fact situations that are different from those civilians will, and as importantly, will require them differently to explain their practical reasoning, making sense of their decisions in different ways, even if, as often seems to be the case, different legal systems achieve the same 'functional equivalent'.[48]

In short, an institution of moral discourse which emphasizes past assimilation of cases in which thick ethical concepts have been applied, continuing exposure to new cases as a source of knowledge, and a commitment to past 'selections' of particular values and the concepts that represent them as ones which are to serve more foundational roles in the discourse of practical reasoning, may count

---

[47] In addition to the interaction between thick and thin ethical concepts discussed above (Part IV of the text), these considerations also go some way to meeting an objection to the morally normative character of thick ethical concepts posed by Simon Blackburn in *Ruling Passions* (Oxford: Clarendon Press, 1998), 100–4. According to Blackburn, by failing to analyse thick ethical concepts into their descriptive and evaluative components, we fail to gain any critical purchase upon them so as to recognize what is wrong with the behavioural direction they provide, for example, failing to see how a thick concept like 'cute' as applied to women should not be treated as a ground of approval but rather as demeaning. Given the plurality of values, thickly conceived, the emphasis by a culture upon some will result in the diminished purchase of others, and it is likely to be the case that certain sorts of emphasis are linked with others. A culture which prizes the more 'intellectual' values and virtues may systematically downgrade the physical or the sensual, and this sort of selection will give an apparent critical purchase by way of the ranking of values. Thus the very existence of a plurality of thick ethical concepts provides critical purchase: we may come to understand the demeaning aspect of applying 'cute' to women by understanding that by placing an emphasis on a woman's appearance we may implicitly or explicitly downgrade other aspects of their identity which are of greater significance. It is also worthwhile pointing out one of the specific features of the example of 'cute' which muddies the waters somewhat. While human beings may be in some deep psychological way 'naturally' sexist, in that humans may be prone to ascribe characteristics to, and differentially value traits when instantiated by men and women differentially, it would also seem clear that there is a great deal of *thin* 'theoretical', or 'religious', or 'cultural' inculcation which lies behind sexist attitudes. By thin here I mean more or less explicit normative tenets such as 'a woman's place is in the home'; the point here is that organizing moral attitudes by way of the ideas generated by *reflective* and *analytic* religious, academic, philosophical, or political practices may result in injustices or other moral failings because the results of these practices displace people's confidence in and reliance upon knowledge or understanding provided by thick ethical concepts—people are blinded by theory or ideology, so to speak. It is one of the themes of much feminist writing that the prevailing philosophical and political orientation towards women effectively silences them by making it difficult to articulate the true moral character of their experience.

[48] These considerations are relevant to our appreciation of the functionality of 'legal transplants', for example the 'transplant' of the civilian concept of 'good faith' in contract law into English law by EU directive. See Gunther Teubner, 'Legal Irritants: Good Faith in British Law or How Unifying Law Ends Up in New Divergences' (1998) 61 MLR, 11–32.

as a genuine case of institutionalized moral expertise. Besides its authority to solve coordination problems, then, the common law may be right to claim, and individual judges and lawyers learned in the common law may be right to claim, that it or he or she is experienced in the application of moral norms in a way which endows it or he or she with moral wisdom. 'Wisdom' here refers to a kind of expertise which exists at a lower level of abstraction than abstract theory, and which depends on the acquisition of correct beliefs about the nature of universal ethical values through long experience with dealing with them, and as well with the particular conventional selections of emphasis which colour but underpin a systematic and sophisticated discourse of practical reasoning.

It is not clear to me the extent to which Raz would disagree with this characterization of thick and thin evaluative concepts in legal and moral reasoning, nor of the suggestion of a basis for a kind of moral expertise which judges and lawyers in the common law represent. His discussion of thick and thin, and parochial and non-parochial, concepts was in the context of papers addressed to different matters, and as I read this work, nothing I have said here is necessarily inconsistent with the views he argued for in those contexts. Yet even if consistent with his views, I have taken his views in directions prompted by my own interests in ways he might not appreciate. In any case, it is also abundantly clear that I stand in his debt, for little that I have written here could have whatever interest or coherence it has in the absence of Raz's own illumination of the issues involved.

6

Raz on Gaps—the Surprising Part

TIMOTHY A.O. ENDICOTT*

In my second-hand copy of *The Authority of Law*, a law student has put an exclamation mark in the margin beside the following passage, which I will call 'the surprising part':

> There is yet a third way in which the sources thesis is responsible for legal gaps and it too arises out of conflict situations. The law may make certain legal rules have prima facie force only by subjecting them to moral or other non-source-based considerations. Let us assume, for example, that by law contracts are valid only if not immoral. Any particular contract can be judged to be prima facie valid if it conforms to the 'value-neutral' conditions for the validity of contract laid down by law. The proposition 'it is legally conclusive that this contract is valid' is neither true nor false until a court authoritatively determines its validity. This is a consequence of the fact that by the sources thesis the courts have discretion when required to apply moral considerations.[1]

I suppose that this passage surprised a lawyer for this reason: in English law there are various ways in which contracts can be invalid or unenforceable because they are immoral—and yet English lawyers know that many contracts are conclusively binding (even non-lawyers know that). They do not need to wait for a court to determine the validity of most contracts.

The first two sources of legal gaps that Joseph Raz identifies do not seem so surprising. Vagueness in the sources of law leads to gaps in borderline cases, and there is a gap if the law includes inconsistent rules, with no way of deciding which is effective. In those situations it seems right to say that the law does not tell people where they stand, so that people may need a court to determine whether, for example, they have a contract, and a court required to resolve a dispute has discretion to resolve it as the judge sees fit. But if Raz is right about the *third* source of gaps, then judges have discretion whenever the law appeals to moral considerations. The English law of contracts subjects the validity of contracts to a variety of moral considerations (I will discuss some in this essay, but I cannot even list them all). So Raz's view seems to mean that no contract is more than *prima facie* valid, and that a court has discretion to hold any contract invalid.

*I benefited from discussing this paper with Michael Spence.

[1] Raz, *The Authority of Law. Essays on Law and Morality* (Oxford: Clarendon Press, 1979), 75.

This essay seeks to make sense of this surprising yet essential fragment of the early articulation of Raz's theory of law. I will argue that the claim it makes needs to be modified: the sources thesis entails that courts have discretion in some cases when required to apply moral considerations. By the sources thesis, there is a gap in the law whenever the law appeals to moral considerations. But gaps in the law do not necessarily confer discretion on judges. I will argue that a legal requirement to apply moral considerations does give courts discretion, but only because moral considerations are vague. In fact, vagueness is the only important source of judicial discretion, aside from express grants of discretion and conventions giving courts power to develop the law.

So courts have discretion only in some of the cases in which they are required to act on moral considerations. Understood in the way I propose, the consequences of the sources thesis are not so surprising.

To evaluate the surprising part, we need to understand the sources thesis and the reasons for it. So section 1 will set out the sources thesis. Section 2 will ask whether there is any such thing as the English law of contract, and will offer some ways of reconciling the sources thesis with the lawyer's sensible view that many contracts are conclusively valid in English law. That task can partly be done without disagreeing with the surprising part of Raz (it is less surprising than it looks at first glance). But Sections 3–5 attempt to set out tentative reasons for a different view of the consequences of the sources thesis. Section 6 is an addendum that raises (but does not resolve) a puzzle about Raz's claim that in a gap in the law a proposition of law is 'neither true nor false'.

First, though, three caveats:

(1) I will talk of 'Raz's views' in the present tense, and that may be misleading—I don't know whether he has changed any of the views he expressed more than twenty years ago. I am not referring to what he thinks now—I am only trying to understand what he has written at various points (I'll argue that work he has done since the 1970s helps to make sense of the surprising part). But of course, I share the vivid concern about his present views that every sensible legal theorist feels.

(2) My argument is that the law gives judges discretion when it appeals to moral considerations, but only because (and to the extent that) those considerations are vague. Many people would claim that moral considerations are not merely vague—there are no *clear cases* for the application of moral terms (there is nothing, for example, that is undeniably fair or undeniably unfair). If my claims are right, those claims are wrong. So I rely on a controversial view of moral considerations, which I will not defend here.

(3) I know that the sources thesis has been a focus of debate about forms of legal positivism, and has focused opposition to legal positivism. Those debates are relevant to what I have to say, but I will not try to come to grips with them. I don't know what legal positivism is, and I actually wonder whether there is any such thing. In *The Authority of Law*, Raz rightly noted 'the difficulty, perhaps the impossibility, of identifying legal positivism at its

source—in a fundamentally positivist philosophical outlook'.[2] Yet even he succumbed to giddy optimism, and subtitled a section of his book 'The Nature of Legal Positivism'.

I can't see that it has a nature. There are many claims that people label 'positivist', and many writers who label themselves and others 'positivist', but this labelling does not convey very much about a claim or about the views of a theorist. To say that so-and-so is a legal positivist is to say next to nothing. And if we decided to endorse legal positivism, we would be no closer to explaining the nature of law. I do not suppose that it is impossible to untangle the skein of articulate and inarticulate ambitions and predilections that no doubt make sense of (some of) the labelling. But I think that it would be a wearisome, complex, and unrewarding task. The strands in the skein only twine together in any significant way momentarily, when accidents of academic culture turn jurisprudence into a team sport. The cultural investigations needed to tease out the strands would make an absorbing pursuit. But I am interested in something more important: the sources thesis, and what it means—and its implications for understanding gaps in the law.

I. BACKGROUND: THE SOURCES THESIS, MORAL CONSIDERATIONS, AND DISCRETION

We want to understand why Raz says that the sources thesis entails that courts have discretion when required to apply moral considerations.

The sources thesis is the claim that the law of a country can be identified by reference to social facts: if I ask you whether a contract is valid in English law, you can answer me by referring to social facts, and you do not need to do any evaluative or moral reasoning. Here is the way Raz formulated it in 1985:

All law is source-based. . . . A law is source-based if its existence and content can be identified by reference to social facts alone, without resort to any evaluative argument.[3]

This claim is supported by (i) Raz's basic assertion that law claims authority, and (ii) his 'service conception of authority,' in which an authority can assist the practical reasoning of its subjects by offering a view of what may or must be done that pre-empts other considerations. I do not think that we should read those two basic insights as empirical generalizations, or as an appeal to points that no one could disagree with. I think that they are an attempt to make sense of the role that law plays in a community and in the reasoning of individuals: law mediates 'between ultimate reasons and peoples' decisions and actions'.[4]

To perform the service that legitimate practical authorities perform, the law must be, or be presented as, someone's view as to what the subject of the law should do; the law cannot perform *that* service if the subject needs to decide what to do in order to decide what the law requires. The subjects of an

[2] Raz, *The Authority of Law. Essays on Law and Morality* (Oxford: Clarendon Press, 1979), 37.
[3] Raz, 'Authority, Law, and Morality', *Ethics in the Public Domain* (Oxford: Oxford University Press, 1994), 194–221, 194–5.   [4] Ibid., 215.

authority 'can benefit by its decisions only if they can establish their existence and content in ways which do not depend on raising the very same issues which the authority is there to settle'.[5]

Now we can see the background to the surprising part of Raz's discussion of gaps. If the law were that contracts are valid if they ought to be valid, then the law would not answer the question of validity (a court might have legal power to do so). There *is no* law of contract (except in the sense that it might be possible to make an agreement legally enforceable by having a court determine that it is enforceable). It would be the same if the law were that the validity of contracts is in the discretion of the court.

The situation is somewhat similar, in Raz's view, if the law provides source-based tests for the validity of contracts, but provides that contracts that meet those tests are invalid if they are immoral. Then we might say that there is a law of contract, but its operation is only *prima facie*, and as Raz puts it, it is neither true nor false that any contract is conclusively valid (until a court determines what the law does not determine).

But that is just what would surprise English lawyers. They know that contracts can be unenforceable when they are immoral, yet they also know that many contracts are conclusively binding even when their enforceability turns on moral considerations. So how can we make sense of the surprising part? Doesn't it mean that there is no English law of contract?

A note on methodology—Why not surprise lawyers?

This essay aims to explain some apparent implications of Raz's views that would surprise English lawyers. Actually, I can only claim that those implications would surprise *sensible* English lawyers. Some lawyers are surprised by nothing. Since H.L.A. Hart, it has been a popular notion that a philosopher who aims to understand a human practice must be able to account for the way in which the people engaged in the practice understand it. I think that is right—but it is not at all necessary or wise to seek to agree with those understandings (to seek a theory that lawyers would agree with). Such a strategy would be incoherent, and that is the least of its defects. A philosopher needs to be able to understand the ways in which people's own self-understanding may be distorted.

I will use the phrase 'sensible English lawyers' to refer to English lawyers who do not suffer from any serious philosophical disorder. I may seem to beg the question, since I seem to appeal to those lawyers to support philosophical claims. But I use them only as an expositional device, and not as an authority. That is, I do not claim that any philosophical thesis is true because the sensible English lawyers would agree with it; I appeal to them when I am going to make an assertion that I think is obviously true and is so important that a philosophical

---

[5] Raz, 'Authority, Law, and Morality', *Ethics in the Public Domain* (Oxford: Oxford University Press, 1994), 203, and see the discussion, ibid., 215.

account of law needs to account for it. So I don't beg the question, although I will leave some claims undefended and vulnerable to an argument that sensible English lawyers would not say what I claim they would say.

Should a philosopher be concerned not to surprise any English lawyer at all? What if Raz were to stick with the surprising apparent implications of his view, and insist that there really are no conclusively binding contracts in English law? I do not think that he should startle sensible English lawyers in that way. For all I know, a sound theory of law may include some surprising insights, but it should not have anything very surprising to say about what the law is on any point. It is a delicate matter to say just how much and in what ways the theory of a social practice ought to resonate with the views of the participants in the practice, and I do not mean to say that no statement of law that surprises sensible English lawyers can be true. But the statement that no contract is conclusively binding would surprise them in the wrong way. English lawyers can distinguish between a conclusively binding contract and a contract that is *prima facie* binding, and the surprising part of Raz's views on gaps seems to deprive the distinction of any use in the practices of English lawyers. It does not make the distinction unintelligible for them (because it still allows them to conceive of a legal system in which contracts *are* conclusively binding because their effect is never subjected to moral considerations). But it would make the distinction useless in understanding their own practice; the distinction would lose the role that it can and does play in the practice of English contract law.

So I think that we should try to reconcile the surprising part of Raz's views with the sensible English lawyer's view that some contracts are conclusively binding in law, even though contracts can be invalid when they are immoral. Doing so will make sense of Raz's third source of gaps.

II. IS THERE ANY SUCH THING AS THE ENGLISH LAW OF CONTRACT?

First we should see the obvious point—that there *is no* principle of English law that all immoral contracts are unenforceable. Suppose an English judge concludes that it is wrong to advertise children's toys by placing them in a hit movie. Suppose that the judge also reaches the conclusion that it is morally proper for a legal system to treat that sort of immorality as a ground for withholding enforcement. Assume that the judge is *right* in both these views. The judge still has no power to interfere with a contract between a filmmaker and a toy manufacturer on the ground of that immorality. Only *certain* immoral contracts are unenforceable, and the sources thesis can account for the factors that determine which contracts a judge can interfere with.

That feature is not a peculiarity of English law. I do not suppose that *any* legal system genuinely gives courts power to interfere with *any immoral contract*, and this fact reflects a significant point about the nature of law. While it may be important for a community (i) that commercial agreements should generally be enforced, and (ii) that some immoral commercial agreements should not be enforced, it will also typically be important for the community (iii) that there should be an authoritative way of deciding in general terms which contracts ought to be unenforceable—a technique that pre-empts the views of each official as to what is right and wrong.

The surprising part of Raz is not so surprising when we remember that there is probably no legal system that satisfies his hypothetical condition 'that by law contracts are valid only if not immoral.' The ways in which the treatment of contracts in real legal systems departs from that condition are reasons for accepting the sources thesis as a claim about law that reflects the role that law generally has in a community, and the value that it potentially (and perhaps generally) has.

So the surprising part is a lot less surprising because it does not abolish the law of contract. But there is more work to do. Even if there is no general power to interfere with an immoral contract, English contract law appeals to moral considerations in such varied and far-reaching ways that Raz's third source of gaps seems to say that most contracts are only *prima facie* enforceable. So we still need to reconcile the surprising part with the sensible lawyer's view.

1. It's common law: the social morality of the judges

Bear in mind that much of English contract law is common law. The rules governing the validity of contracts (including rules making immoral contracts unenforceable) have been made by the courts' own decisions. Assassination contracts are legally invalid because courts have authoritatively held that contracts for the commission of a criminal offence are invalid. So while an English lawyer may say that assassination contracts are invalid because of their immorality, Raz can say that the law prohibiting such contracts is not a rule of morality. The immorality of assassination contracts may be a good reason for the rule. But the rule does not require people to act on moral considerations; in fact it *excludes* considerations of morality by authoritatively invalidating assassination contracts. It is quite true to say that assassination contracts are void because of their immorality—in the sense that it was the courts' conviction that they are immoral that led the courts to deny them validity.

The rule against contracts for the commission of a crime is part of a more general doctrine that contracts 'contrary to public policy' are unenforceable—and any textbook can tell you *which* contracts the law disapproves of. There are facts about which features the courts treat as grounds for finding a contract to be immoral in the relevant sense. Those facts are sources for the law of contract,[6] and they leave a court with discretion only where they are unclear. I think that we could describe this whole body of doctrine in either of two ways:

(1) The common law authoritatively renders *certain sorts* of contract unenforceable on the ground of their immorality; it is the judges' holdings that certain

---

[6] Bear in mind Raz's definition of 'sources' as 'not just law-creating acts but all sorts of facts which make legal statements true or false.' *The Authority of Law* (n. 2 above), 63; cf. ibid., 47–8.

contracts are unenforceable that make the law. By the doctrine of precedent, judges' decisions make rules for the validity of contracts, the justification for which they always mention when they state a rule. The rule is that contracts of that kind are unenforceable; their immorality is a reason for the rule.

(2) The common law is the social morality (or 'positive morality', as Austin called it) of the judges (the judges have legal power not to enforce a contract, and their social morality acquires legal force because it is their way of regulating the exercise of their legal power).

Either description is consistent with the sources thesis; the first because it claims that there is a source for the rule against enforcing any sort of contract that *is* legally unenforceable; the second because, as Raz says, 'Social morality is based on sources: the customs, habits, and common views of a community.'[7] I think either description of the common law is satisfactory; we might say that (1) is part of (2), because the judges' decisions are their principal way of expressing and developing their social morality. Solicitors know (subject to some uncertainties) which types of contract are unenforceable, because they know the customs, habits and common views of the judges (and in particular they know which contracts have been held to be contrary to public policy).

Not all of English law is common law, however. Statutes have modified or restated the law in important respects, and they appeal to moral and evaluative considerations. The Sale of Goods Act (1979) provides that there is an implied term in contracts for the sale of goods in the course of a business, that 'the goods are of satisfactory quality'. How do we explain the sensible lawyer's view that some deliveries of goods conclusively comply with that term? We might say that that statute gave the courts discretion to decide what standard goods should meet, and by the doctrine of precedent their exercises of that discretion have made law according to the sources thesis.

But the sensible lawyer will take the view that many sale of goods contracts were conclusively valid immediately after the enactment of the Sale of Goods Act, *before* the courts had played their role of authoritatively determining the law's view on the quality of goods. So to reconcile the surprising part of Raz with the sensible lawyer's view, we need an account of the effect on the law of new enactments. How do we explain the effect on the law of England of new legislation that appeals to moral criteria for the validity or enforceability of contracts?

2. The effect of new enactments: what the legislature said

The Unfair Contract Terms Act (1977) imposes a 'requirement of reasonableness', which various contract terms (mostly forms of exclusion of liability) must meet. The requirement is 'that the term shall have been a fair and reasonable one to be included having regard to the circumstances . . .'[8]

[7] Ibid., 46, n.7.
[8] S 11(1); there is also a set of guidelines for applying the requirement (Schedule 2); I will ignore them because they complicate matters but do not affect my argument.

What effect did that Act have on English law? The surprising part of Raz suggests the following effect: after the Act was passed, no exclusion clause was conclusively valid. All such terms became only *prima facie* valid, because their validity was subjected to a non-source-based consideration. The Act cast all such contract terms into limbo.

I think that the Act had a different effect—and as always, the sensible English lawyers are with me. Some exclusion clauses are undeniably reasonable; some are undeniably unreasonable. Some are arguably reasonable and arguably unreasonable. The effect of the 1977 Act was to make some terms invalid, to leave some unaffected, and to have the effect that Raz suggests (i.e. to make the validity of a term indeterminate, and subject to determination by a court) only in the case of a term that is neither clearly reasonable nor clearly unreasonable. The undeniably reasonable terms are conclusively binding—even immediately after the passage of the Act. The Act created a good deal of uncertainty, and the law gives the courts discretionary power to resolve the uncertainty—but the Act did not cast all exclusion clauses into limbo.

It is important to see that we can reconcile this view of the effect of the Act with the sources thesis, and Raz's recent work on interpretation can help us to do so. Here's how: the Act was not made in a legal vacuum, but in the context of a scheme of techniques for deciding what is reasonable and unreasonable. That is, the legislation had the effect that I claim it had, because of standards for the interpretation of the notion of reasonableness in contract law *that are part of the law of England*.

This feature of English law is no peculiarity, either. Officials have techniques that they use to decide what legislation means, and those techniques make legislation what it is. Raz has argued that the interpretation of deliberate legislation 'should reflect the intentions of its law-maker'[9]—that is his 'Authoritative Intention Thesis'. But that thesis does not mean that the 1977 Act licensed a judge to invalidate any exclusion clause he or she considers unreasonable. According to Raz,

The thesis requires one to understand the legislation as meaning what the legislator said. What the legislator said is what his words mean, given the circumstances of the promulgation of the legislation, and the conventions of interpretation prevailing at the time.[10]

The effect of the Act was to invalidate contract terms that would be judged to be unreasonable by officials of the legal system, interpreting the appeal to reasonableness in accordance with the principles of the legal system.

That approach makes the surprising part less surprising; it shows that Raz need not say that no exclusion clause was conclusively valid after the 1977 Act was passed. It can also explain the sensible lawyer's view that there *are some* cases in which no conclusive opinion can be given on whether an exclusion clause is enforceable. That is the case because although the techniques of the courts make it perfectly clear what a court will do in some cases (and they make sense of saying that the court is bound to give effect to some exclusion clauses), those techniques are vague,

---

[9] Raz, 'Intention in Interpretation', in *The Autonomy of Law*, ed. Robert P. George (Oxford: Oxford University Press 1996), 249–86, 259.   [10] Ibid., 271.

so that they do not answer all questions as to whether a term is valid under the Act. There are indeterminacies in the effect of the Act to the extent that the techniques of judges give no clear answer to this interpretive question.

III. DOES THE LAW *EVER* APPEAL TO MORAL CONSIDERATIONS?

There is more than a grain of truth in this account of the effect of new enactments. The Sale of Goods Act did not come out of the blue; when it was originally enacted in 1893, it was an attempt to restate and to bring order to some doctrines of the common law. When it came into force, no one thought that it licensed courts to remodel the standards that suppliers of goods must meet. The courts knew that the Act gave them discretion only in unclear cases. And this account offers Raz a way of admitting that even new legislation appealing to moral considerations does not cast all contracts into limbo.

But it risks leading to another surprising conclusion: that the law can *never* make the validity of contracts (or anything else) depend on moral considerations. Some people may not even find that surprising. If legislation says what its wording means given the conventions of the legal culture, then it seems that any legislative attempt to appeal to moral considerations can do no more than to require judges to give effect to their positive morality. Perhaps every legal system has techniques for deciding what is reasonable and unreasonable, and if we treat legislation subjecting legal rules to moral considerations as legislation calling on the officials of the legal system to implement their established, positive norms, we can eliminate the possibility that legislation could ever 'subject legal rules to moral or other non-source based considerations'. Perhaps it is conceptually impossible for a lawmaker to subject legal rights to moral considerations.

Or we might conclude more modestly that it is rare, and legally pathological. In 1994, Britain implemented the European Union's Directive on Unfair Terms in Consumer Contracts. The people in the Department of Trade and Industry did not really know what to do with the Directive, and they wisely decided to let judges sort out its implications for English contract law. So they just copied the text of the Directive into a British regulation. The main clause reads as follows:

An unfair term in a contract concluded with a consumer by a seller or supplier shall not be binding on the consumer.[11]

According to the guidelines for deciding whether a term is unfair, one consideration is whether the term runs 'contrary to the requirement of good faith'.[12] That phrase seems to appeal to a principle of the law—but the Directive is European. There has never been a principle of good faith in English law![13] English judges

---

[11] Unfair Terms in Consumer Contracts Regulations 1994 (SI 1994/3159), s 5(1).
[12] S 4(1) of the 1994 Regulation.
[13] The House of Lords held in 1992 that a 'concept of a duty to carry on negotiations in good faith is inherently repugnant to the adversarial position of the parties when involved in negotiations'. *Walford* v. *Miles* [1992] 2 AC 128, *per* Lord Keith.

keen to interpret the regulation according to their conventions will find no guidance in the practice of the courts: they seem to need to craft a 'requirement of good faith' out of whole cloth, acting directly on moral considerations.

We might think that the courts need to act on genuine moral considerations only rarely: never when they are asked to administer a scheme of regulation that their conventions enable them to comprehend, but only in extraordinary circumstances, when a lawmaker tells them to act on a moral consideration that is alien to their conventions—when the legal culture gives no answer to the question of how to interpret an act of legislation. The law only appeals to moral considerations when worlds collide.

It would be simplistic to reach either conclusion: that it is impossible for the law to appeal to moral considerations, or that it happens only in rare and deviant circumstances. The conventions that affect an enactment expressed in moral terms are *conventions of interpretation* (i.e., ways of deciding what meaning to give to the enactment), not *conventions of morality*. Legislation appealing to moral considerations does not necessarily require judges to apply their positive morality; it requires them to apply their positive conventions for interpreting the legislature's use of moral terms. The task of a court in applying the 1994 regulation is not to ask, '*What do we judges treat as unfair?*' it is to ask, '*What meaning do we judges give to enactments that make unfair terms unenforceable?*'

This important distinction has two consequences: first, as a technique for determining the effect of an enactment on the law, those conventions may be radically incomplete. The constraint they impose on a court may be minimal. That constraint may be enough to make it clear that most ordinary sales contracts are not unfair for the purposes of the regulation, without answering any interesting question of the fairness of a term in a consumer contract. Like the 1977 Act, the 1994 regulation did not cast all consumer contracts into limbo, but it did create a lot of uncertainty. And in resolving the uncertainties, there is no reason to think the judges are doing anything other than asking whether the term is fair, even if they treat their conventions as giving binding answers to some questions of fairness.

Secondly, it is not at all inconceivable, and it may be common, for the courts' techniques of interpretation to require them to treat appeals to moral terms in enactments as calling on them to act directly on moral considerations, rather than to give effect to their own positive morality.

For both these reasons, I think we should conclude that the law *very commonly* does appeal directly to moral considerations. Raz appears to take that view.[14] What are the consequences for the theory of law?

Suppose that a law really does appeal to moral considerations. Perhaps the 1994 regulation is a good example. In that situation, the sources thesis does entail that there is a gap in the law: the law does not answer the question

---

[14] 'The law itself quite commonly directs the courts to apply extralegal considerations' (Raz, 'On the Autonomy of Legal Reasoning', *Ethics in the Public Domain* (n. 3 above), 310–24, 317). Raz had in mind other extralegal considerations besides moral considerations, but I think the discussion of the role of moral reasoning in legal reasoning in that essay supports my claim.

whether a contract with a consumer is binding; it calls on the court to subject a business's legal rights to the moral consideration of fairness. Yet I propose that the judges still do not have discretion in all cases to hold a term in a contract unenforceable against the consumer. Some terms are undeniably fair, and the regulation gives a court no discretion to decline to enforce such a term. The regulation creates a lot of uncertainties because it is so vague; in cases in which it is uncertain whether a term is fair, the court does have discretion. But it was misleading for Raz to say that 'by the sources thesis the courts have discretion when required to apply moral considerations'. They do not have discretion in cases in which the effect of those considerations is unarguable. And it was an over-generalization to say that 'The proposition "it is legally conclusive that this contract is valid" is neither true nor false until a court authoritatively determines its validity.'

I want to say that norms of fairness (and not just conventional legal norms of interpretation) bind the judges, in reasoning according to law, when they give effect to the 1994 regulation. Imagine a case of a contract term X which is clearly fair. I want to distinguish between

> (A) a judge being bound, according to law, to give effect to X because it is fair, and the regulation only makes unfair terms unenforceable,

and

> (B) a judge being bound by a principle for the interpretation of such enactments according to which the regulation is not to be read as making X unenforceable.

Raz can say that a judge may be bound in the second way. My claim is that a judge may be bound in the first way, so that although the sources thesis entails that the 1994 regulation created a gap in the law, it did not give judges discretion over the enforceability of *all* consumer contracts, but only over those whose fairness is unclear. And it gave the courts no discretion over patently unfair contract terms: they do not bind consumers, and a business has no legal right to their enforcement.

A brief explanation of what I mean by 'gaps' and 'discretion' may help to clarify the claim. (It may also show that I am only disagreeing with Raz by employing different notions of gaps and of discretion.)

IV. WHAT ARE GAPS?

There are gaps in the law to the extent that there are questions of law which the law does not answer.

There are many sources of gaps in this sense, besides the law's appeal to moral considerations. Raz has listed some important sources:

Italian law may direct the courts to apply European Community law, or International law, or Chinese law to a case. It may direct the court to settle a dispute by reference to the rules and regulations of a corporation, or an unincorporated association, or by reference to commercial practices or moral norms. In all these cases legal reasoning, understood to mean reasoning according to law, involves much more than merely establishing the law.[15]

Contract law is one big complicated set of gaps. Its organizing point is to enable the parties to reach an agreement to regulate their own legal rights. The law directs courts to treat parties as having the legal rights and obligations that their agreement creates, and to settle disputes by reference to their agreement. If I buy your car, there is no law that answers the question of what price the law requires me to pay; there is a law that gives me a legal obligation to pay the price required by the agreement.

Understood in this way, gaps in the law entail that someone has some form of choice to make, but they do not entail judicial discretion.[16] A judge does not have discretion to decide what price I should pay you; you have a legal right to the price we agreed on. The law leaves terms like that to the agreement of the parties, and it does not give courts discretion. When *do* gaps confer discretion on judges?

V. What is discretion?

Let's keep things simple and say that discretionary decision-making is unbound decision-making.

To have a discretion is to be given power to make a decision, without being bound to decide on a particular outcome.[17]

This simple understanding of the notion leaves ambiguities which a detailed account of discretion would need to explain: there are different ways in which a decision-maker may be bound or not bound.[18]

Suppose I tell you to have something from the fridge for supper. I haven't told you what to eat; I have bound you only by restricting your choices. You have discretion to choose from what's in the fridge (and no discretion to order a pizza). There is a *gap* in my instructions in the sense that I have not told you what to eat. Even if you act on my instructions, it is still up to you to choose from what is in the fridge.

---

[15] Ibid., 317.

[16] For this reason I prefer my definition to Raz's definition in *The Authority of Law* (n. 2 above): 'There is a gap in the law when a legal question has no complete answer.' (70) That definition (which is popular in writing on legal theory) ties gaps to judicial discretion by necessity.

[17] I think that even Ronald Dworkin could accept this understanding of the notion (it differs in some minor respects from what he calls 'the strong sense of discretion' in *Taking Rights Seriously* (London: Duckworth, 1979)). Dworkin's view is that judges virtually never have discretion of that kind; I will not address that view here.

[18] A decision-maker may be restricted to a range of options, or may be bound to reason in a particular way without being bound to reach a particular decision; or may have to proceed in a particular way, or may be supervised by another decision-maker in a variety of ways, and so on.

But suppose I tell you to eat what your babysitter tells you to eat. We might say, once more, that I haven't told you what to eat. But that does not mean that you have any discretion. You have discretion only if your babysitter gives you a choice. My instructions do not give you discretion; they bind you to obey an authority that may or may not give you a discretion. There is a gap in my instructions just in the sense that in order to act on them you need to obey the babysitter. There is no gap in the sense that it is up to you to choose what to eat (unless the babysitter leaves such a gap).

Understanding discretion in this simple way is useful for present purposes. We do not need to resolve the ambiguities in the notion; there is no sense at all in which I give you discretion when I tell you to eat what the babysitter says to eat. I do not tell you what to eat; but I do not give you power to make a decision without being bound to reach one outcome or another; I leave it to the babysitter to give you discretion or not. I do not confer discretion on you, in the way I do when I tell you to have something from the fridge.

Now suppose that I tell you to have something from the fridge, but to be fair to your sister who also needs supper. Do I give you discretion? Probably. It may be unclear whether, for example, it would be fair to your sister to eat all the left-over chicken casserole and leave her the soup and the carrot cake. But I do *not* give you discretion to empty the fridge. If it is clearly unfair, you have no discretion to do it. There *is* a gap in my command (*I* do not tell you what counts as fair; you cannot use my authority to answer that question). But you are not free to fill the gap as you choose. I confer discretion on you only insofar as fairness is vague.

I want to say that when lawmakers appeal to moral considerations, they give discretion just insofar as moral considerations are vague. When English lawmakers tell courts to apply German law, they give no discretion; they leave that to German law, just as I gave you no discretion when I told you to eat what the babysitter tells you to. By the sources thesis, there is a gap in the law when it makes legal rights and duties depend on German law, or on morality; but courts have discretion in such gaps only if German law confers it, or if morality does not demand a particular action.

A court that holds that a contract is unfair when it is clearly not unfair cannot be accused of wrongly identifying the law; but it can be criticized for not reasoning rightly according to law, and for depriving a party of its legal rights, and for failing to carry out its legal duty. If it has failed to carry out its legal duty, there is no useful sense of 'discretion' in which it has exercised a discretion.

VI. ADDENDUM: CAN A STATEMENT OF LAW BE NEITHER TRUE NOR FALSE?

Raz's claim about the third source of gaps is that, when the law makes the validity of a contract depend on moral considerations, 'The proposition "it is legally conclusive that this contract is valid" is neither true nor false until a court authoritatively determines its validity.'[19] I would like to add a note on the 'neither true nor false' part of that claim, because I find it puzzling.

Raz, like several other philosophers, says that vague statements of law are neither true nor false in borderline cases, as other vague statements are neither true nor false in borderline cases.

... it may be neither true nor false that this is a dwelling or a motor vehicle. It may be neither true nor false that this man is bald. Where the facts which are legal reasons are indeterminate, through vagueness, open texture, or some other factors, certain legal statements are neither true nor false.[20]

I have tried and failed to conceive of a man of whom it is neither true nor false that he is bald. Of course, I wouldn't know whether to call some men bald or not. And I think that as a man loses his hair, there is no last hair whose loss makes him bald. So I think that there is no sharp boundary between the bald and not-bald of this world. So I think that there are bound to be some men of whom it is indeterminate whether they are bald or not; let's call such a person 'Charles', in honour of Charlemagne's grandson, Charles the Bald. It is the year 857, and Charles has lost some of his hair, but it is not clear whether he is bald. Is it neither true nor false that Charles is bald? If so, it is not true that he is bald and it is not false that he is bald. But how can we assert either 'it is not true that Charles is bald', or 'it is not false that Charles is bald'? The problem about the application of a vague term in such a case is that it is unclear what is true and what is false.[21]

We can think of statements that *are* neither true nor false. Nonsensical statements are neither true nor false. It is neither true nor false that English law permits the exiculation of arnimodes; but I don't know that such nonsense amounts to a statement of law at all (we might say that it expresses no proposition of law). It is false that English law authorizes capital punishment, and we know what things would be like if it were true. But we cannot conceive what

[19] *The Authority of Law* (n. 2 above), 75. Perhaps he should have said 'The proposition "this contract is valid" is neither true nor false ...'; on Raz's own view, I think, the proposition 'it is legally conclusive that this contract is valid' is *false* until a court authoritatively determines its validity. (On the view I've tried to sketch, both propositions are *true* before a court determines the validity of a contract, if it is clear that the contract satisfies the non-source-based considerations which the law directs the court to apply.)

[20] *The Authority of Law* (n. 2 above), 72. Cf., 'if the content of the law is exclusively determined by social facts, then the law is gap'; that is, there are legal statements which are neither true nor false. 'Legal Principles and the Limits of Law', in *Ronald Dworkin and Contemporary Jurisprudence*, ed. Marshall Cohen (Totowa N.J.: Rowman & Allanhead, 1984), 73–87, 81; cf. also Raz, *The Morality of Freedom* (Oxford: Oxford University Press, 1986), 327. Cf. Jules Coleman: 'Philosophers generally agree that some sentences involving the application of vague predicates are neither true nor false.' ('Truth and Objectivity in Law', *Legal Theory* 1 (1995), 33–68, 49.) I have discussed the question of whether a vague statement of law in a borderline case is neither true or false in 'Vagueness and Legal Theory' *Legal Theory* 3 (1997), 37–63, and my remarks here are partly based on that discussion.

[21] It has also been argued that the 'neither true nor false' description of borderline cases leads to contradiction: in Timothy Williamson, *Vagueness* (London: Routledge, 1994), 187–9.

things would be like if it were true that English law forbids the exiculation of arnimodes. It is not capable of being true or false. 'Charles is bald' is different: even if it is unclear whether it is true or not, we have no trouble conceiving of a situation in which it would be true.

It is unclear to me whether, in saying these things, I am disagreeing with Raz in any significant way. I agree with him that there are questions of law, which a court might have to answer, to which the law does not require one answer. I would be happy to say that the law is indeterminate in such a case, and Raz says so too. That means we agree that the outcome that a judge rightly gives in deciding a case is sometimes (*often*, in fact, although it takes further argument to say that) not determined by the law. But I don't know whether there is a real question that we disagree on—whether the claim that *it is neither true nor false that Charles is bald* differs, in any way worth understanding, from the claim that *it is indeterminate whether it is true or false that Charles is bald*. The difference may only be a difference in taste for two ways of saying the same thing; to work this out, I think that it would be necessary to come up with a way of making something useful out of the notion of 'truth'.

I do think, though, that the notion that some statements of law are 'neither true nor false' can be helpful in understanding discretion. Think of the paradigm case of a gap in the law: an express discretion unbounded by any mandatory standards of exercise. What if a legislature went mad and enacted that the validity of contracts should be in the discretion of the court?[22] Then it would be neither true nor false to say that 'this contract is legally valid'. It is not valid, and it is not invalid. Its force is in the discretion of the court. We might say that the question whether a contract is valid is ill-formed in that situation, like the question whether the law permits the exiculation of arnimodes. I think that the effect of vagueness in the grounds for validity of contracts is different. The question whether Charles is bald is equally well-formed, no matter how much or little hair Charles has. In a borderline case, it does not become clear that it is not false that Charles is bald, or clear that it is not true. But an express discretion over the validity of a contract makes it clear that it is not true that the contract is valid, and not false that it is valid.

We should not say that a vague statement in a borderline case is neither true nor false, unless we can say that it is not true, and that it is not false. If that is right, then there is an interesting difference between express grants of discretion, and the discretion that arises when the law is vague. The 'neither true nor false' formulation is useful in describing the effect of an express discretion on the law, but is not useful in describing the effect of vagueness on the law. I think the difference corresponds to the fact that, while an express grant of discretion to courts over the validity of contracts makes it clear that a contract is not valid or invalid until a court has decided, vague criteria for the validity of contracts

---

[22] Assume for simplicity that by the conventions of interpretation in the legal culture at the time, the enactment has the effect that the validity of contracts *is* in the discretion of the court.

generally do not yield cases in which it is clear that a contract is not invalid and is not valid until a court has decided. Even if there is discretion in borderline cases, it differs from discretion conferred directly by an authority or by conventions, because there are commonly no clear borderline cases. So there may be no cases in which a court clearly has discretion.

VII. CONCLUSION

I have tried to understand a remark that Raz made in the 1970's, and for that purpose I have found it essential to use work that he has done in the 80's and in the 90's. Here are the points on which, if I have understood Raz's views, I think I differ from them:

(1) Judges have discretion only in borderline cases of the application of the moral considerations that the law directs judges (and others) to act upon. Raz's third source of gaps (laws subjecting legal rules to non-source-based considerations) does not confer discretion in all cases.[23]
(2) In a borderline case, we should not say that a vague statement of law is 'neither true nor false', although its truth may be indeterminate.

I have argued that when there is a gap in the law, the law does not answer questions of people's legal rights and duties; but the really interesting kind of gap is a gap in which reasoning according to law does not require a single answer. Let's call this a question which a judge may resolve at his or her discretion. Let's call it that because a judge is not bound to give an answer one way or the other. The law's appeals to moral considerations do not lead to that sort of discretion in all cases, but only in certain cases; and they lead to that sort of discretion only because general moral considerations are vague. In all cases, the appeal to moral considerations in laws requires a decision-maker to act on dependent reasons, and does not perform the law's central function of pre-empting those reasons. But in cases in which the right application of moral considerations is clear, so that a judge can get it wrong, judges have no discretion.

But the law commonly appeals to moral considerations, and by doing so it gives courts a great deal of discretion. The vagueness of general moral and evaluative considerations is very important; first because such considerations are *necessarily* vague,[24] and secondly because it is the most important source of vagueness in law. Lawmakers generally avoid vagueness *except* when they

---

[23] This claim relies on the proposition that moral considerations are vague; I suppose that no one would claim that they are *precise* (so that there are, for example, no unclear cases for the application of the 1994 regulation). But note that an 'epistemic' theory of the vagueness of moral considerations would entail that appeals to moral considerations give no discretion to courts, although in some cases courts cannot know what their duty is; my claim relies on the rejection of such an epistemic theory (in *Vagueness in Law* (Oxford University Press, 2000), I argue that such a theory should be rejected).   [24] I argue that general moral considerations are necessarily vague in ibid.

appeal to moral considerations. They may require fair criminal trials; they may require criminal trials to be held in a reasonable time; they may require them to be held within 7 months of the laying of charges. But no lawmaker ever enacted that they should be held within approximately 7 months.[25]

I am not troubled by whether these conclusions make me a soft positivist or not; perhaps they do and do not, depending on what content we give to the notion of positivism and the notion of softness. The sources thesis is not a distinctively positivist thesis, and by proposing a modified view of its consequences I don't think that I have made it more or less positivistic. It can form part of an account of the nature of law that could intelligibly be called 'positivist'; but I do not think that calling such a theory 'positivist' would say anything interesting about it.

In defending the sources thesis, Raz has left open the possibility that 'additional considerations lead to a complex view of the law lying between the incorporation and the sources thesis'.[26]

Have we found such considerations here? The incorporation thesis is the claim that law includes not only source-based considerations, but also considerations entailed by the sources; it may seem that I have been supporting the incorporation thesis, by saying that a court has no legal discretion under the 1994 regulation to enforce a clearly unfair term in a consumer contract. But I have not. At most we have found reasons for disagreeing with Raz about the consequences of the sources thesis, not reasons to agree with the incorporation thesis; there is a gap in the law when the law appeals to moral considerations, but it is a gap that confers discretion on the judges only in borderline cases (just as, when English law directs courts to apply German law, a court has discretion only when German law gives discretion). The sources thesis is less surprising than it sounds. Labels like 'hard positivism' and 'exclusive positivism' make Raz's theory of law sound extreme. They make it sound as if we should all look for a *via media*. But in fact, the sources thesis should not surprise us sensible, sober-minded lawyers.

---

[25] The vagueness of evaluative and moral considerations is not the only sort of vagueness that is important in law. Vague classificatory schemes that make no explicit appeal to moral considerations are familiar in taxation, in criminal prohibitions on various classes of activity, in building regulations, etc.   [26] *The Authority of Law* (n. 2 above), 214.

PERSPECTIVES ON LIBERAL SOCIETY: EQUALITY, INCOMMENSURABILITY, GROUP RIGHTS, AND MULTICULTURALISM

7

Equality, Incommensurability, and Rights

HILLEL STEINER

In *The Morality of Freedom*, Joseph Raz plausibly proposes the following statement as the general form of strictly egalitarian principles:

All Fs who do not have G have a right to G if some Fs have G.[1]

He thence proceeds to mount a sustained criticism of such principles as being deeply implausible—a criticism which has been nicely summarized thus:

One either values equal shares for their own sake or for the sake of some other values. If the latter, then one cannot claim to be an egalitarian. Those who want equality to relieve misery do not really care about equality, but only about misery. But to care about equality as such, as a purely distributional good, is to be irrational, or envious, or in the grip of a strange aesthetic ideal.[2]

Is this criticism warranted? Can one not care about equality as such *without* being irrational, envious or gripped by a strange aesthetic ideal? One aim of this paper is to show that, under one of two mutually exclusive and jointly exhaustive assumptions about the aggregate magnitude of G, caring about equality as such need not be encumbered with such undesirable baggage. Indeed, it will be part of this argument that, for some Gs, their equal distribution *must* be valued for its own sake if those Gs themselves are valued for their own sake.

The aggregate magnitude of *anything*, we may safely suppose, is either constant or variable. It may, of course, be very difficult to establish in certain instances just what precisely those aggregates are. But such difficulties cannot be taken to falsify claims of their constancy or variability. Perhaps the First and Third Laws of Thermodynamics can respectively serve as sufficient evidence of this general fact.[3] And there is no reason to suppose the case to be otherwise with respect to G, whatever G may be. So let's call goods whose aggregate magnitude is constant CAM-goods or simply *CAMs*, and their variable counterparts *VAMs*.

Now it's probably true that most Gs—most types of thing that are valued or regarded as goods—are *VAMs*. Happiness, trust, friendship, need-alleviation

[1] Joseph Raz, *The Morality of Freedom* (Oxford: Oxford University Press, 1986), 225.

[2] Leslie Green, 'Un-American Liberalism: Raz's "Morality of Freedom" ', *University of Toronto Law Journal* 38 (1988), 317–32, 329.

[3] The First Law states that the total energy of a thermodynamic system remains constant although it may be transformed from one form to another. The Third Law states that the entropy of a substance approaches zero as its temperature approaches absolute zero.

and, for that matter, concern and respect, are each items of which there can plainly be more or less for individuals, whether those persons are taken disjunctively or conjunctively. I can now be less happy than I was half an hour ago. And my being less happy does not entail that someone else has become more happy. Despite occasional gloomy suspicions to the contrary, we don't generally consider the pretty universal quest for happiness to be a zero-sum game.

That said, however, what's also true is that different distributions of happiness are commonly associated with different aggregate amounts of it, and for good reason. Happiness, as an end, requires the deployment of various means to secure it. And these means, themselves in highly variable aggregate supply, can be deployed in distributively diverse ways. There can, of course, be disagreement about the strength of the reasons for favouring some of these distributions over others. But one thing we can all agree on is that giving me and my melancholic neighbour equal amounts of these means will, *ceteris paribus*, result in lower aggregate happiness than would a less egalitarian division. So it would seem that any personal or political morality that embraces happiness among its values will have at least a *prima facie* reason to disfavour that equal division and to follow Raz in excluding any strictly egalitarian principle that enjoins it. After all, if happiness counts as a value, more of it must be better than less.[4] It is this virtual truism that strict egalitarianism is heroically committed to denying.[5] For as Raz notes,

> Egalitarian principles often lead to waste. . . . [They] always permit waste as a way of satisfying them, and in quite common circumstances require it as the only way to satisfy them. . . . Egalitarian principles would be indifferent between achieving equality through taking away from those who have and giving to those who have not . . . If they constitute the entire foundation of morality then the happiness of a person does not matter except if there are other happy people. Nor is there any reason to avoid harming or hurting a person except on the ground that there are others who are unharmed or unhurt.[6]

Persons with a commitment to *levelling down*—to the betterness of wasting some happiness solely for the sake of avoiding its unequal distribution—do, indeed, seem unambiguously to be irrational, envious or in the grip of some strange aesthetic ideal. Hence Raz justifiably concludes that, even in egalitarian theories, the function of egalitarian principles can—at most—be one of supplementing and controlling the application of other principles of entitlement.

Moreover, the domain in which this function is warranted is shown to be far less extensive than many egalitarians suppose. For not all principles of entitlement are appropriate candidates for such regulation, inasmuch as some of them

---

[4] Discussion of the formal properties of the ordering relation 'better than', and of its connection to 'more', can be found in: M.K. Rennie, 'On Hare's "Better" ', *Nous* 2 (1968), 75–9; M.B. Smyth, 'The Prescriptivist Definition of "Better" ', *Analysis* 33 (1972), 4–9; H-N. Castaneda, ' "Ought" and "Better" ', *Analysis* 34 (1973), 50–5; H.S. Silverstein, 'A Correction to Smyth's "Better" ', *Analysis* 34 (1973), 55–6; Hillel Steiner, *An Essay on Rights* (Oxford: Blackwell, 1994), chs. 4 (C,D), 5 (A,C).
[5] *Non-strict* egalitarianism holds that equality, just as such, makes things in one way better.
[6] Raz, *The Morality of Freedom* (n. 1 above), 227, 235.

carry their own in-built standards for the interpersonal distribution of their associated goods. In this regard, Raz's perspicuous distinction between *satiable* and *insatiable* entitlement principles is central. A satiable principle is one whose demands can be completely met, whereas an insatiable principle is one that it is always possible in principle to satisfy to a higher degree. 'Everyone's needs should be met' and 'Everyone should have as much pleasure as they can enjoy' are offered as examples of these two types of principle, respectively.[7]

A key claim here is that all satiable principles are 'diminishing' ones: they embody their own distributive norms and consequently have no need of supplementation by strict egalitarian principles. Thus, if 'Alleviate hunger' is an entitlement principle, then

> if Bess and Bert are equally hungry it makes no difference who gets a slice of bread. But if Bess had it and there is a second slice to be had, Bert should have that one, for now his hunger is worse than hers. This means that diminishing principles lead to an approximately equal distribution in any case. But the equality they give rise to is a by-product of their concern with the alleviation of hunger, and not a reflection of concern for equality.[8]

'Alleviate hunger' is a diminishing principle and entails its own distributive norm because the reason for complying with it in one distributive way becomes progressively weaker, with successive such compliances, than the reason for complying with it in an alternative distributive way. Diminishing principles supply their own verdicts in cases like 'Bess vs Bert'.

Contrast this with the principle 'Maximize wealth for people'. This entitlement principle is an insatiable one 'for it is always possible to increase the wealth available'. But it is also a non-diminishing one and provides no guidance as to which of any two (or more) mutually exclusive distributions will satisfy it.

> Imagine that Abigail's wealth measures £10,000 whereas Andrew has only £1,000 to his name. New wealth valued at £100 becomes available. Who should have it? The wealth-maximizing principle tells us that there is equal reason to give it to each of them. Being a non-diminishing principle it disregards the existing disparity of wealth between them. It is indifferent as to who should get the extra wealth and thus it tolerates extreme inequalities.[9]

Such entitlement principles are 'purely aggregative' and, in Raz's view, it is their widely-presumed foundational presence in our moral and political reasoning that has led to the growing appeal of strict egalitarianism.

> [E]galitarian theories are based on non-diminishing, usually insatiable, principles the operation of which is subjected to egalitarian constraints. Viewed in this way strict egalitarianism is seen as a response to a perceived failure of non-diminishing principles.[10]

What's wrong with non-diminishing principles is that they don't supply their own verdicts in cases like 'Abigail vs Andrew'. So strict egalitarianism is called in to resolve the matter. Accordingly, Raz's strategy for rejecting egalitarian theories

---

[7] Ibid., 235–6.   [8] Ibid., 239.   [9] Ibid., 238.   [10] Ibid., 240–1.

consists in showing that the ideals at the foundation of morality and politics are all diminishing and satiable principles. And the tactic adopted for this demonstration is to argue (persuasively, in my view) that one candidate principle, widely thought to require egalitarian constraint—utilitarianism's pursuit of happiness—is in fact a diminishing and satiable principle.[11]

The question I want to address is one that asks whether this strategy is sufficient to warrant that rejection. Are *all* foundational entitlement principles diminishing and satiable? To find an answer to this question, we need to have recourse to the previous discussion of CAMs and VAMs.

Suppose there is a good, G, which is a CAM. One thing that is guaranteed by the constancy of its aggregate magnitude is that the condition stated in the antecedent of Raz's model formulation of strictly egalitarian principles,

All Fs who do not have G have a right to G if some Fs have G, is almost invariably satisfied. My having no G implies that others have some of it. And if I have all of it, others have none. Hence any entitlement principle pertaining to it—'Everyone should have some G'—qualifies as satiable in Raz's terms because, unlike the case of wealth, it is impossible to increase the G available and the demands the principle imposes can be completely met.

But, contrary to Raz's claim, its being satiable does *not*, in itself, guarantee that this principle is also a diminishing one.[12] It does not guarantee that my getting successive increments of G progressively weakens the reason for giving me G. Of course, if I do have all of it, the reason to give me more is not merely weak: its strength is literally zero. But the impotence of that reason is due, not to my having enough G, but rather to there being absolutely no possibility of increasing the G available: there are no additional units of it to be had, by me or anyone else. Nor is it necessarily true that, if what I have is only *almost* all the G available, the reason for giving me G becomes weaker. For as in Raz's 'Abigail vs. Andrew' treatment of the wealth-maximizing principle, the reason for giving me G can be as good as the reason for giving others G, even if there is an enormous disparity between our respective holdings of G. In short, everything here entirely depends on what that reason is. So the possibility of CAMs at the very least suggests that the dyadic classification of entitlement principles—as either satiable/diminishing or insatiable/non-diminishing—though probably sufficient to cover all VAMs, must give way to a triadic one that further includes satiable/non-diminishing principles.[13]

Are there actually any Gs that are CAMs? Elsewhere I've argued that what some have called 'pure negative liberty' (and others 'crude negative liberty') is at least one such good.[14] Space does not permit a rehearsal of that argument

---

[11] Raz, *The Morality of Freedom* (n. 1 above), 240–4.

[12] Ibid., 236: 'Satiable principles are invariably also diminishing principles'.

[13] Whether a quadratic classification makes sense—whether there can also be insatiable/diminishing entitlement principles—is something I'm currently unable to discern.

[14] Cf. *An Essay on Rights* (n. 4 above), ch. 2 (D); see also Michael Taylor, *Community, Anarchy and Liberty* (Cambridge: Cambridge University Press, 1982), 142; Charles Taylor, 'What's Wrong

here. Nor, let me hasten to add, has it gone undisputed.[15] But for our present purposes, it will suffice to examine the relevant implications of the possibility that there are indeed some Gs that are *CAMs* and that pure negative liberty is one of them.

Pure negative liberty is a good because its possession is a necessary condition for acting: trivially, we cannot perform any actions which others physically prevent us from performing. But pure negative liberty's being a *CAM*, though implying that its entitlement principle is a satiable one, does not imply that it's also a diminishing one. Unlike 'Alleviate hunger' and like 'Maximize wealth', there are no general grounds to imagine that the reason for giving persons pure negative liberty weakens with each additional increment of it that they receive. Neither their capacity nor inclination for acting can be presumed to exhibit this kind of declining tendency. Being non-diminishing, pure negative liberty's entitlement principle thus lacks the feature which, according to Raz, is required to liberate it from any need for supplementation by a strictly egalitarian principle: it lacks an in-built distributive norm.

Now there are, in fact, any number of ways in which pure negative liberty can be distributed. Slave societies exhibit some of them, feudal societies others, and liberal societies still others. The problem, from a Razian point-of-view, with attaching an exogenous (non-in-built) distributive rule to entitlement principles is that it can conflict with the endogenous distributive norms embedded in those principles themselves. In particular, it can be wasteful of valuable goods, implicitly denying intrinsic value to their associated entitlement principles. For those principles to be valued for their own sake, their endogenous distributive norms must be allowed to prevail. But since *non*-diminishing entitlement principles lack such endogenous distributive norms, their application cannot avoid regulation by exogenous ones.

Why should this fact tell particularly in favour of strict egalitarianism? After all, 'Abigail vs Andrew' suggests that any non-diminishing principle entitling persons to some type of good is thereby *indifferent* to how that good is to be distributed: *any* exogenous distributive rule—non-egalitarian as well as egalitarian—looks to be equally eligible to serve in this regulatory capacity. The choice between them seems to be, ineluctably, a purely arbitrary one.

But this appearance of arbitrariness or equal eligibility is deeply deceptive. It's deceptive because there is a highly significant *asymmetry* between egalitarian and non-egalitarian distributions of any particular type of good: namely, that there is only one of the former, but many of the latter. An instruction to distribute a collection of apples unequally among a set of persons is fundamentally indeterminate in a way that its egalitarian counterpart is not. The natural

---

with Negative Liberty', in *The Idea of Freedom*, ed. Alan Ryan (Oxford: Oxford University Press, 1979); Richard Flathman, *The Philosophy and Politics of Freedom* (Cambridge: Cambridge University Press, 1987).

[15] For a particularly detailed challenge, see Ian Carter, *A Measure of Freedom* (Oxford: Oxford University Press, 1999), 258–68.

response to the former instruction is to ask for further guidance: 'Distribute them unequally in accordance with/in proportion to. . . . *what?*'

Put in Razian terms, the importance of this asymmetry is that, regulated by an exogenous *non*-egalitarian distributive rule, any non-diminishing entitlement principle *fails* to be valued for its own sake. Rather, persons' entitlements under that principle are thereby derivatively valued for their contribution to whatever good is represented in the particular proportionality nominated to govern that inequality. If we instruct the non-egalitarian regulator to distribute the apples in proportion to relative degrees of hunger, we are signifying that the apple-entitling principle is valued not for its own sake but rather for the sake of another entitlement principle—in this case, 'Alleviate hunger'. More generally, *non-egalitarian exogenous rules reduce the ostensible plurality of intrinsically valued entitlement principles*—in this case, by one. It is this same plurality-reducing quality that Raz rightly exposes in the application of strict egalitarianism to *diminishing* entitlement principles and that partly motivates his persuasive rejection of any such application.

For a non-diminishing entitlement principle to be valued for its own sake—for it to be an independent citizen in a pluralistic republic of entitlement principles—it *must* be regulated by a strictly egalitarian rule. And this necessity appears to dictate the nature of our valuation of that rule itself. Since that entitlement principle's being valued for its own sake entails its being regulated by that egalitarian rule, that rule must itself be valued for its own sake: the equal distribution of the entitled good is itself intrinsically valuable. Were it not so, were it valued solely for its contribution to the satisfaction of some other entitlement principles, this would imply that the very entitlement principle it regulates is itself one which is instrumentally subservient to those other principles and not one which is valued for its own sake. If changing circumstances can bring it about that the value of an unequal distribution of apples exceeds that of an equal one, we are bound to infer that persons having apples is not valued for its own sake.

It seems plausible to suppose that the presence of a strictly egalitarian rule distributing pure negative liberty would be a *foundational* one, in our moral and political thinking. And this, for essentially two reasons. First, any legal system, whatever else it may be, is *necessarily* a distribution of pure negative liberty. Inasmuch as what distinguishes legal systems from other normative systems is the *enforceability* of their duties, they directly or obliquely determine what actions persons should or should not be physically prevented by others from performing.[16] A set of legal rights, being correlatively entailed by those duties, thereby represents that distribution of liberty.[17] So if pure negative liberty is a

---

[16] 'Directly or obliquely' in the sense that these determinations divide into first- and second-order types, with the latter applying to cases where the former are breached.

[17] This claim is (intended to be!) neutral as between the rival Will and Interest Theories of rights, though I've elsewhere defended the former as possessing greater explanatory/descriptive power; cf. *An Essay on Rights* (n. 4 above), ch. 3 (A), and 'Working Rights', in Matthew Kramer, Nigel

good, and if it must be distributed equally, then it follows that our legal rights should reflect that moral fact. The moral evaluation of any action bearing liberty-distributing properties must make reference to that strictly egalitarian rule.

What about the *other* morally-relevant properties of actions? Here we encounter the second reason for equal liberty's foundational status. A legal system, in attaching enforceability to its duties, thereby assigns to the actions (performances or forbearances) enjoined by those duties some kind of priority over all other possible actions,[18] in circumstances where an enjoined action is incompatible (jointly unperformable) with a legally unenjoined one. It does *not* say 'Comply with this duty, unless the reasons for performing that unenjoined action have a strength of at least *s*'.[19] If an action has the property of being illegal, the fact that it also bears many worthy properties is insufficient, legally, to justify a failure to enforce its forbearance. In this sense, such rules assign *lexical* primacy to their duties. The illegality of an action *trumps* even its weightiest valuable properties, rendering its performance impermissible and its forbearance permissibly—indeed, mandatorily—enforceable. Accordingly, any comprehensive set of moral standards must structurally reflect this formal feature of legal duties and their correlatively entailed rights. Among its various entitling principles, it must assign the status of *primus inter pares* to the principle used specifically for the moral evaluation of enforcement. And equal liberty appears to be that principle.

Does this suggest that such rights as are entailed by the equal liberty principle are *incommensurable* with other moral values? On Raz's understanding of incommensurability, precisely the opposite is true. For him, it is due to a failure of transitivity and the test for its presence is described thus:

Two valuable options are incommensurable if (1) neither is better than the other, and (2) there is (or could be) another option which is better than one but is not better than the other.[20]

Since lexically prime options are, *ipso facto*, better than ones endorsed by lower-ranked values, they must fail this test. Is this what we mean by incommensurability?

Consider two types of valuable option: Es which satisfy the equal liberty principle but not that of benevolence, and Bs which do the reverse.[21] Each of these types includes options whose values vary with the magnitude of their estimated principle-satisfaction—some Es, say, secure the equal liberty of more

Simmonds and Hillel Steiner, *A Debate Over Rights. Philosophical Enquiries* (Oxford: Oxford University Press, 1998), 298–301.

[18] Including ones compliant with other non-enforceable duties.
[19] That is, a legal system that *does* allow performance of an *s*-reasons-backed action to override compliance with that duty is not one in which that action is an unenjoined one.
[20] Raz, *The Morality of Freedom* (n. 1 above), 325.
[21] To keep things simple, we'll suppose that these Es and Bs are *indifferent* with regard to benevolence and equal liberty, respectively.

persons than others, while some Bs bestow more benefits than others—and hence all Es are mutually commensurable, as are all Bs.[22]

Now it obviously doesn't follow from this that all Es *and* Bs are mutually commensurable. If we take an option's subscript to signify the extent to which it satisfies its corresponding principle, then E_1 is straightforwardly worse than E_2, and B_1 than B_2. But although this implies B_9's superiority to both of the latter pair, it tells us nothing about its value relative to both of the former pair: it could be better or worse than one or both of them. Hence B_9 and E_1 might satisfy both of Raz's conditions for being a pair of incommensurable options: (1) neither may be better than the other, and (2) E_2 is better than E_1 but may not be better than B_9. It's important to notice that what accounts for that incommensurability is the fact that *there is no way of unifying, or inter-translating, the E and B metrics*. It's this fact, that there is no basis for judging a unit of securing equal liberty to be of greater or lesser magnitude than a unit of bestowing benefit, that generates incommensurability here, and explains why that pair of options would pass Raz's test.

The point of the foregoing excursus is simply this: the non-unifiability of the E and B metrics remains true even when we bestow lexical primacy on the equal liberty principle and its rights. Despite our thereby embracing transitivity, we still remain unable to compare the magnitude of B_9 with that of E_1, even though that pair of options now *fails* Raz's incommensurability test (since E_1 is now better than B_9 and so is E_2).

Definitions are always, to some extent, a matter of stipulation. And the appropriate definition of 'incommensurability' looks like remaining a subject of lively philosophical controversy and one to which Raz continues to make a major contribution.[23] So perhaps the most that can be said here by way of a conclusion is this. Intransitivity is generally considered to be a stronger condition than *discontinuity*, in processes of rational valuation. Lexical priority implies discontinuity but not intransitivity. Nonetheless, the lexical priority of Es over Bs (and other types of valuable option), is fully adequate to resist the forms of substitutability that are rationally mandated among incontrovertibly commensurable options.[24] So on this view of the matter, it is a failure of continuity—rather than transitivity—that would give us the incommensurability possessed by whatever rights are entailed by the equal liberty principle, and places them in a foundational position in our moral and political reasoning.[25]

[22] I certainly don't mean to suggest here that the number of persons liberated, or of benefits bestowed, is the *only* index for measuring these magnitudes.

[23] Cf. Ruth Chang (ed.), *Incommensurability, Incomparability and Practical Reason* (Cambridge, Mass.: Harvard University Press, 1997).

[24] On continuity and commensurability, see *An Essay on Rights* (n. 4 above), chs. 4 (C, D), 5 (C).

[25] I am grateful to Jerry Cohen for his comments on an earlier draft of this paper.

8

The Intrinsic Value of Economic Equality

ANDREI MARMOR*

Why should we care about economic equality? Some philosophers, prominently Joseph Raz and Harry Frankfurt, claim that we shouldn't, that is, at least not if we think of economic equality as intrinsically valuable. They claim that economic *equality* has no moral value in itself. Harry Frankfurt formulated this point succinctly in saying that 'what is important from the point of view of morality is not that everyone should have the same but that each should have *enough*.'[1] But there is a serious question that arises here: can it be the case that people have enough of what they need if others have much more? The immediate suspicion that perhaps this cannot be the case, stems from the fact that needs are profoundly relative to the norms of flourishing in one's society. A great many needs, for example, are relative to culture. People's needs, and the criteria of sufficiency for those needs, are determined to a very considerable extent by the culture they live in. This, I take it, is widely recognized. But needs are also relative to the actual possessions of others in the same society, or, at least, so I shall argue here. Roughly, the basic idea is this: Above the level of bare subsistence, what people need, and mainly to what extent they need them, is something which is partly, but significantly, determined by the actual availability of those resources to others within an indeterminate distance around them.

If this is true, then it is not so clear anymore that claims of need, and more generally, our concern for people 'having enough', is essentially distinguishable from having not much less than others. In any case, this is precisely what I shall try to argue here, namely, that part of what having *enough* economic resources *means*, is that one does not have much less than most others. This will show that the value of economic equality is actually derivable from those same considerations which were meant to show why equality, as such, has no intrinsic

*I am very grateful to Omri Ben-Shachar, Meir Dan-Cohen, Chaim Gans, Amy Gutman, Leslie Green, Alon Harel, Francis Kamm, Martha Nussbaum, Joseph Raz, Donald Regan, Philip Soper, and Cass Sunstein for their illuminating comments on previous drafts of this paper.

[1] Harry Frankfurt, 'Equality as a moral ideal', reprinted in his *The Importance of What We Care About* (Cambridge University Press, 1988), 134–58, 134. Frankfurt has reaffirmed this line of thought in his recent article, 'Equality and Respect', *Social Research* 64 (1997), 3–15. Joseph Raz makes essentially the same point (among others) in ch. 9 of *The Morality of Freedom* (Oxford: Oxford University Press, 1986), see, particularly, 240.

value, namely, the basic moral concern with the satisfaction of people's needs. In the first section I will try to substantiate this claim. In the second section, I will try to show why this value of economic equality is an intrinsic one. Finally, I shall say a few words about the kind of equality which is entailed by the discussion.

I.

The ultimate concern of humanist moral-political ideals is with people's lives. Eventually, what matters is how well each individual's life is going. What makes one's life go well depends on innumerous things. The possession of economic resources is only one of many factors which contribute to people's well-being. How crucial economic resources are, as compared with other factors which affect people's chances of leading a good life, also depends on a great many things, partly on specific cultural circumstances. It would be safe to assume, however, that the relative significance of the possession of economic resources in the modern world is increasing steadily. For better or worse, the predominance of Western capitalism in the world creates an increasing dependence of people's well-being on their economic resources.

Furthermore, I will assume here that the relation between people's well-being and the resources they possess is both instrumental and intrinsic, or constitutive. Obviously, people need economic resources in order to be able to realize their life plans and the projects they regard as valuable. In this sense, the possession of resources is instrumentally valuable. But I will assume that there is also a deeper, non-instrumental relation between the possession of resources and well-being. What one has and what one is, are not totally detachable aspects of one's life and personality. In other words, my assumption is that the satisfaction of people's needs and interests in material resources is, at least to some extent, intrinsically valuable.[2]

Another assumption needs to be spelled out: Throughout the discussion, I will assume that there is a distinction between the moral grounds for seeking a desirable state of affairs, and the grounds for taking measures to attain it. In particular, a certain state of affairs may well be morally desirable, even if there is no particular agent, private or official, whose responsibility it is to try to bring about such a state of affairs. My argument about the intrinsic value of equality will not assume that if a certain form of equality is valuable, intrinsically or otherwise, then it automatically follows that the state, or anyone else, must take measures to accomplish it. The argument that follows is about values, concerning things we should care about. It leaves the questions concerning the implementation of those values entirely open.

---

[2] It is safe to assume that both Frankfurt and Raz would not object to this last point. Frankfurt, in any case, seems to pre-suppose it.

Now, when we look at the societies we know, and that, I will suppose here, includes the world at large, we see that at least from an economic perspective, many people can lead a decent life. Some people have much more than that; they have more resources than the vast majority can ever hope for. And then, there is a huge number of people at the bottom of the socio-economic scale, whose lives are pretty miserable. These poor people suffer from real deprivations; they don't have enough resources to be able to conduct a decent life. Frankfurt, Raz, and others, who object to the intrinsic value of equality, ask us to realize that it is the urgency of poor people's needs which calls upon our attention, and not the quantitative discrepancy between their possessions and others'.[3] But why, exactly, do we think that certain needs are urgent? What is it that constitutes needs and 'having enough' resources?

The notion of 'need' is often used to indicate something like *fundamental*, or *basic*, interests. My use of the term 'need' is much broader than this. Need, as I shall use the term here, is tantamount to any interest in material resources one might have. But it is crucial to note that interests differ from wants and desires. People can wish to have things they don't need, even things it would be against their interest to have, and *vice versa*.[4] They may not be aware of, or be aware of and not want, things they actually do need, things that are in their interest to have. Furthermore, it is possible to distinguish between what a person needs, and what he thinks that he needs. People may think that they need something which, in fact, they do not need.[5] Does this make needs an objective matter? Perhaps it does. But even if needs are objective, metaphysically or otherwise (though I am not suggesting that they are), needs are still relative, and in several respects.

First, as I have mentioned above, it is generally recognized that at least some needs are culture-specific.[6] There are, however, several ways in which culture affects people's needs and not all of them are important for our discussion. The influence of culture is most evident in shaping the various ways in which people satisfy their needs. One and the same kind of need may be satisfied differently in different cultures. This, however, does not render needs themselves relative to culture. But there are needs which are partly constituted by culture,

---

[3] See also Amartya Sen, 'Poor, Relatively Speaking', in his *Resources, Values and Development* (Oxford: Blackwell, 1984), 325–43.

[4] See, for example, David Wiggins, *Needs, Values, Truth* (Oxford: Blackwell, 2nd ed., 1991), ch. 1.

[5] This is actually not so simple: though people can certainly be mistaken about their needs, it is far from clear that colossal mistakes are possible. Most common mistakes about one's needs stem from mistakes about facts. We may all think, for example, that we need a low cholesterol diet, and this may turn out to be a big mistake: it may turn out to be that cholesterol is actually good for us. But it is less clear that we can all be mistaken about the nature of our needs, if it does not involve mistakes about facts. In other words, metaphysical realism about needs, i.e. those which go beyond biological needs, is not an initially plausible view.

[6] The cultural dependence of needs has often been stressed by the Frankfurt school. See, for example, Herbert Marcuse, *One-Dimensional Man* (London: Routledge, 1964), 4. Marcuse, however, also believed that there are 'real' needs transcending cultural contingencies.

though typically indirectly. In order to see this, it is essential to realize that above the level of biological needs and bare subsistence, needs are inherently relative to what is considered as prosperity, flourishing etc., (and its opposites, i.e. harm, wretchedness, etc.) in one's society. Needs, after all, are always *for* something. People need things in order to avoid harm and attain some forms of flourishing. What constitutes human flourishing is, to a considerable extent, culturally determined.[7] Some cultures value forms of human flourishing which other cultures regard with disdain. To be sure, I am not trying to deny that there are universal human needs, transcending cultural differences. But I believe that it is equally clear that a great many needs are not universal, but relative to culture.

In a similar, but I think much less recognized way, needs are also relative to the socio-economic opportunities which prevail in one's society. Roughly, again, what people need, and mainly to what extent they need them, is something which is partly, but significantly, determined by the actual availability of those resources to others within their social vicinity.

In order to clarify this point, let me distinguish, though somewhat artificially, between several levels of needs. We can construct a simple scale along the following lines. At the very bottom, we would find those needs which are absolutely essential for one's survival. These needs are determined by our biological makeup and environmental realities. We can say that these biological needs are *absolute*, in that they are entirely determined by necessities of survival. Such needs are obviously not relative, either to culture or to socio-economic scales. Now, one step above the bottom, we will find those things people need without which their lives are doomed to be wretched, miserable, almost unbearable. Let us call these 'urgent needs'. These would be the things people need in order to be able to maintain something like a *minimally decent* life. Further up the scale we can identify those things most people need in order to conduct a decent life. Let us call them 'reasonable', or 'average' needs. Satisfaction of such reasonable needs is what would provide most people with the kind of resources they need in order to conduct a decent, prosperous, fulfilling, life. Finally, there are things people may want to have, though, in one clear sense, it would be awkward to say that they need them. We can call them 'luxuries', indicating the fact that the satisfaction of such 'needs' is not really required in order to conduct a decent life. In other words, having luxuries is what distinguishes the rich, or the very rich, from the well-to-do.

Now, my basic claim is, that above the level of absolute needs, this scale of needs is profoundly sensitive to the actual division of resources in the society. Whether someone is warranted in holding that her need of an x is urgent, reasonable, or less than that, crucially (though not exclusively!) depends on the actual availability of x to others. The more readily x is available to others, the more urgent, or important, its possession may become; and *vice versa*, of course.

---

[7] See Wiggins (n. 4 above), 11.

In other words, what I am trying to suggest is, that the scale of needs is basically a matter of social constructions, because there is no truth of the matter about it which is independent of the division of possessions in one's social vicinity.

Let me clarify: I do not wish to claim that just about anything which is readily available to most people becomes, *ipso facto*, a reasonable need. People can have a great many things which they do not need. In order to need something, other conditions would normally have to obtain; relative availability does not form a sufficient condition of something being a need. Needs relate to things people would normally want to have, and they would normally want to have them for reasons. Some of those reasons may be agent-relative, and others may not. In any case, the argument under consideration does not depend on *a definition* of 'needs'. Nor such a definition is intended here. The moral intuition of the Frankfurt–Raz argument concerns the *sufficiency* of needs' satisfaction; it does not depend on any precise definition of what 'needs' are. Frankfurt and Raz claim that we should be concerned with people having enough of *whatever* they need, and the main question I want to raise here is, whether we can know what this 'enough' means, in a non-relative manner.

As a rough illustration, consider this example. Imagine that we discover life on a remote planet, very similar to earth, which is comprised of two groups, the 'rich' and the 'poor'; imagine that the differences between the economic resources of these two groups are considerable, but, nevertheless, the 'poor' in this imaginary alien society are actually better off than most of us. That is, judging by *our* standards of living, the 'poor' in this imaginary society are not poor at all. They are poor, however, relative to the 'rich' in their society. Suppose further, that the 'poor' in this imaginary society do feel poor; judging by the only standards familiar to them, they do feel deprived of many opportunities which are available to the 'rich'. They think that they have some urgent needs, and a great many reasonable needs, unsatisfied.

Now, according to the view which denies the relativity of needs to the actual socio-economic gaps, one would have to maintain that the 'poor' in this imaginary society suffer from some kind of false-consciousness; they only think that they have unsatisfied needs, but as a matter of fact, they actually have enough. But this is quite implausible. After all, nobody would think that the poor people in *our* society should suddenly think of themselves rich and content if we discover yet another, opposite, remote planet, where even the 'rich' are much worse off than they are.

A similar way to think about this is this: take a poor segment of our society, that is, think of people whose biological needs are met, but beyond that, they have very little. Imagine that they are the only ones around, that is, imagine that the whole world is exactly in their situation. Whatever they have is all that there is to have for everybody else. Would you still think of these people as 'poor'? Would you still insist that they have urgent needs? I don't see how you could.

It may be objected that this relativity of needs to the actual distribution of resources in society is only an empirical generalization concerning typical human reactions, and a contestable one at that. This is true about one aspect of the relativity of needs, and false about another. We must distinguish between two questions: how do people *actually form* their conceptions of their needs, and how do we judge their *sufficiency*? People form their own conceptions of what they need on the basis of a very complex combination of factors, some which are culturally determined, and others which are personally variant. The general norms of flourishing in society form an essential part of such need-formations, but only a part, and the extent to which such cultural factors figure in individuals' conceptions of their needs is a contingent matter. It varies between different cultures and between individuals in the same culture.

The relevant question, however, is not about the way people come to form their own conceptions of their needs, which is, indeed, largely an empirical matter. The crucial question concerns the criteria of sufficiency: Can we have objective *criteria* for judging that people have enough (or plenty, etc.) of what they need which are not relative to the possessions of others? A negative answer only to this last question is what I am trying to defend here. And it is not an empirical question. It is a philosophical question about the concept of needs, and particularly, about what it means to have enough, or plenty, etc.

We know what it means to have enough food, since food is needed to satisfy certain biological needs. In such cases, needs are determined by some absolute standards which are simply there, given by the realities of life. But most needs are not like that. People don't need to go to the opera, or to the theatre, etc., or have cars, washing machines, television sets, stereo equipment, etc., in order to survive. These are 'reasonable' needs in our society only because nowadays a great many people can afford them. One who cannot afford most of such standard consumer items would rightly feel that she is unable to conduct a decent life. Such a self-conception of deprivation, however, would be totally out of place if the items in question were considered luxury items. Whether they are luxury or reasonable items crucially depends, however, on who can afford what. The more people can afford an x, the less of a luxury it may become (i.e. assuming that x is something that people actually want to possess).

Consider, for example, the possession of cars. Just a few decades ago, automobiles were considered luxury items because very few people could afford them. Nowadays, however, we no longer think of the private possession of a car as a luxury. In present industrial societies, the possession of cars is something most people need in order to be able to conduct a decent standard of living, and those who cannot afford such a consumer item as a private automobile, are indeed, deprived of something they might reasonably need.[8]

Amartya Sen claims, however, that such examples do not really show that poverty is a relative matter. Poverty, Sen claims, is an absolute notion in what

---

[8] Once again, though, it should be emphasized that widespread availability of an item does not necessarily render that particular item one in need. Relative availability certainly does not constitute a sufficient condition of needs; it only figures in our criteria of what it means to have *enough*.

he calls 'the space of capabilities', though it would often take a relative form in the space of commodities, that is, with respect to people's interests in specific material resources.[9] Admittedly, there is something very important in this distinction. It is certainly true that the widespread availability of cars has actually changed the world, so to speak, in the sense that people can no longer function in society as they could have functioned without cars at the beginning of the 20th century. Therefore, Sen concludes, the relative deprivation of those who cannot afford a car these days is only a failure in the commodity space, leaving the space of capabilities constant.

This conclusion, however, is over-stated. The fact that the same kind of functioning capability may require different commodities in different cultures, does not show, by itself, that capabilities remain constant.[10] In order to deny the relativity of needs, Sen would have to show that we can articulate an absolute, non-relative list of capabilities which are constant across cultures, irrespective of the commodities which are available in them. This seems to me very unlikely. Even less plausible, however, is the thesis underlying Sen's argument here, that the notion of poverty, and more generally, the notion of 'standard of living', is best defined solely in terms of capabilities to function.[11] Such a view entails, for example, that the Bedouin peasant, who only needs a camel to move around, and the suburban American Yuppie, who needs a car, are equally well off if the Bedouin gets his camel and the Yuppie gets his car. Surely we must allow for the intuitive idea that the Bedouin is poor, and the Yuppie is rich.

Admittedly, there is an obvious way in which one could support something like Sen's argument: one could claim that needs are generally satiable. That is, whatever one needs, one can reach a point where one has enough of it in the sense that having more of it would not constitute any improvement. Surely some needs are satiable in this sense. Nourishment, fresh air to breathe, etc., are satiable needs. But it seems extremely unlikely that economic resources, in general, are satiable. One's economic situation can always be improved. This does not mean, however, that there is no such thing as having *enough* economic resources. Only that any judgement about the sufficiency of economic resources is bound to be relative to the actual socio-economic scale which prevails in one's society.

---

[9] 'Poor, Relatively Speaking' (n. 3 above), 335.

[10] Here is a similar example Sen himself provides to illustrate this point. Citing a research which showed that children in Western countries might not be able to follow their school program unless they have access to television, Sen claims that a child in, say, England, without a television set is actually worse off than, say, a child in Tanzania without a television, who, presumably does not need the television in order to fulfil his educational needs. In other words, the widespread availability of televisions in the West, and their role in education, has not created a 'brand new need', Sen claims, but that to meet the same need as that of the Tanzanian children in education, the British child must posses more commodities (ibid., 336–37). In a limited sense, this is true; but of course, it does not entail that one would be indifferent between growing up in England or in Tanzania. Even if there is a loose sense in which education in both countries serves the same functioning capabilities, those are, nevertheless, quite different. The fact that the English child needs a television to accomplish her tasks is rather indicative of the fact that the standard of living in England is, quite simply, much higher than in Tanzania.   [11] Ibid., 334.

Now it is, of course, only the objective judgement about sufficiency that concerns us here. The fact that we can easily envisage very poor people who are content with what they have is beside the point. Only according to rather crude versions of Utilitarianism the subjective state of mind of people about such matters is decisive of anything, and it tells more against such versions of Utilitarianism than against the argument offered here.[12]

Another serious objection, however, might go as follows: people need things for certain *reasons*. Now, according to the objection, whatever the reasons are for needing something, those reasons are also reasons for having a certain amount of it. If x is a reason for A's needing y, then x may provide the grounds for judging how much of y is enough for A. And if this is the case, it would seem to be a decisive argument against the relativity of needs to others' possessions. But the conclusion is premature. The reasons which underlie a particular need are typically *indeterminate* about the criteria of sufficiency of that need. In other words, even if the reason for needing something is independent of any considerations about what others have, the criteria of its sufficiency may well be relative to others' situation. Consider, for example, people's need for lodging. There are good reasons for this need, but those reasons do not entail any particular standard of lodging which could be considered appropriate in any given set of circumstances. The appropriateness, or sufficiency, of one's lodging condition is bound to be relative to the general availability in one's socio-economic vicinity.[13] Similar considerations apply, I believe, to all economic resources. Their criteria of sufficiency are under-determined by the reasons for having the economic resources one needs. This is so, because the basic criterion of sufficiency of economic resources is essentially a comparative matter, largely determined by the norms of flourishing in one's society.

Admittedly, it is very difficult to answer the question of what is the relevant society here. Though the argument assumes that standards of flourishing are relative to a given society, it does not assume that those standards are parochial. Mexican peasants, for example, do not form part of the North American society, but presumably they are affected by the standards of flourishing which prevail in US and Canada. Perhaps nowadays we may safely assume that the world at large is so intertwined by mass media and economic ties, that it is the one society that matters.[14]

[12] For example, such versions of Utilitarianism are committed to the view that if it turns out to be cheaper to convince poor people, say, by indoctrination, to be content with what they have, than actually to improve their economic situation, then such indoctrination is warranted and more desirable than trying to improve people's economic situation. This, I take it, is a very implausible moral stance.

[13] For example, think why would it be so ridiculous if someone said that she 'needs to live in Buckingham palace'? Well, obviously, because most everybody lives in much humbler residence. But it is worth keeping in mind that for millions of poor people around the world, our residence is not unlike Buckingham palace compared to their lodging conditions. Appropriateness of residence conditions is profoundly a relative matter.

[14] It is a difficult question, whether the argument depends on people's knowledge, or awareness, of the others' situation. I tend to think that such knowledge is only relevant if we think about the

There seems to be a further, serious objection that might arise here, with respect to the irrationality of envy. Rawls famously claimed that rational people do not suffer from envy: A rational person 'is not ready to accept a loss for himself if only others have less as well', that is, 'as long as the differences between himself and others do not exceed certain limits.'[15] Now, it may be objected that the kind of relativity of needs I have assumed here goes against this fairly standard assumption about the irrationality of envy. That is so, because if it is true that people cannot really have enough economic resources if others have much more, then it may often be rational for a person to forgo a certain economic gain just in order to prevent an even greater gain to somebody else.

There are several complications here. To begin with, there is an important distinction between individual comparisons and those which relate to socio-economic classes. Although it may be irrational for an individual, as such, to forgo a certain expected gain only to prevent others from gaining more, such a strategy may well be quite rational when the comparison relates to socio-economic classes. For example, if the Dean offers one of his professors an increase of 5% to his salary while increasing the salary of another professor by 20%, the former would probably behave irrationally if he declines the offer just in order to prevent his colleague from getting a higher increase to her salary. But if the government offers an increase to the salary of university professors, say by 5%, conditional upon a much higher increase say, of 30% to the civil service employees, the situation is quite different. Creating, or substantially increasing, a socio-economic gap between classes of people involves moral costs regardless of envy. It creates a class difference which has not previously existed, and this difference may be detrimental to the disadvantaged class in many ways, even if, as is often the case, each and every individual in that class would have personally preferred the modest gain.

Secondly, there is the issue of limits. As Rawls himself admitted (see the quote above), if the expected difference in gains between the parties concerned exceeds a certain limit, the so called 'envy' principle turns to be quite rational. Now, this threshold-proviso may well be quite intuitive, but it is far from clear what its grounds are; why does the *quantity* of the expected difference matter? If the principle of rationality assumes that one should only be concerned with one's own possessions, and one's own expected gains, why does it matter *how much* more the others are going to gain? Where does the threshold come from?

Note, however, that if the argument about the relativity of needs is correct, the rationality of the threshold-proviso is rendered pretty clear. My rational concern with others' expected gains can stem from my concern with my own

---

empirical question concerning the ways in which people come to form their own conceptions of their needs. It is not required for purposes of assessing the sufficiency of their needs. We can form our objective judgement about the poor condition of the Mexican peasants in comparison to their North American counterparts, even if the former are totally unaware of the condition of the latter.

[15] John Rawls, *A Theory of Justice* (Oxford: Oxford University Press, 1971), 143.

situation—if others gain *much* more than I do, then my own gain can easily turn out to be a relative loss.

In other words, Rawls' principle is not necessarily a principle of envy. Envy is a type of motivation, or reason, and there is no swift move from Rawls' principle to the real motivation behind it. A motivation is based on envy only when it is essentially not self-regarding, that is, when the loss which is intended to be inflicted on the other party contributes nothing to the situation of the envious party; A motivation is envious only when it is intended to prevent the other from gaining something which the envious party is in no position to gain himself.

This, however, is not necessarily the case whenever one is willing to forgo a certain expected gain just in order to prevent somebody else from gaining even more. And this is particularly the case when we concentrate on the differences between classes of people, not individuals. If it is true that people cannot have enough if others have much more, the reasons against increasing economic gaps are self-related ones, based on real interests of the disadvantaged party. Thus, the following conclusion seems to be warranted: on the one hand, it is true that the argument about the relativity of needs entails that it can often be rational to forgo certain possible gains only in order to avoid increasing the gaps between the parties concerned. (There is, of course, little wonder about that: it is something which is entailed by all egalitarian principles.) On the other hand, such sacrifices are not necessarily motivated by envy.[16]

Another difficulty which seems to present itself is this: How can we explain the fact that we seem to be much less concerned with the inequalities between the well-to-do and the rich, than with the poor and the rest? Harry Frankfurt claims, not unreasonably I think, that 'we tend to be quite unmoved . . . by the inequalities between the well-to-do and the rich . . . The fact that some people have much less than others is morally un-disturbing when it is clear that they have plenty.'[17]

Does this not show, then, that people can have quite enough even if others have much more? I don't think that it does, and for three different reasons. First, it should be kept in mind that if my argument so far is correct, then 'having plenty' is simply not a judgement we can make irrespective of what others have. From an objective vantage point, 'having plenty' can only mean something like having more, or at least not less, than the average. Secondly, I venture to guess that we are typically unmoved by the discrepancies between the rich and the well-to-do, partly because there are much fewer of the former than the latter. In a society where there are many rich, few poor, and few in between, I am not so sure that we would not be concerned by the discrepancy between the rich and the well-to-do. Relative numbers may matter.[18]

---

[16] Economists often take it for granted that nobody can really object to Pareto improvements. But this is far from clear. Pareto improvements, particularly in successive stages, can easily increase the gap between the rich and the poor to such an extent that the gains to the poor are out-weighted by the cost of the increased gap. This, perhaps, may have been the intuition behind Rawls' proviso.

[17] 'Equality as a moral ideal' (n. 1 above), 147.

[18] See, for example, Larry S. Temkin, *Inequality* (Oxford: Oxford University Press, 1993), ch. 1.

Most importantly, however, the reason for being much more concerned with the relative disadvantage of the poor than that of the well-to-do, stems from special, *additional* disadvantages of being poor, over and above one's relative place on the socio-economic scale. The status of being poor, though essentially a relative matter, is particularly degrading, for reasons which have to do, for example, with the way in which poor people see themselves in relation to the society they live in. Poor people typically feel alienated from their society. At best, they tend to feel excluded from the general advantages of living in society. More often, they also feel humiliated. Such understandable feelings of alienation, exclusion, and humiliation, add an especially urgent demand on our attention, and this provides one important reason to be much more concerned with the discrepancies between the poor and the well-to-do, than with discrepancies between the latter and the rich.[19] There are, of course, many more disadvantages to being poor compared to the other socio-economic segments of society but we need not go into this here.

To sum up so far: I have tried to argue that the value of economic equality derives from the basic moral concern with the sufficiency of people's needs. From a moral point of view, it is important that each person should have enough resources to be able to conduct a decent, autonomous, fulfilling life. The argument was, that this concern cannot be realized without a considerable amount of equality, since the criteria of the sufficiency of needs are essentially relative to others' possessions. People cannot have enough if many others have much more. A crucial question remains open about this argument, however, and it is whether the value of equality which is entailed by it is intrinsic, or merely instrumental. I take up this issue in the next section.

II.

What is the significance of saying that something is merely of instrumental value? The typical case is the following: suppose there is a state of affairs, say A, and we hold that A, as such, is not good in itself, that is, we have no reason to pursue A for its own sake, but, combined with circumstances C, the pursuit of A is likely to bring about some good consequences B, and B is such that it is something we value for its own sake.[20]

Note that there is a good reason for saying that in such cases, the pursuit of A is *merely* of instrumental value (i.e. positive or negative). This normally

[19] It may be useful to compare our intuitions with respect to the poor in our society, and the urgency of their needs, with the way we react to very poor, but also very isolated communities. I think we are much less concerned with the predicament of the latter, because we assume that their poverty does not involve such feelings of alienation and humiliation.

[20] The same structure can be put in negative terms: we can say that A is not bad in in itself, that is, if A obtains, by itself, there is nothing to complain about, but, combined with circumstances Ci ... n, the fact that A obtains tends to bring about bad consequences.

indicates the fact that things could have been otherwise, that is, that the connection between the pursuit (or the avoidance) of A and the things we really value in life, is only contingent. If the circumstances change, the consequences following from A may change as well. It is this element of contingency which warrants our reaction to instrumental values as 'merely' instrumental. Furthermore, contingency, in a sense, admits of degrees. Things can be more or less contingent, depending on the probability that we attach to the occurrence of the relevant causal chain.

Given this line of thought, it is natural to assume that valuable things in our lives can either be instrumentally or intrinsically valuable. If we attach a certain value to an A, then it must mean that A is either something we value for its own sake, or else, it is something we value only because its pursuit (or realization, etc.) is likely to bring about something else which we value for its own sake.

Compelling as this dichotomy may be, it is in need of much further refinements. For our purposes, however, we only need to distinguish between several categories of intrinsic values. Raz's distinctions are very useful here. He suggested three such categories: Things can be intrinsically valuable if they are valuable in themselves, regardless of anything else. Some of these things may be of ultimate value. The relation between these two categories is, as Raz explains, a justificatory one. 'Ultimate values are referred to in explaining the value of non-ultimate goods.'[21] Thirdly, there are 'constituent goods', and these are 'elements of what is good in itself which contribute to its value, i.e. elements but for which a situation which is good in itself would be less valuable'.[22]

It is on this, third category, that I want to concentrate, suggesting that constituent goods can be of two kinds. Things may be valued in this sense because they are instances, or realizations, of goods which we value intrinsically. These are the things which instantiate, non-instrumentally, something which is good in itself. If friendship is of intrinsic value, then my friendship *with Sarah* is a constituent good in this sense. There is, however, another important category, where the constituent good is an *essential ingredient* of something which we value for its own sake. The main difference between these two sub-categories of constituent goods is that non-essential constituent goods are, typically, substitutable. My friendship *with Sarah* is not an essential ingredient of friendship, though it instantiates friendship non-instrumentally.

As an example of the second sub-category, consider the complex relations between the value of choice and the value of personal autonomy. As Raz famously formulated it, 'The ruling idea behind the ideal of personal autonomy is that people should make their own lives. The autonomous person is a (part) author of his own life. The ideal of personal autonomy is the vision of people controlling, to some degree, their own destiny, fashioning it through successive decisions throughout their lives.'[23] Clearly enough, the value of choice figures

---

[21] *The Morality of Freedom* (n. 1 above), 200.   [22] Ibid.

[23] 'Autonomy, Toleration, and the Harm Principle', in *Issues in Contemporary Legal Philosophy*, ed. Ruth Gavison (Oxford: Oxford University Press, 1987), 313–33, 314.

in this picture as an essential ingredient. That it is only one ingredient can be clearly seen from the fact that there is much more to the value of personal autonomy than an aggregate of choices. Furthermore, not all choices are relevant to personal autonomy. Only certain types of choices, and under certain circumstances, form part of the realization of an autonomous life. And it is equally clear how *essential* an ingredient choice is to the ideal of personal autonomy. Part of what it means to be an autonomous person is that one has made certain choices in one's life. Choice is not something that only contributes, instrumentally, to personal autonomy; it actually forms part of what it is to be an autonomous person. Its value consists in being an essential ingredient of personal autonomy.[24]

Similarly, I want to suggest, the intrinsic value of economic equality lies in its being an essential ingredient of the kind of general moral concern Frankfurt has in mind, namely, our moral concern with people having enough of what they need. We should not value economic equality as such, but only as an essential constituent of the value of having enough of what one needs to conduct a decent life.

Let me summarize in brief. I agree with Frankfurt and Raz that the fundamental moral concern is with the idea of need: what we should really care about is with people having enough of what they need. A considerable amount of economic equality, however, forms an essential ingredient of this general concern. Generally speaking, people cannot have enough of what they need in a society where many other people have much more. Part of what 'having enough' means, is that one does not have much less than most others. Equality, on this account, is not of instrumental value; its value lies in being an essential ingredient of the general concern with people's needs, which *is* something we should value for its own sake.[25]

III.

What kind of economic equality is entailed by our discussion so far? There are two distinctions, or contrasts, which I would like to dwell on in order to answer this question. First, it is noticeable that the kind of economic equality which is entailed by the considerations I have mentioned in the first section, is very rough. If the basic moral concern is with people having enough of what they need, and all we have shown so far is that people cannot have enough if others have much more, it certainly does not follow that total economic equality is required. Only a very rough amount of economic equality is what is needed.

---

[24] By this I do not mean to exclude other values we may attach to choice, values which do not derive from choice being part of autonomy.

[25] None of this, of course, excludes the possibility that equality is also of great importance in terms of the instrumental values it serves, in, for example, containing the relative political power of some people over others, and the like.

Now, many egalitarians would be happy to concede that equality is, anyway, only an ideal. Part of what we mean when we say that P is a moral-political ideal is, that P need not, or cannot, be implemented in full. Note, however, that there is an important difference between 'need not' and 'cannot', and that there are, accordingly, two categories of *ideal* principles. Let me call them *guiding* ideals, and *limit* ideals, respectively.[26]

A guiding ideal principle is one which does not require, on its own moral grounds, full implementation. Limit ideals, on the other hand, would require full implementation, if only that were possible. That is, anything that falls short of full implementation is due to the obstacles imposed by the realities of life. A good example of a limit ideal principle is the principle of equality of opportunity. This principle, on its own moral grounds, requires the elimination of *all* possible factors which would give anyone an unfair advantage or disadvantage over another. But in most contexts, we know that life is too complicated, and no matter what we do, some people will have an unfair advantage over others, since it is simply impossible to eliminate all the relevant factors. The principle sets an ideal limit that we can only try to approximate.

Guiding ideals, on the other hand, do not require full implementation. That is, not because we have given up on something in advance, but because the grounds of the principle itself are such that they do not call for strict implementation. What such principles do require, however, is that there be no gross deviations from the standards they set. Furthermore, such guiding ideals are typically non-perfectionist principles, in that attempts to implement them in full tend to be self-defeating, neurotic, or ridiculous. Consider, for example, ideals such as 'reasonable care' (i.e. the avoidance of negligence), charity, authenticity, or spontaneity. Only that much of spontaneity is enough; one who tries to be spontaneous whenever possible tends to look rather ridiculous. Similarly, excessive caution is not always a symptom of rationality.[27]

The ideal of economic equality which is entailed by our discussion in the first section belongs to this latter category. It is a guiding ideal. On its own grounds, it does not call for full implementation of economic equality. It only tells against gross deviations from economic equality, since such deviations undermine the basic moral concern we should have for people's needs. The argument was, that people cannot have enough of what they need if others have *much more*; but surely they can have enough if others have just a little more, or perhaps even if very few people have much more. Rough economic equality is all that the principle requires.

In order to introduce the second contrast, it may be useful to draw on Derek Parfit's distinction between two main kinds of egalitarian concerns: the Telic and the Deontic views.[28] On the Telic view, inequality is bad, regardless of how

[26] I use the term 'limit' here in deference to the Renaissance notion of *idea limis*.

[27] The Kantian distinction between 'perfect' and 'imperfect duties' is very similar to the idea I have in mind here. But I don't think we need the specific Kantian grounds for it.

[28] See Derek Parfit, 'Equality and Priority' in *Ideals of Equality*, ed. A. Mason (Oxford: Blackwell 1998), 1–20, 1.

it came about. On the Deontic view, inequality is unjust, injustice being a special kind of badness, one which necessarily involves wrong-doing. On this rough dividing line, the value of economic equality I have argued for above certainly belongs to the Telic view. What is bad about inequality is not that it results from some injustice that had been done, but from the fact that it is a *bad state of affairs* if people don't have enough of what they need, combined with the fact that people cannot have enough if others have much more. Thus, if we care about people having enough of what they need, we should also care about economic equality. Needless to add, economic equality is not the only distributive concern we should care about. Furthermore, the implementation of equality, even as a guiding ideal, is often a wasteful policy, and it certainly may happen that the waste is too big to be ignored.

9

Past and Future: The Case for a Threshold Notion of Harm

LUKAS H. MEYER*

I. INTRODUCTION

Liberal cosmopolitans[1] often take the view, first, that currently living people, wherever they may live, and future people, whenever their lives take place, have, *qua* human beings, the same moral status.[2] Cosmopolitans, at any rate where attributing this moral status to future people is concerned, are inclined to deny the relevance of the special features of our relations to future people. One way of expressing this conviction is to say that both our contemporaries and future people have general (human) rights vis-à-vis us.[3] Secondly, liberal cosmopolitans often take the view that currently living people cannot be said to have claims to compensation because their predecessors were badly wronged in the past. Instead, they claim that the significance of history lies in the consequences of

*I am grateful to Arthur Applbaum, Brian Barry, Brian Bix, Catherine Elgin, Axel Gosseries, David Heyd, Erin Kelly, Rahul Kumar, David Lyons, Avishai Margalit, Larry May, Jeff McMahan, Stanley L. Paulson, Thomas W. Pogge, Joseph Raz, Adam Swift, Andrew D. Williams and, last but by no means least, Barbara Reiter, for their written and oral comments on a longer version of this paper. Earlier versions of the paper were the subject of a workshop at the University of Maryland, Committee on Politics, Philosophy, and Public Policy, as well as at one of the sessions of the workshop 'Ethics and Future People' at the Columbia Law School Center for Law and Philosophy, from which I greatly benefited. I am also very indebted to the members of the Faculty Seminar at the Harvard University Center for Ethics and the Professions for a lively and rewarding discussion.

[1] Liberal cosmopolitanism is broadly consequentialist in character, endorses the position of value-individualism and understands value-individualism to hold universally. There are as many variants of this position as there are theories of value compatible with these features. For this characterization see Thomas W. Pogge, 'Cosmopolitanism and Sovereignty', *Ethics* 103 (1992), 48–75, 48 f. See also my 'Cosmopolitan Communities', in *International Justice*, ed. Anthony Coates (Aldershot and Brookfield: Ashgate), 89–110, 89–92.

[2] See, for example, Brian Barry, *Theories of Justice. A Treatise on Social Justice*, vol. 1 (Berkeley: University of California Press, 1989), 347; Barry, *Justice as Impartiality. A Treatise on Social Justice*, vol. 2 (Oxford: Clarendon Press, 1995), 195–7; Onora O'Neill, *Towards Justice and Virtue* (Cambridge: Cambridge University Press, 1996), 115.

[3] In this paper I discuss what we owe to future people in terms of both their rights vis-à-vis us and our correlative duties. However, some of our concerns for future people are best understood in terms of duties towards them with which no rights of future people correlate—or so I have argued in 'More Than They Have a Right to: Future People and Our Future Oriented Projects', in *Contingent Future Persons. On the Ethics of Deciding Who Will Live, or Not, in the Future*, ed. Nick Fotion and Jan C. Heller (Dordrecht, Boston and London: Kluwer Academic Publishers, 1997), 137–56. See n. 13 below.

past events for the well-being of currently living and future people. In short, the past matters causally. I will refer to this view as the forward-looking understanding of the significance of past wrongs.[4]

It can be shown that these cosmopolitan views bear systematic connections to each other. I will distinguish between a subjunctive-threshold and a subjunctive-historical interpretation of the right not to be harmed. I will also distinguish between (i) the present generations' duties not to violate the rights of future generations and (ii) the present generations' duties to compensate currently living people for the harms inflicted upon them through the lasting impact of injustices committed against their predecessors. My thesis is that by employing a subjunctive-threshold notion of harm we can justify conclusions about both types of present generations' duties—conclusions that appeal only to rights-based considerations and that are acceptable to cosmopolitans.

My defence of the cosmopolitan view on the status of future people, turns on the adoption of a subjunctive-threshold notion of harm (sections II and III). On the basis of such a notion of harm, I develop, second, the following analysis of historical claims: the normative relevance of past wrongs today depends upon their causal relevance for the well-being of currently living (and future people). This is a way of making sense of the cosmopolitan analysis of the moral relevance of historical injustices (section IV). I then undertake what is at any rate a partial defence of this understanding of our duties towards past and future by considering several objections (sections V and VI).

II. RIGHTS OF FUTURE PEOPLE?

The cosmopolitan view on the status of future people has been challenged. I begin here by summarizing the results of my earlier discussions in so far as they are relevant to the argument in this paper.[5] First, some philosophers have denied that future people can have rights, pointing out that they live in the

---

[4] The importance of the forward-looking assessment of the significance of past wrongs has been stressed by, for example, David Lyons, 'The New Indian Claims and Original Rights to Land', *Social Theory and Practice* 4 (1977), 249–72; Jeremy Waldron, 'Superseding Historic Injustice', *Ethics* 103 (1992), 4–28; Bruce A. Ackerman, *The Future of Liberal Revolution* (New Haven: Yale University Press, 1992), 72 f. For a theory of justice that bases our obligations in backward-looking reasoning see Robert Nozick, *Anarchy, State, and Utopia* (Oxford: Blackwell, 1974), 152 f. For epistemic problems in determining what holdings people would have today if the injustice (committed against previously living people) had not taken place, Nozick proposes Rawls' difference principle—a forward-looking principle, specifying what the future should be like—as a 'rough rule of thumb for rectifying' historical injustice (ibid., 231). This idea does not address the problem of the inapplicability of an identity-dependent notion of harm as discussed in secs. 3 and 4 below. See also George Sher, 'Ancient Wrongs and Modern Rights', in *Justice between Age Groups and Generations*, ed. Peter Laslett and James S. Fishkin (New Haven and London: Yale University Press, 1992), 48–61.

[5] See my 'More Than They Have a Right to: Future People and Our Future Oriented Projects' (n. 3 above); id., 'Can Actual Future People Have a Right to Non-Existence?', *Archives for Philosophy of Law and Social Philosophy, Beiheft 67: Rights* (1997), 200–9.

future. Consider the following claim: 'Future generations by definition do not exist now. They cannot now, therefore, be the present bearer or subject of anything, including rights.'[6] Claiming that we can violate future people's rights now does not, however, imply that future people have rights now.[7] That implication would hold only if it were contended that presently existing rights alone constrain present action. But we can safely assume, first, that future people can be bearers of rights in the future; second, that the rights they have will be determined by the interests they have then; and, third, that our present actions and policies can affect their interests. Thus, if we can adversely affect future people's interests, we can violate their future rights. By causing damage to an embryo today, we can harm the interests and violate the rights of a future person. By causing damage to the environment today we can harm the interests of future people and violate their rights.[8]

Second, the fact that the composition and, indeed, the very existence of future people depend upon our decisions has given rise to doubts about whether they can be said to have any rights whatsoever that have their basis in duties required of us.[9] Indeed, we often find ourselves in decision-making situations in which future people are possible people for us insofar as their existence, identity and number depend upon our decision.[10] Can considerations based on

[6] Richard de George, 'The Environment, Rights, and Future Generations', in *Responsibilities to Future Generations. Environmental Ethics*, ed. Ernest Partridge (New York: Prometheus Books, 1981), 157–66, 161; see also Ruth Macklin, 'Can Future Generations Correctly Be Said to Have Rights?', in ibid., 151–6, 151 f.

[7] But see Ernest Partridge, 'On the Rights of Future People' in *Upstream/Downstream. Issues in Environmental Ethics*, ed. Donald Scherer (Philadelphia: Temple University, 1990), 40–66, 54 f. (suggesting that future people have rights in the present).

[8] See Norbert Hoerster, *Abtreibung im säkularen Staat. Argumente gegen den § 218* (Frankfurt: Suhrkamp, 1991), 98–102.

[9] See Thomas Schwartz, 'Obligations to Posterity', in *Obligations to Future Generations*, ed. R. I. Sikora and Brian Barry (Philadelphia: Temple University Press, 1978), 3–13; Gregory Kavka, 'The Paradox of Future Individuals', *Philosophy & Public Affairs* 11 (1982), 93–112; Derek Parfit, *Reasons and Persons* (Oxford: Clarendon Press, 1984), part iv.

[10] Here and in the following I rely on the distinction between *actual* and *possible* future people. If we take a decision on an action or a policy, and the likelihood of the existence of future people is (relatively) *independent* of our performing the action or carrying out the policy in question, then these future people are *actual* future people for us in this decision-making context. If, on the other hand, we take a decision on an action or a policy, and the likelihood of the existence of future people is (highly) *dependent* on our performing the action or carrying out the policy, then these future people are *possible* future people for us in this decision-making context. In short, the distinction between actual future people and possible future people turns on the decision-making context; these contexts differ, one from another, and because they do, the ways in which we relate to future people differ, too. In characterizing this distinction I follow the accounts as given by Trudy Govier in her 'What Should We Do About Future People?', *American Philosophical Quarterly* 16 (1979), 105–13, 106, and, particularly, David Heyd in his *Genethics. Moral Issues in the Creation of People* (Berkeley: University of California Press, 1992), 97–103. However, my wording differs from both. Govier distinguishes between 'epistemically possible people', and 'volitionally possible people'. She wants to stress that all future people are in an epistemic sense possible: we can only claim to have good reasons to believe that it is highly probable that there will be future people. Though this fact is of relevance both to the types of rights we can attribute to future people as well as to the weight we should assign to these rights, I believe the likelihood that there will be people in the foreseeable future

the rights of future people guide us in decision-making contexts in which future
people are possible future people for us with respect to their number and
identity? A decision that at least indirectly affects the identity and number of
future people can be guided, at least in part, by the rights of future people. This
is possible only if attributing rights to people does not require us to make reference to individual persons where the individuating properties of these persons
are fixed at the time at which we attribute rights to them. In such decision-
making contexts we can refer to future people as human beings. In doing so, we
attribute *some* identity to them. We attribute general and universal rights to
people for what they are: human beings, and not with an eye to the question of
which particular human beings they are, or to when and where they live. If in
such a decision-making context it is legitimate to refer to future people—
whoever they will be and in whatever numbers they will exist—as human
beings, then we refer to them under the description that is required for our
relating morally to them as human beings. If people, *qua* human beings, have
claims on us, then those future people who are actual for us with respect to their
existence have claims on us.[11] Thus, it may be the case that rights-based considerations do not bear merely upon 'same people choices' but will bear also
upon both types of 'different people choices' that Derek Parfit distinguishes,
including what he calls 'different number choices'. In 'same people choices' the
number and identity of people who are likely to be affected by the action we
choose to carry out are independent of our performing the action. In 'different
people choices' the identity of future people and in 'different number choices'
both the identity and number (that is, the composition) of future people are
dependent on our performing the action we choose.[12] If we assume that future
people have general (human) rights vis-à-vis us, our correlative duties set a
normative framework for most of our decisions concerning future people.[13]

is so great that it is not misleading to speak of *actual* future people as long as we keep in mind that
what we can know of future people can be expressed only in terms of probabilities. Heyd distinguishes between 'actual future people' and 'potential future people'. In certain contexts foetuses have
been called potential future people, relying on an Aristotelian concept of something's developing into
something else in the course of normal circumstances. I am not concerned here with questions
concerning the criteria for identifying something as a person.

[11] For attributing specific rights to a future person (or future people) one has to decide, *inter alia*,
what the relevant description of the person's identity is, and this will depend upon the particular
context at hand.

[12] Parfit, *Reasons and Persons* (n. 9 above), 355–6. For the purpose of explaining the idea that currently living people may face different people choices, Parfit adopts the genetic identity view of personal identity: the identity of a person is at least in part constituted by the DNA the person has as a
result of which ovum was fertilized by this or that spermatozoon in the creation of this person. Under
normal circumstances of reproduction the personal identity of a person depends upon the moment of
conception. However, adopting an alternative view of personal identity will not undermine the argument as long as the view allows that we face different people choices. We can be in decision-making
situations in which the composition of people who will come into existence, that is, the identity and
number of people who live in the future, depends upon the action or policy we choose.

[13] A rights-based approach can account for the asymmetry of our procreational duties: while we
have no obligation to procreate, some prospective parents should refrain from procreating, namely,
owing to the plight of the would-be child. When prospective parents learn that their child would have

III. HARMING FUTURE PEOPLE:
A SUBJUNCTIVE-THRESHOLD NOTION OF HARM

My claim that rights-considerations can guide us in making decisions on the composition of future people relies upon a subjunctive-threshold interpretation of harm. The contingency upon our decisions of the number of future people, as well as their specific identity, is immaterial when the question concerns our ability to harm future people's interests and to violate their rights. We know, of course, that when such instances of harm occur, specific people are harmed. But the decision we take counts as a necessary condition of the very existence of this genetically and numerically specific set of people at some future point in time. A subjunctive-threshold interpretation of harm, as suggested by my discussion, can be expressed in the following formula:

> (I) (subjunctive-threshold) Having acted in a certain way (or having refrained from acting in that way) at a time t_1, we thereby harm someone only if we cause this person's life to fall below some specified threshold.[14]

This interpretation of harm differs from both a diachronic interpretation of harm and an interpretation that requires a subjunctive comparison with a historical baseline (hereinafter subjunctive-historical interpretation of harm).[15] Both the diachronic and the subjunctive-historical interpretations of harm

---

a life not worth living, they should refrain from having it, for by bringing the child into existence they would cause harm to it (see Meyer, 'Can Actual Future People Have a Right to Non-Existence?' (n. 5 above)). But see Heyd, *Genethics* (n. 10 above), 102, 105 f., 241 f.

However, a framework of future persons' rights and currently living persons' correlative duties does not provide a complete moral theory of intergenerational relations. There are concerns for future people shared by many of us that cannot be accounted for by rights-based considerations: many of us believe that future people should have a life that is well above a minimal level of well-being or that they will share with us a particular way of life. Also, many of us believe that it is important that there be future people. However, we cannot, on the basis of considerations of rights of future people, prefer a future with people all of whom have lives far above the level of decency to a future with no people. Possible people have no right to be brought into existence (and we do not have the correlative obligation to procreate) (Meyer, 'More Than They Have a Right to: Future People and Our Future Oriented Projects' (n. 5 above), secs. 1. 1–3). I have suggested that the widely shared concerns about the continuation of human life on earth at a high level of well-being can, at least in part, be accounted for by an obligation towards future people to which no rights of future people correspond (ibid., sec. 2).

[14] See Joseph Raz, *The Morality of Freedom* (Oxford: Clarendon Press, 1986), 414.

[15] For the distinctions see Parfit, *Reasons and Persons* (n. 9 above), 487–90; James Woodward, 'The Non-Identity Problem', *Ethics* 96 (1986), 804–31, 818; E. Haavi Morreim, 'The Concept of Harm Reconceived: A Different Look at Wrongful Life', *Law and Philosophy* 7 (1988), 3–33, 23; James S. Fishkin, 'Justice between Generations: Compensation, Identity, and Group Membership' in *Compensatory Justice* (Nomos 33), ed. John W. Chapman (New York and London: New York University Press, 1991), 85–96; Fishkin, 'The Limits of Intergenerational Justice' in *Justice between Age Groups and Generations*, ed. Peter Laslett and James S. Fishkin (New Haven & London: Yale University Press, 1992), 62–83, 63–4; Sheana Shiffrin, 'Wrongful Life, Procreative Responsibility, and the Significance of Harm', *Legal Theory* 5 (1999), 117–48. For the wording of these notions of harm see Thomas W. Pogge, ' "Assisting" the Global Poor' in *The Ethics of Assistance: Morality*

require that the existence of the harmed person or people *qua* individuals is independent of the harming act or policy. The diachronic interpretation of harm can be expressed in the following formula:

> (II) (diachronic) Having acted in a certain way (or having refrained from acting in that way) at a time t_1, we thereby harm someone only if we cause this person to be worse off at some later time t_2[16] than the person was before we acted in this way, that is, before t_1.

The subjunctive-historical interpretation of harm can be expressed in the following formula:

> (III) (subjunctive-historical) Having acted in a certain way (or having refrained from acting in that way) at a time t_1, we thereby harm some-one only if we cause this person to be worse off at some later time t_2 than the person would have been at t_2 had we not interacted with this person at all.[17]

In decision-making contexts in which future people are possible future people, both the diachronic and the subjunctive-historical interpretations of harm will exclude the possibility of our harming future people. In such a decision-making context, currently living people cannot claim that the people whose interests and rights they are required to respect are in a particular state of well-being at the time they take their decision, or that specific future people will be better or worse off depending upon what decision they take. The former claim is implied by the reading of harm at (II), the latter by the reading of harm at (III). Reading of harm at (II) runs: unless we can claim that the person is in a particular state of well-being at the time of our decision, that is, at t_1, we cannot say that the person is worse off at t_2 owing to our decision at t_1. The reading of harm at (III) runs: unless we are in a position to claim that there is a specific person who

---

and the Distant Needy, ed. Deen K. Chatterjee (Cambridge: Cambridge University Press, forthcoming 2003).

[16] The formulation might be misleading in suggesting that by t_2 we refer to a moment of a person's life. Rather, the readings of harm as distinguished in this entry should be understood to allow for differing interpretations of the relevant unit of well-being (e.g., the life of the affected person as a whole, or future periods of her life). For discussions of how to interpret and measure the well-being of people see James Griffin, *Well-Being. Its Meaning, Measurement and Moral Importance* (Oxford: Clarendon, 1986), part i; Thomas Hurka, *Perfectionism* (New York, Oxford: Oxford University Press, 1993), ch. 6; Thomas M. Scanlon, *What We Owe To Each Other* (Cambridge, MA: Harvard University Press, 1998), ch. 3.

[17] We prefer 'had we not interacted with this person at all' to David Gauthier's 'in our absence' (Gauthier, *Morals by Agreement* (Oxford: Clarendon Press, 1986), 203–5). Both formulations are problematic and it is beyond the scope of this entry to discuss their respective problems at length. Gauthier himself points out that his formulation has difficulties in dealing with situations in which a person has assumed a certain social role, e.g., the role of a life-guard that is, in part, defined by positive duties vis-à-vis others. If a person assumes such a role, her 'absence' in a situation where she is duty-bound to intervene can worsen the situation of others (ibid., 205). For the formulation we prefer, it seems plausible to suggest that assuming such a role does constitute an 'interaction' of the then duty-bound person with those to whom she owes the fulfilment of the duties of her role.

would have been better off at t_2 than the person would have been at t_2 had we not interacted with this person at all, this notion of harm makes no sense.

Adopting either the diachronic or the subjunctive-historical interpretations of harm excludes the possibility of our harming future people when we choose among long-term policies with significantly differing consequences for the quality of life of future people. But if we adopt the subjunctive-threshold reading of harm at (I), future people can be said to be wronged by our having chosen a policy that harms them, notwithstanding the fact that the existence of the specific people who are said to be harmed is caused by our having chosen to pursue this policy.[18]

To be sure, we will still have to specify a standard for judging the adoption of a long-term policy as wrong owing to its likely consequences for future people. The identity-independent interpretation of harm presupposes our being able positively to describe a standard of well-being in such a way that we violate a person's right when we cause this person to fall below the standard specified or when this person fails to reach the standard owing to a lack of causal intervention on our part.[19]

IV. CURRENTLY LIVING PEOPLE'S CLAIMS TO COMPENSATION OWING TO INJUSTICES COMMITTED AGAINST THEIR PREDECESSORS

I now turn to the question of whether currently living people can be said to have just claims to compensation owing to the fact that their predecessors were badly wronged. There is, for example, the case of African Americans, whose

[18] This is why this type of notion of harm is also called identity-independent. See Fishkin, 'The Limits of Intergenerational Justice' (n. 15 above), 63–4.

[19] Such a standard can specify a *sufficientarian* threshold defined in terms of absolute, non-comparative conditions. Then currently living people harm future people by causing them to fall below this threshold or by not helping them to reach the threshold. Shiffrin outlines such a threshold notion of harm in 'Wrongful Life, Procreative Responsibility, and the Significance of Harm' (n. 15 above), 123 f. For a discussion of such a rights-based understanding of the threshold see Jeff McMahan in 'Wrongful Life: Paradoxes in the Morality of Causing People to Exist' in *Rational Commitment and Social Justice. Essays for Gregory Kavka*, ed. Jules Coleman and C. Morris (Cambridge: Cambridge University Press, 1998), 208–47, 223–9. However, I do not mean to exclude the possibility of *egalitarian* conceptions of subjunctive-threshold harm. According to one interpretation of an egalitarian reading of the standard employed by a subjunctive-threshold notion of harm, currently living people harm future people by causing them to realize a (much) lower level of well-being than their contemporaries. In 'Compensation and Transworld Personal Identity', *Monist* 62 (1979), 378–91, 389, George Sher suggests that the standard could be specified by reference to the well-being realized by the average member of the society to which the claimant belongs whose existence and low level of well-being was caused by the wrong committed against his predecessors. A subjunctive-threshold notion of harm could also be egalitarian in requiring that each generation stand under the duty to 'leave people in the future with the possibility of not falling below' its level of well-being. See Brian Barry, 'Sustainability and Intergenerational Justice' in *Fairness and Futurity. Essays on Environmental Sustainability*, ed. Andrew Dobson (Oxford: Oxford University Press, 1999), 93–117, 109.

ancestors were subjected to terrible injustices in being kidnapped in Africa and
then enslaved. Do their descendants have a just claim to compensation?[20] I will
set aside a host of specifically legal questions concerning, for example, statutes
of limitations and the question of who is liable. Also, I shall assume that in a
specific case concerning an individual person, let us call him Robert, his parent-
age has been settled. He is a descendant of those who were forcefully brought
to America as slaves.[21]

   People can make claims to compensation for harms suffered by them. As a
descendant of slaves, has Robert been harmed owing to the injustices suffered
by his ancestors? First, I shall turn briefly to the subjunctive-historical reading
of harm at (III). According to this interpretation of harm, a person is fully compensated for an act or policy (or event[22]) when she is as well off as she would
be if the act had not been carried out. According to this interpretation of harm,
it is not the case that Robert has been harmed for the reason that his ancestors
were kidnapped and enslaved. If his ancestors had not been kidnapped and
enslaved, Robert would not exist today. His existence depends on the fact that
the genealogical chain was not broken at any point. Hence, the initial kidnap-
ping in Africa, the transport to America, and the slavery of his ancestors are
(most likely)[23] necessary conditions for Robert's having come into existence at

---

   [20] For recent contributions to this debate see, for example, part 6 'Slavery', part 7 'Jim Crow' in
When Sorry Isn't Enough. The Controversy over Apologies and Reparations for Human Injustice,
ed. Roy L. Brooks (New York and London: New York University Press, 1999); Wole Soyinka,
'Reparations, Truth, and Reconciliation' in Soyinka, *The Burden of Memory, the Muse of
Forgiveness* (New York: Oxford University Press, 1999), 23–92, 44–69; Robert Fullinwider, 'The
Case for Reparations', *Philosophy & Public Policy* 20 (2000).
   [21] See Fishkin, 'Justice between Generations: Compensation, Identity, and Group Membership' (n.
15 above), 91–3.
   [22] People can be harmed by events, say, by a natural catastrophe. The following reasoning applies
when such an event occurs before the person who makes the claim for compensation in light of the
event comes into existence.
   [23] The moment of conception does not necessarily determine the genetic identity of a child. More
than one directly reproductive act can give rise to the same child. A couple having sexual intercourse
at different times could still give rise to the same child, as long as the ovum is the same, that is, within
one period. Even within the same period, a couple having sexual intercourse at different times is likely
to give rise to different people, given the huge amount of competing spermatozoa at stake and the high
likelihood of the ovum being fertilized by a different spermatozoon. Then alternative actions that are
non-reproductive but affect the reproductive behaviour of people and thus the moment of conception
do not necessarily give rise to genetically different people. Also, in the laboratory a technician might
be able to bring about now or at a different time, the genetically identical person by using the same
spermatozoon and the same ovum. Then a probabilistic and a necessarian reading of Parfit's 'Time-
Dependence Claim' (*Reasons and Persons* (n. 9 above), 351–2) can be distinguished and, thus, the
scope of the non-identity problem. According to the necessarian reading it matters that the same person or people could have existed had we not carried out the act or policy. Whether it is in fact likely
or unlikely to have happened does not matter. According to the probabilistic reading, if it were
extremely unlikely and the probability was close to zero, it is reasonable to hold that the same person
would not have existed. The latter view can be attributed to Parfit (ibid., 352). For discussion whether
it normatively matters that genetically identical people can be brought about by different acts and
under different circumstances, see A. John Simmons, 'Historical Rights and Fair Shares', *Law and
Philosophy* 12 (1995), 149, 178–9; Melinda A. Roberts, *Child versus Childmaker. Future Persons and
Present Duties in Ethics and the Law* (Lanham: Rowman & Littlefield, 1998), secs. 3.4 and 3.5.

all. He would not have been better off had his ancestors not been badly wronged. Thus, we cannot rely upon this interpretation of harm and its accompanying interpretation of compensation in claiming that Robert has been harmed and should be compensated; the required state of affairs implies the nonexistence of the claimant in question.[24]

Secondly, we might briefly consider the subjunctive-threshold reading of harm at (I). According to this interpretation of harm, a person is fully compensated for an act or policy (or event) if that person does not fall below the specified standard at a particular time. Robert can be harmed because his ancestors were kidnapped and enslaved. Whether Robert has been harmed due to the way his ancestors were treated depends upon whether the way they were treated has led to Robert's falling below the standard of well-being specified. That this is true in the case of Robert, however, will turn on his current state of well-being. Employing this interpretation of harm and its accompanying interpretation of compensation requires a forward-looking assessment of what we ought to do today. When we analyse historical claims on the basis of such a subjunctive-threshold interpretation of harm, the normative relevance of past wrongs will depend upon their causal relevance for the well-being of currently living (and future people). Fulfilling our duties to currently (and future) living people might well require that we counteract the consequences that stem from the fact that their predecessors have been badly wronged. That their predecessors were wronged, however, does not by itself give rise to just claims to compensation by their descendants today.

A forward-looking analysis of this character, directed to the moral relevance of historical injustices, is endorsed by liberal cosmopolitans. As shown, such an analysis is based on a subjunctive-threshold notion of harm. Liberal cosmopolitans also claim that future people have general human rights vis-à-vis us. This claim, too, is best understood as based upon a subjunctive-threshold interpretation of harm. By means of the subjunctive-threshold interpretation of harm, the forward-looking understanding of the relevance of historical injustices is tied to the cosmopolitan endorsement of future people's general human rights.

In what follows, I will discuss what are the most challenging objections to the understanding of harmful acts and policies in intergenerational relations, as it is sketched in this entry. In responding to these objections I will delineate two alternative readings of the relation between the subjunctive-historical and subjunctive-threshold interpretations of harm introduced above. According to the first reading, the subjunctive-threshold interpretation and the subjunctive-historical interpretations of harm are mutually exclusive. This will be called the 'exclusive subjunctive-threshold' or the 'exclusive subjunctive-historical view of harm': we will have to adopt either the subjunctive-threshold or the subjunctive-historical interpretations of harm as specifying alternative necessary conditions

---

[24] We cannot rely on the diachronic notion at (II) either. It presupposes that we can attribute a state of well-being to the descendant at the time his or her ancestors are being wronged.

of harm; if we adopt one of these, we have to deny that the other interpretation specifies necessary (or sufficient) conditions of harm. According to the second interpretation, the subjunctive-threshold interpretation of harm and the subjunctive-historical interpretations can be combined. According to the 'combined view', the necessary condition for harming is the disjunction of the conditions for harming as set out by the readings of harm at (I) and (III).[25]

V. Problems for a threshold conception of harm

The following set of objections is meant to show that the subjunctive-threshold interpretation of harm is both over- and under-inclusive. On the one hand, the interpretation is said to assess acts as objectionably harmful that seem clearly not to be so. On the other hand, the subjunctive-threshold interpretation of harm does not seem to allow us to count acts as harmful that most of us would firmly describe as such. In response, I will attempt to defend the subjunctive-threshold interpretation of harm against these objections. I will initially consider the subjunctive-threshold interpretation of harm as the only sound interpretation of harm. I will then propose and discuss an understanding of harm that combines the subjunctive-threshold and subjunctive-historical interpretations of harm. While the combined view of harm will be shown not to be open to the objections discussed in this section, this understanding of harm raises difficult questions of interpretation of its own. I will consider then whether the combined view of harm is compatible with what Parfit has called the 'no-difference view'.

The first of these objections proceeds as follows: according to the subjunctive-threshold interpretation of harm, I could be in a position in which *whatever* I do at t_1, I will harm a person by causing this person to be worse off at some later time t_2 than the person should then be, or I will allow the person to be worse off than he should be. For example, a physician might face a situation in which he either allows a patient to die of natural causes or he intervenes, thereby improving the patient's condition, but still leaving him below the threshold, since the intervention requires, say, a disfiguring medical procedure.[26]

The idea that, in such a situation, whatever I might do at t_1, I thereby cause or allow harm to happen and violate a person's right not to be harmed is

---

[25] It is worth noting that in discussing the combined view, it is superfluous to consider notion (II): when notion (II) is applicable, notion (III) is applicable as well; notion (II) is applicable when counterfactual considerations play no role in the application of notion (III).

[26] For this example see McMahan 'Wrongful Life: Paradoxes in the Morality of Causing People to Exist' (n. 19 above), 221–2. As used here, the example presupposes that if the person had not died, this would have been better for her even though she would have been disfigured. Saying this does not require that we compare the value of the state of being dead to the value of continuing to exist for the person in question. See Raz, *Value, Respect, and Attachment* (Cambridge: Cambridge University Press, 2001), 85.

counterintuitive and clearly mistaken. In the situation as described, the physician cannot avoid acting in a way that is harmful to other people in the sense of not preventing them to fall below the threshold. In such a situation, attributing to a person the obligation of not causing such harm makes no sense. Such an attribution would violate the minimal requirement understood in '"ought" implies "can"': it does not make sense to require that people do what is impossible.[27] In response to the objection as stated, we do not have to give up the reading of harm at (I).

However, even in a situation in which we cannot prevent other people from falling below the threshold, we might still be in a position to choose among courses of action that differ in terms of the severity of the harm we cause. We should prevent a person from falling to the worse sub-threshold state where we are in a position to cause the person to be in a different and better, but still sub-threshold, state. As the subjunctive-threshold notion of harm at (I) does not imply this, we will want to amend this understanding by the requirement that people ought to minimize harm.

In the context of procreational decision-making we might face a situation where we cannot appeal to having fulfilled the duty of minimizing harm in order to justify our decision to cause the existence of a person. In this context it may simply not be true that whatever we do at t_1, we will harm a person by causing this person to be worse off at some later time t_2 than the person should then be. By refraining from procreation, we do not harm anybody. Then we cannot justify our decision on the basis that the person we bring into existence is better, or at least as well off, as the other possible people whom we could have brought into existence. However, the duty to minimize (subjunctive-threshold) harm can be relevant in 'different people' and 'different number' choices (section 2 above). When we face such a situation we might well be in a position in which we can neither hinder the coming into existence of a future person or future people nor prevent them from falling below the threshold. At the same time, we might be in a position to exercise influence on, or to determine, how far below the threshold the person or people will stand. We are then under the duty to minimize the subjunctive-threshold harm to 'these' people.

I now turn to the second objection: the threshold conception of harm is under-inclusive in interpreting which acts we consider harmful. Again, we will have to appeal to an obligation to minimize harm in interpreting cases that present clear cases of harmful acts to many of us. Taken by itself, the subjunctive-threshold interpretation is under-inclusive by not qualifying these acts as objectionably harmful. In the first type of case, the person is living a life below the threshold as specified and nothing we can do will improve the person's life in such a way that he has a life with well-being above the threshold. If, under these circumstances, someone acts in a way that diminishes the well-being of such a person to an even lower level, this act cannot be described, according to

[27] As opposed to what people could perfectly well do if they chose to and made a serious effort.

the reading of harm at (I), as causing harm to the person. This, however, seems to be strongly counterintuitive. For example, we clearly harm a person who is severely handicapped by causing pain to him. By appealing to an obligation to minimize harm to other persons, we can argue that we are forbidden to cause another person to fall to an even lower level of well-being as measured by the specified threshold.

In the second type of case, the person is living above the threshold as specified and we can act in a way that diminishes the well-being of the person, but to a level that is still above the threshold. For example, someone breaks into the garage of a mansion and steals the new convertible while the wealthy owner is at his penthouse in the city. Whatever the owner's attachment to his new car, the theft is not likely to cause the wealthy person's well-being to fall below any plausibly construed threshold of harm; the act cannot be described as causing harm to this person according to the reading of harm at (I). Again, we can appeal to an obligation of minimizing harm to other persons. The obligation requires that we not cause another person to fall to a lower level of well-being quite independently of the level of well-being the person already realizes. What counts as a lower level of well-being can be measured by the specified threshold.

If the first objection is meant to show that the threshold conception of harm is over-inclusive, the second objection is supposed to show that it is under-inclusive in interpreting which acts we consider harmful. In defending the subjunctive-threshold reading of harm at (I) against these objections, I have assumed that we should interpret this reading of harm as specifying a necessary condition for harming someone (and the subjunctive-historical reading at (III) as specifying neither necessary nor sufficient conditions). In defending this exclusive view of what it means to harm someone, I introduced, first, the idea that we have an obligation to minimize harm where we have an obligation to avoid doing harm; and, second, in response to objection one, the notion that if in certain situations you cannot prevent a person from suffering (subjunctive-threshold) harm, you do not cause harm—you do not, that is, if you fulfill the duty of minimizing harm.

These points are, I think, satisfactory as replies to the objections as stated. However, what I called the combined view makes it possible for us to avoid the problem of the under-inclusiveness of the subjunctive-threshold reading of harm as exemplified by objection two. The proposal is this: instead of interpreting readings of harm at (I) and (III) as providing alternative necessary conditions for harming, we can understand the readings at (I) and (III) as sufficient conditions; the necessary condition for harming is then the disjunction of the conditions for harming as set out by the readings at (I) and (III). This is the combined view (CV) of what it means to harm someone:

(CV) Having acted in a certain way (or having refrained from acting in that way) at a time t_1, we thereby harm someone only if either (I) we cause this person's life to fall below some specified standard, and, if we cannot avoid causing harm in this sense, do not minimize the harm; or (III) we cause this person to be worse off at some later time t_2 than the person would have been at t_2 had we not interacted with this person at all.

We ought clearly to prefer the combined view to the exclusive subjunctive-historical view according to which the subjunctive-historical reading of harm specifies necessary conditions of harm (and the subjunctive-threshold reading at (I) specifies neither necessary nor sufficient conditions). The combined view is compatible with the thesis of this essay that relies upon us employing a subjunctive-threshold interpretation of harm where the subjunctive-historical and the diachronic notions cannot be employed to interpret the cases as cases of harm.[28]

Ought we to prefer the combined view to the exclusive subjunctive-threshold view according to which the subjunctive-threshold interpretation of harm specifies the necessary and sufficient conditions of harm? Assuming that my response to the first objection is satisfactory with respect to those cases to which the subjunctive-historical notion of harm is inapplicable (that is, to 'different people' and 'different number' choices), the advantage of the combined view is that this understanding of harm allows us to rely on the subjunctive-historical interpretation of harm whenever it is applicable, that is, when we will harm an already existing person. In these cases, notion of harm at (III) provides us with a straightforward interpretation of the harm caused. We will not have to appeal to the duty to minimize harm. Objections one and two present cases in which the affected person is clearly harmed—namely, when we harm an already existing person and the conditions are according to the subjunctive-historical reading at (III).

However, this combined view of harm raises difficult questions of interpretation of its own. In the next section I consider whether the combined view is compatible with what Parfit has called the 'no-difference view'.

VI. DEREK PARFIT'S NO-DIFFERENCE VIEW

The exclusive subjunctive-threshold view of harm is compatible with Parfit's no-difference view, which, on one understanding, states that it makes no difference

---

[28] Of course, not only our (CV) as stated above fulfills this requirement. Any combined view that entails notion of harm at (I) as a sufficient condition for causing harm will fulfill this requirement. Thomas W. Pogge suggested to me an understanding of the combined view that gives priority to the subjunctive-historical notion of harm:

(CV*) Having acted in a certain way (or having refrained from acting in that way) at a time t_1, we thereby harm someone only if either (III) we cause this person to be worse off at some later time t_2 than the person would have been at t_2 had we not interacted with this person at all; or this test is inapplicable and (I) we cause this person's life to fall below some specified standard, and, if we cannot avoid causing harm in this sense, do not minimize the harm.

For discussion see ns. 30 and 33 below.

to how we should act, all things considered, whether the size and identity of future generations depend upon our decision. Parfit illustrates this view by considering two medical programmes.[29] One involves pregnancy testing. If the test comes out positive, foetuses are treated for a rare condition. The other involves preconception testing for an incurable condition of women that will result in the same particular handicap in the children these women might have. The women found to have this condition are told to postpone conception for at least two months after which the condition will have disappeared. The available funds can be spent on one or the other programme. Assuming that both pro- grammes have equivalent effects on parents, that the conditions lead to the same particular handicap in children, and that the two programmes will achieve results in as many cases, the programmes differ only in affecting actual people (pregnancy testing) or possible people (preconception testing). The no-difference view in its practical reading says: the objection of our not preventing the harm- ing of possible future people (those who might be conceived) is as strong as the objection of our similarly not preventing the harming of actual people (those already conceived who will develop from the already existing foetuses in due course). The two medical programmes in Parfit's example are equally worthy and it makes no moral difference which is cancelled.

Is the combined view of harm compatible with the no-difference view, thus understood? Here I cannot discuss the implications of the combined view in any detail. I might first observe that both the subjunctive-historical and sub- junctive-threshold readings of harm can be employed to interpret many core cases of harm. That is to say, both sets of conditions as specified by the two readings of harm will arguably be satisfied in many cases where most people agree that harm was caused—at least under plausible interpretations of both readings of harm. Second, in the cases in which not all sets of conditions obtain, we still find that harm was caused, namely, as long as at least one set of condi- tions obtains. If the subjunctive-threshold reading of harm applies, we find that harm was caused. The combined view entails that cancelling either test causes harm.

However, the combined view does not entail that it makes no moral differ- ence which test we cancel. A plausible interpretation of the combined view might be the following: satisfying each set of the conditions (as specified by each reading of harm) provides a reason for objecting to the harm caused; if two sets of conditions obtain, we have two reasons for objecting and thus, the objection is presumably stronger than if only one set of conditions obtains.[30]

---

[29] Parfit, *Reasons and Persons* (n. 9 above), 367.

[30] According to (CV*) (see above n. 28) only one set of conditions (as specified by each reading of harm) can obtain. (CV*) might also imply that it makes a moral difference which test we cancel. It might well make a moral difference in view of the particular reason we have for objecting to the cancellation of either test. However, (CV*) will not give us two reasons for objecting to the cancel- lation of pregnancy testing. Thus, we could not interpret the supposed difference in terms of there

According to this understanding of the combined view and assuming that—in Parfit's example of the two medical programs—the children, if either they or their mothers are not treated, will suffer under a severe handicap, the objection to cancelling pregnancy testing is stronger than the objection to cancelling the preconception testing program. Because the handicap is severe, the children will fall below the threshold and the subjunctive-threshold notion of harm provides the same reason for objecting to cancelling either programme. If pregnancy testing is cancelled this will be worse for the children who are not treated. The subjunctive-historical notion of harm applies. Cancelling the programme means allowing these children to suffer under the particular handicap. The subjunctive-historical notion does not provide a reason for objecting to the cancellation of the preconception testing. The children who will be born handicapped would never have existed if there had been testing prior to conception.[31] Then this understanding of the combined view may not be compatible with the no-difference view. Harming possible future people can be less objectionable than harming actual people even if we cause the people to be in the same state. Harming the latter is more objectionable because the subjunctive-historical notion is applicable. At least, this is one reading of the combined view. An alternative reading would deny that where both notions of harm are applicable, this strengthens the objection to the harmful act.

The exclusive subjunctive-threshold view of harm is also compatible with a second and stronger reading of the no-difference view: there is no theoretical difference in harming possible future people and harming actual people since we have the very same reasons for objecting to harming possible future people and harming actual people.[32] This is true only if we rely on one and the same reading of harm in identifying all cases of harmful acts. The combined view is clearly incompatible with the theoretical interpretation of the no-difference view. According to the combined view, it would often not be true that we have the same reasons to object to harming possible future people and to harming actual people. When we object to the harming of actual people we will

being two reasons for objecting to the cancellation of the pregnancy testing and just one reason for objecting to the cancellation of preconception testing.

[31] It is assumed here that in the context of taking a decision on whether or not to treat the foetuses, the foetuses are actual future people (see sec. 2). In other words, the treatment of the foetuses will not have the compositional effects as might be induced by post-conception genetic interventions. For the feasibility of such post-conception genetic therapy and surgery and their implications for interpreting wrongful life claims, see Allen Buchanan, Dan W. Brock, Norman Daniels, and Daniel Wikler, *From Chance to Choice. Genetics & Justice* (Cambridge: Cambridge University Press, 2000), 6 and ch. 6. If pregnancy testing leads to post-conception intervention that has compositional effects, Parfit's two medical programmes become indistinguishable with respect to the applicability of the subjunctive-historical notion of harm.

[32] For the distinction between and a discussion of these two versions of the no-difference view, see Woodward, 'The Non-Identity Problem' (n. 15 above), secs. ii and iii; Derek Parfit, 'Comments', *Ethics* 96 (1986), 832–72, 856–9.

often have additional reasons that reflect the fact that the subjunctive-historical readings of harm apply.[33]

However, the thesis of this paper is compatible with the combined view of harm and does not depend upon either version of the no-difference view.[34] Present generations have obligations not to violate the rights of future people against being harmed even if—as the combined view implies—the reasons offered as to why harming possible future people is objectionable are different from (and possibly less weighty than) the reasons for objecting to acts that cause harm to actual people. Accordingly, present generations have obligations to compensate currently living people for the harms that accrue to them owing to the lasting impact of injustices committed against their predecessors, even if the reasons for providing them with compensation are different from (and possibly less weighty than) the reasons for compensating people whose identities are not caused (or changed) by the harmful acts.

VII. CONCLUSION

Two claims, characteristic of the cosmopolitan position and of some importance for assessing claims of currently living people wherever they might live, are, I believe, systematically related. Cosmopolitans typically claim that future people have general (human) rights vis-à-vis us. And they claim that the significance of history lies in the consequences of past events for the well-being of currently living and future people. I have offered an interpretation according to which both of these claims are based upon a subjunctive-threshold notion of harm. If we adopt either the exclusive subjunctive-threshold view of harm or the combined view, future people can be said to be wronged by our having chosen a policy that harms them even where the existence of the specific people said to be harmed is caused by our having chosen this policy. Secondly, currently living people (and future people) can be said to have been harmed because wrongs suffered by their predecessors cause them to fall below a certain standard of well-being. Such a forward-looking understanding of the grounds for our relating to

---

[33] Note that (CV*) (n. 28 above) is also incompatible with the theoretical reading of the no-difference view. According to (CV*) we have different (but not additional) reasons for objecting to the harming of actual people.

[34] There are other reasons for preferring the combined over the exclusive view. The combined view is compatible with the central understanding of harm and compensation as these notions are normally understood in tort law. In cases which do not involve the non-identity problem and in which the harmful act reduces the well-being of the victim to a level that is still above the threshold, the identity-dependent notion of harm provides the relevant standard for restitution and compensation. For a discussion of how to apply the standard where counterfactual considerations play an important role, see *The Commonwealth of Australia v. Amann Aviation PTY. Limited (1992) 174 CLR 64 F.C. 91/043*; and Alberta Law Reform Institute, *Should a Claim for the Loss of a Chance of Future Earnings Survive Death?*, Report No. 76 (December 1998).

both past and future reflects the broadly consequentialist, value-individualistic and universalistic framework of the (liberal) cosmopolitan.[35]

---

[35] I might add two qualifications. First, we will be able to determine whether future people are being wronged and whether currently living people have legitimate claims to compensation owing to wrongs suffered by their predecessors only if we succeed in working out an interpretation of harm that specifies the necessary and sufficient conditions for wrongful harm-doing. In this paper I have presented neither an understanding of wrong-doing nor a substantive view of what counts as subjunctive-threshold harm. Second, the forward-looking interpretation of the relevance of historical injustices is incomplete when understood as a statement of how we ought to respond to the fact that past people were severely wronged. The forward-looking understanding should be seen as providing an understanding of the significance of historical injustices for the specification of currently living persons' rights and their correlative duties. If we allow that intergenerational relations are not governed exclusively by duties with correlative rights, the notion that we can have moral duties towards dead people who are not bearers of rights is compatible with the forward-looking understanding of the significance of historical injustice. Our relations to future people are not exclusively governed by considerations of rights of future people either. However, and unlike past people, people who will live in the future can be said to have rights vis-à-vis us.

10

Group Rights

JAMES GRIFFIN

I. THREE GENERATIONS OF RIGHTS

Political theorists sometimes speak of different generations of rights. The first generation are the classic liberty rights of the seventeenth and eighteenth centuries—freedom of expression, of assembly, of worship, and the like. The second generation are the welfare rights of the mid-twentieth century—positive rights to aid—in contrast, it is thought, to the purely negative rights of the first generation. The third generation, the rights of our time, of the last twenty years or so, are 'solidarity' rights, including most prominently group rights.[1] A people, a nation, a race, an ethnic or cultural or linguistic or religious group are now often said to have rights. Group rights—at least the most interesting form of them—are supposed not to be reducible to the individual rights of their members. They are supposed to be rights that groups have as groups.

The appearance of group rights seems to me regrettable. It is part of a widespread modern movement to make the discourse of rights do most of the important work in ethics, which it was neither designed to do nor should now be made to do. That is the burden of this paper.

II. INDIVIDUAL RIGHTS

Let me start—to set the scene—with a few remarks about first and second generation rights.

According to the tradition, a human right is one that a person has, not by virtue of any special status or relation to others, but simply by virtue of being human. But to apply the term 'human right' we have to be able to tell what rights we have simply by virtue of being human, and we have little agreement about the relevant sense of 'human'. There are very many cases in which we have no agreed criteria to determine whether the term is being correctly or

---

[1] See Karel Vasak, 'Pour une Troisième Génération des Droits de l'Homme' in *Studies and Essays on International Law and Red Cross Principles*, ed. Christophe Swinarski (The Hague: Martinus Nijhoff, 1984), 837–43. The fit between what Vasak says about solidarity rights and what, in recent discussion, philosophers have tended to say in definition of group rights is not perfect. But the two notions are close, and there is a virtually complete coincidence in examples. In any case, my interest is in group rights.

incorrectly used. That is why supposed human rights have proliferated with so little control. Of course, 'human right' is what has been called an 'essentially contestable concept', but that a concept is essentially contestable does not relieve it of the need to be tolerably determinate.

Now, there are, I think, plausible ways of making the term 'human right' tolerably determinate and useful. What seems to me the best account of human rights is this. It is centred on the notion of agency. We humans have the capacity to form pictures of what a good life would be and to try to realize these pictures. We value our status as agents especially highly, often more highly even than our happiness. Human rights can then be seen as protections of our human standing, our agency. They are protections, then, of that somewhat austere state, the life of an agent, and not of a good or happy or perfected or flourishing life. It is not that what human rights protect is clearly the most important aspect of our life; the nature and degree of its importance remains to be seen. But it is what various Renaissance and Enlightenment philosophers have marked off with the notion of 'human dignity'. We attach special importance to it, and that is reason enough to mark it off, too, with the language of human rights.

To link human rights to what I just called the somewhat austere state of human agency seems to be both what the tradition supports and the proper stipulation to make. If we had rights to all that is needed for a good or happy life, then the language of rights would become redundant. We already have a perfectly clear and compact way of speaking about individual well-being and any obligations there might be to promote it.

Personhood is *one* ground of human rights, but it could not be the only one; it leaves rights still too indeterminate. Personhood tells us that each of us has a right to *some* political voice. But in what form? It tells us that we have a right to *minimum* material resources. How much is that? We have a right to security of person. What does that exclude? Would it exclude forcibly taking a little of my blood? Pricking my finger would hardly destroy my personhood. But what happens if we up the stakes? Does the right to security of person not protect me against, say, the health authority that wants one of my kidneys? After all, the few weeks that it would take me to recover from a kidney extraction would not prevent me from living a recognizably human life either. Where is the line to be drawn? What is clear is that, on its own, the personhood consideration is not up to fixing anything approaching a determinate enough line for practice. And unless we had something determinate enough to work as an effective, socially manageable claim on others, it is doubtful that we should say that a right yet exists. There are practical considerations: to be effective the line has to be clear and so not take too many complicated bends; we should probably have to leave a generous safety-margin. So to make the right to security of person determinate enough, we need another ground, call it practicalities. We also need to consult human nature, the nature of society, and so on, in drawing the line.

The existence conditions for a human right would then be these. One establishes the existence of such a right by showing, first, that it protects an essential feature of human standing and, second, that its determinate content results from the sorts of practical considerations that I have very roughly sketched.

This is not the only way that one might go about attaching existence conditions to human rights, although it seems to me the best. I mention these particular existence conditions solely as an example of the sort of thing we need, and I shall not later assume their correctness. I think that we can, in the end, make 'human rights' a useful term in ethics. I doubt, however, that we can do the same for the term 'group rights'.

III. No quick way of dismissing group rights

It is not that there is a simple flaw in the very idea of a group right, although some say there is. Some think that only persons (or agents) can have rights (I am not talking about human rights here, but rights in general) and that this fact alone rules out animals, trees, and most human groups from having rights. For instance, some say that one can have rights only if one can also have duties,[2] because they think that the ability to bear rights is necessarily part of a package that includes the capacity to discharge duties. Others say that most rights should themselves be seen as packages, that many of them can be analysed into, among other things, liberties and powers[3] (Hohfeldian components). Therefore, both groups conclude, only persons can bear rights because only persons can have duties or exercise liberties or powers. The word 'person', they concede, must be understood here in a broad sense that includes 'artificial persons'. For example, it should be understood as including legal persons such as corporations, schools, and clubs. These legal persons are person-like in the necessary sense, because they too can decide, act, accept responsibility for their actions, have duties, make amends, and so on.

Groups, then, are said to be person-like only if they have the kind of fairly complex internal organization that allows them to decide, act, and so on. Corporations, schools, and clubs can have it. Parliament has it, which is why it made sense for the English Declaration of Rights of 1689 to assert the rights of Parliament against the Crown. But it is striking that many groups for which nowadays group rights are often claimed lack it.[4] Recent Hispanic immigrants to the United States, blacks, women, and the elderly all lack the requisite

---

[2] E.g. Roger Scruton, 'Groups Do Not Have Rights', *The Times*, London, 21 December 1995.

[3] Although he does not regard it as a conclusive objection to group rights, this is Carl Wellman's 'most fundamental' doubt about them in his book *The Proliferation of Rights* (Boulder: Westview Press, 1999) ch. 2, which has influenced other parts of my discussion too.

[4] What sorts of groups are said to have (group) rights? Some group rights seem to be claimed simply for humanity at large (rights to peace and to the integrity of the environment). Other group rights are attributed to a 'people' or a 'nation' (Article 1 of the *Universal Declaration of the Rights of Peoples* says: 'Every people has the right to existence'). Yet other rights are attributed to a cultural or ethnic group—for instance, to the survival of its culture (which will be very similar to the preceding right if, as is likely, that is meant to go beyond mere physical survival to survival *as*

internal organization. It is true that occasionally a non-agent-like group acts collectively. A mob might spontaneously collect in the streets and, united by strong common grievance, act as one and, say, storm the Bastille or the Winter Palace. It is doubtful, though, that having this sort of ephemeral unity would be enough, on this conception, to have rights, but recent Hispanic immigrants, blacks, women, and the elderly lack even ephemeral unity. So they clearly do not (or do not as such) have rights. Or so this attack on group rights goes.

It is an attack which, to repeat, does not seem to me to succeed. Many people have already extended the use of the word 'rights' beyond persons—for instance, to foetuses, animals, and eco-systems. They have already abandoned the requirement that rights-holders be agents. And why not? The use of words changes. The question is whether this change gives us a more helpful moral vocabulary. And the answer to that question cannot be quick. We have to look at what sort of case there is for introducing group rights, and whether it yields a tolerably clear and useful term.

IV. A CASE FOR GROUP RIGHTS: THE GOOD-BASED ARGUMENT

What seems to me the best case for *individual* human rights takes this form: it finds a class of goods (in the case of human rights, the individual goods comprising agency) with the sort of importance that attracts the protection afforded by rights. One case for group rights mimics this case for individual rights; it claims to find goods that can be attributed only to groups, then tries to show that this new kind of good attracts the protection of a new kind of right, namely group rights.

If this form of argument is successfully to yield rights not reducible to individual rights, then we need group goods of a quite special kind. They cannot, for instance, be merely what economists call *public goods*. The term 'public good' lacks sharp boundaries, but three important features that contribute to a good's being 'public' are that it is non-excludable (that is, it cannot be designed so that it benefits some people but not others), non-rivalrous (that is, its enjoyment by

a 'people' or 'nation'). There are rights attributed to various deprived groups (rights to equal treatment to women, blacks, the poor, the disabled, the old). There are rights attributed to a society (a right to fraternity, tolerance, and to the conditions for achieving a certain degree of prosperity). Then sometimes rights are attributed to any group, membership of which is important enough to be part of one's self-respect (a right for the group not to be defamed or reviled, not to be made the object of hate-speech).

What is striking about the items on this short-list, and what lends some force to the quick way of dismissing group rights, is that virtually none of them is, as such, agent-like. A 'society' may be an exception; it all depends upon what kind of organization is required by the concept. A 'nation' may look like another exception, but the word is not used here of anything that need have political organization but could be applied, say, to the Apache nation, whether or not the Apaches constituted a political entity.

For an examination of how corporations and less formal associations (down to mobs) can act as groups, see Larry May, *The Morality of Groups* (Notre Dame: University of Notre Dame Press, 1987), 31–57.

some does not compete with its enjoyment by others), and jointly produced (or, at least, produced by many). Clean air and secure defence are standard examples. Although the entities to which we should most naturally attribute clean air and secure defence are fairly large groups, the values involved in public goods are individual in both their enjoyment and conception. The benefit of clean air and secure defence is enjoyed by each member of the group individually. And to the extent that public goods support rights, they seem to support only familiar individual rights—in the case of clean air, a right to basic health; in the case of secure defence, a right to security of person or to liberty.

So, we need to look for group goods of a special kind. Consider this example. Some dinner parties are good because they generate an atmosphere of conviviality.[5] Conviviality seems to be public, not just in the sense of non-excludable, non-rivalrous, and jointly produced, but in a more thoroughgoing way. Conviviality is a property of the party, not of each individual guest. That a group is involved is part of the very concept of conviviality: Jack enjoys himself partly because Jill is enjoying herself, and Jill is enjoying herself partly because Jack—or some other guest—is enjoying himself, and so on.[6] Conviviality is enjoyment together and interactively. Admittedly, the word 'conviviality' is not always used in this narrow sense, but there is such a phenomenon of joint and interactive enjoyment and 'convivial' is a good way to describe it. And that a group is involved is also part of the felt character of conviviality: one is partly—though not necessarily especially consciously—enjoying others enjoying themselves.[7] We must concede, of course, that the only experiences that constitute this enjoyment take place entirely inside the minds of individuals.[8] But we might still think that the other features of conviviality already noted are enough to mark it off as different from mere public goods. One might put it like this. An account that reduced the value of conviviality to the values of the individual experiences of enjoyment of which, admittedly, it is composed:

. . . would be an unsatisfactory account since, as we have seen, each of these experiences refers beyond itself to the wider group . . . An account, then, of the value of these things that was sensitive to what it was like to enjoy them would have to focus on their communal character.[9]

And:

. . . no account of their *worth* to anyone can be given except by concentrating on everyone together.[10]

It does not matter that our example, the conviviality of a party, is of negligible ethical interest. There are heavy-weight group goods that are thought also to have this special character: for example, fraternity, solidarity, mutual tolerance, and the value of a society with a common culture.[11]

---

[5] I borrow this example from Jeremy Waldron, and I have an argument of his chiefly in mind in what immediately follows. See his 'Can Communal Goods Be Human Rights?', *Liberal Rights* (Cambridge: Cambridge University Press, 1993), 339–69, especially sect. IV. [6] Ibid., 355. [7] Ibid., 356. [8] As Waldron does; ibid., 355. [9] Ibid., 357. [10] Ibid., 358–9. [11] Ibid., 357–8.

The next step in the argument is an inference from these special group goods to group rights. In much recent writing[12] the inference is made using a particularly influential definition of a right, which we owe to Joseph Raz.[13] To say that a person has a right, his definition goes, is to say that, other things being equal, an aspect of that person's well-being is a sufficient reason for holding some other person, or persons, to be under a duty. Given that definition, it seems clear that I, as only one person, do not have a right to, say, fraternity because the benefit to me alone is insufficient to justify holding the rest of you to be under the considerable burden of a duty to produce a fraternal society.[14] One might, then, add the individual benefit to me to the individual benefit to you and so on, until, if we eventually include enough individuals, our reason for imposing the duty on others becomes sufficient.[15]

I shall come back to Raz's account of rights shortly. For now, I want to make only two comments.

First, there does not seem to be any general inference from a *group good* of the special type so far isolated to a *right* to it. For instance, it is thoroughly counter-intuitive to think that from the claim *conviviality is a good of a party* we can infer *a party has a right to conviviality*. That is not because of the lightweight nature of the example; we do not think so in the case of the heavy-weight examples either. From the claim *fraternity is a good of a community* we cannot infer *a community has a right to fraternity*. Fraternity, solidarity, and tolerance are highly desirable qualities in a society, and we members of it should, no doubt, be willing to work hard to bring them about. But what seems deeply counter-intuitive is to think that they are a society's *by right*. What we need is not just a good that is special in some way or other but one that is special in a particular way: that it is the sort of good that attracts the protection of a right.[16]

---

[12] E.g. Denise G. Réaume, 'The Group Right to Linguistic Security: Whose Right, What Duties?', in *Group Rights*, ed. Judith Baker (Toronto: University of Toronto Press, 1994), 118–41, 121; Waldron, 'Can Communal Goods Be Human Rights?' (n. 5 above), 359.

[13] See e.g. Joseph Raz's *The Morality of Freedom* (Oxford: Clarendon Press, 1986), 166, but also 44–5, 278.   [14] See Waldron, 'Can Communal Goods Be Human Rights?' (n. 5 above), 359.

[15] Ibid.

[16] Waldron offers further reasons for thinking that group goods give rise to group rights. One is that there is an analogy between how individuals stand to larger bodies and how groups stand to larger groups. Both of them can be oppressed, denied autonomy or liberty, be treated unequally, and so on. In these situations we reach for the language of rights in the case of individuals. Why not do the same in the case of groups? (See ibid., 361–6.) However, it does not seem enough to argue that, like individuals, groups can be oppressed. That ignores the large question of whether, either for individuals or groups, the remedy for all injustice is rights. I should say that not all matters of justice or fairness or equality are matters of rights. There is no inference from *there is an issue of justice here* to *there is an issue of rights here*. I return to these questions below, especially in sect. 5.

Waldron also offers a second, negative reason: namely, that group rights are at least not ruled out conceptually. So long as a group has a sufficiently agent-like status, as a business corporation does, then it is the kind of thing that can hold rights. But to gesture at business corporations does nothing to meet the serious doubts about the agent-like status of the groups for whom rights are usually claimed. One has either to show that they are agent-like too (a difficult job) or come up with an acceptable account of 'rights' that cuts ties with agency (another difficult job).

My second comment is this. What is special about these supposedly strong group goods is merely that their *description* refers to several individuals together as interacting parts of a functioning whole. It is not that their *value* cannot be reduced to individual values. The value of conviviality resides in the enjoyment that each individual experiences singly. The specialness in these goods is something conceptual. The point seems to be that we do not properly describe conviviality without introducing how the enjoyment of one person works to enhance the enjoyment of another, and so on. That, it is said, is an important part of what conviviality *is*. Similarly, we do not properly describe fraternity without acknowledging that Jack's benevolent concern for Jill is strengthened by his recognition of Jill's benevolent concern for him, and so on through much of the group.

That conceptual point seems to me correct. But exactly the same is true of many individual goods and of the individual rights that they give rise to. Autonomy and liberty are two of the classic goods of first-generation rights. Part of what is meant by autonomy is not being dominated or controlled by others; much of what we mean by liberty is not being blocked by others. The same conceptual point applies in their case: one will have no grasp of these two goods unless one understands certain things about how people interact in groups. That interaction is built into the concepts. And these goods support not only basic rights to living autonomously and at liberty but also derivative rights that are equally conceptually dependent upon group interaction: rights to minimum education, to exchange of ideas, to assembly, and so on. Take the basic right of autonomy. In certain social circumstances the most appropriate manifestation of my autonomy might be my having a voice in decisions that significantly affect me. If a society respects this good, then we shall all have a voice in decisions that significantly affect us all. An obvious form for the recognition of this good to take in many modern circumstances is a derived right to vote. This social good—our having an equal voice in decisions—repeats all of the features of the supposed group goods. Any social structure for fair influence on decision is non-excludable: all agents in the group may avail themselves of it. It is non-rivalrous: your voting does not stop me from voting. It is jointly produced: it is because we all (or most of us) play by the rules that it exists. And it has that additional feature that group goods, in this further special sense, are supposed to have: that the only accurate description of the good must bring in not just the good to members of the group considered as individuals, or even as an aggregation, but as individuals considered together as interacting parts of a functioning whole. The description would have to include how one person accepts the weight given to the views of a second *because* the second person accepts the weight given to the views of the first, and so on.

So we have not yet managed to identify the kind of group good that will underpin a group right. To that end, let me now return to Raz's definition of a right, in particular to how he elaborates it into the conditions for the existence of a group right—just what we need but have not yet found.

To the core of his definition of rights in general, he adds this further condition. In the case of a group right, he says,

> the interests in question are the interests of individuals as members of a group in a public good and the right is a right to that public good because it serves their interests as members of the group.[17]

For instance, a 'nation' can, in certain circumstances, have a right to self-determination. Each member of the nation may have an interest, as an individual, in its self-determination, because its self-determination may be bound up with the flourishing of its culture on which the individual's sense of identity depends.[18] The individual alone, however, does not have a right to the group's self-determination, because that single person's interest is not sufficient to justify imposing such a considerable burden upon others. The interest of the whole group, however, might be. And the interests of the individuals that might build up sufficiently to justify imposing that burden upon others would be, Raz thinks, not individual goods that accrue to them as individuals but more diffuse group goods that accrue to them only in virtue of their being members of the community. Membership of certain groups, especially cultural groups, is of great importance to its members. A good life depends importantly upon the successful pursuit of worthwhile goals and relationships, and they, in turn, are culturally determined.[19] So the 'pragmatic' and 'instrumental' case, as Raz describes it, for the existence of a group's right to self-determination would go along these lines.[20] The 'prosperity and self-respect' of what Raz calls 'encompassing groups'—say, cultural groups, membership in which has a large role in one's self-identification and one's sense of possibilities—are of enormous value to us.[21] An encompassing group does not necessarily have to be self-determining in order to prosper; it may prosper as part of a liberal multi-national state. But in less favourable historical circumstances, the only, or the most satisfactory, way of ensuring its prosperity may be through its being self-governing. Then one has all that one needs for the existence of a group right to self-determination.[22]

That, I think, is Raz's well-wrought argument. It has the great merit of seeing the kind of thing that is needed in order to establish the existence of a group right. Still, I have my doubts about it.

First, are Raz's existence conditions sufficient? Why do they not prove too much? According to Raz, we have a claim, in certain historical circumstances,

---

[17] *The Morality of Freedom* (n. 13 above), 208. In fact, Raz has three existence conditions for a group right: (1) 'it exists because an aspect of the interest of human beings justifies holding some person(s) to be subject to a duty', (2) [as quoted in the text], (3) 'the interest of no single member of that group in that public good is sufficient by itself to justify holding another person to be subject to a duty'. The first condition is just the condition for any right. The third is an additional requirement, which I shall not ignore in the discussion that follows.   [18] Ibid., 207.
[19] Raz and Avishai Margalit, 'National Self-Determination', in Raz's *Ethics in the Public Domain* (Oxford: Clarendon Press, 1994), 125–45, 133–4.   [20] Ibid., 138.
[21] Ibid., 129–32, 134, 141.   [22] Ibid., 139–41.

to self-determination because we have a more general interest in 'the prosperity and self-respect' of our encompassing group, and we have that interest because each of us has a major interest in having a healthy sense of identity and a satisfactorily large array of forms of life open to us. This suggests that standing behind the proposed right to self-determination, in those special circumstances in which such a right arises, is a broader right that one has to the prosperity and self respect of one's encompassing group. And that broader right seems, indeed, to qualify as a group right on Raz's list of existence conditions. Our interests in a healthy sense of identity and in having a good array of options from which to choose seem to justify imposing on certain agents (namely, those political entities with the power to allow or deny our group a political setting in which it can prosper) the burden of allowing it. And the interests involved are our interests as members of the group in a public good. And the interest of a single member would not be sufficient on its own to justify imposing that heavy burden on others. The trouble with this is that it seems to justify a right to even quite high levels of 'prosperity'. It seems to justify any level, no matter how high, in which the benefits are great enough to justify imposing the burden. Now, the word 'prosperity' here does not mean just material wealth, although that must be a large part of it; it means whatever contributes to an encompassing group's prospering. Still, the benefits of a robust sense of identity and a rich array of options in life are characteristically so enormous that they are likely to justify imposing the burden on others to allow it. But this loses what seems to me an important intuitive feature of both individual human rights and, presumably, closely related categories of rights such as group rights: namely, that such rights have to do not with any increase in the satisfaction of interests capable of justifying a duty on others, but with the satisfaction of only special kinds of interests and with their satisfaction only up to a certain point. In the case of human rights, for instance, we have a claim not to any form of flourishing but to that more austere condition: what is necessary for our status as agents, which includes autonomy, liberty, and some sort of minimum material provision. That element of austerity, that reference to a minimum, must not be lost. We have a right to material and cultural resources up to a point beyond which, though more would importantly enhance our lives, they are not a matter of right. How does Raz accommodate that essential feature?

The answer, I think, must be: through his notion of a 'duty'. The interests, he says, have to be sufficient to impose a duty on others, and a duty is not merely another reason for action, able to be merged in an overall balance of reasons for action. It is, rather a reason of a special kind, one that excludes a certain range of reasons from consideration. It is likely that not any aspect of a person's well-being will have this exclusionary effect. Still, it is not at all easy to see how this particular deontic notion is supposed to work in ethical thought, nor when it is present. A paradigm case of an exclusionary reason is a promise. The fact that one has promised excludes then giving weight to every consideration of one's convenience that in other circumstances would have weight. That is precisely the point of a promise: to bind oneself in this way. But where on the spectrum from the most modest provision of material and cultural resources to the most lavish do we pass from interests that impose a duty, in this sense, to those that do not? Raz would say, I suppose: when the interests stop supplying an exclusionary reason. But the case of material and cultural resources has none of the clarity of the case of promising; it is not that the whole point of the reasons present here is to exclude a certain range of other reasons. And one kind of reason can exclude others in many different senses: by totally silencing them, by outweighing them in all but the most extreme circumstances, by characteristically outweighing them, and so on. We must know which sense is relevant to rights. We do not understand what a right is until we understand roughly where along such spectra we are to make the break. Of course, there are ways of explaining this. One can say, as I am inclined to do, that in the example before us the break comes when the material and cultural resources are no longer necessary for one's status as a person, no longer necessary for one to live as an agent. That is, one may add content to Raz's fairly formal existence conditions: interests justifying the imposition of duties. But, of course, if one resorts to this more substantive explanation, one returns to old familiar first generation rights.

My second, closely related doubt is that when Raz gives us examples of group rights, he makes them plausible as rights just to the extent that he appeals to familiar first generation rights. Consider again his case for a right to self-determination. In certain historical circumstances, says Raz, I would have an interest in the self-determination of my encompassing group. 'At least in part', he says, 'that interest is based on a person's interest in living in a community which allows him to express in public and develop without repression those aspects of his personality which are bound up with his sense of identity as a member of his community'.[23] I have an interest in membership in a developed culture, because it supplies me with options in life, and they are protected by the right of the individual to autonomy. I have an interest in openly expressing, without fear of repression, what I am and wish to be, because that is central to my agency, which is protected by our individual right to liberty. This begins to look like a case for rights because it stresses our being able to choose and our being free to live as we choose. But those are familiar cases of first generation rights. It is true that these rights are based on interests that we have as members of a group, but so is our right to a vote, which is also first generation. Much the same can be said of another example that Raz gives. The British people, he says, have a right to know how Britain was led into the Falkland War.[24] This, too, we have as members of our group; the citizens of France, for instance, do not have a right to this information about Britain. But a British citizen has a right to it because a citizen of any country cannot have an effective voice in

---

[23] *The Morality of Freedom* (n. 13 above), 207.
[24] *The Morality of Freedom* (n. 13 above), 209.

important political decisions without such knowledge. But that too is a first generation right.

Let me mention one more doubt. Raz's most sustained argument for a group right is his case (made jointly with Avishai Margalit) for national self-determination.[25] But it seems to me just that: a moral case (and a good one too) for granting self-government to certain nations.[26] The further claim that it is a matter of *right* need not, and should not, be made. A right can be outweighed by another right or by sufficiently important considerations of the general good. But Raz's case for self-determination is not like that. It does not first establish a right, and then consider possible overriding conditions. It is, rather, an all-in moral case. According to Raz, what we must show is that, in particular historical circumstances, self-government is necessary both for the prosperity of a certain encompassing group and for its members' participation in it,[27] that the encompassing group forms a substantial majority in the territory to be governed, that the new state is likely to respect the fundamental interests of its inhabitants, that it will not gravely damage the just interests of other countries, and so on until the all-in case is made.[28] The analogy with the case for individual human rights, therefore, breaks down here; Raz makes no claim that a nation, by virtue of its nature, attracts the protection of a right (compare: a person or an agent, by virtue of what they are, attract the protection of individual human rights). It is appropriate that he makes no such claim. A nation, as such, does not have a right to govern itself, even a right that can be overridden. A nation that is respected and flourishing as part of a liberal multi-national state does not have a right to secede. If there is a right here at all, it seems to me to be a right that, as I suggested earlier, is only one element in a case for self-determination: namely, a right to the conditions necessary for the members of an encompassing group to have an acceptable array of options in life and the freedom to pursue the ones they choose. But this is just the right that reduces to various first generation rights. My final doubt, then, is this: self-determination does not seem to me a *right*, and the right that is part of its backing does not seem to me a *group* right.

I wonder whether Raz is not taking as group rights what are really derived individual rights—rights derived from applying basic individual human rights to particular social circumstances. In any case, his attempts to motivate his proposed examples of group rights appeal to what are no more than such derived rights.

So, to sum up my thoughts so far, the first general kind of case for group rights—their derivation from group goods—seems to me unsuccessful.

---

[25] 'National Self-Determination' (n. 19 above).

[26] According to Raz and Margalit at the start of their article, their subject is whether 'a moral case can be made in support of national self-determination' (110). To my mind, it would have been better if they had not gone on to make self-determination a matter of a right.

[27] Ibid., 141, 143.   [28] Ibid., 141.

V. ANOTHER CASE FOR GROUP RIGHTS:
THE JUSTICE-BASED ARGUMENT

Other writers arrive at group rights in a different way. They base them on considerations of justice. My view is that this second case largely succeeds but that it is not a case for group rights. What this second case says is better said, I think, not forced into the language of rights.

The argument that I have primarily in mind has some claims in common with Raz's, but its direction is quite different. Will Kymlicka puts it like this.[29] The survival of a people or culture or ethnic or linguistic group is of enormous value to its members. It is the basis of their sense of identity—their sense of who they are and what they might become. The range of options open to one is determined by one's culture, by the examples and stories that it provides, from which one learns about the courses of life it is possible to follow. We all 'decide how to lead our lives by situating ourselves in these cultural narratives, by adopting roles that have struck us as worthwhile ones, as ones worth living . . .'.[30] 'Loss of cultural membership, therefore, is a profound harm that reduces one's ability to make meaningful choices'.[31]

For society at large to treat a minority culture as of negligible importance, for it to reflect back upon its members a demeaning picture of themselves, for it to deny the culture any concern for whether it lives or dies can, as Charles Taylor has put it, 'be a form of oppression, imprisoning someone in a false, distorted, and reduced mode of being'.[32] To be held in low esteem by society at large easily translates into holding oneself in low esteem, and persons then become compliant accomplices in their own oppression.[33] Lack of recognition for one's group can be a grave harm, which society at large should not inflict upon any of its members.

There is a constant danger that, in one way or other, a dominant culture in a society will stifle minority cultures. The markets and majority rule will usually work in its favour, and its very vitality can sap the strength of minority cultures, even to the point of their extinction. Minority cultures can unfairly, though by no one's conscious wish, end up with many fewer resources than the majority culture. Unfair deprivation is a *prima facie* ground for erecting special protections around a minority group or for giving it special privileges. For instance, if its voice is unheard in the legislature, perhaps it should be given

---

[29] Will Kymlicka, *Multicultural Citizenship* (Oxford: Clarendon Press, 1995), ch. 3.

[30] Will Kymlicka, *Liberalism, Community, and Culture* (Oxford: Oxford University Press, 1989), 165.

[31] Will Kymlicka, 'Individual and Community Rights', in *Group Rights* (n. 12 above), 17–33, 25. Views like this are not uncommon: see e.g. Raz and Margalit, 'National Self-Determination' (n. 19 above); Allen Buchanan, 'Liberalism and Group Rights', in *In Harm's Way. Essays in Honor of Joel Feinberg*, ed. Jules L. Coleman and Buchanan (Cambridge: Cambridge University Press, 1994); Charles Taylor, 'The Politics of Recognition', in *Multiculturalism. Examining the Politics of Recognition*, ed. Amy Gutman (Princeton: Princeton University Press, 1994), 32–6.

[32] Charles Taylor, 'The Politics of Recognition' (n. 31 above), 25.   [33] Ibid., 26.

special representatives;[34] or perhaps its central government should adopt a federal structure or find some other way of devolving powers to smaller communities. Or if the market works to their disadvantage, perhaps minorities should be given special subsidies. The acknowledgement of minority rights can, in these ways, serve to prevent or correct the injustice.[35] These are just some of the possible means; the end, however, is always the same: rectificatory justice.[36]

By grounding group rights in justice, we can explain why there are also minority cultures that do *not* attract protection. When the Boers in South Africa sought, through *apartheid*, to protect their minority culture against being swamped by the black majority, they had no case. *Apartheid* itself was unfair. And that is also why a group is usually not justified in imposing certain restrictions internally on its own members, such as a ban on leaving the group, even if it promotes its own survival. Such bans are usually violations of liberty. So, as Kymlicka puts it, we 'should endorse certain external protections, where they promote fairness between groups, but should reject internal restrictions which limit the right of group members to question and revise traditional authority and practices'.[37]

This second case seems to me stronger than the first. But what is it a case *for*?

First, as it stands, the case is grossly oversimplified. The loss of cultural membership does not, in itself, reduce one's ability to make meaningful choices. All that one needs for meaningful choice is *some* culture, and if, as is often the case, a minority culture is in decline because it is being supplanted by a majority culture, one can, depending upon how much dislocation is involved in the process, still have *a* culture available to one. And the better the culture is—that is to say, the richer it is, the more examples it supplies and stories it tells, the more humane those stories are—the better off one is in that respect. It is true that there may well be things that could be said in one's original language that cannot be said in the language that supplants it. But the question is not whether there are such things but to what extent they are central to one's being able to conceive the important choices in life. They might be; they might not be; and even if they are, one might still on balance be better off in the new language. We cannot tell in advance. All of that has to be decided case by case.

And one must not oversimplify, or sentimentalize, what it means to people to abandon an old culture for a new one. Cultures can, and must, be criticized. Some cultures are authoritarian, intolerant, sexist, distorted by false belief, dominated by unjust caste or class systems. Some people willingly immigrate, leaving behind one culture for another, as they hope, better one. They might have a small sense of loss and a great sense of gain. Other people—say, natives who see their culture destroyed by colonists—may have a great sense of loss and

---

[34] I take the example from Kymlicka, *Multicultural Citizenship* (n. 29 above), 36.

[35] Kymlicka, 'Individual and Community Rights' (n. 31 above), 23–7.

[36] It is not that, according to this argument, justice is the only ground for group rights. Some (legal) rights can be grounded in historical agreement: charters, treaties, and so on.

[37] Kymlicka, *Multicultural Citizenship* (n. 29 above), 37.

a small sense of gain. People's experiences are hardly uniform. And there is the important question of what sense one *should* have when one's original culture changes substantially, or becomes mixed with another, or gives way to another. One will not know what one *should* feel until one evaluates what is happening, and in all of these cases what is happening is likely to be immensely complex and the proper assessment of it hard to make.

Also, it is easy to exaggerate the extent to which our deliberation about our options in life depends upon our *particular* culture. What that deliberation most needs is a sense of what things in general make a human life good. I have written about this elsewhere, so I shall merely state my view.[38] There are certain things that make *any* characteristic human life good: accomplishing something in the course of one's life, deep personal relations, certain kinds of understanding, enjoyment, and so on. Each of the terms on this list needs a lot of explanation, so much so that they become in effect terms of art. There are not always words in English, as it is now, that will quite serve to name these individual values; to some extent, one has to invent a vocabulary. And this new vocabulary applies to characteristic human life: not British or American or Chinese or Sudanese life but *human* life. It is a grotesque oversimplification to say that having a sense of meaningful options in life requires access to one's original culture, when no culture or language, as it stands, has the vocabulary we need, and when the vocabulary that deliberation can lead us to is, with qualifications, cross-cultural.[39]

There is something worryingly passive about the agent who figures in these arguments for the importance of cultures. According to these arguments, our culture gives us our options; we merely receive them as an inheritance. But this picture leaves out our active critical life. We examine life; we criticize our inheritance. Of course, we do it in our own language. But this does not mean that we are condemned to a life *either* so deeply embedded in our particular culture that we have no access to views originating outside it, *or* so detached from any particular culture that we have critical resources too feebly abstract to settle much. We do not have to be either inside or outside a culture; that is a false dichotomy—one the wide acceptance of which is puzzling in our current cosmopolitan conditions, in which most of us would be hard put to name the culture of which we are ourselves members. A very great deal of our critical vocabulary for ethics has still to be developed, and much of it will be neither

---

[38] See my *Well-Being* (Oxford: Oxford University Press, 1986), chs. I–IV; *Value Judgement* (Oxford: Oxford University Press, 1996), ch. II.

[39] Of course, one's list of good-making features of life is not independent of the world one thinks one inhabits, and world views are likely to vary from culture to culture. But they can vary within a culture too. And the variations are hardly above criticism. My own list is out of a particular tradition: modern, Western, and atheist. A cloistered monk might well have a very different list: for many of the items on my list he might have almost the opposite. Lists change with one's metaphysical views. And metaphysical views can be better or worse, acceptable or unacceptable. Variation in lists is caused by more than just different metaphysical views, but these other social differences are not immune to cross-cultural assessment either. See a somewhat longer discussion in ibid., 150.

the thick terms from a particular cultural perspective nor the thin terms of the spare rational agent of much modern philosophy. What we especially need are the key terms of a successful account of human well-being, largely still unsettled, and of realistically described agents living satisfactory lives in a realistically described society, also largely still unsettled. Once this critical vocabulary has been developed and we look back on our original conceptual framework and ask whether we are inside or outside it, I think that we are likely to drop the question as ill-drawn. We shall have substantially expanded our original conceptual framework; it is enough to say that. We can expect other people in other cultures to have been equally critically active. And we can, with some justification, expect points of convergence between us.[40]

So far I have been concentrating on the sources of personal identity (in the suspect, loose sense of the term found in these discussions) and capacity for choice. But there are, of course, many other reasons for protecting cultures than those. If one's culture dies, especially if records of it are few or destroyed, one loses touch with one's roots. For some people this is not felt as a great loss, but for others it is. Often one's sense of loss will depend upon how secure one's sense of self is within one's current society and how much respect the society shows one. And often one's loss of cultural roots is something that is inflicted upon one. There is a great difference ethically between one's voluntarily abandoning one's culture and a dominant group's destroying it. In general, no one should deny another autonomy—for instance, the autonomy to amend their culture, as *they* see fit. But the values here are not the survival of a culture, admirable or not, but autonomy and good ways of life. What we should cite here is not the right of a group that its culture survive, but one's right autonomously to choose and freely to pursue one's conception of a good life, both of which are individual human rights.

And that seems to me the trouble with all of these arguments. They are arguments about matters of the greatest importance, but they are not arguments for anything as general as a right of a group that its culture survive.

Without doubt, for society at large to deny a minority group proper recognition, to regard it as of little importance, inflicts a great harm upon its members. But this is not a reason to confer upon it and upon all cultural groups a general right to the survival of their culture,[41] but a reason to give it, and indeed

---

[40] See ibid., ch. VIII, sect. 4, especially, 134–5; on convergence see ch. IV sect. 2.

[41] There are considerable problems about individuating cultures. It is by no means clear even that each of us is a member of *a* culture, let alone clear which culture it is. A culture is, roughly, a linguistic group with its own art, literature, customs, and moral attitudes, transmitted from generation to generation. I do not doubt that we can individuate *some* cultures. The ideal conditions for the use of the term are when groups develop largely independently of one another. One could apply the term to an isolated Indian tribe just discovered in the depths of the Amazon. One can properly say that Cortes destroyed Aztec culture. One can say that certain cultures are threatened today: for example, the East Timorese Council of Priests recently described Indonesia's occupation of East Timor and its imposition of its own language as 'killing the culture' (quoted in a letter to the editor, *The Independent*, 27 January 1997).

everyone, equal respect: every human life matters and matters equally, regardless of gender, race, or ethnic group. This is a case for the irrelevance of a culture, not for society's guaranteeing its survival. It may be that in some cases the only practicable way for a society to avoid inflicting this harm on people is to ensure the survival of the identity of their group. But as it is certainly not always so, this argument cannot be an argument for the right of cultures, in general, to continued existence. Every individual must be granted equal respect. Individuals and groups must be granted autonomy. But cultures must be open to criticism and therefore to constant change, even to the point of a natural death.

Indeed, a culture is alive only if it is open to any change that its members think desirable, even if what survives is no longer the 'same' culture. A society intent on preserving a minority culture is actually severely limited in its options. Once one tries to preserve a culture, one has to decide what constitutes it, and that very decision tends to fix it as it happens to be at one moment in time. Embalming is a form of preservation, but it is not a form of life.

My appeals to the politics of sameness (for example, the *universal* human right to autonomy) run the risk, of course, of missing the point of someone such as Charles Taylor, who is promoting, precisely, a new 'politics of difference'. '. . . with the politics of difference', he says, 'what we are asked to realize is the unique identity of this individual or group, their distinctness from everyone else'.[42] His idea is that when this distinctness is destroyed by a dominant or majority identity, the group loses touch with the ideal of authenticity; it loses touch with its own authentic ways of being. Individuals should be accepted as what they are and not made to conform to a model appropriate to someone else;

But, presumably, when people claim a certain group's right to the survival of its culture, they have in mind a universal right: that everyone is a member of some culture, and that everyone equally has the right (though, no doubt, only some cultures are threatened enough for anyone to bother to claim it). But it gets increasingly difficult to speak in those terms in modern conditions: with easy communication, travel, and trade; with the global spread of popular forms of art, of ways of life, of political ideals. (This is a point made by Jeremy Waldron in 'Minority Cultures and the Cosmopolitan Alternative', in *The Rights of Minority Cultures*, ed. Will Kymlicka (New York: Oxford University Press, 1995), 93–119, though Waldron is more sceptical about talk about 'a culture' than I am.)

One might reply that, for all the globalization of ways of life, there are still differences in ways of understanding the world because those ways are embedded in the language. It is very easy to exaggerate on both sides of this dispute, so let me take a concrete (egocentric) example. To what culture do I belong? To the United States, where I was born and raised? Is there a single United States culture? Should I say New England? Or do I belong to the culture of Britain, where I have spent my adult life? Or should I say England, to exclude Scotland and Wales? Or is there now only an omnibus 'Western' culture? To what culture does a Japanese belong who listens to Mozart and reads Dostoevsky, Flaubert, and Henry James? To several? Which ones?

My point is that none of the answers to these questions is easy, and that it is not easy because the criteria for the use of the term 'a culture' do not comfortably fit very many modern conditions. It is not that one simply could not give answers to these questions, but that the answers would have to be arbitrary to a high degree. We can certainly, and comfortably, speak of the cultural side of our lives, meaning that part that has to do with literature, music, and so on. But are many people any longer able to speak of the entity—their 'culture'? Similar problems arise with the terms 'a people', 'a nation', and 'an ethnic group'.

[42] 'The Politics of Recognition' (n. 31 above), 38.

for example, women should not be forced, on pain of failure in their careers, to adopt modes of being appropriate for men. Still, when we autonomously choose a conception of a good life, whether or not it is compatible with the models given to us by our cultures, we are hardly sacrificing our authenticity.

The second case for group rights can be summed up like this: our culture is the source of our identity; some cultures are at an unfair disadvantage to others and need protection. What is important in this argument is not best expressed in terms of the right of a group that its culture survive. To say that a group has a right to the survival of its culture is to suggest that a culture deserves the strong sort of ethical protection that overrides all but the most pressing competing ethical concerns. But the demands on a society to protect a culture are not of this nature. The story is much more complicated than that; the demands upon society are much more complex, less categorical, than that.

Nor is the fact that some cultures are at an unfair disadvantage a case for a general right to the survival of one's culture. Rights do not cover the whole moral domain, nor even the whole domain of justice. Not all legal rights that legislators enact have corresponding moral rights. Not all moral claims that one person makes upon another, or one group upon another, involve rights. Minorities often have successful moral claims upon the majority society, but it is often better to see those claims as based on considerations of justice—usually on fair distribution—rather than on rights. These last claims raise general issues, to which I now want to turn.

VI. EXCLUSION

One suggestion that has emerged so far is that many supposed group rights are best not seen as rights at all, and some others can be reduced to individual rights. Let me say a little more about these two possibilities: exclusion and reduction.

It may seem high-handed of me to dismiss many supposed minority rights as not *really* rights. Or it may seem that I am making only a trivial verbal point—namely, that whereas I choose to define 'rights' so as to exclude many reputed minority rights, others choose to define 'rights' in a way that includes them. But I am not just arbitrarily choosing a definition of rights. Of course, there is an element of stipulation in anyone's claim about what 'rights' are, but there are constraints on this stipulation. A case must be made for it—in terms of fidelity to the tradition, or of theoretical or practical pay-off, or so on. Well chosen stipulations are not high-handed; in the case of rights, they are urgently needed.

I said before that human rights do not exhaust the whole moral domain, or even the whole domain of justice. For example, if you free-ride on the bus because you know that no damage will come to anyone as all the rest of us are paying our way, you act unfairly, but you do not violate my rights. Or suppose that I am deciding what to leave my children in my will, and my thoughts go like this: the obvious basis for the distribution is equal shares, and as none of them has behaved in a way, or ended up in a condition, that would justify an unequal share, that is what I shall do. Now my line of thought here turns on an appeal to equal distribution, the moral consideration at the centre of many supposed minority rights. But though it turns on equal distribution, it is not intuitively a matter of rights. No child of mine can claim that an equal portion is his or hers *by right*. I do not want to claim more for this point than it deserves: it is just an appeal to intuition. But its force, such as it is, cannot be evaded by proposing that *some* considerations of justice are grounds for human rights while *others* (say, my making my will) are not. What would it be about those cases of justice that give rise to rights to distinguish them from the cases that do not? A gap opens in the story, and there is no obvious material on hand to fill it. It is not that there are no ways at all to fill the gap. One could appeal to individual rights: for example, one might suggest that everyone has a human right to equal minimum material resources necessary for living a recognizably human existence, but not to many other forms of equal distribution. That suggestion seems to me entirely plausible: human rights give us a claim to certain basic equal provision but not to equal distribution generally. But to fill the gap in that way is to appeal to the ground for human rights in our idea of personhood or agency, and to abandon a ground in mere equality of distribution or one of its forms.

It would be useful now to look at a concrete example of a supposed minority right. Take a minority culture that is losing out in the marketplace and in the normal workings of a democratic legislature; the majority culture, say, gets a great deal of financial support, while the minority culture gets none and its art and literature are decaying from neglect. The principle of equal distribution of resources may well require some sort of rectification, say in the form of special subsidy. Now it seems to me that there will often be a strong case to that effect, but a case, I am suggesting, based in equality, not in rights. There is an obvious reply to me. The deprived minority, it says, has a *claim* on moral resources, and a natural way to express a claim is in terms of rights. After all, when Hohfeld made his taxonomy of rights, the class of rights that he called rights 'in the strictest sense' were claim rights. The weakness in this reply, however, is that it is not natural to express *all* claims in terms of rights. If a husband is being nasty to his wife, the wife has a (moral) claim on her husband to stop; that is, he ought to stop. But not all moral obligations give rise to rights; this one, for instance, does not.

Of course, we can use the word 'rights' so that its domain of application coincides with the whole domain of moral obligation,[43] but I think that we ought not to. It seems to me that an account of general moral rights should be able to pass a redundancy test. The word 'rights' should not just provide another way

---

[43] As I think do, e.g., Mary Anne Warren, 'Do Potential People Have Moral Rights?', *Canadian Journal of Philosophy* 7 (1977), 275–89, 277, n. 4; T.L.S. Sprigge, 'Metaphysics, Physicalism, and Animal Rights', *Inquiry* 22 (1979), 101–43, 103; Thomas Auxter, 'The Right Not to Be Eaten', *Inquiry* 22 (1979), 221–30, 222.

of talking about what we can already talk about perfectly adequately. 'Rights' should mark off a special domain within morality, and there should be sufficient motivation to mark it off. The pass level for the redundancy test is, of course, a bit fuzzy.[44] It is obviously a matter of judgement when a motivation is 'sufficient'. But making the domain of rights co-extensive, by definition, with the whole domain of moral obligation, for which we already have a perfectly adequate vocabulary, fails the test. True, we could use the word 'rights' to mark the contrast between obligation and supererogation. But I myself doubt that this motivation is sufficient. We already have vocabulary to mark the distinction between duty and supererogation without conscripting the word 'rights' for the job. Besides, this use would be at variance with the philosophical tradition of rights. Certainly, in the mainstream of the tradition, the term 'rights' has a different and more specific job.

This hardly exhausts ways to resist my programme of exclusion.[45] But I cannot myself find any compelling reason, all things considered, to include

---

[44] I think that we should make the pass level fairly low. Ronald Dworkin suggests that the word 'rights' marks off that special moral consideration that operates as a check on maximizing the general good. Rights play the role of 'trump' in the game of moral reasons; indeed he often speaks as if they have no point at all except in that role (see his *Taking Rights Seriously* (London: Duckworth, 1978), 139, 269). Robert Nozick thinks that they play the role of 'side-constraints' (see his *Anarchy, State, and Utopia* (Oxford: Blackwell, 1974), 28–35). Either account more than passes the redundancy test. In fact, claims for rights can be a good deal less strong than that, I think, and still be regarded as passing the test. For instance, a broadly utilitarian account that made rights the protections of specially high-potency utilities would pass.

[45] Much more can be said. What this sort of claim account of rights needs, in order to pass the redundancy test, is a convincing distinction between the special sort of claim associated with rights, on the one side, and moral claims generally, on the other. This distinction will then yield a correlative distinction between kinds of duty. Now, there is an old distinction in philosophy between duties of perfect obligation and duties of imperfect obligation. In one version, it is roughly the distinction between what is morally required and what is merely supererogatory. In that version, it is no help to us here. Kant has a different version: duties of perfect obligation (for example, to do what one promised) specify what one must do and for or to whom; duties of imperfect obligation (for instance, to help the needy) are ones that allow considerable leeway in what one does: for instance, one might be inclined to help the sick, or instead the destitute, or instead the tortured, and so on; and one might choose to help this particular sick person rather than that one, and so on. But Kant's version of the distinction does not seem to help us either.

To explain summarily: there are rights the only specification of which is that the moral agents in a certain subset bear a duty of aid, but which particular agents are members of that subset cannot be specified. Two examples are a right to minimum education and a right to life (if the latter is thought to include, as I think it must, not just a negative duty not to take life without due process but also a positive duty to assist in certain ways in its preservation). In the case of these rights, it is just that somebody should come forward to help, not necessarily everybody (some may not be in a position to help without great hardship) and not necessarily everybody in the subset of those who can help without hardship (only a few may be needed); all that is required is that a large enough number of persons (unspecified) should respond. The positive duties associated with these rights are in this respect much like duties of charity, and the class of duties of perfect obligation cannot therefore be used to isolate the sort of claims associated with rights.

Or one can appeal to what is called the choice account of rights. That account would distinguish the two kinds of duties like this: I have a right to something from you, it says, whenever the reasons for holding you to be under a duty to me are also reasons for thinking that I have the power to release you from the duty if I so wish. This account of rights works well with promises: if you promised me,

claims to rectificatory justice, as such, in the class of rights. It is better—if for no other reason than so much clearer—to go on speaking of *justice* for deprived groups rather than of their having *group rights*.

VII. REDUCTION

Other group rights, I think, can be dissolved by reduction. I shall take a quick look at just one example: the right of a state to non-intervention in its internal affairs. In international law this right is closely related to the 'sovereignty' of states. According to the United Nations *Declaration* of 1970, all states enjoy 'sovereign equality', which among other things includes the inviolability of their territorial integrity and political independence.[46] The *Declaration* also announces a 'principle concerning the duty not to intervene in matters within the domestic jurisdiction of any State', which bans 'armed intervention and all other forms of interference' in a State's 'political, economic and cultural elements'.[47] The overlap in content of the principle of sovereign equality and the duty of non-intervention is obvious.[48] Now, as individuals, each of us has

---

then you have a duty, relative to my right, to do what you promised, unless I waive my claim. But, as is well-known, this account does not work well in many other cases. I have a right to life, a right not to be tortured, a right to minimum material provision, none of which I can waive. These may be thought to be welfare rights, which some regard as doubtful claimants to rights status, but the same applies to undisputed liberty rights. I have a right to autonomy and to liberty. It is not enough to justify your denying me autonomy and liberty that I said you could. Autonomy and liberty constitute the central values of what we think of as human dignity. You may not destroy my dignity just because I am deluded, or desperate, enough to give you permission.

I doubt that we shall find the distinction we are after simply by looking at formal features: whether the duty is waivable or not, whether the individual or entity who owes a duty and the beneficiary are specifiable or not, and so on. We need to put more *content* into the distinction.

[46] *Declaration on Principles of International Law Concerning Friendly Relations and Co-operation among States in accordance with the Charter of the United Nations*, adopted by the United Nations General Assembly, 24 October 1970, see the sect. entitled 'The principle of sovereign equality of states.' The principle of 'sovereign equality' was well established before the United Nations. It was strongly asserted by the League of Nations. Some trace it back to the Treaty of Westphalia, which ended the Thirty Years' War in 1648.

The right to non-intervention also has links in the *Declaration* with the right to self-determination, despite the fact that the latter right is said to be a right of 'peoples' and the former a right of 'states' (and 'peoples' and 'states' are clearly not the same). One part of the explanation of the right to non-intervention is that 'peoples' are not to be deprived of their 'national identity', which colonialism, the paradigm violation of the right to self-determination, would typically constitute. See the section entitled 'The principle concerning the duty not to intervene in matters within the domestic jurisdiction of any State, in accordance with the Charter'. The *Declaration* of 1970 elaborates the principles of the *Charter of the United Nations* (1945). The *Charter* says: *Article 1.2*: '[The Purposes of the United Nations include] To develop friendly relations among nations based on the respect for the principle of equal rights and self-determination of peoples . . .'.

[47] See the section entitled 'The principle concerning the duty not to intervene in matters within the domestic jurisdiction of any State, in accordance with the Charter.'

[48] On certain accounts of 'sovereignty' the link with non-intervention is conceptual. 'It [a sovereign state] has undivided jurisdiction over all persons and property within its territory . . . No other nation may interfere in its domestic affairs.' See article on 'Sovereignty', *The New Columbia Encyclopedia* (New York: Columbia University Press, 1975), 2578.

various rights to non-interference: a right to autonomy (not to have our major decisions taken for us) and a right to liberty (not to be blocked from carrying out our decisions). It is an obvious thought, then, that a state's sovereignty and right to non-intervention might just be, in some way, an aggregation of these individual rights. Perhaps it is because, and only because, all of its citizens have the right that we are willing to say that a state has it.

But if the group right to non-intervention were thus reducible to these individual rights, a state would not have the right to non-intervention unless what it wanted to do expressed what its citizens wanted to do. But that is not the way that this particular group right is commonly understood. It is thought to be unconditional. As the *Declaration* of 1970 puts it: 'No State or group of States has the right to intervene, *for any reason whatsoever*, in the internal or external affairs of any other State.'[49] If this common understanding is correct, then the group right is not reducible to these individual rights.

I doubt, though, that it is correct. One can, of course, create a legal right— say, in international law—to be understood like that, but we are interested in moral rights. And a country's *prima facie* moral right to non-intervention depends, I want to argue, upon its expressing the wishes of its citizens, and that *prima facie* right itself can be overridden by other moral considerations. I think that this is the understanding of the right that best explains our quite complex considered beliefs on this subject.

It is true that we accept that we often, perhaps even generally, ought not to intervene in the affairs even of a country that does not express the wishes of its citizens. But the case for that, I think, is pragmatic. Any wish to intervene runs up against enormous problems of knowledge. We seldom know enough about the intricacies of the local situation to be reasonably confident that we can see what justice requires or, even more to the point, how to bring it about. And even if we can be tolerably assured about the short-run, it is notoriously difficult in complex social and political matters to know what will happen in the long-run. There is also the cold test of results. Though recent 'humanitarian interventions' have aimed at bringing relief, they have in most cases brought more harm than benefit. Then there is the main concern of the United Nations: a firm ban on intervention makes a major contribution to world peace. These, and other considerations, mount up into a strong practical case against intervention. Indeed, they also have an important role in fixing the boundaries of the (moral) right to non-intervention.[50]

---

[49] See the same section as cited above (n. 47); my italics.

[50] See C.A.J. Cody, 'Nationalism and Intervention', in *Introducing Applied Ethics*, ed. Brenda Almond (Oxford: Blackwell, 1995), for a fuller statement of the practical case. See also J.S. Mill's classic argument in the same general direction, 'A Few Words on Non-Intervention', in his *Essays on Politics and Culture*, ed. Gertrude Himmelfarb (New York: Anchor Books, 1963); and Michael Walzer, *Just and Unjust Wars* (New York: Basic Books, 1977). Coady's case seems to me the most persuasive.

They do not, however, make the right absolute. When the genocide began between the Hutus and the Tutsis, there were calls, answered only late, for intervention. In certain cases, cases of genocide or of gross oppression or extreme disregard for the good of the people, what needs moral justification is not intervention but non-intervention. Sometimes non-intervention will be justified by the practical considerations that I just mentioned. But when one's knowledge is reasonably full, when one can help appreciably at smallish risk, then the moral case for intervening is strong. Non-intervention can then be just as morally remiss as a community's not intervening in the internal affairs of a family when the parents are so physically abusive as to endanger their child's life.

The view that I have sketched can be summed up like this. The right to non-intervention depends upon a country's wishes manifesting its individual citizens' wishes. If that is missing, then the right does not even exist. Even if it does exist, the right can still be overridden, though the practical case shows that exceptions should be only in extreme cases. This, in effect, constitutes a reduction of the group right to non-intervention to individual rights to autonomy and liberty. It is hardly the whole story about when intervention is justified, but it is the prologue to the story.

VIII. What is left?

There are other accounts of human rights than the personhood account. There are other possible conceptions of, and arguments for, group rights than the ones we have lately been given and I have discussed here. So I can end only with a challenge.

After the combined workings of exclusion and reduction, are any compelling examples left in the class of group rights? Can we attach sufficiently clear criteria to the term 'group rights' to make it a helpful, non-redundant addition to our moral vocabulary? Are we not better off without the third generation of rights?

11

Against Collective Rights

YAEL (YULI) TAMIR*

In recent years, the notion of collective rights has been gathering considerable support.[1] Collective rights, it is argued, are necessary to protect and promote the interests of members of minority groups. This latter claim is supported by theoretical and political arguments; the former suggest that unless bestowed upon a collective, the existence of some rights cannot be justified; the latter assert that unless granted to a collective, some rights cannot be protected. I will take issue with both claims and argue that one can, and should, justify all rights in terms of individual rights. This does not imply that all the rights referred to as 'collective rights' can be reduced to individual rights. The 'missing rights', are institutional arrangements which to begin with, shouldn't have been justified by using rights discourse.

Not all just and desirable political arrangements could be, or should be, defined in terms of rights. Rights language should delineate basic liberties, powers, and immunities; it should not specify the particular political arrangements that must be installed in order to realize and protect these rights. For example, while individuals have a right to be protected, they do not have a right to a particular kind of protection; while they have a right to be represented in the public sphere, they do not have a right to a particular system of representation, and so on.

It is important, then, to distinguish between rights and the political arrangements that ought to be put in place in order to defend and promote rights: the former ought to reflect the nature of moral and political agents; the latter must take into account contingent limitations embedded in particular social and political circumstances. Expanding the language of rights so that it will cover all desirable social policies weakens rights claims. It places a wide range of

*This paper has a long (and tormented) history. I started writing it while I was a visiting scholar at The Center for Human Values at Princeton University, and returned to it while I was a visiting scholar at The Program in Ethics and the Profession, at Harvard University. I am grateful to Lea Brilmayer and the participants of the International Jurisprudence Colloquium at NYU, and to Susan Dwyer, Robert Fullinwider, Ken Greenawalt, Richard Fallon, Judith Lichtenberg, Nancy Rosenblum, Dennis Thompson, Sue Uniacke, and Noam Zohar for their many instructive comments, good advice and productive discussions. Special thanks to Tamar Meisels for her many helpful comments.

[1] As it will become clear when the discussion unfolds, this paper examines the theoretical and political implications of rights which are bestowed on a collective *as a whole* rather than on individual members of the collective. The adequate term to use was *collective's right*. In this paper I use the more common, but misleading term *collective rights* in order to be able to relate to the literature I'm criticizing without confusing the reader.

social demands on an equal footing, disallowing us to distinguish between demands which are worthy of special protection and those which do not merit such treatment.

I. SOME SOCIOLOGICAL OBSERVATIONS

Demands for collective rights commonly arise when the walls of traditional communities start crumbling down unveiling the external world. Exposure to alternative ways of life threatens social cohesion and cultural continuity and forces the community to seek ways of securing its existence. It is in these moments of transition that we ought to decide whether to side with the community or with its individual members (especially with those who wish to dissent from the traditional way of life).[2] Those who endorse the notion of collective rights side, intentionally or unintentionally, with the former.

Supporters of collective rights may find this claim objectionable and argue that they do not side with the community against its members; their aim is to support those individual members who wish to retain the communal identity. These individuals must be helped in their struggles against trends of assimilation, conversion, language transformation, as well as against moves to reform the communal tradition resulting from pressures exerted by the dominant culture(s). Group rights are offered as a way of countering these pressures. This may indeed be a noble goal. And yet, attempts to protect individuals from external influences by legal means which expropriate their rights and prevent them from following their preferences open the door for dangerous paternalism, and violations of basic human rights. This is the main political danger embodied in collective rights.

Why are these dangers so commonly ignored? The answer seems to be of a sociological nature: those who favour group rights come from two entirely different backgrounds. The first group, which dominates the academic world and produces most of the relevant literature, consists of liberal social thinkers who observe with horror the social, political and cultural disintegration of their society and wish to reestablish communal life as a means of confronting loneliness, alienation, and apathy. Their fears are reflected in essays such as Putnam's 'Bowling Alone', and Walzer's 'Multiculturalism and Individualism'. Rates of disengagement from national, ethics, and cultural associations for the sake of private pursuit of happiness (or desperate search for economic survival) are so high these days, Walzer observes with deep concern, 'that all groups worry all the time about how to hold the periphery and ensure their own future'.[3]

---

[2] In periods when communities can shut themselves off and shelter their members from external influences there is little practical difference between granting cultural, religious or linguistic rights to individual members or to the community as a whole.

[3] Michael Walzer, 'Multiculturalism and Individualism', *Dissent*, Spring 1994, 188.

Authors belonging to the first group feel they live in an atomized society which could benefit from the strengthening of communal life, and are ready to lend a hand to those who strive to pursue this goal.

The second group is comprised, mainly, of leaders of traditional communities who see and fear the destruction of their own communities. These include, among others, leading members of the Native-American nations, of the Amish community, of ultra-orthodox Jewish communities and fundamentalist Moslem communities. Members of this group seek to assure the stability, continuity, and often the economic prosperity of their communities. For that purpose they are ready to overlook the interests of some dissenting individuals whose personal choices contradict communal interests.

What are the social and political implications of collective rights? Are they used to reinvigorate communal life or to prevent members of marginalized sub-groups—women in traditional societies, liberal Jews in Israel, converts to Christianity among Indian tribes—from dissenting from the traditional way of life. Unfortunately all too often they are used for the latter purpose.

This paper is, then, a word of caution, calling upon liberal political theorists, and liberal political activists to acknowledge the fact that rights can rarely help to rebuild a community but can easily be used to strengthen dominant sub-groups, privilege conservative interpretations of culture over reforms, and disadvantage all those who wish to diverge from accepted social norms and question the traditional role of social institutions.[4] Liberals should then be aware of the price embedded in bestowing rights on groups and be more cautious in their support of such rights.

II. COMMUNAL SURVIVAL AND VIOLATIONS OF INDIVIDUAL RIGHTS

In those cases in which the welfare or the interests of the community are at stake, rights should be granted to the community rather than to its individual members or else the community is left defenceless and might face destruction. This is the main argument adduced in support of group rights.

Risks to the community increase, McDonald argues, if individuals may, on their own, without prior community agreement, exercise rights. 'This expresses a slide from *ours* to *mine* that should be resisted. In particular, on a conservative notion of community as a union of past, present, and future generations. I would argue that the claimant's role in collective rights is one of stewardship, and this is best played by the present generation which is mindful of its history and its future.'[5]

---

[4] I have developed this argument in greater details in 'Against Collective Rights', in *Multicultural Question*, ed. Steven Lukes and Christian Joppke (Oxford: Oxford University Press, 1999).

[5] Michael McDonald, 'Should Communities Have Rights? Reflections of Liberal Individualism', *Canadian Journal of Law and Jurisprudence* 4 (1991), 217–37, 232.

What are the implications of McDonald's argument for the ability of individuals to exercise their rights? An example may clarify the issue: in the political debate over a possible withdrawal of Israel from the territories it occupied in the 1967 War, some opponents of withdrawal put forward a claim very similar to the one professed by McDonald. The territories in question, they argue, were promised by God to the Jewish people as a whole—past, present and future generations included. The present generation cannot, without the approval of all other generations, surrender rights grounded in this divine promise. As such an approval cannot possibly be achieved, no withdrawal can ever be morally justified.

In fact, even if members of all past generations as well as members of the present one, prefer a withdrawal it will not be justified, as it is impossible to know the preferences of future generations. The present generation, if it is no more than a steward of a trans-generational whole whose will cannot be confirmed, is therefore deprived of its ability to re-interpret, amend or waive its rights. Collective rights thus turn into individual duties: duties which may be imposed on individuals not only by their own community but also by the state against which the community claims rights.

Note that if collective rights exist, those from whom the rights are claimed—usually state institutions—acquire correlative duties, the most important of which is the obligation to preserve the collectives whose existence is a necessary condition for the protection of the rights. One way of fulfilling this obligation is to impose on individuals duties to act in ways which would guarantee the continued existence of the collective.[6] Consequently, the idea of rights as trumps which could be used by individuals to defend themselves against the community becomes meaningless, and with it collapses one of the most important distinctions between theories of rights and utilitarianism.[7]

Van Dyke also grounds collective rights in arguments which undermine the power of individual rights. Many individuals' rights, he argues, should be seen as derivative from communal rights, especially from the community's right to self-preservation. 'For example, individual freedom of expression can often be interpreted in terms of the right of a linguistic community to preserve its language. But taking individual rights as exhaustive of all rights would not allow us to defend the interests of communities, and particularly their interest of self-determination.'[8]

Like McDonald, Van-Dyke gives priority to the interests of the community over the rights of individuals. One should examine the implications of this argument especially when it is entangled with the notion of survival. Even those who are suspicious of group rights often claim that when the very existence of

---

[6] I am grateful to Sue Dwyer for her helpful discussion on this issue.

[7] See Rawls' discussion of utilitarianism. Classical utilitarianism, he argues, 'fails to take seriously the distinction between persons. The principle of rational choice for one man is taken as the principle of social choice as well' (*A Theory of Justice* (Oxford: Oxford University Press, 1972), 187).

[8] Vernon Van Dyke, 'Collective Entities and Moral Rights: Problems in Liberal Thought', *Journal of Politics* 44 (1982), 21–40, 29.

a collective is endangered, collective rights must prevail over individual ones. It is important to distinguish in this context between two very different meanings of the term 'survival': the first refers to cases in which the survival of the community is endangered irrespective of the will of its members; the second to cases in which the survival of a community is endangered as a result of its members' will. Obviously there are good reasons to protect the community in the first type of case, one may wonder, however, whether it is legitimate to protect 'a community' against its own members. More precisely, is it just, or desirable, to allow those who aspire to preserve the community—often members of the dominant and privileged elite—to force others to preserve a way of life to which they have grown indifferent or even hostile?

The dangers embodied in adopting the second interpretation are clearly exemplified by the case of the Pueblo Indians. In this case, members of a dominant group within the tribe use powers granted to them by collective rights to persecute dissenters. Svensson provides us with the testimony of one of these dissenters, Delfino Concha. Mr Concha claims he was subject to a cruel injustice as he was exposed to 'intimidation, and isolation from social affairs enjoyed by the community simply because I did not conform to the religious function'.[9] Svensson's response to this testimony is sympathy not with the persecuted individual, but with the persecutors. The tribe's reaction to religious dissent is more understandable, he writes, 'when it is remembered that in tribal societies, and even more particularly in one which is a theocracy, religion is an integral part of the community's life which cannot be detached from other aspects of the community. Violation of religious norms is viewed as literally *threatening the survival* of the entire community'.[10]

The term *survival* seems to be doing most of the justificatory work here; when the freedom of an individual is contrasted with the survival of the community, the latter seems to have much more weight. This, however, would not have been the case if the dissenter's interests were weighed against those of other individuals, especially if they were weighed against the external preferences of others concerning the behaviour of the dissenter.[11]

How should we interpret the term 'survival' as used in this context? Taylor's use of the term sheds light on this question: 'It is axiomatic for the Quebec government that the *survival* and flourishing of French culture in Quebec is a good . . . It is not just a matter of having the French language available for those who might *choose* it . . . Policies aimed at *survival* actively seek to *create* members of the community, for instance, in their assuring that future generations continue to identify as French speakers.'[12]

[9] Frances Svensson, 'Liberal Democracy and Group Rights: The Legacy of Individualism and its Impact on American Indian Tribes', *Political Studies* 27 (1979), 421–39, 432.   [10] Ibid., 433.
[11] See Ronald Dworkin's discussion of external preferences in *Taking Rights Seriously* (London: Duckworth, 1978), 234.
[12] Charles Taylor, 'The Politics of Recognition', in *Examining the Politics of Recognition*, ed. Amy Gutman (Princeton: Princeton University Press, 1994), 58–9 (my emphasis).

In the Canadian case, as in many others, the term *survival* refers not to the actual survival of the community or its members but to the survival of the traditional way of life. Is there a reason to defend a particular way of life from undergoing change? Should one protect a community against cultural revisions or reforms, even radical ones, if these are accepted by its members?[13]

Note that in discussing matters regarding social-cultural changes in terms of a threat to the survival of the community, one serves orthodox voices within the community which seek to justify taking extreme measures, including disregard for individual rights and forceful suspension of internal criticism, for the sake of preventing change.

As this discussion exemplifies, in periods of social and cultural transition, when collective rights are most needed to protect a community from external pressures, they pose a threat to social reformers. If rights are granted to the group as a whole then feminists, religious reformers like liberal Jews or Moslems, social activists like the opponents of the Indian caste system, etc. are deprived of their rights. This cannot happen if rights are granted to individuals. It thus makes a considerable difference who is the bearer of rights. Kymlicka disagrees with this claim; theoretical debates concerning the distinctions between collective rights and individual rights are sterile, he argues, 'because the question whether the right is (or is not) collective is morally unimportant'.[14] Is Kymlicka right? In order to answer this question we should examine his own arguments in some details. Kymlicka draws a distinction between community rights understood as the rights of a group against its own members, and community rights as rights against the larger society. He rejects the former and endorses the latter kind of rights which he terms *group differentiated rights*.[15] Group-differentiated rights, he argues, could be 'accorded to individual members of a group, or to the group as a whole, or to a federal state/province in which the group forms a majority'.[16]

Is it really the case that the question of how rights are allocated bears no moral significance? Kymlicka himself acknowledges that the language of differentiated citizenship rights may be abused. This was the case with laws supporting racial segregation and ethnic discrimination in South Africa (before the abolition of Apartheid), the USA, and Israel. They may also be abused in some of the cases Kymlicka himself endorses. A by-product of granting land rights to Indian tribes as a collective, Kymlicka argues, is that individual members lose control over their property, and are thus prevented from borrowing money or selling assets if they wish to leave the community.[17] As hunting rights

---

[13] One can claim that individuals have no choice but to accept the change if they want to enjoy the benefits offered by the surrounding society. This may indeed be true yet accepting this claim may lead to a slippery slope, which leads to a dangerous paternalism.

[14] Will Kymlicka, *Multicultural Citizenship* (Oxford: Oxford University Press, 1995), 45.

[15] Will Kymlicka, 'Individual and Community Rights', in *Group Rights*, ed. Judith Baker (Toronto: University of Toronto Press, 1994), 17–33.

[16] Kymlicka, *Multicultural Citizenship* (n. 14 above), 45.   [17] Ibid., 43.

are given to Indian tribes as collectives rather than to their individual members 'an Indian whose hunting is restricted by her council cannot claim that this is a denial of her rights, because Indian hunting rights are not accorded to individuals'.[18] Unfortunately, Kymlicka concludes, this 'seems to be a natural by-product' of protecting the rights of minority cultures.

One may wonder, however, how natural or unavoidable this 'by-product' is. Note that if the above rights had been granted to individuals rather than to groups, these individuals could have used these rights to protect themselves against the group. The language of collective rights deprives them of this possibility. This is true even if the justifications offered in defence of these rights are liberal ones.

This paper then is a word of caution, calling upon liberal political theorists, and liberal political activists to acknowledge that group rights strengthen dominant sub-groups within each culture and privilege conservative interpretations of culture over reformative and innovative ones. Women rarely belong to the more powerful groups in society, and protectors of women's rights do not affiliate themselves with conservative segments. It follows then, that women, and those who strive to protect their rights and equal status, are among the first to be harmed by group rights. Their plight, however, is not unique. It is shared by all those who wish to diverge from accepted social norms and question the traditional role of social institutions.

As Okin argued, there is an inherent conflict between feminism and group rights 'which persists even when the latter are claimed on liberal grounds, and are limited to some extent by being so grounded'.[19] Her claims can be expanded to cover a large number of cases in which collective rights come into conflict with the rights of other powerless groups: dissenters, reformers, converts, and the like.

The conflict is not restricted to matters concerning the interpretation of certain rights but also covers the more crucial question of who can claim or waive a right. When individuals are unable to waive their rights, these rights turn into duties which restrict personal autonomy rather than protecting it. Individuals who are deprived of their ability to decide which rights to demand and which to waive, who cannot determine for themselves whether to retain their communal tradition, strive to bring about a change, or assimilate, who cannot decide in which language to educate their children and what to teach them are deprived of their most basic liberties.

The more one inquires into actual case studies, the more one comes to the conclusion that the category of collective rights which are harmless to individual members, is (for all practical purposes) an empty one. It thus seems that the debate between defenders of collective rights and supporters of individual rights is not a vacuous semantic controversy but a crucial debate which bears significant theoretical and practical consequences.

---

[18] Ibid.

[19] Susan Okin, 'Feminism or Multiculturalism', *Boston Review of Books*, October 1997.

Moreover, terminological questions are, in themselves, not unimportant. It is nowadays commonplace to claim that language not only expresses reality, but also shapes it. The language of rights one uses has educational and political implications which shouldn't be overlooked. One of the few social and political tools we can use in order to raise consciousness among oppressed individuals of their rights is to teach them to think of these rights as individual rights, as trumps that can be used against communal oppression and discrimination. The language of collective rights might prevent us from conveying this message. We should then be wary of using it.

III. Collectives and associations

Before we continue the discussion, the concept *collective rights* needs to be clarified. In the recent literature this term has been used to describe a wide range of rights. Van Dyke sees collective rights as corporate rights: the view I have in mind, he writes, 'is suggested by the idea of a corporation, which has rights and liabilities distinct from those of the persons composing it'.[20] Kymlicka rejects this interpretation and prefers the term 'minority rights', as it focuses attention on 'the claims of "natural" groupings, rather than the rights of voluntary or contractual associations such as unions and corporations'.[21] Others, like Raz and Margalit favour the term *group rights*.[22]

I do not attempt to settle this terminological dispute; let me however clarify my own terms. The notion *collective* as used in conjunction with *rights* can be understood in two distinct ways: as the rights of a collective, or of individuals who are members of a certain collective. While the latter term refers to different kinds of individual rights, the former refers to rights granted to a particular kind of agent—a collective one.

In order to analyse the notion of a collective's right it is imperative to distinguish between two kinds of collectives: unorganized, informal collectives and organized ones which constitute legal personalities.[23] My main criticism focuses on bestowing rights to informal collectives like national, religious, ethnic or gender groups. I shall therefore refrain from addressing issues concerning the nature of obligations or rights granted to legal personalities.[24] I take it for

[20] Vernon Van Dyke, 'The Individual, the State, and Ethnic Communities in Political Theory', *The Rights of Minority Cultures*, ed. Will Kymlicka (Oxford: Oxford University Press, 1995), 31–56, 33.

[21] Kymlicka, *Multicultural Citizenship* (n. 14 above), 33.

[22] Joseph Raz and Avishai Margalit, 'The Right to National Self-Determination', in Raz's *Ethics in the Public Domain* (Oxford: Clarendon Press, 1994), 110–30.

[23] In the legal sense a corporation can own property, make contracts, or commit torts, but 'it is not a group: it is a single-fictitious-person, distinct from all the members of the group and from the group itself' (Michael Hartney, 'Some Confusion Concerning Collective Rights', in *The Rights of Minority Cultures* (n. 20 above), 202–27, 214).

[24] I follow here Larry May's distinction between unorganized collectives which he calls *mobs* and organized collectives which he calls *corporations*. Yet I will not follow his terminology. As the term

granted that in order to claim that states, corporations or associations are entitled to some legal rights and could be burdened with some legal duties, one need not introduce collectivist concepts. Such rights and obligations are deeply embedded in the legal system of most states and international organizations. The notion of *collective rights* is of theoretical and political value only if it succeeds in enlarging the scope of the existing rights discourse by applying it to a new type of agent.

One should however note that the distinction between formal and informal associations is not as straight-forward as it may seem. In the United States, Young argues, 'civic groups, more often than not, are organized along the lines of gender, race, religion, ethnicity or sexual orientation, even when they have not explicitly aimed to do so.'[25] And most of these groups are neither purely voluntary nor purely prescriptive; many of them have a loose formal structure and a set of unwritten norms and practices.[26] No wonder, then, that in the literature the discussion swings back and forth between groups, communities, and civic associations. Despite these difficulties, I shall concentrate on the rights of informal collectives.[27]

---

mob often carries pejorative connotations I will use the terms *collectives* or *groups*, terms that would be used interchangeably. (See May, *The Morality of Groups; Collective Responsibility, Group Based Harm, and Corporate Rights* (Notre Dame, Indiana: University of Notre Dame Press, 1987).)

[25] Iris Young, 'Social Groups in Associative Democracy', in *Associations and Democracy*, ed. Erik Olin Wright (London: Verso Press, 1995), 209.

[26] I must stress then that while I argue against the notion of *collective rights* and claim that it is theoretically inconsistent and politically dangerous, I endorse the notions of *associational and corporate rights*. The purpose of this paper is, in fact, to urge liberal political theorists to surrender the language of collective rights not only in favour of individuals rights but also in order to examine the kinds of rights that legal entities—be they states, associations or corporations—are entitled to.

[27] I shall not enter here into a discussion concerning the rights of associations. Nevertheless, let me make one brief remark in order to prevent misunderstandings: I do not adopt a libertarian line according to which as long as the right to exist is protected, associations are allowed to adopt any policies they wish even if these violate the basic rights of their members. Associations and corporations possess rights—and among the rights they possess is the right to determine the rights and duties of their members—and liberal societies acknowledge the existence of certain fundamental rights that all individuals must possess and cannot be lost through corporate membership. Hence, while in reference to a large range of interests, members of associations may be legally invisible to the government, membership ought not render them wholly invisible. A liberal-democratic government must be ready to protect the basic rights of its citizens against incursion; for example, unions are granted rights in order to protect the interests of their members. Consequently, the interests of those who deviate from the union's line could be harmed. For example, those who feel they are better off bargaining on their own are unable to do so. Under a regime of collective bargaining and union shop, individual workers become legally invisible to the courts, and even to their own employers, with respect to a vast range of economic interests. Their interests are mediated by the union, which becomes their spokesperson and agent. Their rights and duties are defined by the union's by-laws and by the agreements that the unions exact from the industry. Union bargaining is legitimate as long as it does not violate the basic rights of its members. If the union will accept an agreement which will force Jews to work on a Saturday, women to be paid less than men, or Blacks to do only manual work, then there will be good reason to overrule that agreement. If, on the other hand, the agreement reached by the union disallows some individuals to earn more than they could have earned if they had bargained individually, then no basic rights have been violated as no individual has a right to earn more than his fellow workers.

IV. CAN COLLECTIVES BE RIGHTS-HOLDERS?

When rights theories were born, the range of rights-holders was narrow and comprised white males who were property owners. In the last two centuries it has been expanded first to non-property holders, then to women, Blacks, and members of minority groups; should we now expand it to include collectives? Note that the traditional description of a rights-holder could be easily extended to include members of the above-mentioned groups. It could, in fact, be claimed that in these cases the social-political applicability of theories of rights was expanded while their theoretical scope remained constant. This, however, is not the case with collective rights.

Can collectives be *rights-holders*? Unfortunately this question is rarely discussed.[28] Let's look at this issue from the point of view of the two dominant theories of rights: the choice theory and the interest theory. The choice theory is described by H.L.A. Hart. Hart interprets the claim 'P has a right to X' as: P has a right to do X if he so chooses. If P has a right to X, others require special justifications for limiting P's freedom in pursuing X, while P has a justification for limiting the freedom of others in the course of his pursuit of X.[29] The role of a right then, is to secure a realm of choice in which rights-holders are free to act without external intervention.

Who can qualify as a rights-holder? According to Hart, a rights-holder is 'an adult human being capable of choice', whose activities depend on his ability to make rational decisions.[30] For the choice theory, then, rationality and autonomy are indispensable features of rights-holders. This description makes it particularly hard to apply the choice theory to collectives, as it would demand that collectives be seen not only as active, intentional agents but also as rational and autonomous ones.

The interest theory of rights may offer better support for group rights. According to this theory, 'X has a right if and only if X can have rights and, other things being equal, an aspect of X's well-being (his interest) is a sufficient reason for holding some other person(s) under a duty.'[31] This is a purely formal view which needs to be supplemented by a specification of the type of agents that can have rights and the types of interests that can produce sufficient reason for holding others under a duty.

According to Raz, an agent is entitled to have rights 'if either his well-being is of ultimate value or he is an artificial person (e.g. a corporation).'[32] The collectives discussed here fall under neither of these definitions. Are they the

---

[28] One could, at this stage of the debate, turn to international legal documents in which the rights of peoples are recognized; but these documents are notoriously ambiguous both in their definition of rights-holders and in the definition of the rights that could be attributed to them. I therefore choose not to base my argument on these documents but to seek an independent justification.

[29] H. L. A. Hart, 'Are There Any Natural Rights?', *Philosophical Review* 64 (1955), 175–91.

[30] Ibid., 175.

[31] Raz, *The Morality of Freedom* (Oxford: Oxford University Press, 1986), 166.   [32] Ibid.

kind of agents whose interests, or parts thereof, can be seen as sufficient grounds for holding others under a duty?

Raz obviously believes they are. Belief in the existence of rights, he claims, 'does not commit one to individualism. States, corporations and groups might be right-holders. Banks have legal and moral rights. Nations are commonly believed to have the right of self-determination, and so on'.[33]

He restates his assumption that groups can have rights in his discussion of the right to national self-determination (together with Margalit) in which the following question is asked: 'Assuming that self-determination is enjoyed by groups, what groups qualify?'[34] This question presupposes that groups, some groups, could qualify as rights-holders.

Margalit and Raz ground their justifications for national self-determination in the importance of membership in encompassing communities for the self-identification and prosperity of individual members. These arguments are used to explain why membership in such communities is an individual interest worthy of protection. But how can arguments grounded in the interests of individuals be used to support a '*collective's right*'?

In order to answer this question we have to take a closer look at Raz's definition of collective rights. According to Raz, a collective right exists when the following three conditions are met: First, there exists an aspect of the interest of human beings that justifies holding some person(s) under a duty; second, the interest(s) in question are interests in a public good and the right is a right to that public good; and lastly, the interest of no single member of that group in that public good is sufficient, by itself, to justify holding others under a duty.[35]

The first condition is strictly individualistic; it depends on the existence of an individual interest which justifies holding some person(s) under a duty. The second condition brings in a communal dimension which relates to the nature of the interest—an interest in a public good. The third condition brings in consequential considerations. A right is a collective one if its realization imposes far-reaching duties on others. As the interest of no single individual can justify imposing such duties, no individual can be a holder of this right. This latter condition is stated by Raz in the following form:

If B's interest does not justify holding A to be under a duty to do X then B has no right that A shall do X even if A has a duty to do X based on the fact that the action will serve the interests of a class of individuals of whom B is one. Thus a government may have a duty to try and improve the standard of living of all its inhabitants even though no single inhabitant has a right that the government shall try to improve his standard of living.[36]

This definition embodies a cost-benefit analysis. The nature of rights is then to be defined in a two-step procedure: the first identifies the kind of individual interests that could, in principle, give rise to a right; the second evaluates the

---

[33] Ibid.
[34] Raz and Margalit, 'The Right to National Self-Determination' (n. 22 above), 113.
[35] Raz, *The Morality of Freedom* (n. 31 above), 208.   [36] Ibid., 182, fn. 1.

burdens imposed by rights defending these interests and weighs them against the benefits of protecting that interest. Only if the result of the weighing process is of a certain kind (unspecified by Raz) can we claim that there is a sufficient reason to impose the relevant duties on others.[37]

The precise nature of both steps is unclear. As I cannot develop here a fully-fledged criticism of Raz's approach, let me concentrate on one issue only. Can this theory be applied to the kind of collective agents with which I am interested here? A theory that places interests at its core must have an underlying theory of agency which will allow one to identify the kinds of interests worthy of protection. In Raz's writings such a theory is implied (though never fully stated) by the relations between X's ability to be the holder of rights and the fact that X's well-being is of ultimate value. It is unlikely that this kind of theory—which seems to be a derivative of Kant's kingdom of ends—could be extended to corporations, associations, social groups or collectives. The existence of collectives may indeed be of value and their preservation could impose certain duties, but unless one is ready to claim that collectives are the kind of agents whose existence is of ultimate value, the Razian definition collapses.

And yet, Raz's theory demands that collectives will be granted rights lest a whole set of rights will go unrecognized. This phenomenon results from the fact that according to Raz's definition, the very existence of a right depends on it being a sufficient reason for holding other(s) under a duty. In those cases in which the realization of a certain right imposes a too-heavy burden on others, such a right can be defended only if it is enjoyed by a large enough number of individuals whose accumulated benefit justifies the imposition of duties. Consequently, no single individual could be the holder of this right.

There are two problems with this account: first, while it makes the very existence of a right dependent on a cost-benefit analysis, it does not specify what should be placed on both sides of the scale. In determining the nature of rights, should we make a general a priori estimate as to what the cost-benefit analysis might be under normal circumstances, or should we look for particular cases in which the right is about to be implemented? If we take the latter route we will not be able to make decontextualized, a priori, judgements about rights— not even about basic rights. All we would be able to say is that under certain circumstances X has a right to freedom of speech whereas under some other circumstances he does not. But this will rule out rights discourse as an educational, corrective or guiding tool. Moreover, instead of promoting justice, this interpretation of Raz's theory would motivate individuals and institutions to hinder justice.

A real-life example might clarify this point: In the thirty years since Israel has occupied the West Bank, it has settled hundreds of thousands of individuals in the occupied territories. The settlers have established a life for themselves and their children in these territories, and developed expectations to continue living

---

[37] I am grateful to Tamar Meisels for discussing this issue with me.

in their houses, working their fields, and sustaining their communal life. All these activities have raised the costs of an Israeli withdrawal from the West Bank. According to Raz's theory, raising costs has two effects: first, in order to justify the duties imposed on Israelis, the number of Palestinians who enjoy the right to national self-determination must constantly be on the rise, and second, there might be a point at which the costs will be so high that the right will disappear altogether. In this latter case the right will not be violated, or overridden, but will cease to exist.

The ability to cause a right to vanish must motivate those who oppose it to raise the costs of its implementation. This is not an unknown procedure. Consider the following example: suppose that in a certain community there will be enough anti-abortion fanatics who will attempt to kill a member of the personnel of an abortion clinic every time an abortion is being performed. Under these circumstances the price of protecting women's rights to perform abortions might be exceedingly high. If we accept the interpretation of Raz's theory offered so far, we might have to conclude that under these circumstances women's right to control their bodies has been expunged. It follows that in such cases women's inability to gain control over their bodies does not constitute a violation of their rights.

One could, however, argue that Raz does not endorse the above interpretation, rather he sees the qualification 'other things being equal' as referring to some hypothetical set of 'normal' circumstances. How can we evaluate the burdens imposed by the interest of women in having control over their bodies under such 'normal' circumstances? We may start by assuming that the term *normal* ought to refer only to those actions which are morally justified. The costs imposed by immoral acts should not be taken into account. This would imply that women's right to their bodies is a right which immoral acts cannot negate.

Collective rights, then, are the kind of rights the realization of which, under normal circumstances, is too costly if only one person can benefit from them (provided that the costs calculated are solely moral and normal ones). Which rights fall under this description? The answer depends on an account of the nature of 'normal' circumstances and the costs involved in the implementation of a right under such circumstances. What would the costs of freedom of speech, or of the right to national self-determination be under normal circumstances? The answer depends on the scope of the right. If freedom of speech demands that individuals should be able to speak on any topic, at any time, in any place, in any volume, then the social costs of such a right might be unreasonably high (e.g., if the right includes the right of secret agents to disclose, at times of war, national secrets). Similarly, if the right to self-determination demands that each individual would be given a state of her own the costs might indeed be exceedingly high. However, the fact that realizing one's right in the most satisfactory and expanded form would impose far too heavy burdens on others should not imply that a more modest and restrained realization of this right should not be defended. No right ought to be realized regardless of its costs, but no right should be eliminated just because it is impossible to implement it in the most extended form.

As all rights could be realized at different points along a continuum, how can we define the point along this continuum at which we should situate ourselves in order to evaluate the costs of each right? Raz seems to use different standards for evaluating individual and collective rights. In the case of the former he takes the more modest forms of realization to be the standard for the implementation of the right while in the case of the latter, he takes the more extreme version to be the standard. This leads to the conclusion that collective rights are the kind of rights that cannot exist at all, when applied to individuals. This leaves Raz with a real worry. How could some rights, which have moral and political importance, come into being? His answer is given in terms of collective rights.

One must remember that this conclusion is valid if, and only if, we endorse Raz's theory. If, however, we accept the claim that cost-benefit analysis should not enter into the definition of basic rights, or argue that theories of rights must take into account the fact that each right can be implemented in different forms, then the theoretical vacuum created by Raz's theory disappears and with it the need to turn to collective rights.

The claim that cost-benefit analysis should not play a role in determining the rights we have concurs with the view that the nature of a right should be defined by its justifications rather than by its modes of implementation. Namely, that rights which are justified by making reference to individual interests are individual rights even if, most commonly, they cannot be implemented by single individuals. We should then distinguish between matters of principle and matters of policy. As a matter of principle, rights which are meant to protect the interests of individuals are individual rights; as a matter of policy, a decision to protect individuals in exercising these rights might be justified only if there is a certain threshold number of beneficiaries. Hence, the size of the group deriving benefits from a particular right might influence the prospects of its realization: the larger the number of beneficiaries, the stronger the justification to burden others with the relevant costs.

Another way of understanding Raz's notion of collective rights is to merge his interest theory of rights—according to which a right is seen as an interest-based reason for imposing some duty(ies) on others—with the claim that groups have interests which are non-reducible to those of individuals, thus claiming that groups should be seen as independent rights-holders. But in order to do so, the argument must start not with the well-being and interests of individuals but with that of groups. Yet Raz supports the importance of collective rights by making reference to the importance of group membership for individuals and dedicates little space to the more crucial question of groups' interests: Do such interests exist at all? Margalit and Raz claim they do, and that due to their relative independence of individual interests there is no a priori way of correlating the former with the latter. Their arguments seem unconvincing. But suppose, for the sake of argument, that some interests could best be described as group interests; does it follow that groups should be seen as bearers of rights defending these interests?

According to Kukathas, the claim that groups have independent interests is insufficient to establish that groups can be rights-holders, as the particular nature of groups' interests excludes the possibility of seeing such interests as grounds for rights. Group interests, he argues, 'exist or take their particular shape, only because of certain historical circumstances or because political institutions prevail and not because they are part of some natural order'.[38] But surely Kukathas does not think that individuals' interests are part of some natural order or that they are formed free of all historical circumstances or social influences. The reason to respect individual rather than group interests cannot possibly be the fact that the former are natural while the latter are not.

Moreover, Kukathas' argument invites an unnecessary discussion concerning the origin of individual interests. Yet, the debate between supporters and opponents of collective rights is not grounded in different views of the origins of individual interests, preferences or motivations. It would be misleading to claim that supporters of moral individualism see individuals as essentially atomized, autonomous, self-creating agents, while communitarians see individuals as totally encumbered by their communal setting. The real debate concerns the following question: how should the facts, recognized by both supporters and adversaries of collective rights, that individuals are contextualized, that they find meaning and pleasure in communal affiliations, and that their interests are structured (at least partly) by membership in various collectives, influence our theory of rights?

Note that liberalism, even in its more traditional forms, is committed to protecting personal autonomy, yet it is not committed to defending only those interests and preferences which are autonomously formed. It is quite obvious that many of the basic liberties liberalism defends, are, by definition, community-bound; including religious and political rights. The claim that ethical individualism fails to respect persons bound by duties derived from sources other than themselves is, therefore, unfounded.

The reason we should respect the interests of individuals and not of groups derives from the nature of the agents who have these interests, and not from the nature or the origins of the interests themselves. Here we can find support in Raz's own definition of rights-holders. An individual is capable of having rights, he argues, 'if and only if, either his well-being is of ultimate value or he is an "artificial person" (e.g. a corporation).'[39] If we apply this definition to Raz's and Margalit's own argument, a disturbing inconsistency emerges. Their argument in support of the right of groups to self-determination is grounded in the claim that the prosperity of encompassing groups is 'vital for the prosperity of their members'.[40] This line of argument suggests that group interests should be

---

[38] Chandran Kukathas, 'Are There any Cultural Rights?', *Political Theory* 20 (1992), 105–39, 111 (my emphasis).   [39] Raz, *The Morality of Freedom* (n. 31 above), 166.
[40] Raz and Margalit 'The Right to National Self-Determination' (n. 22 above), 119.

198 Yael (Yuli) Tamir

protected because groups are *instrumental* to the interests of individuals, not because their well-being is of ultimate value. Hence, on his own grounds Raz's argument fails to establish the status of groups (which do not constitute themselves as artificial persons) as potential rights-holders.

Consequently, asking which collectives qualify as rights-holders is asking the wrong question. And yet this question has attracted much attention. Supporters of collective rights like Kymlicka, Van-Dyke, Margalit, Raz, and Svensson, as well as opponents of collective rights like Kukathas and Reaume, devote lengthy discussions to establishing distinctions between different kinds of collectives. Supporters of collective rights attempt to find 'the right kind of collectives', which are entitled to be rights-holders—according to Van Dyke these include ethnic communities, nations, and the populations of political dependencies and sovereign states and trade unions, and exclude 'chance aggregates and even social and economic classes, [which] may have group interests, but not group rights'.[41] According to Raz and Margalit the collectives that qualify as rights-holders are encompassing groups, while Kymlicka prefers the term national minorities.

Opponents search for deficiencies in each other's definitions, trying to claim that the collectives mentioned cannot qualify as holders of rights, that the concept of a collective is too vague, its identity undetermined and so on. The chief concerns about according rights to groups are an interrelated set of problems of indeterminacy, Reaume argues: 'First, there may be indeterminacy concerning the group's boundaries, which in turn threatens to give rise to indeterminacy vis-à-vis its interests. Second, it may be difficult to identify group actions and decisions of the sort normally associated with exercising and waiving rights.'[42]

This unnecessary debate results from the fact that efforts to define the characteristics of those collectives that are entitled to enjoy collective rights are discussed prior to discussions of the much more fundamental question: can any collective qualify as a rights-holder? If the answer to this preliminary question is negative, as I have argued, the rest of the debate is vacuous.

Nevertheless, some may insist that despite the objections raised so far, the language of collective rights cannot be surrendered, as the language of individual rights simply does not makes sense in certain cases. In what follows I shall challenge these claims.

V. Are collective rights indispensable?

Is the notion of collective rights indispensable? I'll answer this question by raising, and answering, four possible objections to my own position, all of

---

[41] Van Dyke, 'The Individual, the State, and Ethnic Communities in Political Theory' (n. 20 above), 33.
[42] Denise Reaume, 'The Group Right to Linguistic Security; Whose Rights? What Duties?', in *Group Rights* (n. 15 above), 118–41, 124.

which make a similar claim: no matter how convincing arguments against collective rights are, if we are to defend certain kinds of interests we simply cannot do without them. The first two objections take individuals' interests as their starting point but claim that these interests would be best served by granting rights to collectives rather than individuals. The last two draw on the notion of collective goods, and claim that rights protecting the pursuit of such goods must be collective ones.

Objection A.: Collective rights are the kind of rights that could be realized only within a collective framework. It makes no sense, it is argued, to grant an individual a right to pursue a communal practice. Is this claim well-founded? Let us look at one of the most common examples of a collective right, that of national self-determination. At the heart of this right lies an interest to preserve and express one's communal identity and culture. Does it make sense to grant such a right to an isolated individual? The answer depends on the different ways the right can be realized. It is quite clear that one can declare oneself Israeli, Palestinian, Basque or French even when alone, and that some features of the national culture and tradition can be retained in complete solitude; reading to oneself in one's own language, reciting poems, practising some traditional ceremonies etc. The ability to enjoy these benefits in solitude is indeed restricted; it grows relative to the size of the group, and reaches full expression in the presence of a community.

The fact that a certain right can be realized in its fullest form within the framework of a community does not imply that it is worthless to isolated individuals. Modern technology opens up new opportunities that allow individuals to communicate with distant communities: they can read daily newspapers on the Internet, listen to radio programmes or watch TV shows, talk on the phone to their relatives, fax them written material, and fly back home for a visit. Such individuals can remain in touch with their community of origins even when they reside miles away from home, and consequently they may wish to preserve the communal traditions and way of life to the best of their ability.

Acknowledging the full spectrum of possible expressions of identity and culture is of utmost importance in an age of massive immigration in which individuals struggle to retain their identity even when detached from their homeland. For such individuals, being granted rights which allow them to preserve their identity—in the restricted form dictated by their separation from other members—is the only barrier against the pressures of assimilation and feelings of uprootedness.[43]

There are, however, some rights one can enjoy only within the framework of a group. For example rights which are dependent on the existence of a certain institutional setting such as the right to be elected, the right to due process, or the right to enjoy a fair system of criminal justice. As no isolated individual can

---

[43] Telecommunication can also allow for a form of electronic immigration in which the emigrant need not usurp his/her culture to reside in another.

form her own set of institutions these rights seem to be dependent on the existence of a group. Are these rights to be seen as collective rights? Hartney rejects
the claim that rights which are grounded in a social setting only a group can
establish are group rights. This faulty conclusion, he maintains, leads to the following implausible consequences: 'since a fair system of criminal justice is something only a group, and not an individual, can have, it would follow that
individuals cannot have any right to a fair system of criminal justice, and that no
individual's right would be violated if the system is not fair'.[44] One can conclude
then, that the fact that a right cannot be enjoyed outside the existence of a socio-
political system, and that no isolated individual can construct such a system on
his own, is no evidence that the rights the system protects are collective rights.

   Objection B.: Some individuals' interests can best be served by allocating the
relevant right to a group. The apparent plausibility of this objection is grounded
in confusion between two claims: that some individual interests can be better
pursued within a collective framework, and that some individual interests will
be better served if granted to the community rather than to its individual
members. There is a world of difference between these two claims. The first is
commonplace, and poses no threat to an individualistic conception of rights.
After all, the desire to secure for oneself the most individualistic right of all–the
right to self-preservation—leads individuals to contract and form political
frameworks, as they believe that this right will be best served within such
frameworks. It would be ludicrous to claim that for that reason we should see
this right as a collective right.

   The second claim is not only more problematic but embodies an actual threat
to individuals' rights and liberties. Its plausibility depends on a particular interpretation of the term *individuals' interests*, which presupposes that all members
of a collective have at least some identical interests and that the collective would
use the rights granted to it to defend these interests and these interests only.
There is, however, no reason to accept either of these claims. Collectives are not
undifferentiated wholes, and their members may entertain radically different,
even conflicting, interests. Granting the right to 'the collective' in order to protect 'its interests', forces 'the collective' to define a uniform set of interests—a
process which is likely to provoke among members of the dominant sub-
group(s) the motivation to repress dissenting or marginalized individuals, and
the power to do so. An interesting example comes out of Svensson's discussion
of the case of the Pueblo Indians. Difficulties had arisen, he argues, 'when a few
individuals among the Indians, under various types of pressures and influences,
particularly conversion to Protestant Christianity, chose to withdraw from certain communal functions while at the same time demanding their 'share' in the
community and its resources'. Svensson's wording reflects the way dissidents
are portrayed; they are seen as weak-willed individuals who, under pressure,
betray the group. Those who conform to the norms of the group, on the other

---

[44] Hartney, 'Some Confusion Concerning Collective Rights' (n. 23 above), 218.

hand, are viewed as authentic, loyal and virtuous individuals. These images place social, religious and cultural reformists and dissenters at a clear disadvantage. They are often excluded from the centres of power, and are deprived of their ability to pursue their own interpretation of the collective's norms, traditions, way of life.

This is well exemplified by an analysis of the difficulties reformist and liberal Jews face in Israel. In Israel, religious rights are granted to religious communities rather than to individuals. The chief rabbinical authorities thus determine for all Jews the acceptable ways of practice. Consequently, reform and conservative Jews who disagree with the orthodox interpretation of Judaism are deprived of their religious rights; they do not get a fair share of the state's support for religious practice, they are unable to get land for burial, the marriages and conversion they perform are not recognized by the state, they are never invited to perform official ceremonies and the like. No surprise then that these movements have failed to establish a strong hold in Israel. In the USA, on the other hand, where religious rights are granted to individuals, each Jew can decide to which of the existing Jewish congregations he/she will adhere. All American Jews thus enjoy equal religious rights, and use them to form institutional settings in which they can follow the practices of the community of their choice. As a result, the reform and conservative movements flourish in the USA.

One can summarize this section by claiming that functionalist attempts to defend collective rights by making reference to the interests of individuals fail. Indeed many rights cannot be realized outside of a community but this is no evidence that these rights belong to the community. There are many enabling arrangements without which rights are meaningless, but these arrangements, in themselves, need not be the bearers of rights.

One could still claim that as some goods cannot be given to individuals they must be the subject of collective rights. The next two objections refer then to the nature of the good the rights serve to protect and argue that there could be no individual right to a collective good.

Objection C.: According to Waldron the justification of a right depends on the good it promotes. Those rights which protect the pursuit of a collective good cannot be a matter of individual right, as the value of a collective good can only be appreciated with reference to its benefit to the group as a whole. A claim of right does two things, Waldron argues: 'it specifies a good, and it specifies a person—a beneficiary, a rights-holder—for whom, or for whose sake, the good is to be brought about'.[45] As no account of the worth of common goods to any particular individual can be given except by concentrating on what they are worth to all, 'the duty to realize such goods must be grounded in an adequate characterization of their desirability, and that is their worth to members of the group considered together not as individual recipients of benefit . . . So

---

[45] Jeremy Waldron, 'Can Communal Good be Human Rights?' in *Waldron's Liberal Rights* (Cambridge: Cambridge University Press, 1993), 339–69, 355.

202 _Yael (Yuli) Tamir_

since no adequate account of its desirability can be pinned down to either X or Y or Z, there can be no _point_ in saying it ought to be pursued as X's or Y's or Z's right.'[46]

Waldron suggests that the worth of communal goods cannot be measured for each individual. The worth of culture, solidarity, or shared language is larger than its cumulative worth to each individual. These experiences are unintelligible without reference to the mutual experiences of the participants. I certainly agree that the full worth of culture can be appreciated only if we take into account the importance of interpersonal exchanges; nevertheless I argue that the worth of culture to individuals can be measured and should be the only criterion for the allocation of cultural rights.

The claim that cultural rights should be grounded only in the value of culture to its individual members has far reaching implications, as non-members may also favour the preservation and flourishing of a certain culture. Suppose a small community of Latin speakers exists on some remote island. Members of this community may believe they would be better off, for both financial and cultural reasons, if they gave up their original language and assimilated into the English-speaking community that surrounds them. Yet, others who are not members of this community may think that keeping Latin alive is of great cultural value and that members of the community should continue to preserve and develop the Latin language. As the community of Latin speakers is very small and the number of non-members who are interested in the survival of the language is very large, taking external preferences into account might justify forcing members of the community to preserve their culture.[47] To call such an oppressive attitude a right is absurd.

I therefore agree with Dworkin's claim that external preferences should not count and cannot provide a justification for a right. Rights ought to be justified only with reference to their internal value to individuals even if this justification will fail to capture the full worth of the good in question.

Objection D.: As collective goods are non-exclusive it makes no difference who is their holder. Indeed, collective goods are provided in ways which makes exclusion almost impossible; nevertheless, it does make a difference whether they are granted to individual members or to the collective as a whole. Granting the right to individuals protects their freedom and promotes pluralism within groups as well as among them. It makes a difference whether I have a right to language which I can use or waive at will, or whether the community has a right to language which I cannot waive, or demand on my own. In the first case I am recognized as an independent agent who can determine her life plan and pursue it; in the second I am but an organ of a whole I cannot control. We are then

---

[46] Jeremy Waldron, 'Can Communal Good be Human Rights?' (n. 45 above), 339–69, 355, 359.

[47] Similarly, taking into account external preferences might justify refusing members of some other community a right to preserve their language or tradition on the grounds that non-members consider this language and tradition to be of inferior value, or even dangerous.

back to the claims that opened our discussion, regarding the political importance of the ability to demand and waive rights and the educational importance
of the kind of rights language that is being used.

VI. CONCLUSIONS

Some may argue, that despite the reservations raised so far, the language of
group rights should be preserved, as it has symbolic importance; it signifies the
role groups ought to play in social life. The decision whether to adopt the language of individual rights or of group rights, Glazer argues, is of great importance, as it reflects the model of social life a state endorses: 'If the state sets
before itself a model that group membership is purely private, a shifting matter
of individual choice and degree, something that may be weakened and dissolved
in times as other identities take over, then to place an emphasis on group rights
is to hamper this development . . . If, on the other hand, the model a society has
for itself, today and in the future, is of a confederation of groups, with group
membership as central and permanent, and with divisions among groups making it unrealistic or unjust to envisage these group identities weakening in time
to be replaced by common citizenship, then it must take the path of determining what the rights of each group shall be.'[48]

The debate between supporters of individuals' rights and groups' rights is
thus portrayed as a debate between two camps. One camp consists of those
who believe that members of ethnic and national groups should be protected
against discrimination and prejudice, and should be free to maintain whatever
part of their ethnic heritage or identity they wish to maintain, but believe that
these 'efforts are purely private, and it is not the place of public agencies to
attach legal identities or disabilities to cultural membership in ethnic groups'.[49]
The other comprises those who think that ethnicity should be displayed in the
public sphere and that the state should support public measures aimed at
protecting or promoting an ethno-cultural identity.

This may have been an adequate portrayal of the state of the debate in the
seventies when Glazer wrote the above passage, but in recent years the debate
has shifted elsewhere: it is no longer a debate between liberals who claim that
pluralism is a historically contingent fact of social life which societies ought to
overcome and communitarians who see it as an enduring feature of modern
societies.[50] Instead it is a debate which takes the fact of pluralism as its starting
point and asks what is the best way to assure to individuals, rooted in their own
cultural, linguistic, and religious communities, their rights.

---

[48] Nathan Glazer, 'Individuals' Rights Against Groups' Rights', *The Rights of Minority Cultures*
(n. 20 above), 123–38, 134.   [49] Will Kymlicka, 'Introduction', in ibid., 1–27, 9.
[50] See John Rawls' discussion of the fact of pluralism in *Political Liberalism* (New York:
Columbia University Press, 1995).

It is from this point of view that I have analysed the distinction between rights granted to collectives and rights granted to individual members of collectives and endorsed the notion of individual rights. Granting rights to collectives rather than to individuals, I have argued, too often leads to the violation of basic individuals' rights.

The fact that collectives cannot be the holders of rights does not mean that policies adopted in order to protect members of disempowered groups, to promote social justice, or to remedy injustice are undesirable: but it seems advisable *to avoid* defining such arrangements in terms of collective rights, as individuals do not have *a right* to any particular political arrangement, but only to a just one. Nor does my argument imply that there is no room in the public sphere for any other associations but the state. Individuals have a right to form associations or corporations, which allow them to pursue their rights collectively. But in order to deal with these agencies there is no need to turn to the language of collective rights. For all these reasons the language of collective rights should be abandoned.

12

Communal Groups and Cultural Conflict

BERNHARD PETERS

In certain ways, Joseph Raz's distinct version of a liberal moral and political theory seems to be particularly congenial to political conceptions of 'multiculturalism', understood as political support for a variety of cultural communities.

For Raz, notions like personal well-being, freedom or autonomy, leading a successful life are the central elements of normative political theory. Freedom and the chances of leading a successful life are crucially dependent on certain cultural and social conditions. Freedom requires the availability of meaningful options, and such options are (to a large degree at least) provided by group membership, the participation in group cultures or in collective ways of life, and the immersion in 'social forms'.[1]

Another important condition is the fact of pluralism, and more specifically of value pluralism. Pluralism, for Raz, means the fact that 'our societies consist of groups and communities with diverse practices and beliefs, including groups whose beliefs are inconsistent with each other . . .'.[2] Value pluralism, as understood by Raz, has two aspects. First, there is a variety of different, partly incompatible, but valid values which are embedded in the social practices of different societies, or social groups.[3] Second, these values are in large part not only incompatible (in the sense that they could not all be fully realized in any individual life), but also incommensurable or incomparable, in the specific sense that Raz has given these terms.

Now we know already from the various debates about conceptions of multiculturalism that statements about culture as a condition of individual freedom

---

[1] Raz even maintains that 'social forms do more than determine the availability of valuable options. They constitute them.' (Joseph Raz, 'Facing up: A Reply', *Southern California Law Review*, 62 (1989), 1218.) In an earlier text, Raz explains why he prefers the concept 'social forms' over notions like social practices or conventions: 'These appear to be concerned exclusively with behaviour, and attitudes to behaviour. I mean social forms to consist of shared beliefs, folklore, high culture, collectively shared metaphors and imagination, and so on.' (*The Morality of Freedom* (Oxford: Clarendon Press, 1986), 311.) This comes close to E.B. Tylor's famous 'anthropological' definition of culture (E.B. Tylor, *Primitive Culture: Researches in the Development of Mythology, Philosophy, Art, and Custom* (London: J. Murray, 1871), Vol. 1, 1)—and is maybe open to some of the objections which have been directed at this conception (especially with regard to its apparent assumptions of coherence and so on).

[2] Raz, *Ethics in the Public Domain* (Oxford: Clarendon Press, 1994), 60.   [3] Ibid., 174.

or autonomy only support the claim that individuals should be able to participate in *some* group or group culture. Whereas they do *not* yet support the claim that different individuals would need to participate in *their own* various cultures. However, Raz provides additional considerations which give support to the normative validity of cultural *pluralism*, and the undesirability of assimilation, or at least of rapid and 'forced' cultural change and assimilation. One consideration pertains to individual identity: for many people, membership in the cultural group into which they were socialized contributes to their sense of personal identity. Abandonment of *their* group, even if generally feasible, would bring about considerable problems for their sense of self. The other consideration pertains to the facilitating role of shared culture for social interaction, above all for close personal relationships, like that between parents and children: '. . . in one's relation with one's children and with one's parents, a common culture is an essential condition for the tight bonding we expect and desire'.[4]

From these assumptions, Raz can in a relatively straightforward way derive normative principles of policy recommendations with respect to cultural and group pluralism: 'Given those beliefs, multiculturalism requires a political society to recognize the equal standing of all the stable and viable cultural communities existing in that society.'[5] This implies some kind of 'affirmative multiculturalism', which goes beyond toleration or policies of non-discrimination. Specific recommendations are: the young of all cultural groups should, 'if their parents so desire' be educated in the culture of their groups, but also be made familiar with the other cultures within their society. The customs of groups should 'within the limits of permissible toleration', be recognized and accommodated in law, as well as in all institutions or organizations which serve the public. The link between poverty and ethnicity should be broken. Autonomous cultural institutions should be supported by the state, and public spaces should be made available to all the cultural groups.

Many of these principles or recommendations will probably be shared by other liberal theories of multiculturalism, even if the philosophical foundations of these principles are certainly contested. Of course, as Raz himself notes, there remain many problems of application or implementation in specific circumstances.

But I do not want to take issue here either with Raz's philosophical position in general or with his general conception of liberal multiculturalism. Instead I am mainly interested in some problems of empirical application, and in some of the empirical assumptions or presuppositions of Raz's writings on multiculturalism. This interest, however, brings me first to some conceptual questions: what exactly does Raz mean by 'cultural pluralism' or 'value pluralism', and

---

[4] Ibid., 162f Raz, however, acknowledges the inevitability of cultural change: 'So long as the process is not coerced, does not arise out of lack of respect for people and their communities, and is gradual, there is nothing wrong with it. The dying of cultures is as much part of normal life as the birth of new ones.' (Ibid., 167)   [5] Ibid., 159.

which groups, or what kinds of groups does he have in mind as carriers of different cultures and values? His main references go to different 'ways of life' or 'styles of life': 'Views and opinions, activities, emotions, etc., expressed or portrayed (in forms of public expression) are an aspect of a wider net of opinions, sensibilities, habits of action or dressing, attitudes, etc., which, taken together, form a distinctive style or form of life.'[6] Carriers of different ways of life may be occupations or professions, life forms constituted by family status (single, or member of a large family), lifestyle communities which consist of members who have important preferences in common (country or urban living).[7] But most importantly, cultural or value differences are found between 'encompassing groups' with 'pervasive cultures'.[8]

How do these kinds of group pluralism relate to *value* pluralism, and in which ways can values or other cultural features compete or conflict? Here, Raz mainly relies on his concepts of incompatibility and incommensurability. Values are incommensurable or incomparable, if they cannot be ranked (to put it very briefly). This becomes a problem only if these values, or the ways of life in which they are embedded, are also incompatible: 'They are incompatible in that no person can combine all of them in one single life, as they call on different qualities and require the relative neglect or even suppression of other qualities which are good in themselves. It is this value multiplicity, this incompatibility of much that is valuable, that I mean by value pluralism.'[9] These descriptions and conceptual distinctions are by and large intelligible and clear enough. Some clarifications or amplifications might still be in order.

First, it should be emphasized that value pluralism and cultural, or group pluralism are overlapping, but not identical phenomena. In principle, there could be value pluralism (i.e. a pluralism of incommensurable and partly incompatible values) without cultural pluralism, or at least without a pluralism of distinct and encompassing group cultures. And there could be group pluralism, even a pluralism of encompassing groups, without value pluralism. Finally, incompatible values, even if not held by one individual, but by different groups, do not necessarily lead to conflict. These propositions depend, of course, on the precise meaning given to terms like value pluralism, group pluralism, and incompatibility (or rivalry) of values.

If we mean by group pluralism a plurality of encompassing groups, or at least a plurality of groups in the stricter sociological sense of the term (in contrast to mere social categories, members of groups must have some sense of common

---

[6] Ibid., 138.   [7] Ibid., 117, 119.

[8] Ibid., 118. There is some similarity with Kymlicka's notion of encompassing or societal cultures 'meaningful ways of life across the full range of human activities, including social, educational, religious, recreational, and economic life, encompassing both public and private spheres.' (W. Kymlicka, *Multicultural Citizenship* (Oxford: Oxford University Press, 1995), 76.) But Kymlicka's definition seems to be stronger (at least in this passage). I have some doubts about how we should understand these terms, and if we understand them in a strong sense, how many real examples of such encompassing and distinct culture really exist. But that would be another topic.   [9] Ibid., 119.

membership, or collective identity—they must be groups 'für sich', not only 'an sich'), there could be kinds of value pluralism which are independent from divisions between groups. There may be cultural commonalities within certain social categories and differences between them, without a corresponding sense of group identity. Raz himself gives the example of occupations, professions, or lifestyles (or 'milieus', to add another term which again has become popular among sociologists studying forms of social and cultural differentiation). These *could* be, but *must not* be groups in the sense just mentioned. At least, it seems implausible to see them (or most of them) as encompassing groups. Not only because membership in them is chosen, or achieved, and not simply a matter of belonging. Also, because occupational or professional cultures nowadays only rarely cross over into other aspects of life. Typically there is a certain distance and variability in the relations between occupational role, family roles, leisure activities and so on. On the other hand, groups and group identities are not always, or not always primarily based on their cultural differences in comparison with other groups (as I will explain in more detail later).

In addition, imcompatibility of values may not only exist as incompatibility between individual or collective ways of life, which cannot be pursued at once, or at least not to the same degree, by the same individual. Incommensurable values do not exist solely as constituent parts of different 'ways of life'. Incommensurabilities may happen to all of us in a different way: Even *within* our individual or collective way of life, there might be tensions or conflicts between values—if we look at our private life, between, for example, occupational or family values, or within our common political life between liberty and security.

Incompatibility, as defined by Raz (i.e. as impossibility to pursue certain values fully in one individual life) obviously need not necessarily lead to conflict. Different people might each just choose one kind of career, maybe with some slight disdain for people in certain other careers. But conflict will only occur if there is competition for scarce resources or social space, or contempt and disrespect, or some conflict of normative prescriptions in areas where those different people interact, or in the case in which one individual or group tries to impose his/its values or principles on the other. All this is somewhat trivial theoretically, but of course very important in practice. Also, these statements do not necessarily contradict Raz's more general position.

However, some of the distinctions just made are important to avoid certain misconceptions about the realities of group or cultural conflicts in contemporary Western societies. All too often, notions of cultural difference, pluralism and conflict are used in somewhat vague ways. Cultural or group pluralism is often both evaluated positively and seen as threatened by homogenizing tendencies. Group cultures are seen as still existing or resurrected repositories of meaning and sources of identity. But they are in danger of being marginalized and undermined by the forces of modernity (or capitalism, or statism, or other culprits), and therefore in need of special legal and political protection.

But cultural differences, or at least certain forms of difference and pluralism, are also seen as a problem—as a threat to social unity or political order, or at least as posing special problems of conflict resolution and integration. So it now seems that the problem is not primarily a loss or lack of culture and community, but a proliferation of cultures and communities, possibly of the wrong sort, or with some problematic features. Not lack of all conviction, but passionate intensity seems to be the trouble.

This view is often expressed in statements about 'cultural conflict', 'conflicts of identity' or 'ethnic conflict'. In these statements, cultural conflicts or identity conflicts appear as very special types of conflict, which seem particularly difficult to resolve. Allusions are to images of 'religious war', referring to historical experiences in the West, or to clashes with 'fundamentalist' movements in some parts of the contemporary world.

Both versions seem to me somewhat misleading. To make this clearer, I would like to present some kind of heuristic, descriptive account of the goals or claims of cultural groups and of cultural conflicts. By cultural groups or communal groups (as I prefer to call them), I refer to a general type of social association which has similarities to Raz and Margalit's definition of 'encompassing groups'. The groups in question are large groups: most of their members do not know most other members personally. They are not organized around a small set of specific goals and do not have an encompassing formal organizational structure tied to those goals. The goals that they have are multiple and diffuse, the organizational structure is somewhat loose. Communal groups are enduring or intergenerational groups. Membership in these groups is long-term for most individuals. Like many groups or organizations, they survive changes or gradual replacements of their membership. As intergenerational groups, they comprise members of different generations (or whole families). Concerning the group, this means it comprises members of all ages. Looking at individual members, membership is a life-long affair for most. For most or many members, membership is acquired by birth. Looking again at the group level and the longer term, one could say that a large part of the membership is made up by family lineages. In any case, this is how current members *see* their group and their membership. It does not necessarily imply that the group has actually existed over many generations. But at least the members expect it to continue after their individual lifetimes.

One type of communal group, which figures prominently in the literature, includes groups where a particular history or genesis is a primary focus of collective identity. (Therefore they are often labelled 'ethnic' groups.) These are groups which look back to a longer common history that has had the effect of binding them as a distinct group, and see themselves as incorporated, either voluntarily or involuntarily, into a modern state, while retaining some kind of collective identity with historical, cultural and political elements.[10] In some

---

[10] Their long common history is an element of their current collective identity. The veracity of these historical memories is not an issue here.

cases, they see themselves as part of a larger historical group, where the other parts are majority or minority populations of different states. These are usually referred to as nationalities or national minorities, or as indigenous populations (or people), or sometimes as historical 'regions' or regional movements. Also in this category are groups which evolved in the context of migrations into some established modern state-bounded society. Migration may have been more or less voluntary, or a result of expulsion, or even forcible transportation. Another type, often overlapping with the foregoing, are certain religious communities with a strong collective identity and some continuous communal life (the Jewish diaspora, Protestant sects in the U.S.).

In all these cases it is an open empirical question, to what degree they show the features of communal groups, what kinds of collective identity exist and what degrees of cultural distinctiveness. It will be obvious, for example, that immigration does not invariably lead to the formation of communal groups, and that groups of immigrant origin can be of very variable strength and continuity. In other cases (like certain regions), we may be dealing more with temporal (possibly recurring) social and political movements, than with more permanent communal groups.

More importantly, it is not clear at all what kinds of interests or demands are pursued by such groups and what kinds of conflicts they are involved in. To clarify the problem, I will tell three stories about these conflicts and the group interests which are involved. They are named here as the 'culture war' story, the 'endangered culture' story, and the 'blood and belonging' story. These stories are meant to bring out, in a simplifying and partly exaggerated way, several *distinct* interpretations of cultural or identity conflict. These distinctions are sometimes neglected, or left implicit in the literature.

I. THE 'CULTURE WAR' STORY. CULTURAL DIFFERENCES AND CONFLICT

In this story, like in the following versions, we are looking at some society of the contemporary Western type, with a liberal-democratic constitutional system. The membership is divided in two groups, A and B. To simplify things, we assume throughout that the Bs (the members of group B) are in a minority (even if this is not a necessary or important feature in all of the following cases).

Now groups A and B are said to be involved in a cultural struggle, a deep cultural conflict. Observers alarmingly speak of a 'clash of cultures', or a 'culture war'. What could they mean?

Let us first note that almost all conflicts are 'cultural' in the sense that the parties have some differences or disagreements in beliefs, evaluations, interpretations of the situation and so on, and *not only* incompatible goals or demands. This is sometimes neglected by observers who see a basic difference between 'value conflicts' and 'conflicts of interests', where the latter appear to be conflicts about the distribution of goods or resources which are equally valued by the parties. But it is only in certain cases of distributional conflict that parties are unconcerned about the justification of their case, and coolly try to push aside opponents, or try to strike bargains in a morally neutral way, without any occasion for complaint, accusation, or justification. In other cases (probably in most cases of collective conflict), opponents may be convinced, or make proclamations that they are in their right, that they are entitled to what they demand, or that what they demand is generally the right thing to do, or that they are somehow wronged by their respective opponents, that an injustice occurred, or something like that. These claims and convictions may come into play even if the immediate demands are quite narrow, e.g. aiming at some moderate redistribution of resources.

Let us also note that such differences and disagreements, as elements of conflict, are quite likely to emerge even in cases where there is a very large degree of cultural homogeneity and general consensus between parties. If complex belief systems are applied to specific and possibly new situations, there is always enough indeterminacy to make conflicting interpretations possible. New problems and conflicts may also provoke a questioning of an established consensus and a revision of beliefs and convictions. In addition, some partiality of perspective and interpretation is likely in conflict situations.

But certainly, our observers were not thinking of *these* kinds of disagreement when they talked about cultural conflicts or culture wars. One fact about the As and the Bs which they certainly had in mind was the following: A and B show deep and important cultural differences. They show large differences in their beliefs and values, leading to different prescriptions and practices, which are incompatible.

This alone, however, does not necessarily lead them into conflict. The As and Bs might just stick to their own beliefs and practices, and leave each other alone. Conflict exists if they try to impose those beliefs, values, prescriptions or practices on each other. To speak of conflict, instead of mere disagreement, one has also to suppose that they not just try to convince each other, to change their beliefs and convictions by some kind of argument or by some other unobtrusive means of persuasion. Instead, they must either aim at binding decisions, practical resolutions, changes of practice, or they must use other means, like sanctions or the threat of sanctions, to change either beliefs or practices. The sanctions might be legal and political ones, but also other, informal means, including moral condemnation or contempt, shaming, ridicule and the like.

So our 'culture war' story unfolds. A and B have deeply different and divergent cultures, and try to impose certain elements of their culture (principles and norms of conduct, prescriptions or proscriptions, goals and so on), or certain demands backed by their culture on each other. These conflicting cultural programmes may involve whole conceptions of the social and political order, or certain central elements thereof. But the underlying deeper differences may also aggravate conflicts about seemingly smaller issues.

But here the story divides in two versions. Because the conflict situation can be of two kinds. In one situation, both A and B literally try to impose their cultural-political programme on each other, by making it binding for everybody, by making it the law of the land. In another situation, one of the groups (say B) just wants to follow its own standards in certain areas of life, to regulate its own internal affairs, without trying to impose it on the other group (A), without making it obligatory for the whole society. However, A does not accept this demand of non-interference from B, but insists on imposing certain contested standards or norms on the members of B.

Now, to make a brief digression from our story, why should the As and Bs do so, and not leave each other alone? There are structural and cultural limits to this latter solution. The cultural limits consist in the conviction of the As or Bs that certain values, principles, or norms are so important that nobody, or at least nobody within the same polity may be allowed to disregard them. To give an example of the second version of the story: the As may hold certain principles of individual liberty and equality as self-evidently valid and inviolable. They think this implies equal rights of men and women in all areas of life. Being the majority, they put this into law. The Bs may hold to certain principles of male authority, and may disagree. The As will disapprove, and think about enforcing the law. However, the As, or the government which is predominantly influenced by the As, are generally reluctant to interfere in what could be described as affairs between consenting adults. They may tend to see the case in this light, and be a little lax about enforcement. The situation changes, however, if individual women of B start to protest against the custom. Not willing to accept exit or exclusion from B, they appeal to the As, or to the government, for support. Now the As feel compelled to interfere. For similar reasons, the As may show special concern if they feel that important interests of B's children are at stake.

The structural limits of mutual non-interference are determined by relations of interdependence. These may consist in forms of cooperation and exchange, or all other kinds of interaction. Interdependence also exists where the activity of one group has harmful effects for the other, or where the groups compete for resources. In all these cases, some kind of common normative framework is necessary, which enables coordination, secures expectations, and provides norms and procedures for the prevention or resolution of conflict.[11]

---

[11] It would be interesting to ask how these structural conditions have changed with the emergence of modern societies. It has been pointed out that these societies are characterized by wide-ranging interdependencies and chains of interaction. Therefore, they need certain kinds of cultural homogeneity or conformity, many common rules, tight discipline. What is sometimes overlooked, however, are certain forms of internal differentiation. Especially the differentiation between areas, where wide-ranging networks and chains of interaction between strangers are actually found (like the economy), on the one hand, and other areas of private, or associational life, where mainly like-minded people get together and where there is hardly a 'structural' reason for them not to do whatever their particular area of activity. This gives lots of room for certain kinds of cultural variation and mutual non-interference.

It is, however, not always easy to determine in which areas of social life inter-dependence occurs in such a way that uniform regulations are necessary, and where there is enough separation or independence of activities to make mutual non-interference possible. One cause for difficulty is the fact that in contempo-rary societies, groups are always in a relation of interdependence or interaction in *some* areas, whereas in others, they may live separately. This leads to many spill-over effects between these areas. It may also often be contested just how much uniformity is necessary to make smooth interaction and coordination possible. The As, for example, may think that it is not enough to have common rules of conduct, but that it is necessary to instill certain attitudes and beliefs in all members of the polity, to make cooperation more secure. They may want to design language policies, educational policies and other measures with this in mind. The Bs may object. Finally, it will often be contested just what *counts* as interdependence or interference, e.g. what counts as harm done to the Bs from the As, or conversely.[12] This brings the cultural component back in. Obviously the line between cultural and structural limits of mutual non-interference is blurred in certain areas.

After these more theoretical considerations, let us recount our main story, in its two versions. In the first version, A and B have deep cultural differences, deeply divergent beliefs, values, goals, models of social order and interaction. Both A and B want to make some principles and rules of conduct, which derive from their respective cultures and which are incompatible, into the law of the land. They want to make them binding for the whole society and polity. This leads to deep disagreements and conflicts in certain issue areas or even with respect to more general principles of the legal and political order. In the second version, the As and Bs again have deeply different cultures. But now the Bs just want to realize some important principles, norms and practices within their own group, and demand non-interference by the As. But the As, or the govern-ment which is mostly controlled by them, will not let the Bs have their way in certain matters, for one of the reasons indicated above.

What questions could be asked about the story? Of course, it only gives a very sketchy account. If more details were filled in, many more variations would emerge, as would some conceptual questions.[13] For instance, there will be a broad range of cultural differences and resulting political disagreements, from moderate or shallow to extreme or deep, and it might not be so easy to distinguish degrees of difference. Also, the relations between cultural difference

---

[12] This is well known from the debates about J.S. Mill's 'harm principles', or from R. Dworkin's treatment of 'external preferences'.

[13] It should be noted, for instance, that there is a third general version of the story. Instead of aiming either at one set of rules which should be binding for everyone, or for different sets of rules for A and B, the As and Bs could devise three sets of rules: one for A, one for B, and one specifically regulating interactions between A and B, or between individual As and Bs. For our purposes, it is not necessary to examine the possibilities in more detail.

(in the sense indicated above) and political disagreement and conflict might be complicated at times. Different comprehensive belief systems might not always, in all areas, lead to very different policy prescriptions. And most importantly, groups A and B might not be quite so homogenous internally as was presupposed by our story. These possible complications apart, the story seems to be coherent and intelligible.

So the most interesting question becomes: are there plausible empirical applications of this story, to real cases in contemporary Western societies? Very briefly: classic cases that fit the description might be comprehensive and political ideologies. The most important example in Western (especially European) societies, after the demise of national socialism and fascism, was the conflict between Marxist, or communist and various versions of liberal-democratic belief systems and political programs.[14] Interestingly, conflicts between these or other political ideologies are rarely described as 'cultural' conflict. It is not clear if there are any particular reasons for this. But ideologies may be seen as very specific and rationally elaborated political belief systems, therefore not qualifying for the term 'culture', where culture is imagined as something more comprehensive and diffuse, extending to spheres other than merely the political.

More recently, social scientists and commentators have debated whether new political cleavages and alignments are developing in Western societies, which are based on deeper differences of values and metaphysical (religious, or secular) world views. In the United States, for example, the 'culture war' metaphor has been applied to an alleged division between cultural-political camps which adhere to comprehensive religious or secular, or conservative or progressive general world views, or more specifically to orthodox or 'fundamentalist' religious movements with political aspirations (references). This particular version of the 'culture war' thesis has been roundly criticized on empirical grounds, however, and other, more general variants of this 'value conflict' thesis remain disputed. Apart from this, most of the diagnoses about 'cultural conflict' which were mentioned at the beginning do not seem to have these, but other phenomena in mind. This is apparent from the fact that they usually refer to certain 'groups' or 'minority groups'. This terminology seems to mean something different from the broad camps or social milieus with very diffuse boundaries which the 'value conflict' hypothesis refers to. Before taking up the question, if *group* conflicts (conflicts between communal groups) of this type are really widespread in contemporary Western societies, we should first ask about other possible meanings of 'cultural conflict' or 'identity conflict'. This brings us to our second, and then to the third story.

---

[14] If we discount ideologies of the contemporary radical right, a more diffuse and heterogeneous phenomenon.

II. THE 'ENDANGERED CULTURES' STORY. SPECIAL
SUPPORT FOR CULTURAL GROUPS

Again we are looking at a majority group, A, and particularly at a minority group, B. Observers describe B as a group with a distinct culture, quite different from A's culture. B's culture comprises systems of values and beliefs, common practices and customs, distinct ways of doing things in various aspects of life (family and intimate relations, work, recreation, communal activities, artistic activities, and so on). B is said to have a peculiar 'way of life',[15] different from A's 'way of life'. Presumably this means not only that the Bs do various things differently and have different beliefs and values, but also that all these things hang together in some way, making up something like a coherent whole. There seem to be certain common cultural threads running through their various customs, practices or beliefs. So the Bs cannot easily change or give up one piece of their culture without adapting the other pieces, or else without experiencing some sense of contradiction or incoherence. B is also said to be a 'comprehensive', or 'encompassing' group or community.[16] This means not only that its culture or way of life ranges over larger parts of individual and social life, as already stated. It means also that people largely grow up and are socialized or educated within the group and that their personalities, or, as some observers prefer to say, their identities are formed by that cultural environment.

However, there is no 'cultural conflict' in the sense of the first story. The As are not trying to change B's ways, neither by political nor by other means. The government is not concerned about anything in B's way of life. The Bs are considered to be good citizens, and they enjoy equal rights and liberties. Group B is not pursuing any very controversial political aims. The Bs accept the constitutional principles of the polity, obey the laws of the land, follow the rules of the political game. Of course they may have certain different political objectives, different interpretations of constitutional principles and so on. But this is in the range of general political disagreement, or controversy, or political competition.

Nevertheless, members of group B feel that the survival of their culture is endangered. So they demand special protection or support. To make a credible claim, members of group B (or speakers for group B) have to show what negative influences threaten their culture. This is important for normative reasons, with respect to attributions of responsibility, as well as for pragmatic reasons: can something be done about the problem? They also have to explain why a decline of their culture would violate important interests. And they have to specify their demands for protection or support. So speakers for B put forward

---

[15] Bhiku Parekh, 'Equality, Fairness and Limits of Diversity', *Innovation* 7 (1994), 289–308.
[16] Philip Selznick, *The Moral Commonwealth. Social Theory and the Promise of Community* (Berkeley: University of California Press, 1992), 358; Raz and Avishai Margalit, 'National Self-Determination', in Raz's *Ethics in the Public Domain* (n. 2 above), 110–30.

a series of concerns or complaints. They describe several situations, of the following kinds.

Group A ignores group B, or its ways (its culture), is not interested, shows indifference. There are no signs of particular aversion. Members of A, if in contact with members of B, politely ignore B's group membership and do not want to be bothered with it. At most, the As show some mild, sometimes slightly astonished curiosity. Members of group B complain. They feel ignored in some important part of their life or identity. They want to get attention, acknowledgment, signs of respect for their culture from the As. Sometimes, the Bs feel that there is not just indifference. Members of group A let it show that they do not care much about the ways of group B, as a matter of opinion. They find B's culture somewhat alien, a little odd, perhaps a little distasteful. There may even be slight indications that group A finds its own ways somehow superior, more truly cultivated. Even so, the As are not intentionally trying to change B's ways, to impose their own culture. They do not find this worth their while, or would even regard it as a hopeless task. Things may become worse, in certain situations. Members of group A insult or denigrate the culture of group B. There is ridicule, there are nasty jokes. B's members feel hurt by remarks and jokes about their group or about their culture, even if they are not directed at them individually. Some Bs at least see this as some kind of pressure to give up their culture, and become more like the As. The majority of the Bs want to put up some kind of collective defence. They may just retaliate in kind, as it were, and declare themselves superior to the As and make jokes about *them*. But as a minority, they see some dangers for themselves in this kind of competition. So they ask for public protection.

Members of group A may also tend to avoid personal contact, sociability, marriage, friendship with members of group B, teach their children to avoid children of group B and so on. The Bs are very ambivalent about this. On the one hand, they may largely want to keep to themselves, too, and may want their children to marry within the group. On the other hand, they feel snubbed and rejected. The As want to keep to themselves for the wrong reasons. They want to keep the Bs out because they see them as inferior, not good enough for them. Again a few Bs accept the judgement and are tempted to hide their membership or defect from the group, to join the As. Other Bs are again thinking about ways to rub the As' noses in the dirt, or about other ways of purging their arrogance.

The younger Bs are doing less well in the educational system, on average, and the Bs are on the whole less successful in their occupational careers. The Bs explain this as an indication of, or a result of discrimination. The schools and universities are more oriented to the A's children and their cultural dispositions, than to B's children. The As which dominate the educational institutions hold low opinions about the average abilities of the Bs, which damages the self-confidence of the Bs and works in this and other ways as a self-fulfilling expectation. Members of group A are reluctant to give jobs to members of B, or to promote them. Either because they just dislike them because of their cultural characteristics and do not want them near, or because they think (rightly or wrongly) that members of B are *on average* less qualified for certain positions. Similarly, members of A are reluctant to rent apartments or houses to members of B, or to let them join some private, but publicly accessible associations (like sport clubs and so on). Prejudice in the sense of false and incorrigible *perceptions* of cultural characteristics of B may be involved, but not necessarily so.

Group A and group B have different languages, religions, and social rituals (e.g. historical commemorations, holidays and so on). The language of group A is the official language in the state. There are some public holidays with connections to the religion, or the rituals, or the history of group A. The Bs feel that their culture is disadvantaged by this. They also feel that their culture is not given enough attention in the educational system, in courses about literature and history, and in the public broadcasting media. There are also certain general provisions which for culturally neutral reasons prescribe or proscribe certain practices, which the Bs would like to maintain for cultural reasons. There are certain regulations for the slaughtering of animals, for example, or certain dress codes in work environments or public institutions. The Bs again see this as a disadvantage for their culture.

In a final version, the Bs complain that their beliefs and cultural practices are slowly dying out, because B's members increasingly adopt A's ways. Among the causes for this development are the following (at least as seen by many loyal members of B): group A is richer and more numerous. B's children are required to go to public schools, where they are confronted with many cultural options, which confuses and distracts them. B's children are also unduly impressed by the (in the eyes of children) more glamorous or entertaining lives of A's children, and the cheap thrills of A's culture. Group A, being richer and bigger, can support more radio and TV programmes, more theatre companies, more magazines and newspapers, more pop groups and more advertising campaigns. There is more variety, a larger pool of talent and innovation. For these or other reasons, B's cultural production is at a disadvantage, and loses support among B's members. And finally, many of B's cultural practices are somewhat dependent on neighbourly relations, a certain residential density or separation. But now A's members are moving in everywhere. Possibly, the B-loyalists also maintain that their culture includes certain ways of work (e.g. running farms, or trapping wild animals), certain professional traditions, certain ways of making a living. Because of economic competition, these are no longer sustainable. Many members of B sell their land or other property to outsiders, and many have to take jobs elsewhere, and have to adapt to working environments where they are not able to keep some of their own habits.

Now speakers for B claim that these treatments and relations give unfair disadvantages to their group culture, and to their interest in maintaining and developing their own culture and way of life. Therefore the Bs put forward certain policy proposals or demands, to rectify these situations. Among them are legal protections against insults and denigrations of their group, policies against discrimination in the educational system, in the labour market, the housing market and other areas. The Bs demand that their group culture be publicly acknowledged and honoured, by public holidays, commemorations, or other public symbols or symbolic activities. They want certain language rights (in education and use in public institutions) and demand more space for their culture in the educational curricula and in public broadcasting. They want exemptions from regulations which constrain some of their ritual practices. Referring to the last-mentioned situation, B's loyal members even demand their own schools with their own curriculum, subsidies or protected markets for their own mass media and other cultural productions, restrictions for the settlement of non-members in their own residential areas, and market protection and subsidies for economic activities. The Bs may even think it necessary to gain political control over important policy areas, to defend their interests.

When pressed to explain a little more clearly why the impending demise of their group culture should be a public concern, speakers for B first give some reasons why preservation of their culture is important for the Bs. They first say that B's culture provides meaning for their lives. By this they mean that there are stocks of cultural meanings which they can use to make sense of themselves and their social relations, form self-conceptions and construct or remake their life-projects, cope with the difficulties of life and so on. There are cultural values, patterns of relationships, formulas or scripts for conduct in typical life situations, and so on. We may call this the 'cultural repertoire' argument.

They go on to argue that the members of B are influenced and formed by their culture from infancy on, and that they later develop their personalities or personal identities by using that cultural repertoire. Thereby they acquire habits, dispositions, routines, skills, competencies, and make personal investments in individual and collective life-projects. They can change these elements of their personality or identity, and possibly also their life-projects, only slowly, and at a cost, if at all. Most of these things function well for them only in the social and cultural context of the group. They cannot easily be transferred to other contexts. So if the Bs lose their cultural context, by leaving the group, or because the group culture dissolves, they are at a severe disadvantage. We could call this the 'cultural investment' interest.

The Bs may also give this argument a more collective twist, as it were. Taking part in the collective cultural life of B, in their distinct rituals and cultural practices may be an important good in itself for many members, an important part of their lives, which they do not want to give up. We may call this the 'cultural participation' interest.

Next, the Bs state that they wish to transmit their culture to their children, that they want their children to be educated and socialized so that they acquire the cultural repertoire of the group, are formed by it, learn how to use it. This is important for them because it forms a special bond between them and their children, a basis for close relations. If the children acquired some other culture, the parents would fear that they would become estranged from them, not being able to really understand them any more, and be understood and respected by them. We could call this the 'generation gap' argument.

Finally, some speakers state that they are not just thinking of their own children or grandchildren. They want the group culture to be preserved and developed indefinitely, for other reasons than just commonality with their off-spring. They see the group culture as some kind of heritage or trust that they want, or feel obliged, to preserve and develop, in order to pass it on to later generations. They claim that it provides an essential element of meaning to their life to take part in this transgenerational cultural endeavour and to make a contribution to it, however small. We may call this the 'cultural trust' interest.

Now, after these accounts of their own interests, the Bs still have to argue why these interests should be protected by special legal or political measures, especially if this involves burdens or sacrifices for the As. Presumably, they could do this in various ways, especially by arguing from principles of equality. They could, for example, point out that, given their minority situation and other disadvantages for which they are not responsible, they have a much poorer chance of realizing their most important interests than the As.[17] Of course, the As may disagree with the Bs about that. With this kind of disagreement, we would be back to a 'cultural conflict' in the general sense, as described in the first story. But that would not necessarily be a very deep conflict, rooted, for example, in large differences of normative convictions between the As and the Bs. It might be a much more limited disagreement, e.g. about the interpretation of principles of equality, and their application to the problem at hand.

Now, what questions could be asked about this second story? We may first note that certain parts of the story could be read in other ways, or do not seem to entirely fit into the general frame of the story. This was meant to be a story about the preservation of distinct and comprehensive group cultures. But not all situations which were described above need have much to do with this kind of cultural difference, and not all interests involved need primarily be directed at the survival of such a distinct culture. If the As look down on the Bs, or dislike them, they may not do this because B's culture is so different and is not appreciated as a whole by the As. The As may just dislike some particular, ephemeral feature of B. Or the Bs may have low status because they are concentrated in certain low-status occupations. Discrimination may also have other causes than some kind of negative appreciation of B's culture, or some maladaptation of institutions and workplaces to B's cultural features. More importantly, the Bs may be upset about experiences of contempt, insult or discrimination not primarily because they fear for the stability of their culture (although this may be *one* of their concerns, for example, if they fear defection of their members).

---

[17] Some clever members of B, with academic degrees, may also point out to the As that it might be pleasant for *them* to have a larger degree of cultural variety in their society, and to be able to look at some different way of life. Not all As may be convinced, however, especially if they do look at B's way of life and do not like, or appreciate it much.

They will see this more immediately as violations of their integrity (as individuals, or as group members, or of the integrity of the group, if they think in these terms), and of their rights to fair and equal treatment. Consequently, demands for protection against insults or discrimination need not be grounded in an interest in cultural survival. It seems more likely that these demands will be justified by some principle of individual equality, or fairness, or some notions of dignity.

Other demands may also not primarily have to do with cultural survival as such, but with recognition of the worth of B's culture. The Bs may argue that it is important for their self-esteem that their culture be publicly recognized by certain symbolic acts (like public holidays or rituals). Or even, that the worth of their culture is generally acknowledged by the As. It is not so clear, however, how they would propose to enforce this. But maybe they have some hopes that this can be achieved through the educational system.

But this is no very important objection to the story. One could just keep the topic of discrimination somewhat separately. More interesting problems lie with the descriptions of the interests which are involved, and with the initial description of B's culture. We may ask if the descriptions of these interests are plausible, and if they are plausibly linked to the continued existence of a distinct and encompassing culture. If there is no necessary link, they cannot justify policies of cultural preservation. If there *is* a necessary link, another problem emerges. What if B's culture, as it exists, does not fit the description in the first place?

Let us take the above mentioned interests in turn. There is a quite obvious answer to the 'cultural reservoir' argument: why not take A's cultural reservoir, or some other? Does the 'cultural investment' argument provide an answer? People have a personal investment in their own culture, in the ways described. Certainly they would be disadvantaged if this cultural context were lost. But this is a slippery argument. Surely the Bs cannot expect that their culture will not change. It probably keeps changing, and they keep adapting, even over their individual lifetimes. (Of course, the Bs, being somewhat conservative, may have an interest, or wish, that there be no change. But this is largely illusory, or could be pursued in earnest only with somewhat unpleasant and costly means.) But if there is to be change anyway, what does it matter for their investments if this change goes in one direction or another? Why should they object if the change goes in the direction of A's culture? At least if this does not happen too rapidly? If we look closer, we may also note that cultural change is quite uneven, more rapid in some areas, slower in others. Does this produce contradictions, tensions, incoherence? Do the Bs suffer from this? Possibly, but not necessarily. The empirical evidence may point to a considerable capability of internal adaptation, to a loose coupling of cultural elements. This weakens arguments that the encompassing culture as a whole has to be protected and preserved, in order to avoid cultural difficulties for the Bs.

These observations also affect the 'generation gap' argument. If there is to be a generation gap anyway (as has to be expected), what does it matter in which direction the younger generation takes off? Again, change may be more rapid or more gradual, and group B might be able to influence this to a degree, given adequate means. But this provides no argument for a long-term preservation of B's distinct culture.

What about the 'cultural participation' interest? This one is trickier. The Bs may have a vested interest to participate in *their* own culture, the culture of their group. But it is not so clear if the stress here lies on 'culture', or on 'group'. If the Bs are mainly interested to maintain certain communal cultural activities or practices, it is more important to maintain group boundaries and group cohesion than to maintain a *distinct* culture. But they may also have an interest in some kind of identification with a certain distinct character of their culture, and they may want it to develop in a certain direction, and not in others (not towards A's culture, for example). This neatly links with the 'cultural trust' interest. Here, the Bs are equally concerned that their culture keeps a certain distinct character, that a recognizably distinct cultural tradition be continued, but now they are also looking to the long term.

So the last two seem to be better candidates for genuine interests in cultural preservation. If they are to be starting points for normative arguments, it is of course relevant how important these interests really are for the Bs, and if there really is an encompassing and coherent culture to preserve. And even if this is the case, it might be asked, if the interest in question is compelling enough to demand special public support. Couldn't it be seen as some kind of expensive taste? One peculiarly expensive conception of the good among other possible ones (even for the Bs)? Why should it be subsidized? The Bs may retort that they do not demand *special*, but just *equal* protection. But there the debate becomes complicated, and as I said, the normative arguments will not be discussed here in detail.

Concerning the second story, too, our last question will be: Are there plausible empirical cases? Again, I will come back to it at the end. First, we should look at our third story about group politics and group conflict.

III. THE 'BLOOD AND BELONGING' STORY. IDENTITY POLITICS

There is another story about a minority group B. It has some overlap with the last one, but is still significantly different. The Bs show a strong sense of belonging to the group, feelings of group solidarity, strong sentimental attachments to their group. They rally together to defend against perceived violations of vital interests and demands, not least against what they see as denigration or insult or violation of their collective integrity. They have pride in what they see as achievements of the group, and these may not just be cultural achievements, but also economic or technological ones, or military prowess, or other things. They see their bonds as rather profound or somehow natural, their membership as unchosen, their commitments to the group as unconditional. They see their community as continuing in time, as transgenerational, transcending their individual lifetimes. In particular, they refer to a common collective past, to memories of collective activities and achievements, or to past sufferings or defeats. And they look forward to a future for the group, beyond their individual lifetime. This transgenerational solidarity they often frame in terms of genealogy or descent. So they talk about their ancestors, and their future descendants. It is often not very clear how they understand this: whether they see some kind of kinship between group members, in a literal way, or if they see themselves connected to the history of the group through their own family lineage, through membership of their personal ancestors and descendants in the group.

Now, in this story, group B has some of the same complaints as group B had in our last story, and some of the same demands. They complain about being ignored, or not respected enough by members of A. Their sense of dignity or honour is violated, because their group does not enjoy enough public recognition. There are no (or not enough) public holidays or other commemorations, no place names, no memorials celebrating achievements of the group, or mourning its sufferings. Possibly they feel harassed, or discriminated against in various ways. Politically, they do not feel that their influence, or representation is adequate. Economically, they may feel disadvantaged, because, say, their average income is lower compared to A's. There may be various explanations for this (the Bs may stick to certain occupations or be stuck in them, or they may have recently settled as immigrants and may still be in a process of adjustment, or they may suffer from past or present discrimination). In any case, and separate from the question of explanation, the Bs see this disadvantage as intolerable, as a blow to their collective pride or sense of equality.[18] The Bs also complain that their youth are defecting in growing numbers. They ascribe this (in part at least) to lack of recognition or respect for their group. So many young people try to escape from a position of low status by giving up or hiding their affiliation with B.

So, similarly to the last story, the Bs demand their own holidays, memorials and place names, a quota for jobs, political offices and parliamentary representation, possibly subsidies or market protections for the regions or occupations where they are heavily represented. They demand their own radio programmes. And they want their own schools, or special classes or courses in public schools, to instil loyalty and group pride in their offspring. Or at least they want the history of their group to be taught in the school curriculum. And finally, if they are geographically concentrated, they may go further and demand certain forms of self-government, or even complete political independence and sovereignty.

What distinguishes this story from the earlier ones is that *cultural difference* does not play any essential or important role in it. Neither in the sense of the

---

[18] In a somewhat different scenario, the Bs actually may enjoy economic advantages over the As, and may claim to be unjustly exploited by them, because of redistributive measures applied by the state.

first story: there are no incompatible, comprehensive belief systems or deep disagreements about general norms and values, no conflicts about the principles of social and political order. Nor in the second sense, where a group wishes to save a distinct culture or way of life against forces of assimilation. In our story here, group B lives just like the members of A live. There is no comprehensive culture which is different from A's culture, no shared and distinct way of life. Sure, there are *certain* cultural differences. Group B has some community rituals, celebrating community solidarity, certain culinary traditions. Also, the collective beliefs and representations which were mentioned above are all cultural elements which are unique features of the group: collective memories about a distinct group history, group solidarity, collective aspirations, collective grievances and demands. But that is not what is usually meant by a distinct, or different group culture, or a way of life. If you looked at the everyday lives of B's members, at occupational work, family life, voluntary associations, recreation, personal values and life-goals, political opinions on general constitutional principles or most policy matters and so on, you could not really tell them apart from the As. However, there might also be some differences which would help to distinguish the As from the Bs in some contexts, some kind of dialect or slang, some manners of dress or outer appearance. But there is a distinct impression that these features are not really valued as such, but are valued as signs of group membership, as demarcations of group boundaries. Or there might be somewhat deeper differences, in that most members of A, and most members of B belong to different religious congregations. But this difference does not seem to be of much concern to them, as such. The Bs are not too concerned about a possible decline of their religion (which they may share with many people elsewhere, if not with most members of A), or if there is a decline, they do not attribute it to their relations with A and their situation as a minority in the social and political system which they share with group A. Religious convictions and practices are largely private affairs. They become relevant only in a secondary manner, by reinforcing group solidarity and group boundaries between A and B, especially if there is tension and conflict. But these conflicts do not have anything to do with religion as such. On their marches, the As and Bs may carry religious banners, without having any religious thoughts.

There might be also the interesting case where the Bs do have their own language (not just a dialect). Now there is certainly a cultural difference. But still, having a different language does not imply that there are any further differences with respect to way of life, social behaviour, norms, values, and so on. Sure, there might be, for example, certain differences in framing personal experiences or personal relationships, due to a certain vocabulary and repertoire of interpretations. But in general it might just not be the case that having a different language necessarily means having any profound differences of world view. But of course, with language comes at least a literary tradition, and possibly certain oral traditions of narratives, proverbs and so on. So if we have different languages, the story begins to resemble the 'survival of group culture' version.

But still, the cultural differences, the distinct cultural repertoires which are based on the distinct language might be small. And observers who look at various demands of B might gain the impression that the Bs are stressing the importance of language not *because* of the cultural differences which are linked to that language, but because they want to stress the distinctiveness of their group for somewhat different reasons—for the kind of reasons which were described in our third story. Maybe they are even trying to *revive* a language which is no longer spoken in their group. Or they more or less invent a new language, in order to stress their distinctiveness and strengthen the identity and solidarity of their group.[19]

So, in our third story, the Bs do not demand greater control over resources, larger political influence, or political autonomy and self-government in order to protect or save their culture. They just act on the basis of certain understandings of group solidarity and collective identity, from a sense of belonging, out of concern about the welfare and status of the group. None of this has to be based on cultural distinctiveness with respect to general values, world-views, or way of life. They want to govern themselves (to take their most extreme demands), instead of taking part in a common democratic order with the As, because they have a strong sense of commonality and identity and therefore see themselves as a permanent minority, permanently ruled by a majority, and they want to direct what they see as *their* own affairs as members of *their* group.

What questions could be asked about this version? Many observers (social scientists, historians) have looked at the story with suspicion. They have pointed out, for example, that the kind of group solidarity described in the story has often found very nasty expressions. Groups of this kind have been known to suppress internal difference and dissidence and to severely constrain the individual liberties of their members. They have also acted in aggressive and ruthless ways against outsiders.

Apart from these observations (which might only apply to some, not all cases), there is a more systematic reason for these suspicions. Many social scientists see the phenomena of group identity and solidarity, which are described in the third story, as somehow anomalous, if they occur in modern societies. Roughly, they see these societies as dominated by the principles of individual choice and rational calculation of individual interests, or similar characteristics. Unchosen group solidarities obviously do not fit this picture. There are various ways to deal with this perceived anomaly. They could be seen as some kind of pathology, a regression from normal behaviour to irrational behaviour patterns. They could be explained as results of manipulation, where rationally acting, but ruthless elites or political and cultural entrepreneurs have invented some group-myth,

---

[19] See Brian Barry's telling remark on the case of Quebec nationalism: '. . . if the concern were exclusively for the integrity of French language and culture, an independent Quebec would not merely accept but welcome the loss of those areas occupied by anglophones and native Americans. Yet Quebec nationalists are unwilling to give up any territory . . .' (Barry, 'The Limits of Cultural Politics', *Review of International Studies* 24 (1998), 307–19, 312).

and have talked gullible masses into these group fantasies, to gain some advantage. Or they could be explained as a veil for different group interests, where group members pursuing more mundane political and economic goals drape themselves, consciously or semi-consciously, in ethnic costumes. They may do this because it affords them a greater chance of acceptance or legitimacy, under some circumstances, or because it gives an additional push to group cohesion, which is useful to overcome free-rider problems in collective action. All these re-interpretations could also be applied to the second version of our story, of course.

Now some of these interpretations might be empirically true, in various cases. We may note, however, that a certain prejudice may be involved. It seems to be a mere prejudice, or an unwarranted theoretical generalization, to assume, that it is somehow more rational, or modern, to strive individually for money, political power, or status, or just fun, than to care about life in certain communities, their flourishing and continuance, and to wish that one's children might have the option to continue a similar communal life. This might just be an erroneous picture of modernity, or rationality. In any case, empirical observations should not be guided by such a preconception, and experiences or expressions of group solidarity should not be regarded as *principally* suspicious, not a priori as a manifestation of false consciousness or bad faith.

IV. SOME LESSONS

Obviously, the three stories represent something like ideal types, or stylized descriptions (and there exists some overlap between the three stories). In reality, we will probably find many cases in which features of the three stories are combined in various ways. Probably the stories were also not comprehensive, in the sense that there are other features of groups, group interests and group conflict which may be relevant in this context. But the stories, as they stand, still shed some light on the current, somewhat alarmed diagnoses about 'cultural conflicts' or 'identity conflicts' mentioned.

Deep cultural conflict, in the sense of the two versions of our first story, seems to be very rare. General political goals of communal groups, or demands for non-interference, seem only in rare cases to be based on deep cultural differences and disagreements. The diagnosis of deep conflict in this sense may apply to some religious movements, or political movements inspired by certain religious convictions (Protestant, Islamic, or Jewish). Among communal groups, certain Islamist tendencies come to mind. Not much is known, however, about the influence of these tendencies among Islamic communities in the West. But this influence does not appear to be strong. Immigrant communities with predominantly Islamic orientation generally do not pursue or support radical political goals. There are also very few cases where the internal practices of communal groups collide with the general political principles and basic norms of contemporary Western societies. At least cases of open conflict, where governments or courts try to impose liberal principles on recalcitrant groups, seem to be extremely rare.[20]

Are there empirical instances where the 'endangered culture' story applies? If we take our initial description of encompassing cultures or ways of life seriously, probably seldom. Some aboriginal communities in settler societies (North America and Australia) may come close, as may a few religious communities (like the Amish). Not surprisingly they are also the favourite examples of philosophers who talk about cultural rights. But even there, we will probably not find that cultures are quite as coherent as was suggested in our description. There will probably be quite a jumble of cultural elements, some cherished and more or less preserved (possibly on the basis of cultural participation and cultural trust interests), some changing quite rapidly. But if the 'participation' and 'cultural trust' interests are the only plausible ones anyway, we may have no need for truly encompassing and coherent cultures. All we need are *some* cultural traditions (religious or otherwise), which the group wants to preserve. If we look for further real-world cases where those interests may be involved, there are other candidates: the Jewish community or communities outside Israel, for instance, or certain national minority groups in Europe, or possibly some immigrant groups (most probably with a strong religious background).

Are there groups and group conflicts in the contemporary world which might fit the third story? As to real examples, look to ethnic groups of immigrant origin in the United States. Or to the French-Canadians. Or to regional movements in Western Europe (e.g. the Bretons). Or look to Northern Ireland. The cases may not fit our third story exactly, but there are similarities.[21]

In most cases, however, we find communal groups whose communal ties largely resemble our third story, but who have a mixture of shared or common interests. They are not really based on a *distinct* encompassing culture and their main goal does not really seem to be the preservation of a distinctive way of life with deep differences from the dominant culture and way of life. Instead they pursue a mixture of other goals. Many immigrant communities seem to strive both for emancipation in the sense of non-discrimination and equal treatment, of public *disregard* of their group affiliation in many contexts (occupational, educational and so on) and for the preservation of some collective life within the group (for which they may demand protection and support). Often, economic or occupational disadvantages are very important, because they make immigrant groups vulnerable also in other areas, for example, with respect to matters of recognition. Regional groups or movements in the Western world

---

[20] There are a few examples: some Indian nations in the U.S., or the question of clitoridectomy and polygamy within certain immigrant communities in Europe.

[21] There are more impressive examples in other regions of the world. What is the cultural difference between the Hutus and Tutsis in Rwanda? What where the cultural differences between Serbs and Croats? Sure, there were religious differences, but who noticed them *before* the conflict? Of course, there were very different *historical memories*. And that's exactly the point. Which does not mean, of course, that we necessarily have here the causes of the war between these groups.

also show a mixture of motives or goals, which is often hard to analyse. Distributive goals may sometimes have some impact. Equally, or more important, seem to be collective identities with a strong historical component, which fuel demands for political influence or autonomy, even if a holistic and distinctive culture does not really exist in the everyday life of its members.

It is not obvious why these demands should be 'non-negotiable', or pose insurmountable difficulties for conflict resolution in liberal democracies, as some of the diagnoses about cultural conflict seem to assume. The accommodation of group demands, and group differentiated policies are nothing new, but belong to the standard political repertoire of liberal democracies. And political theorists have demonstrated that it is possible to evaluate or justify many group demands (of the kinds which were listed above) in a broadly liberal framework.

Of course there will be specific controversies. Some of them may involve difficult normative problems and disagreements.[22] There might be wider disagreements or uncertainties about the claims of communal groups than about many other political problems. One of the reasons for this is the fact that the normative assessment of group demands is often very closely linked to difficult empirical assessments.

One interesting example is the 'test of viability', which Raz mentions. He rightly says that the size and viability of cultural groups is relevant for the justification of 'multicultural' political measures. In particular, there is 'no point in trying to prop up by public action cultures which have lost their vitality . . .'.[23] The criterion of 'viability' is certainly a plausible one. But the task of actually distinguishing viable and non-viable cultures or communal groups may not be so easy, to say the least. Another example is the determination of complex causal relations. This is most visible in demands for policies of anti-discrimination (like affirmative action). For their moral justification, both with respect to the allocation of responsibility and to the appropriateness of proposed remedies, it is important to show in what ways, by which mechanisms and so on discrimination actually occurs (or has occured in the past). It cannot simply be determined, for instance, whether a group of recent immigrants is discriminated against, by making comparisons between their level of welfare or their status positions (in various relevant dimensions) with those of the resident population. That is because there are many possible alternative causes for certain disadvantages of such a group (like the unavoidable effects of changing from one set of economic, social and cultural circumstances to another, and so on)—causes which do not *necessarily* constitute an injustice done to the group.[24]

---

[22] One important example are the conflicts and controversies surrounding affirmative action policies, especially in the United States. This is largely a debate about different interpretations of liberal principles.

[23] Raz, 'Multiculturalism' (n. 1 above), 198; Raz, *Ethics in the Public Domain* (n. 2 above), 190.

[24] Of course, these sorts of difficulty are well known from the field of *legal* adjudication. But they are relevant also for the moral justification of political claims.

My last case will be the relevance of *actual intent* for the justification or adjudication of claims to multicultural rights or policies. If cultural groups demand public support for the preservation and development of their culture, it is quite crucial to determine if this interest is actually, and sincerely held, by relevant parts of the membership. If most members are not really so committed, public support is not likely to be forthcoming with respect to its stated goal. And there is always the possibility that support (e.g. in the form of material resources) is claimed for different, and hidden purposes. Should this be so, then the moral justification for such claims vanishes. As in the case of the 'test of viability', it might not be so easy to determine actual intent. Especially if we consider that different members of communal groups might have different interpretations of their collective interests. Demands which are made by elites or particularly committed subgroups might not really be representative of what the general membership thinks and feels to be in its interest. In the case of demands for public resources or other support for group development, it is generally not possible to determine from the outside, as it were, what the legitimate interests of such a group are. This is so because members do not *have* to have an interest in the preservation of their group culture. For them, it may be equally legitimate to strive for assimilation into some other culture. Nobody can make this decision for them. But the process of forming and expressing their intent in this area is obviously difficult. And in many cases there are obvious incentives for the strategic misrepresentations of group interests. For it might be very tempting to parade mere distributional or similar interests as genuinely collective interests that are vital in ensuring cultural survival and flourishing.

In his writings, Raz has always shown his sensitivity to these relations between normative considerations and empirical facts, in his own unobtrusive way. Thereby he has given me many incentives to take up these questions and pursue them in the ways indicated above.

13

Liberal Theories of Multiculturalism

WILL KYMLICKA*

The last ten years have seen a remarkable upsurge in interest amongst political philosophers in the rights of ethnocultural groups within Western democracies. Joseph Raz's writings, particularly his article on 'Multiculturalism: A Liberal Perspective', have played an important role in this debate. My aim in this paper is to give a (very) condensed overview of the philosophical debate so far, and to suggest how Raz's theory fits into the larger debate.

I. THE FIRST STAGE: MULTICULTURALISM AS COMMUNITARIANISM

I think we can distinguish three broad positions in the debate over multiculturalism or minority rights[1]. The first position to emerge, and the one that dominated the debate in the 1970s and 1980s, viewed multiculturalism as a form of, or application of, communitarianism. It was assumed that the debate over multiculturalism was therefore essentially equivalent to the debate between 'liberals' and 'communitarians' (or between 'individualists' and 'collectivists'). Confronted with an unexplored topic like multiculturalism, it was natural, and perhaps inevitable, that political theorists would look for

*This paper draws on my 'The New Debate on Minority Rights' in Kymlicka, *Politics in the Vernacular: Nationalism, Multiculturalism, Citizenship* (Oxford: Oxford University Press, 2001), ch. 1.

[1] I will use the term 'minority rights' and 'multiculturalism' interchangeably, to refer to a wide range of public policies, legal rights and constitutional provisions that relate to the accommodation of ethnocultural minorities. Common examples of such policies and laws in Western democracies include language rights and self-government powers for national minorities, multicultural educational reforms and religious exemptions for immigrant groups, treaty rights and land claims for indigenous peoples. This is obviously a heterogeneous category, but the various measures have two important features in common: (a) they go beyond the familiar set of common civil and political rights of individual citizenship which are protected in all liberal democracies; (b) they are adopted with the intention of recognizing and accommodating the distinctive identities and needs of ethnocultural groups. For a helpful typology, see Jacob Levy, 'Classifying Cultural Rights', in Ian Shapiro and Will Kymlicka (eds.), *Ethnicity and Group Rights* (New York: New York University Press, 1997), 22–66. I should emphasize that many of the measures that I am describing as 'minority rights' are not 'rights' in Joseph Raz's technical sense.

analogies with other, more familiar, topics, and the liberal-communitarian debate seemed the most relevant and applicable.

The liberal-communitarian debate is an old and venerable one within political philosophy, going back several centuries, so I won't try to rehearse it in its entirety. But to dramatically oversimplify, one strand of the debate revolves around the priority of individual freedom. Liberals insist that individuals should be free to decide on their own conception of the good life, and applaud the liberation of individuals from any ascribed or inherited status. Liberal individualists argue that the individual is morally prior to the community: the community matters only because it contributes to the well-being of the individuals who compose it. If those individuals no longer find it worthwhile to maintain existing cultural practices, then the community has no independent interest in preserving those practices, and no right to prevent individuals from modifying or rejecting them.

Communitarians dispute this conception of the 'autonomous individual'. They view individuals as 'embedded' in particular social roles and relationships, rather than as agents capable of forming and revising their own conception of the good life. Rather than viewing group practices as the product of individual choices, they tend to view individuals as the product of social practices. Moreover, they often deny that the interests of communities can be reduced to the interests of their individual members. Privileging individual autonomy is therefore seen as destructive of communities. A healthy community maintains a balance between individual choice and protection for the communal way of life, and seeks to limit the extent to which the former can erode the latter.

In this first stage of the debate, the assumption was that one's position on minority rights was dependent on, and derivative of, one's position on the liberal-communitarian debate. That is, if one is a liberal who cherishes individual autonomy, then one will oppose minority rights as an unnecessary and dangerous departure from the proper emphasis on the individual. Communitarians, by contrast, view minority rights as an appropriate way of protecting communities from the eroding effects of individual autonomy, and of affirming the value of community. Ethnocultural minorities in particular are worthy of such protection, partly because they are most at risk, but also because they still have a communal way of life to be protected. Unlike the majority, ethnocultural minorities have not yet succumbed to liberal individualism, and so have maintained a coherent collective way of life.

This debate over the priority and reducibility of community interests to individual interests dominated the early literature on minority rights.[2] This

---

[2] For 'communitarian' defenders of minority rights, see Vernon Van Dyke, 'The Individual, the State, and Ethnic Communities in Political Theory', *World Politics* 29 (1977), 343–69; Van Dyke, 'Collective Rights and Moral Rights: Problems in Liberal-Democratic Thought', *Journal of Politics* 44 (1982), 21–40; Ronald Garet, 'Communality and Existence: The Rights of Groups', *Southern California Law Review* 56 (1983), 1001–75; Michael McDonald, 'Should Communities Have Rights? Reflections on Liberal Individualism', *Canadian Journal of Law and Jurisprudence* 4 (1991), 217–37;

interpretation of the debate was shared by both defenders and critics of minority rights. Both sides agreed that in order to evaluate minority rights we needed to first resolve these ontological and metaphysical questions about the relative priority of individuals and groups. Defenders of minority rights agreed that they were inconsistent with liberalism's commitment to moral individualism and individual autonomy, but argued that this just pointed out the inherent flaws of liberalism.

In short, defending minority rights involved endorsing the communitarian critique of liberalism, and viewing minority rights as defending cohesive and communally-minded minority groups against the encroachment of liberal individualism.

II. THE SECOND STAGE: MULTICULTURALISM WITHIN A LIBERAL FRAMEWORK

Partly as a result of Raz's influential contributions, it has been increasingly recognized that this first stage represented an unhelpful way to conceptualize most minority rights claims in Western democracies. Equating minority rights with communitarianism seemed sensible at the time, but assumptions about the 'striking parallel between the communitarian attack of philosophical liberalism and the notion of collective rights' have been increasingly questioned.[3] There are two problems with this approach: first, it misinterprets the nature of ethnocultural minorities; and second, it misinterprets the nature of liberalism.

In reality, most ethnocultural groups within Western democracies do not want to be protected from the forces of modernity unleashed in liberal societies. On the contrary, they want to be full and equal participants in modern liberal societies. This is true of most immigrant groups, which seek inclusion and full participation in the mainstream of liberal-democratic societies, with access to its education, technology, literacy, mass communications, etc. It is equally true of most non-immigrant national minorities, like the Québécois, Flemish or Catalans.[4]

Darlene Johnston, 'Native Rights as Collective Rights: A Question of Group Self-Preservation', *Canadian Journal of Law and Jurisprudence* 2 (1989), 19–34; Adeno Addis, 'Individualism, Communitarianism and the Rights of Ethnic Minorities', *Notre Dame Law Review* 67 (1992), 615–76; Dimitrios Karmis, 'Cultures autochtones et libéralisme au Canada: les vertus mediatrices du communautarisme libéral de Charles Taylor', *Canadian Journal of Political Science* 26 (1993), 69–96; Frances Svensson, 'Liberal Democracy and Group Rights: The Legacy of Individualism and its Impact on American Indian Tribes', *Political Studies* 27 (1979), 421–39. For 'individualist' critics, see Jan Narveson, 'Collective Rights?', *Canadian Journal of Law and Jurisprudence* 4 (1991), 329–45; Michael Hartney, 'Some Confusion Concerning Collective Rights,' *The Rights of Minority Cultures*, ed. Will Kymlicka (Oxford: Oxford University Press, 1995), 202–27.

[3] Marlies Galenkamp, *Individualism and Collectivism. The Concept of Collective Rights* (Rotterdam: Rotterdamse Filosofische Studies, 1993), 20–5.

[4] By national minorities, I mean groups that formed complete and functioning societies on their historic homeland prior to being incorporated into a larger state. The incorporation of such national minorities has typically been involuntary, due to colonization, conquest, or the ceding of territory from one imperial power to another, but may also arise voluntarily, as a result of federation.

Some of their members may seek to secede from a liberal democracy, but if they do, it is not in order to create an illiberal communitarian society, but rather to create their own modern liberal democratic society. The Québécois wish to create a 'distinct society', but it is a modern, liberal society—with an urbanized, secular, pluralistic, industrialized, bureaucratized, consumerist mass culture.

Indeed, far from opposing liberal principles, public opinion polls show there are no statistical differences between national minorities and majorities in their adherence to liberal principles. And immigrants also quickly absorb the basic liberal-democratic consensus, even when they came from countries with little or no experience of liberal democracy.[5]

As Raz rightly emphasizes, the commitment to individual autonomy is deep and wide in modern societies, crossing ethnic, linguistic and religious lines. To be sure, there are some important—and visible—exceptions to this rule. For example, there are a few ethno-religious sects that voluntarily distance themselves from the larger world—for example, the Hutterites, Amish, Hasidic Jews. And perhaps some of the more isolated or traditionalist indigenous communities fit this description as 'communitarian' groups. The question of how liberal states should respond to such non-liberal groups is an important one, to which I will return.

But the overwhelming majority of debates about minority rights within Western democracies are not debates between a liberal majority and communitarian minorities, but debates amongst liberals about the meaning of liberalism. They are debates between individuals and groups who endorse the basic liberal-democratic consensus, but who disagree about the interpretation of these principles in multi-ethnic societies—in particular, they disagree about the proper role of language, nationality, and ethnic identities within liberal-democratic societies and institutions. Groups claiming minority rights insist that certain forms of public recognition for their language, practices and identities are not only consistent with basic liberal-democratic principles, including the importance of individual autonomy, but may indeed be required by them.

This leads to the second problem with the pre-1989 debate—namely, the assumption that liberal principles are inherently opposed to minority rights claims. We now know that things are much more complicated, particularly under modern conditions of ethnocultural pluralism. We have inherited a set of

---

[5] On the political values of Canadian immigrants, see James Frideres, 'Edging into the Mainstream: Immigrant Adult and their Children', in *Comparative Perspectives on Interethnic Relations and Social Incorporation in Europe and North America*, ed. by S. Isajiw (Toronto: Canadian Scholar's Press, 1997), 537–62; for American immigrants, see John Harles, *Politics in the Lifeboat. Immigrants and the American Democratic Order* (Boulder: Westview Press, 1993). On the convergence in political values between Anglophones and Francophones in Canada, see Stéphane Dion, 'Le Nationalisme dans la Convergence Culturelle', in *L'Engagement Intellectuel: Mélanges en l'honneur de Léon Dion*, eds. R. Hudon and R. Pelletier (Sainte-Foy: Les Presses de l'Université Laval, 1991). In fact, on many issues, national minorities tend to be more liberal than the majority. For example, Scots, Québécois and Catalans tend to be more liberal than their majority counterparts on issues regarding gay rights, gender equality or foreign aid. See Kymlicka, *Politics in the Vernacular: Nationalism, Multiculturalism, Citizenship* (Oxford: Oxford University Press, 2001), chs. 10–15.

assumptions about what liberal principles require, but these assumptions first emerged in eighteenth-century United States, or nineteenth-century England, where there was very little ethnocultural heterogeneity. Virtually all citizens shared the same language, ethnic descent, national identity, and Christian faith. It is increasingly clear that we cannot rely on the interpretation of liberalism developed in those earlier times. We need to judge for ourselves what liberalism requires under our own conditions of ethnocultural pluralism.

This then has led to the second stage of the debate, in which the question becomes: what is the possible scope for minority rights *within* liberal theory? Framing the debate this way does not resolve the issues. On the contrary, the place of minority rights within liberal theory remains very controversial. But it changes the terms of the debate. The issue is no longer how to protect communitarian minorities from liberalism, but whether minorities that share basic liberal principles nonetheless need minority rights. If groups are indeed liberal, why do they want minority rights? Why aren't they satisfied with the traditional common rights of citizenship?

Raz's 1990 article on national self-determination (co-authored with Avishai Margalit)[6] and his 1994 article on multiculturalism[7] are paradigm examples of this new approach, and both played a pivotal step in moving the debate forward. Drawing on the account of autonomy developed in *The Morality of Freedom*, Raz insisted that the autonomy of individuals—their ability to make good choices amongst good lives—is intimately tied up with access to their culture, with the prosperity and flourishing of their culture, and with the respect accorded their culture by others. Other liberal writers like David Miller, Yael Tamir and Jeff Spinner and myself have developed and elaborated this theme.[8] The details of the argument vary, but each of us, in our own way, argues that there are compelling interests related to cultural membership and cultural identity, which are fully consistent with liberal principles of freedom and equality, and which justify adopting measures for 'fostering and encouraging the prosperity, cultural and material, of cultural groups, and respecting their identity'.[9]

---

[6] Avishai Margalit and Raz, 'National Self-Determination', *Journal of Philosophy* 87 (1990), 439–61.

[7] Raz, 'Multiculturalism: A Liberal Perspective', *Dissent*, Winter 1994, 67–79.

[8] Yael Tamir, *Liberal Nationalism* (Princeton: Princeton University Press, 1993); Jeff Spinner, *The Boundaries of Citizenship: Race, Ethnicity and Nationality in the Liberal State* (Baltimore: Johns Hopkins University Press, 1994); David Miller, *On Nationality* (Oxford: Oxford University Press, 1995); Kymlicka, *Liberalism, Community, and Culture* (Oxford: Oxford University Press, 1989); Kymlicka, *Multicultural Citizenship* (Oxford: Oxford University Press, 1995).

[9] Raz, 'Multiculturalism', *Ratio Juris* 11 (1998), 193–205, 197. Even Charles Taylor's account of the 'politics of recognition', which is often described as a 'communitarian' position, can be seen as a form of 'liberal culturalism', since he too argues that people demand recognition of their differences, not instead of individual freedom, but rather as a support and precondition for freedom (Charles Taylor, 'The Politics of Recognition', in *Multiculturalism and the 'Politics of Recognition'*, ed. Amy Gutmann (Princeton: Princeton University Press, 1992), 25–73). However, Taylor mixes this liberal argument for multiculturalism with another more communitarian argument about the intrinsic value of group survival, and his policy recommendations reflect this hybrid mixture of liberal and communitarian reasoning.

We can call this the 'liberal culturalist' position, and I think it has quickly become the dominant position amongst liberals working in this field.[10]

Critics of liberal culturalism have raised many objections to this entire line of argument: some deny that we can intelligibly distinguish or individuate 'cultures' or 'cultural groups'; others deny that we can make sense of the claim that individuals are 'members' of cultures; yet others say that even if we can make sense of the claim that individuals are members of distinct cultures, we have no reason to assume that the well-being of the individual is tied in any way with the flourishing of the culture.[11] These are important objections that must be answered if liberal culturalism is to be properly defended.

However, since I am sympathetic to Raz's line of argument, I will set these objections aside, and assume that there is indeed an important sense in which the well-being and autonomy of individuals is tied to their cultural membership. This still leaves some difficult issues even for those who accept the liberal culturalist position. The first relates to illiberal minorities. As I noted earlier, there is a small subset of minority groups within Western democracies which seek to suppress the autonomy of their members, and such illiberal groups would presumably use minority rights almost exclusively for this purpose. Second, there are illiberal strands in every culture, even the most liberal and democratic, and this raises the worry that some forms of minority rights could be misused, even within generally liberal-minded groups, to undermine, rather then support, individual autonomy. Indeed, many liberals have supposed that 'group rights' are inherently a threat to individual rights. This raises two fundamental problems for any liberal theory of minority rights:

(a) how should the state respond to the claims of groups which are illiberal? Should they be entitled to claim minority rights, or should these rights be restricted to groups that have embraced the liberal consensus? This is a question about the kinds of groups entitled to minority rights;

(b) what sort of restrictions or conditions must be set on minority rights to ensure that they serve to supplement or strengthen individual rights and individual liberty, rather than restrict individual rights? This is a question about the kinds of rights that should be accorded to groups.

Any liberal theory must address these two questions, and of course Raz has done so. To oversimplify, he answers them as follows:

(a) illiberal groups have no claim to support: only groups that respect and enable the autonomy of their members deserve support. If illiberal groups desire support, they must abandon or neutralize their illiberal practices;

---

[10] It is an interesting question why this liberal culturalist view—which is a clear departure from the dominant liberal view for several decades—has become so popular so quickly. For some speculations, see Kymlicka, *Politics in the Vernacular: Nationalism, Multiculturalism, Citizenship* (n. 5 above), ch. 2. For a recent spirited defence of the older liberal view that opposes multiculturalism and minority rights, see Brian Parry, *Culture and Equality* (Cambridge: Polity Press, 2001).

[11] For a pithy statement of these points, see Jeremy Waldron, 'Minority Cultures and the Cosmopolitan Alternative' in *The Rights of Minority Cultures* (n. 2 above), 93–121.

(b) the key restriction on minority rights is that they must allow for a right of exit. Granting rights to (generally liberal) groups is not a threat to individual liberty so long as individuals have an effective right of exit (which includes knowledge of the options available in the larger society, and the general skills needed to succeed in it).

These two answers are controversial, even amongst 'liberal culturalists' who are otherwise sympathetic to Raz's view. Regarding the first question, many liberal culturalists would be more generous to non-liberal groups, particularly if they are either ethno-religious sects (like the Amish) or indigenous peoples (like the Inuit). In the case of groups like the Amish, some authors argue that religious toleration is a distinct liberal value which may sometimes conflict with, and take precedence over, autonomy.[12] In the case of groups like the Inuit, some authors argue that, as conquered or colonized peoples, indigenous groups have rights to self-government which predate the rise of the state established by colonizing settlers, and that the state therefore has not acquired the right to impose liberal norms on them.[13] While Raz implicitly assumes that states have the right to impose liberal norms on the indigenous peoples that they have colonized, he does not explicitly address the question of how or why this assertion of state authority over colonized peoples is legitimate.[14]

Regarding the second question of restrictions on minority rights, virtually all liberal culturalists would agree that a right of exit is crucial to any liberal theory of minority rights. However, there remain disputes about the meaning and preconditions of such a right. Chandran Kukathas, for example, argues that it only requires a formal legal right of exit, and he therefore objects to Raz's requirement that the children of minority groups must learn a core curriculum, national language or set of general skills.[15] Okin, on the other hand, insists that a truly effective right of exit, particularly for women, requires not only formal rights and minimal education, but also active state intervention to eliminate sexist cultural practices and stereotypes which make it difficult or impossible for women to leave a community, even when they are oppressed within it.[16] She argues that Raz's account of a right of exit is therefore too weak.

---

[12] E.g., Jeff Spinner, *The Boundaries of Citizenship* (n. 8 above); William Galston, 'Two Concepts of Liberalism', *Ethics* 105 (1995), 516–34. This is particularly likely to be the view of those who endorse a more 'political' conception of liberalism, in Rawls' sense, rather than the more 'comprehensive' conception that Raz adopts (and I share).

[13] E.g., James Tully, *Strange Multiplicity. Constitutionalism in an Age of Diversity* (Cambridge: Cambridge University Press, 1995). Note that neither of these arguments applies to the (non-religious) practices of voluntary immigrants. In such cases, most liberal culturalists agree with Raz that it is appropriate for the state to insist on respect for liberal norms. This would apply to many controversial issues regarding immigrant groups, such as female circumcision or forced arranged marriages.

[14] See Raz, *The Morality of Freedom* (Oxford: Oxford University Press, 1986), 423–4.

[15] See Chandran Kukathas, 'Cultural Toleration', in Ian Shapiro and Will Kymlicka (eds.) *Ethnicity and Group Rights: NOMOS 39* (New York: New York University Press, 1997), 69–104.

[16] See Susan Okin, 'Mistresses of Their Own Destiny? Group Rights, Gender, and Realistic Rights of Exit' (presented at the annual meeting of the American Political Science Association, Sept. 1998).

Much more could be said about these two questions. I have quibbles with Raz's answers to these questions, but I will not pursue them here. Instead, I want to raise a more general concern about the framework underlying this second stage of the debate, including Raz's contributions. To recap, in this second stage, the question of minority rights is reformulated as a question within liberal theory, and the aim is to show that some (but not all) minority rights claims actually enhance liberal values. In my opinion, this second stage reflects genuine progress. We now have a better understanding of the claims being made by ethnocultural groups, and of the normative issues they raise. We have moved beyond the sterile and misleading debate about individualism and collectivism.

However, I think this second stage also needs to be questioned. While it incorporates a more accurate understanding of the nature of most ethnocultural groups, and the demands they place on the liberal state, it misinterprets the nature of the liberal state, and the demands it places on minorities.

III. A THIRD STAGE? MINORITY RIGHTS AS A RESPONSE TO NATION-BUILDING

Let me explain. The assumption—generally shared by both defenders and critics of minority rights, though not by Raz himself—is that the liberal state, in its normal operation, abides by a principle of ethnocultural neutrality. That is, the state is 'neutral' with respect to the ethnocultural identities of its citizens, and indifferent to the ability of ethnocultural groups to reproduce themselves over time. According to this view, liberal states treat culture in the same way as religion—that is, as something which people should be free to pursue in their private lives, but which is not the concern of the state (so long as they respect the rights of others). Just as liberalism precludes the establishment of an official religion, so too there cannot be official cultures that have preferred status over other possible cultural allegiances.[17]

Indeed, some theorists argue that this is precisely what distinguishes liberal 'civic nations' from illiberal 'ethnic nations'[18]. Ethnic nations take the reproduction of a particular ethno-national culture and identity as one of their most important goals. Civic nations, by contrast, are 'neutral' with respect to the ethnocultural identities of their citizens, and define national membership purely in terms of adherence to certain principles of democracy and justice. For minorities to seek special rights, in this view, is a departure from the traditional operation of the liberal state. Therefore, the burden of proof lies on anyone who would wish to endorse such minority rights.

---

[17] See, e.g., Michael Walzer, 'Comment', in *Multiculturalism and the 'Politics of Recognition'*, ed. Amy Gutmann (Princeton: Princeton University Press, 1992), 100–1.

[18] See Michael Ignatieff, *Blood and Belonging. Journeys Into the New Nationalism* (New York: Farrar, Straus and Giroux, 1993).

This is the burden of proof which liberal culturalists try to meet with their account of the importance of cultural membership in securing individual autonomy and self-respect. Liberal culturalists try to show that minority rights supplement, rather than diminish, individual freedom and equality, and help to meet legitimate interests that would otherwise go unmet in a state that clings rigidly to ethnocultural neutrality.

The presumption in the second stage of the debate has been that advocates of minority rights must demonstrate compelling reasons to depart from the norm of ethnocultural neutrality. This is not the way Raz himself describes the issue— he has never accepted that liberal states are or can be ethnoculturally neutral— but even he seems to accept that the burden of proof falls on those who seek to deviate from 'difference-blind' institutions or procedures.[19]

I would argue, however, that the idea that liberal-democratic states (or 'civic nations') are ethnoculturally neutral is manifestly false, both historically and conceptually. The religion model is altogether misleading as an account of the relationship between the liberal-democratic state and ethnocultural groups. Once we abandon this model, and adopt a more accurate conception of the liberal state, we will also have to rethink our theory of minority rights, and address a range of issues not present in Raz's theory.

Why is the ethnocultural neutrality model inaccurate? Consider the actual policies of the United States, which is often cited as the prototypically 'neutral' state. Historically, decisions about the boundaries of state governments, and the timing of their admission into the federation, were deliberately made to ensure that Anglophones would be a majority within each of the fifty states of the American federation. This helped establish the dominance of English throughout the territory of the United States. And the continuing dominance of English is ensured by several ongoing policies. For example, it is a legal requirement for children to learn the English language in schools; it is a legal requirement for immigrants (under the age of 50) to learn the English language to acquire American citizenship; and it is a de facto requirement for government employment that the applicant speak English.

These decisions about the drawing of internal boundaries, the language of education and government employment, and the requirements of citizenship are profoundly important. They are not isolated exceptions to some norm of ethnocultural neutrality. On the contrary, they have shaped the very structure of the American state and of American society.

These policies have been pursued with the intention of promoting the integration of American citizens into what I call a 'societal culture'. By a societal culture, I mean a territorially-concentrated culture, centred on a shared language which is used in a wide range of societal institutions, in both public and private life (schools, media, law, economy, government, etc.). I call

---

[19] See his discussion of the 'Why multiculturalism?' question in 'Multiculturalism' (n. 9 above), 200.

it a *societal* culture to emphasize that it involves a common language and social institutions, rather than common religious beliefs, family customs or personal lifestyles. Societal cultures within a modern liberal democracy are inevitably pluralistic, containing Christians as well as Muslims, Jews and atheists; heterosexuals as well as gays; urban professionals as well as rural farmers; conservatives as well as socialists. Such diversity is the inevitable result of the rights and freedoms guaranteed to liberal citizens—including freedom of conscience, association, speech, political dissent and rights to privacy—particularly when combined with an ethnically diverse population. This diversity, however, is balanced and constrained by linguistic and institutional cohesion; cohesion that has not emerged on its own, but rather is the result of deliberate state policies.

The American government has deliberately created and sustained such a societal culture: it has systematically promoted a common language, and a sense of common membership in, and equal access to, the social institutions operating in that language. It has encouraged citizens to view their life-chances as tied up with participation in common societal institutions that operate in the English language, and nurtured a national identity defined in part by this common membership in a societal culture. Nor is the United States unique in this respect. Promoting integration of citizens into a societal culture is part of a 'nation-building' project that all liberal democracies have engaged in.

Obviously, the sense in which English-speaking Americans share a common 'culture' is a very thin one, since it does not preclude differences in religion, personal values, family relationships or lifestyle choices. But it is far from trivial. On the contrary, as I discuss below, attempts to integrate people into such a common societal culture have often faced serious resistance. Although integration in this sense leaves a great deal of room for both the public and private expression of individual and collective differences, some groups have nonetheless rejected the idea that they should integrate into a common societal culture, and view their life-chances as tied up with the societal institutions conducted in the majority's language.

So we need to replace the idea of an 'ethnoculturally neutral' state with a new model of a liberal democratic state—what I call the 'nation-building' model. To say that states are nation-building is not to say that governments can only promote one societal culture. It is possible for government policies to encourage the sustaining of two or more societal cultures within a single country—indeed, as I discuss below, this is precisely what characterizes multi-nation states like Switzerland, Belgium, Spain or Canada.

However, historically, virtually all liberal democracies have, at one point or another, attempted to diffuse a single societal culture throughout all of its territory.[20] Nor should this be seen purely as a matter of cultural imperialism

---

[20] To my knowledge, Switzerland is perhaps the only exception: it never made any serious attempt to pressure its French- and Italian-speaking minorities to integrate into the German majority. All of the other contemporary Western multination states have at one time or another made a concerted effort to assimilate their minorities, and only reluctantly gave up this ideal.

or ethnocentric prejudice. Nation-building serves a number of important liberal-democratic goals. For example, a modern economy requires a mobile, educated and literate workforce. Standardized public education in a common language has often been seen as essential if all citizens are to have equal opportunity to work in this modern economy. Also, participation in a common societal culture has often been seen as essential for generating the sort of solidarity required by a welfare state, since it promotes a sense of common national identity and membership. Moreover, a common language has been seen as essential to democracy—how can 'the people' govern together if they cannot understand one another? In short, promoting integration into a common societal culture has been seen as essential to promoting social equality and political cohesion in modern states.

Indeed, one could argue that the only sort of liberal democracy that exists in the world has arisen through efforts to create liberalized societal cultures. Liberal reformers have generally, if implicitly, accepted that the relevant unit or context within which to pursue liberal principles of freedom and equality is societal cultures consolidated by state nation-building policies. In this sense, as Tamir puts it, 'most liberals are liberal nationalists'.[21]

Of course, nation-building can also be used to promote illiberal goals. As Margaret Canovan puts it, nationhood is like a 'battery' which makes states run—the existence of a common national identity motivates and mobilizes citizens to act for common political goals—and these goals can be liberal or illiberal.[22] The 'battery' of nationalism can be used to promote liberal goals (such as social justice, democratization, equality of opportunity, economic development) or illiberal goals (chauvinism, xenophobia, militarism, and unjust conquest). The fact that the battery of nationalism can be used for so many functions helps to explain why it has been so ubiquitous. Liberal reformers invoke nationhood to mobilize citizens behind projects of democratization and social justice (e.g., comprehensive health care or public schooling); illiberal authoritarians invoke nationhood to mobilize citizens behind attacks on alleged enemies of the nation, be they foreign countries or internal dissidents. This is why nation-building is just as common in authoritarian regimes in the West as in democracies. Consider Spain under Franco, or Greece or Latin America under the military dictators. Authoritarian regimes also need a 'battery' to help achieve public objectives in complex modern societies. What distinguishes liberal from illiberal states is not the presence or absence of nation-building, but rather the ends to which nation-building is put, and the means used in pursuit of nation-building.

So states have engaged in this process of 'nation-building'.[23] Decisions regarding official languages, core curriculum in education, and the requirements for

---

[21] See Yael Tamir, *Liberal Nationalism* (n. 8 above), 139.

[22] See Margaret Canovan, *Nationhood and Political Theory* (Cheltenham: Edward Elgar, 1996), 80.

[23] For the ubiquity of this process, see Ernest Gellner, *Nations and Nationalism* (Oxford: Blackwell, 1983); Benedict Anderson, *Imagined Communities: Reflections on the Origin and Spread of Nationalism* (London: New Left Books, 1983).

acquiring citizenship, all have been made with the express intention of diffusing a particular societal culture throughout the territory of the state, and of promoting a national identity based on participation in that societal culture.

If this nation-building model provides a more accurate account of the nature of modern liberal democratic states than the ethnocultural neutrality model, how does this affect the issue of minority rights? I believe it gives us a very different perspective on the debate. In particular, it changes the burden of proof. As I noted earlier, during the second stage of the debate both advocates and critics of minority rights tended to assume that the onus was on advocates to show compelling reasons why states should deviate from ethnocultural neutrality. Once we recognize that states are not ethnoculturally neutral, but rather engage in the promotion and diffusion of a dominant societal culture, we must ask whether these nation-building policies create injustices for minorities. The burden of proof falls on the state to show that minority rights are not required to remedy or counteract injustices which arise from state nation-building.

This would be a new approach to the debate, which I am trying to develop in my own recent work. I cannot explore all of its implications, but let me give two examples of how this new model of the liberal state may affect the debate over minority rights. I will first try to develop this new model in my own terms (section 4), and then consider the extent to which this new model requires the revising or expanding of Raz's account (section 5).

IV. Two examples

How does nation-building affect minorities? As Charles Taylor notes, the process of nation-building inescapably privileges members of the majority culture:

If a modern society has an 'official' language, in the fullest sense of the term, that is, a state-sponsored, inculcated, and defined language and culture, in which both economy and state function, then it is obviously an immense advantage to people if this language and culture are theirs. Speakers of other languages are at a distinct disadvantage.[24]

This means that the members of minority cultures face a choice. If all public institutions are being run in another language, minorities face the danger of being marginalized from the major economic, academic, and political institutions of the society. Faced with this dilemma, minorities have (to oversimplify) three basic options:

(i) they can accept integration into the majority culture, although perhaps attempt to renegotiate the terms of integration;

---

[24] Charles Taylor, 'Nationalism and Modernity', in J. McMahan and R. McKim (eds.), *The Morality of Nationalism* (Oxford: Oxford University Press, 1997), 34.

(ii) they can seek the sorts of rights and powers of self-government needed to maintain their own societal culture—that is, to create their own economic, political and educational institutions in their own language;

(iii) they can accept permanent marginalization.

We can find some ethnocultural groups that fit each of these categories (and other groups that are caught between them). For example, some immigrant groups choose permanent marginalization. This is true, for example, of the Hutterites in Canada, or the Amish in the United States. But the option of accepting marginalization is only likely to be attractive to ethno-religious groups whose theology requires them to avoid all contact with the modern world. The Hutterites and Amish are unconcerned about their marginalization from universities or legislatures, since they view such 'worldly' institutions as corrupt.

Virtually all other ethnocultural minorities, however, seek to participate in the modern world, and to do so, they must either integrate or seek the self-government needed to create and sustain their own modern institutions. Faced with this choice, ethnocultural groups have responded in different ways.

National minorities

National minorities have typically responded to majority nation-building by engaging in their own competing nation-building. Indeed, they often use the same tools that the majority uses to promote this nation-building—for example, control over the language and curriculum of schooling, the language of government employment, the requirements of immigration and naturalization, and the drawing of internal boundaries. We can see this clearly in the case of Québécois nationalism, which has largely been concerned with gaining and exercising these nation-building powers. The same is true of Flemish or Catalan nationalism. But it is also increasingly true of indigenous peoples in various parts of the world, who have adopted the language of 'nationhood' and 'nation-building'.[25]

Intuitively, the adoption of such minority nation-building projects seems fair. If the majority can engage in legitimate nation-building, why not national minorities, particularly those which have been involuntarily incorporated into a larger state? To be sure, liberal principles set limits on *how* national groups, whether majority or minority, go about nation-building. Liberal principles preclude any attempts at ethnic cleansing, or stripping people of their citizenship, or the violation of human rights. These principles will also insist that any national group engaged in a project of nation-building must respect the right of other nations within its jurisdiction to protect and build their own national institutions. For example, the Québécois are entitled to assert national rights vis-à-vis the rest of Canada, but only if they respect the rights of Aboriginals within Quebec to assert national rights vis-à-vis the rest of Quebec.

---

[25] See Gerald Alfred, *Heeding the Voices of our Ancestors: Kahnawake Mohawk Politics and the Rise of Native Nationalism* (Toronto: Oxford University Press, 1995).

These limits are important, but they still leave significant room, I believe, for legitimate forms of minority nationalism. Moreover, these limits are likely to be similar for both majority and minority nations. All else being equal, national minorities should have the same tools of nation-building available to them as the majority nation, subject to the same liberal limitations.

What we need, in other words, is a consistent theory of permissible forms of nation-building within liberal democracies. I do not think that political theorists have yet developed such a theory. One of the many unfortunate side-effects of the dominance of the 'ethnocultural neutrality' model of the liberal state is that liberal theorists have never explicitly confronted this question.

I do not have a fully developed theory about the permissible forms of nation-building.[26] My aim here is not to promote any particular theory of permissible nation-building, but simply to insist that this is the relevant question we need to address. That is, the question is not 'have national minorities given us a compelling reason to abandon the norm of ethnocultural neutrality?', but rather 'why should national minorities not have the same powers of nation-building as the majority?' This is the context within which minority nationalism must be evaluated—i.e. as a response to majority nation-building, using the same tools of nation-building. And the burden of proof surely rests on those who would deny to national minorities the powers of nation-building which the national majority takes for granted.

Immigrants

Historically, nation-building has been neither desirable nor feasible for immigrant groups. Instead, these groups have traditionally accepted the expectation that they will integrate into the larger societal culture. Indeed, few immigrant groups in any Western democracy have objected to the requirement that they must learn an official language as a condition of citizenship, or that their children must learn the official language in school. They have accepted the assumption that their life-chances, and even more the life-chances of their children, will be bound up with participation in mainstream institutions operating in the majority language.

However, this is not to say that immigrants do not suffer injustices as a result of nation-building policies. After all, the state is not neutral with respect to the language and culture of immigrants: it imposes a range of de jure and de facto requirements for immigrants to integrate in order to succeed. These requirements are often difficult and costly for immigrants to meet. Since immigrants cannot respond to this by adopting their own nation-building programs, but rather must attempt to integrate as best they can, it is only fair that the state minimize the costs involved in this state-demanded integration.

[26] I offer guidelines for distinguishing liberal and illiberal forms of nation-building in Kymlicka and Magda Opalski, *Can Liberal Pluralism be Exported? Western Political Theory and Ethnic Relations in Eastern Europe* (Oxford: Oxford University Press, 2001).

Put another way, immigrants can demand fairer terms of integration. If a country is going to pressure immigrants to integrate into common institutions operating in the majority language, then it must ensure that the terms of integration are fair. To my mind, this demand has two basic elements:

(a) we need to recognize that integration does not occur overnight, but is a difficult and long-term process which operates inter-generationally. This means that special accommodations are often required for immigrants on a transitional basis. For example, certain services should be available in the immigrants' mother tongue, and support should be provided for those organizations and groups within immigrant communities which assist in the settlement and integration process;

(b) we need to ensure that the common institutions into which immigrants are pressured to integrate provide the same degree of respect, recognition and accommodation of the identities and practices of immigrants as they traditionally have of the identities of the majority group.

This requires a systematic exploration of our social institutions to see whether their rules, structures and symbols disadvantage immigrants. For example, we need to examine dress-codes, public holidays, or even height and weight restrictions to see whether they are biased against certain immigrant groups. We also need to examine the portrayal of minorities in school curricula or the media to see if they are stereotypical, or fail to recognize the contributions of ethnocultural groups to national history or world culture. And so on. These measures are needed to ensure that liberal states are offering immigrants fair terms of integration.[27]

Others may disagree with the fairness of some of these policies. The requirements of fairness are not obvious, particularly in the context of people who have chosen to enter a country, and political theorists have done little to illuminate the issue. Here again, the dominance of the 'ethnocultural neutrality' model of the liberal state has blinded liberal theorists to the importance of the question. My aim here is not to promote a particular theory of fair terms of integration, but rather to insist that this is the relevant question we need to address. The question is not whether immigrants have given us a compelling reason to diverge from the norm of ethnocultural neutrality, but rather how can we ensure that state policies aimed at pressuring immigrants to integrate are fair?

I believe that we could extend this method to look at other types of ethnocultural groups that are neither national minorities nor immigrants, such as African-Americans, the Roma in Central Europe, or Russian settlers in the Baltics. In each case, I think it is possible—and indeed essential—to view their claims to minority rights as a response to perceived injustices that arise out of

---

[27] Kymlicka, *Finding Our Way: Rethinking Ethnocultural Relations in Canada* (Toronto: Oxford University Press, 1998), ch. 3.

nation-building policies.[28] Each group's claims can be seen as specifying the injustices that majority nation-building has imposed on them, and as identifying the conditions under which majority nation-building would cease to be unjust.

If we combine these different demands into a larger conception of ethnocultural justice, we can say that majority nation-building in a liberal-democracy is legitimate under the following conditions:

(a) nation-building is inclusive: that is, no groups of long-term residents are permanently excluded from membership in the nation. Everyone living on the territory must be able to gain citizenship, and become an equal member of the nation if they wish to do so. This condition responds to and remedies the injustice which groups such as metics or racial caste have faced as a result of nation-building in many Western democracies;

(b) the concept of national identity and integration must be pluralistic and tolerant: i.e., the sort of socio-cultural integration which is required for membership in the nation should be understood in a 'thin' sense, primarily involving institutional and linguistic integration, not the adoption of any particular set of customs, religious beliefs, or lifestyles. Integration into common institutions operating in a common language should still leave maximal room for the expression of individual and collective differences, both in public and private, and public institutions should be adapted to accommodate the identity and practices of ethnocultural minorities. This condition responds to and remedies the injustice that many immigrant groups have faced as a result of nation-building;

(c) all national groups within a state, not just the majority nation, are allowed to engage in their own nation-building, to enable them to maintain themselves as distinct societal cultures. This condition responds to and remedies the injustice that many national minorities have faced as a result of nation-building.

These three conditions have rarely been met within Western democracies, but we can see a clear trend within most democracies towards greater acceptance of them. And I think that the major task facing any liberal theory of multiculturalism is to better understand these conditions of ethnocultural justice, by showing how particular minority rights claims are related to, and a response to, state nation-building policies.

V. RAZ ON NATIONALISM AND NATION-BUILDING

How does this relate to Raz's theory? At one level, I think that there is no inherent conflict between Raz's approach and the one that I have just sketched.

---

[28] I explore the claims of these other types of groups in Kymlicka and Opalski, *Can Liberalism Pluralism Be Exported?*, (n. 26 above), ch. 3.

Indeed, his account of appropriate multiculturalism policies for immigrant groups,[29] and his account of the rights of national groups to self-determination,[30] can easily be (re)described in the terms I have just outlined.

For example, consider his list of multicultural policies which immigrant groups can rightly seek:[31]

- while children should be educated to be familiar with the history and traditions of the dominant culture of the country, they should also be educated in the culture of their group, if their parents so desire;
- the customs and practices of different groups, within the limits of permissible toleration, should be recognized;
- the link between poverty, under-education and ethnicity should be dissolved;
- there should be generous public support for cultural institutions (museums, theatre etc.);
- public space should accommodate all cultural groups.

Each of these policies can be redescribed, I believe, as helping to ensure fairer terms of integration into the dominant societal culture of a new country.

Similarly, Raz's account of the right of self-determination for national groups can be seen as a defence of the right of national minorities to engage in a range of nation-building policies so as to maintain their distinct societal cultures, with their own public institutions operating in their own language.[32]

So most or all of what Raz says regarding the substantive rights of immigrants and national minorities is consistent with the sort of model I am advancing. His account can be seen as putting flesh on the skeletal framework that I have outlined; conversely, my framework can be seen as providing further support for his substantive claims about the legitimate claims of immigrants and national minorities.

However, at another level, Raz's account is in some tension with mine. For he insists that his conception of multiculturalism requires not only this or that substantive policy for this or that group, but also a complete revision in our very understanding of the nation-state. In particular, he argues that multiculturalism 'calls on us to radically to reconceive society, changing its self-image', in two respects:

(a) it requires that 'we should learn to think of our societies as consisting not of a majority and minorities, but as constituted by a plurality of cultural groups'.[33] Indeed, he says that multiculturalism is *primarily* a matter of such a change in self-image, rather than of specific policies.[34]

---

[29] See Raz, 'Multiculturalism' (n. 9 above), 193–205.
[30] See Margalit and Raz, 'National Self-Determination' (n. 6 above), 439–61.
[31] Raz, 'Multiculturalism' (n. 9 above), 198–9.
[32] See Margalit and Raz, 'National Self-Determination' (n. 6 above).
[33] Raz, 'Multiculturalism' (n. 9 above), 197.   [34] Ibid., 200.

(b) it also calls on us to 'replace the ideology of nationalism', and 'reject common nationality as the common bond on which political units must be based'.[35]

It's important to note that my conception of minority rights does not involve either of these two claims, and in a certain sense rejects both. First, the whole point of my approach is precisely to emphasize the extent to which most liberal democratic societies *do* consist of a majority, which uses state power to engage in nation-building, and various minorities, who then have to decide how to respond to these nation-building policies. If there were no majority, and hence no majority nation-building, we could not think of minority rights as a response to the potential injustices of majority nation-building.

Indeed, I would argue that the major advances in thinking about multiculturalism and minority rights in the past decade have arisen precisely out of an awareness of the pervasiveness and significance of majority/minority relations—i.e. an awareness of the benefits accrued by majorities in majoritarian, nation-building states, and the subsequent pressures and disadvantages faced by minorities. It is often the critics of multiculturalism, at least in the North American context, who say that we don't have a (privileged) majority and (disadvantaged) minorities, and therefore don't need multiculturalism policies.

Perhaps Raz would agree that contemporary societies can only be understood through the lens of majority/minority dynamics, but would insist that the point of multiculturalism would be to eliminate these dynamics. This then leads us to Raz's second claim: namely, that multiculturalism challenges nationalism, and the privileging of national identities as the locus of political community. I'm not sure what precisely Raz means by this, but one obvious interpretation would be to say that multiculturalism challenges the very legitimacy of state nation-building policies, and seeks to prevent majorities from using state power to promote the integration of citizens into common societal cultures.

If this is what Raz means (and I'm not sure it is), then I think it is problematic, both empirically and normatively. Empirically, I see no evidence that either immigrants or national minorities are challenging the basic legitimacy of nation-building policies, or the legitimacy of states trying to integrate citizens into societal cultures. It is obvious that national minorities are not challenging this, since the whole aim of minority nationalism is precisely to gain these nation-building powers for themselves, and to use these same powers to consolidate their own societal culture in their own region of the country. They are insisting that they live in multi-nation states, in which two or more national groups are able to exercise nation-building powers on a regional basis. This insistence that they live in a multi-nation state is, in one sense, a challenge to the traditional ideal of a (mono-national) 'nation-state'. But a multi-nation state is not a *post*-national state: it is still organized along national lines, and still

---

[35] Raz, 'Multiculturalism' (n. 9 above), 196, 202.

asserts that national groups have the right to self-government—i.e. to form their own autonomous political communities within the larger state. It therefore accepts the legitimacy of nationalism as an ideology, and accepts that nations form a basic context of liberal political community.[36]

It might seem that the claims of immigrants are more of a challenge to the legitimacy of nation-building. But in fact the vast majority of immigrants also accept the validity of nation-building. For example, as I noted earlier, few immigrant groups in any Western democracy have objected to the requirement that they must learn an official language as a condition of citizenship, or that their children must learn the official language in school. They have accepted the assumption that their life-chances, and even more the life-chances of their children, will be bound up with participation in mainstream institutions operating in the majority language. What they are seeking is fair terms of integration into the dominant societal culture.

So far as I can tell, therefore, neither immigrants nor national minorities are challenging the centrality of national cultures and national identities to political life, or the legitimacy of using state power to consolidate these national cultures and identities.

I'm not sure whether Raz really disagrees with any of this. After all, he agrees that immigrants should learn a 'common culture',[37] in part through a 'common education'[38] which includes knowledge of the basic skills required to have equal opportunity in the economy and to participate in mainstream political life. It is difficult to see what this could possibly mean other than the sort of linguistic and institutional integration into a common societal culture that has been the aim of traditional nation-building policies. How else could immigrants achieve economic equality of opportunity except by knowing the dominant language, and participating in integrated institutions of higher education conducted in the dominant language? Indeed, how would we measure equality of opportunity except by seeing whether immigrants are succeeding in such institutions? And how else can they participate in politics?

Given Raz's call for a common culture and a common education, and for equality of opportunity in economics and politics, it is quite possible that he endorses much if not all of what I have been calling 'nation-building' policies. Perhaps we simply disagree about whether to use the terms 'nationalism' and 'nation-building'. Perhaps he thinks that if liberal states allow national minorities to be self-governing, and allow immigrants to integrate rather than assimilate, then they have distanced themselves so far from traditional forms of nationalism that it is tantamount to 'rejecting the ideology of nationalism'.

If this is his view, then our dispute is merely semantic. In my view, if liberal states accord rights of self-government to national groups, and pressure

---

[36] For evidence that the claims of national minorities are indeed driven by nationalism, see Michael Keating and John McGarry, *Minority Nationalism and the Changing International Order* (Oxford: Oxford University Press, 2001).   [37] Ibid., 202.

[38] Raz, 'Multicultarlism' (n. 9 above), 203.

immigrants to integrate linguistically and institutionally into the societal culture of a host nation, then liberal states are still very much imbued with the ideology of nationalism. To be sure, this is a distinctive form of nationalism: it is, in fact, a distinctively liberal form of nationalism. Indeed, one way to define liberal nationalism is precisely that it accepts the legitimacy of minority nationalism and of immigrant multiculturalism. But this is still nationalism, and it still involves nation-building, both by the state and by national minorities.

But our dispute may not be purely semantic. Perhaps I've put too much weight on Raz's brief references to 'common culture' and 'common education'. Perhaps he only means by this that the state can require minimal levels of knowledge (e.g. of one's rights, or of mathematics) but not any sort of linguistic or institutional integration. Perhaps he really does think that it is impermissible for the state (or national minorities) to engage in nation-building, or to seek to integrate immigrants linguistically and institutionally into a societal culture. If so, then I think he is going far beyond the actual demands of most minorities in Western democracies. Moreover, I'm not sure what sorts of rights minorities would have in such a non-national or post-national state. Imagine that the liberal state rejected nation-building policies, and abandoned the goal of the linguistic or institutional integration of citizens. Would national minorities still have rights to self-determination? Would immigrants still have the right to inclusion and representation in public media or school curriculum? Or would it be enough to simply ensure that minorities have rights of non-discrimination in the distribution of public funds?

Raz insists that multiculturalism isn't simply a matter of non-discrimination, and I agree. But on my view, part of the reason why justice requires more than non-discrimination is that liberal states are nation-building states. For example, it is because states are nation-building that justice requires granting comparable nation-building powers to national minorities. If majorities never used state power to pressure national minorities into integrating into majority institutions, then national minorities wouldn't have the same need to control their own levers of state power. Whether national minorities need rights of regional self-government depends, in least in part, on the prior question of whether the majority is prone to using centralized power to promote nation-building.

Similarly, it is at least partly because states pressure immigrants to integrate linguistically and institutionally that immigrants have a right to respect and accommodation within the institutions that they are being pressured to integrate into. If majorities weren't pressuring immigrants to integrate into common public institutions in the dominant language—if, for example, immigrants didn't have to learn the dominant language to become citizens, or to have their professional qualifications recognized—then they would have a weaker claim to accommodation within majority institutions.

To be sure, both immigrants and national minorities would have certain claims to respect and accommodation even in such a non-national state. But it is likely, I believe, that in a world where majorities renounced their nation-building

projects, minorities would also have to give up many of their claims to multiculturalism and minority rights. In my view, these are two sides of the same coin:
the legitimacy of minority rights depends, at least in part, on the legitimacy of
nation-building. I would defend a robust set of minority rights, not because
nation-building is illegitimate, but precisely because it is legitimate. I believe it
is legitimate for states to engage in robust forms of nation-building—nation-
building is necessary to achieve liberal values of freedom and equality in complex
modern societies—and just for that reason, we must also defend a robust set of
minority rights, in order to remedy any inequalities which might arise as a result
of (legitimate) nation-building policies.

Raz's claim that liberal multiculturalism involves 'learning to think of our
societies as consisting not of a majority and minorities, but as constituted by a
plurality of cultural groups'[39] sounds attractive at first glance, but I think it is
actually a more accurate description of pre-liberal and pre-modern societies than
of liberal democracies. In the past, multi-ethnic empires were often content to
simply let a plurality of groups alone, so long as they paid their taxes or tributes,
obeyed the laws, and co-existed peacefully with other ethnic groups. No one
group tried to use state power to consolidate or diffuse its language and culture
as the societal culture for all citizens. Today, however, few states around the
world are content with this sort of co-existence. They want groups to exhibit a
stronger sense of identification or loyalty with the state, so that they will actively
participate and cooperate in the projects of the state, be they militaristic wars,
economic modernization, or social justice. And to gain the active support of
citizens, states around the world have adopted nation-building programmes
which aim to turn co-subjects, bound only loosely to each other by certain common laws and taxes, into co-nationals, who share a strong bond by virtue of a
common national identity and a common commitment to national projects.

I suspect that this historical shift from multi-ethnic empires to nation-building
states was necessary for liberalization and democratization. The consolidation of
liberal democracy required shifting from the earlier model of society as a loose
plurality of cultural groups to a modern model of a nation-building state in
which the majority attempts to diffuse its national language and culture throughout the state. And in my view, current demands for self-government by national
minorities and for multiculturalism by immigrant groups do not represent a
rejection of that basic shift, but rather an attempt to remedy the injustices which
accompanied it. Far from rejecting or repudiating the legitimacy of nation-building,
they are intended precisely to create the qualifications and conditions under
which it is legitimate. As I said earlier, these conditions can be summarized as:

(a) there are no groups of long-term residents which are permanently excluded
    from membership in the nation, such as metics or racial caste groups;

---

[39] Raz, 'Multiculturalism' (n. 9 above), 197.

(b) the sort of socio-cultural integration which is required for membership in the nation should be understood in a 'thin' sense, primarily involving institutional and linguistic integration, not the adoption of any particular set of customs, religious beliefs, or lifestyles;

(c) national minorities are allowed to engage in their own nation-building, to enable them to maintain themselves as distinct societal cultures.

So far as I can tell, none of these claims repudiate the necessity or legitimacy of majority nation-building. Rather, they presuppose the historical shift away from the model of society as a loose plurality of groups towards a model of a nation-building state, and seek only to ensure that this shift is not unfair to minorities.

Perhaps Raz thinks that nation-building was not needed to secure democratization, mass participation and equality of opportunity. Or perhaps he thinks that while it was needed in the past, it is no longer necessary, and that we can give up nation-building without reverting to this older pre-democratic model of the (mere) coexistence of a plurality of groups. Or perhaps he only rejects the term, rather than the substance, of nation-building. Clarifying these issues will help determine the extent to which Raz's theory differs from other emerging theories of liberal multiculturalism.

COMMENTS AND RESPONSES

Comments and Responses

JOSEPH RAZ

It is gratifying to be the occasion for such a rich collection. In philosophy more than in any other area, many regard themselves as teachers in a special way, not primarily transmitters of knowledge, but provokers of inquiry, stimulators of questions and of questioning. Perhaps not quite in the manner of Socrates, but recognizably descendent from it. There can, therefore, be few rewards greater than to be a partial stimulant of a collection of inquiring and challenging articles about such a variety of topics. The editors asked me to add comments. I think that the reader will be served best if I do not scatter what would inevitably be half-argued-for comments on everything, but confine myself to reflections on direct criticism of my work, and related points. For this reason, for example, I will not comment on the rich and suggestive paper by **Robert Alexy**, who surveys the terrain of legal philosophy as a whole. For a different reason, I will not comment on **Timothy Endicott**'s paper which takes us deep into some of the mysteries beguiling legal philosophy. His paper is generally sympathetic to my views. It has the advantage of thinking and arguing seriously on points which so many treat in a rather off-hand manner. He reflected on these matters more than anyone I know, more than I have done. I hope to learn from his analysis myself, but will reserve its discussion to an occasion which would allow for a longer consideration of his arguments than is possible here.

I should, however, take advantage of the opportunity to plead guilty to one methodological accusation he levels against me: I agree that I should not have succumbed to the temptation of suggesting that there is 'a nature' to legal positivism (100–1). I should have known better and stuck to the view I expressed (in *The Authority of Law*[1]) that we should think of legal positivism as a historical tradition containing writings some of which bear greater similarity in their central tenets to writings outside it (e.g. to Finnis, and to Aquinas as he understands him) than to each other, a tradition which cannot be characterized by adherence to any central tenet or tenets. This would have made it clear that there is little value, other than historical, in using the classification of writings into positivist and non-positivist when considering various accounts of the nature of law (if it has a nature).

[1] *The Authority of Law* (Oxford: Clarendon Press, 1979).

I.

Rüdiger Bittner criticised two claims I made in *Practical Reason and Norms*.[2]
Simplifying somewhat, they are:

(1) To say that one ought to do A is to say that one has a reason to do A.
(2) (a) To say that of two reasons one is stronger than the other is to say that
      it overrides the other whenever they conflict.
    (b) If P is a reason for doing A, and Q a reason for refraining from doing
      A then P overrides Q, if and only if P&Q is a reason for doing A, and
      not a reason for refraining from A.

Bittner objects to (1) on the ground that, if the reason is overridden it is not the
case that where there is a reason for an action one ought to perform it. At the
time I wrote the book I suggested that pragmatic implicatures explain away
such objections. They explain why we would not, when speaking sincerely and
helpfully, say that one ought to perform an action where we believe the reason
for it to have been overridden, even though it is strictly speaking true that we
ought. I agree that that was a mistake. I tried to correct it in 1978 in the
Introduction to *Practical Reasoning*[3] in which I suggested that statements of the
general form 'In circumstances C, agents X ought to do A' state that there is a
reason for agents X to do A in C, which is not defeated on all the occasions
when agents X have an opportunity to do A in circumstances C.

This takes account of the fact that 'ought' statements range from very general
statements to statements specific to a particular agent and a particular occasion.
Specific 'ought' statements are, or are close to, statements of what we have unde-
feated reason to do. Saying to my child 'you ought to eat this soup now' is not only
saying to him that there is a reason to eat the soup. It is inconsistent with there
being any factor which defeats the reason for his eating the soup now. On the
other hand, saying 'one ought not to lie (or to deceive people)' is not inconsistent
with there being reasons which defeat the reason against lying and make lying (or
deceiving) the right action on some occasions. But it is inconsistent with there
being a better reason to lie than not to lie whenever one has a choice between the
two. Inevitably the more general 'ought' statements allow for more exceptions,
whereas the more specific 'ought' statements leave less room for exceptions,
meaning cases where they are defeated. The account finds a middle way between
regarding 'ought' statements as statements of what we have reason to do all told,
and treating them as being statements of what we have reason to do.

It is possible that this account requires further refinement. But I think that it is
right in one aspect which it shares with the view I took in *Practical Reason and
Norms*, which Bittner rightly criticizes, namely it takes 'ought' statements to be
statements about reasons, rather than being statements of reasons. When told
what I ought to do I am told what I have reasons to do, but I am no wiser about

---

[2] *Practical Reason and Norms*, 3rd edition (Oxford: Oxford University Press, 1999).
[3] *Practical Reasoning* (Oxford: Oxford University Press, 1978).

why I am to so act, I am not told what these reasons are. This is an important point to understanding the divide between the normative and the evaluative, at least as that distinction applies to a division between types of statements. Principles tell us what we have reason to do, but they are not themselves reasons.

Bittner also takes me to task about (2), more specifically about (2)(b). Here I think that he is only partly right. Today, as much as at the time of writing, I am struck by the flexibility of our 'reasons' discourse. Possibly this should discourage us from regarding the concept as a theoretically pivotal one, be that as it may. Given the pivotal role which I, and others, assign it, it is important to keep the flexibility of its use in mind, even while theoretical purposes require a certain streamlining in the philosophical explanation of the concept, and its derivatives. One complication relevant here is that while philosophers have offered various ideas about what are reasons, we refer to many other 'things' as reasons. More specifically, there is no suggestion that what is referred to as a reason contains neither more nor less than one complete reason. Recent press criticism may be cited by the management as a reason for dismissing a worker. The very same criticism may also have been a reason for not dismissing that very worker. On the one hand, the criticism makes it desirable to fire the worker, to show that one is responsive to public opinion. On the other hand, dismissing a worker because of criticism may be seen as a sign of weak management. Hence, it is a reason for not dismissing a worker who has recently been subjected to press criticism. So the facts referred to as reasons for an action are part of a complete reason for that action, but also part of a complete reason against it. But if the management deems that on balance the better reason is the one to dismiss the worker, it will cite the event which is reason both for and against the action as reason for it, thus indicating that, as they see it, the reason for the action defeats or overrides the reason against it.

This is just one example of how we often refer to a complex of reasons for and against an action as a reason for it. Hence my claim (2) above, which Bittner criticizes. He is right, of course, in saying that utterances of the form specified in (2) are not always felicitous. I suggested that pragmatic implicatures can explain when such utterances are and when they are not appropriate. Possibly this will not be enough to deal with all cases and additional semantic distinctions are needed. Whatever we think of that, Bittner is certainly right that there is more to be said about what makes one reason override or defeat another. It was not the purpose of my claim (2) to provide an answer to that question.

Bruno Celano's article provides the occasion for another reminder about the flexibility and complex nuances of normative language. He quite rightly points to the importance of explaining the connection between judgements about what reasons exist and judgements about which actions would be reasonable, sensible, or rational and what would be reasonable, sensible or rational for a person to do. I find two difficulties with his argument. First, he assumes that there are two types of judgements (about reasons and about rationality) where I think there are several more, and when setting out the problem he will discuss he assumes that these judgements have to be understood as either made true (or false) by how things are in the world or by the agents' beliefs, whereas as he later acknowledges, there are several other alternatives, and as it turns out, they hold the key to the explanation of the rationality of agents' action.

Taking the first point first, Celano regards the two questions: 'Did she act rationally? Did she do the right thing?' as one. But they are not. In fact, without context we cannot be sure what question is asked by the utterance of either sentence. But, for purposes of illustration, we can imagine very common circumstances in which the second question is more or less identical with 'was there adequate reason for the action she took?' Whereas the first is not a question about her action at all, but about her, her 'performance' in forming the intention to do what she did: was she weak-willed? Was she rash or negligent in forming the view that there is adequate reason for the action? Etc.

The second point I mentioned above, that is that there is a third basis for these judgements other than what reasons there are and what people believe about their reasons, has already been illustrated in my previous remark: people's judgements about the agent's rationality typically depend not only on what they believe, and how it fits how things are, but also on how they formed their beliefs, and how they hold them: are they rash or negligent? Should they have known better? Should they have tried harder to find out how things are? Without attending to these questions and distinctions we cannot hope to explain when people act rationally, and therefore nor can we explain the relations between judgements of what reasons there are and judgements about rationality.

When Celano introduces considerations relating to the ways agents form or hold judgements he does so in the name of unnamed writers who introduce them to show that agents may have excuses for acting irrationally etc. I do not know which writers he has in mind, and I doubt that there is anyone who holds the view he dubs 'pure objectivism' which the excuse-account is meant to defend. However, the important point is that these factors affect the rationality of the agent in holding the judgement, and in relying on it in action. They determine the answers to these questions, but not the answers to the question whether there was a reason for the action, or for the judgement which led to it. The result is somewhat unfortunate, for while Celano is right to reject the position he constructed under the title 'pure objectivism', his reasons for doing so, in ignoring important distinctions, fail to establish his contention that the views 'that (i) reasons are facts, and (ii) being facts, they are belief-independent, are inherently unstable.'

Celano, quoting me, says: ' "we use explanatory reasons in judging the agent's rationality in doing what he did—rationality is measured in the light of the agent's own beliefs and goals" (39). But this seems too harsh. There has to be some connection between rationality in action and what (normative) reasons the agent has.' Maybe, but it will take an argument to show what the connection is and why there is one. My own view is that in most contexts, so-called 'explanatory reasons' are facts explaining the agents' actions and intentions via their beliefs about what reasons they have. These beliefs can be false, and there may be no connection between rationality in action and what reasons the agent has, in the sense that one may act rationally even when acting for no reason at all. There is no necessary connection between reasons I can rationally believe that I have and reasons which I do have. That does not mean that I can rationally believe anything; it means, for example, that circumstances can conspire against me and make it rational for me to have erroneous beliefs about my situation, and therefore about the reasons I have. Celano would not deny that. He thinks that beliefs affect reasons in some other way than getting them right. But his case remains to be made.

Celano expresses doubts about my view, which is to my mind quite independent of the matters he discusses in the rest of his article, which he calls the conformity thesis:

the conformity thesis (reasons for action are, fundamentally, not reasons to comply, but only reasons to conform) may be held to have counter-intuitive implications. Since "in order to be guided by what is the case a person must come to believe that it is the case", we would have to grant that reasons for action are not—not primarily, nor fundamentally—guides to action; that their point is not—not primarily, nor fundamentally—to guide behaviour. That is, we would have to give up the view that "reasons are there to guide action"— that "their very nature is that they should guide". (41)

This is the first, and the most plausible, of three grounds of doubt which he expresses, but I think that it is based on a misunderstanding. Reasons are essentially guides; this is what makes them reasons: we can be guided by them. That does not mean that we are at fault when we conform to them without being guided by them. Think of reasons for refraining from certain actions. For example, reasons not to murder, or not to use the Internet to steal money. Other things being equal, I am glad that when I went out to do my shopping a short while ago I did not murder anyone not because of the reason not to murder but because the thought of murdering anyone never crossed my mind. I would start worrying about my morality or sanity were this not so. Similarly lots of people do not use the Internet to defraud anyone because, given that they do not know how to do so, the thought never crossed their mind. Should we say that they must learn how to defraud using the Internet and then refrain from doing so because they should not, or else they fail to do what reason requires them to do?

II.

James Penner's essay takes us beyond these abstract reflections about practical reasons towards their application in the law, given the fact that the law claims to be authoritative. His main contention is that the courts have authority based on their moral expertise. En route he touches on many points relevant to various aspects of my work, which he discusses all too generously. This provides me with an opportunity to clarify one or two points where our views may, perhaps, seem to diverge more than they do, or where the appearance of difference may be created by the wrong reasons. Penner is quite right in emphasizing that so-called 'thick' ethical concepts can be universal if that means that the conditions for their application can be specified without the use of any singular expressions. Just about all the moral concepts we know are universal in this sense. But Penner's concern is not with universality, thus understood, but with the universal accessibility of ethical concepts. His contention is that 'thick' concepts can be universally accessible, which I assume he understands as I do (in the passages from *Engaging Reason* which he considers), namely, as meaning that it is possible for everyone capable of knowledge, whatever the circumstances of his/her life, to possess the concepts.

This contention seems to me doubtful, and Penner's examples do nothing to allay my doubts. 'What human culture, for example, would not have acquaintance with and formed a concept of courage, or could not think about brutality or promises or greed?' (88) Many, seems to me the only answer. Many cultures have no use for these concepts. That need not, however, matter, since, on my view, once the concept emerges it becomes accessible to everyone who can in principle have knowledge of the culture in which it emerged. The problem is that only concepts, access to which is coextensive with the capacities to have knowledge and to act intentionally, are non-parochial, for only they were available to all knowers. The concepts mentioned by Penner by way of illustration do not meet this condition.

Penner seems keen to establish that thick concepts are not parochial in order to show that the intelligibility of values does not depend on their subsumption under more abstract values: those referred to as thin concepts. It is important here to avoid the equivocation between the two senses of 'universal', that is 'universal' as defined above, and as non-parochial. If we are, as both Penner and I think we should, to allow that values have a temporal history we need to explain how that can be. Part of the explanation, I believe, is in showing how the more local and parochial values, while distinct, generate new ways of instantiating more general values. For example, literary forms have distinct modes of excellence, which are distinct values. These values come into existence with the genre. Novels, for example, are a relatively recent literary form. Until the genre emerged, neither novels nor the modes of excellence that only novels can display existed. But our understanding of the emergence of these new forms of excellence depends on our appreciation of more general values, the value of humour, of insight into human psychology, of story-telling, etc. and it is through understanding them that we understand the forms of excellence specific to novels as a particular way of instantiating them. That form of the dependence of our understanding of less general values on understanding more general values is an essential part of our ability to understand how values can come into being. That is why I think that not all values can be very specific, and that particularly those which are the product of history must be subsumable under more general ones. So far as I can see there is no conflict between these points and any of the wider goals that Penner wishes to reach.

Waldron offers thoughtful and challenging ideas about the authority of legal political authorities. I will not examine them in detail. My own account of authority (its core in *The Morality of Freedom*,[4] with some additions elsewhere) is meant as a general explanation of the central sense of 'having authority' in practical matters—authority over what to do, which can readily be adjusted to apply to theoretical authority as well. To the extent that Waldron doubts the adequacy of my account he focuses mainly on two of my more far-reaching claims: (1) that all practical authorities, parental, political, legal, within voluntary associations, in international law, etc., are of a type, that one abstract account can explain them all, with the differences being revealed at a less abstract level of analysis. (2) that my account applies not only to the relations between government and citizens, but also to the relations between different organs of government. I will try to reply to the criticism, and also to suggest one needed modification of my previous position. But first a few observations on points where Waldron's generally meticulously accurate and fair, not to say generous, presentation of my views may nevertheless leave one somewhat puzzled.

First, as Waldron mentions, while I take coordination to be one of the central functions of government, I do not believe that people who are in situations where they should coordinate their actions are necessarily aware of this fact. Nor do I understand 'coordination' in the rather impoverished sense given the term by Lewis (in his book *Convention*—these points are explained in 'Facing Up'[5]). I therefore think that sometimes it is part of the function of political authorities to determine whether a situation justifying or requiring coordination exists. But, of course, I do not think that political authorities always have that power. That would amount to giving political authorities power over all matters, provided they believe them to require coordination—dangerously close to granting them unlimited authority. They have the power to determine that a given situation justifies or requires coordination when the general doctrine of authority determines that they do. For example, when the normal justification thesis vindicates their possession of the power, namely, when people or institutions would better conform to reason if that power were exercised by an authority than otherwise.

Second, one of the most tantalizing difficulties in explaining practical authorities has to do with explaining how their existence can change the reasons facing people subject to them; that is, how they can do so not through the mere fact of their actual power which people have to take into account, nor simply by the fact that people have reason to support valuable institutions. Part of the answer requires explaining how and why the issuing of directives issued by legitimate authority (laws, commands, regulations, etc.) is binding on those subject to their authority. But obvious though it appears that legitimate directives are binding and one has reasons to conform to them one did not have

---

[4] *The Morality of Freedom* (Oxford: Oxford University Press, 1986).
[5] 'Facing Up', *Southern California Law Review* 62 (1989), 1153–1235.

before, that in itself is a puzzle, for the question arises: how can someone other than yourself make it so that you have a new reason just by saying so, a reason you would not otherwise have? This puzzle has led some to suppose that practical authorities are really theoretical authorities, just telling people what they have reason to do anyway. That view encounters decisive objections, whose consideration does not belong here. So we need an explanation of how authorities can make a difference to the reasons people have. Part of the explanation is in the fact that, according to the normal justification thesis, the justification of authority relates to its *general* success in enabling its subjects to track reason over certain classes of cases better than they would be able to do without it. Such general success usually falls short of success in every case. This in itself leads to the fact that those subject to authority have reasons to act in ways they would not otherwise have. But Waldron is right in implying that that cannot be the whole story. The existence of an authority, i.e. its de facto power, enables it to achieve desirable goals which would be unachievable without it, and often that is enough to endow it with authority to do so. Does not that violate my 'dependence thesis' which claims that the legitimacy of authorities depends on their acting for reasons which apply anyway? If their existence creates new opportunities how can reasons to pursue them exist anyway? Once you pose the question in this way the answer appears obvious. Reasons, often of an abstract character, exist even when the opportunities to pursue them are limited. The coming into being of new opportunities, including those created by the de facto power of political authorities, gives rise to new reasons which are ways of following the more abstract reasons which existed before. An example not relating to authority illustrates the point: many have reason to save for their old age. The creation of pension schemes gives them a new way of following that reason by giving them reasons to join a pension scheme. Similarly, the existence of political authorities creates opportunities to achieve forms of coordination which will secure goals we always had reasons to pursue, but no opportunity to do so. Thus authorities can make a difference to the reasons we have while doing no more than acting for reasons we had anyway.

Third, another question arises out of the previous one: are we bound by reasons which concretize reasons applying to each of us, or are we bound by reasons which apply to the community as a whole? Writing about authority I tended to emphasize that authorities have legitimate authority over a person only to the extent that they concretize reasons which apply to *that* person anyway. But it seemed to me, and still does, that the conflict just mentioned is illusory, for people have duties towards others, including towards communities, and that political authorities are speaking for communities largely to the extent to which they act in areas where the reasons of people coincide, not necessarily because their self-interest, narrowly conceived, coincides but because they have duties towards each other, including duties for collective, joint and common actions, of the kind recently analysed by a number of writers, such as Margaret Gilbert and Michael Bratman.

Finally, Waldron's discussion is focused on the normal justification thesis. It is therefore worth mentioning that its name 'normal justification' is meant to remind us that its central idea (how can one best track reason, independently or by following another) was never presented as the sole argument bearing on the legitimacy of authority. There are several other subsidiary arguments I discuss, and there can be others. Here it is worth mentioning that the desirability or undesirability of deciding for oneself, independently of authority, is a major enhancer and qualifier of the scope of authority. The normal justification thesis has regard only to degrees of conformity with reason. It disregards the advantages and the disadvantages of the ways, the process, by which that conformity is secured, in particular it disregards the desirability of making up one's mind unaided, or at any rate unbound by authority, as well as the disadvantages of doing so. The burden of deciding for oneself may sometimes justify the legitimacy of an authority over people and matters where the normal justification condition by itself would not be enough to do so. It may be, in some cases, that one would be marginally better deciding for oneself, but the disadvantages will be great. Some people find some decisions agonizing and difficult. All of us find some decisions time-consuming, demanding many resources, and incurring high opportunity costs. On the other hand, in certain matters it is important, or important to some agents, to decide for themselves rather than decide well. Because they would not decide well, the normal justification thesis may suggest that someone is in authority over them, but nevertheless, because of the importance of deciding for oneself, that person has no authority.[6]

Many of Waldron's illuminating observations seem to me to be sound, but sound because, and to the extent that, they successfully apply my account of practical authority to some fairly general types of situations, for example, those involving what he calls the condition of institutional settlement, or to relations among legal institutions. Waldron seems to think that my account is not suitable to explain when one institution is under the legitimate authority of another. But his reasons are not clear to me. The authority of the institutions of the European Community, for example, is governed by, among others, a principle of subsidiarity that says:

In areas which do not fall within its exclusive competence, the Community shall take action, in accordance with the principle of subsidiarity, only if and in so far as the objectives of the proposed action cannot be sufficiently achieved by the Member States and can therefore, by reason of the scale or effects of the proposed action, be better achieved by the Community.

The principle, applying between national and Community institutions, is an adaptation of the central aspect of the normal justification thesis; that is, that

---

[6] In a rare lapse, Waldron seems to forget these points when he writes: 'For example: I have made a number of disastrous romantic choices, and on many of these choices I would have done better following the instructions of my closest friends than trying to figure things out for myself. Do we want to say therefore that my friends had authority over me in this regard?' as if this is an objection to my view, rather than an illustration of the limits it imposes on the normal justification thesis.

an institution is subject to the authority of another only if tasks which the lower authority has, would be better discharged if it were subjected to higher authority than if it were acting independently of such authority. This is an example of how my general account of authority fits the way we do, and should, think of the legitimate relations between lower and higher authorities. The example does not exhaust all aspects of my account, but it illustrates its relevance to the relations between institutions, and provides some grounds for confidence in its adequacy for the task.

But is not my account open to the challenge that according to it, the U.S. Congress is subject to the authority of the American Conference of Catholic Bishops, assuming as he does that their decisions on welfare issues are regularly better and fairer? Not so, and for several reasons. One is, of course, the fact that an authority may be better only if it succeeds in achieving coordination around the better policy, and it is far from clear that the U.S. Congress, were it to acknowledge the authority of the Conference of Catholic Bishops, would be able to secure compliance with its laws. It could, of course, follow the advice of the Conference—that is a different matter altogether—but even that, were it to do so too slavishly, might undermine its ability to secure compliance with its legislation. This may be regrettable, but the normal justification thesis is about achieving results, and that is unlikely to happen. There is, however, a more significant reason why the U.S. Congress is not under the authority of the Conference of Catholic Bishops: its constitution precludes it, or so I assume, from acknowledging any such authority. Again, this may or may not be regrettable. The important point is that when we deal with institutions, what they can or cannot do is determined, to a large degree, by their constitution, formal or informal.

This is a point of general relevance for the discussion of the relations among institutions. Not all of them are relations of authority to its subject. But many of them are determined by the constitution of the relevant institutions. If I would track reasons better if I followed someone's directives, then that someone has authority over me, if I can follow his or her directives. The same is true of an institution, but whether one institution can follow the directives of another depends, *inter alia*, on its constitution, a point of difference between individuals and institutions which far from undermining my account of authority, helps to establish its application to institutions.[7] It therefore seems to me that my account of authority applies successfully to test the legitimacy of the authority of an integrated structure of institutions (as well as of individual components of it, but that depends on the possibility of making judgements which sever one element of the structure from the rest). It is also possible to apply my account to the authority relations among institutions within the structure, remembering that the relations between individuals and the government, and among governmental institutions are not exclusively relations of authority.

---

[7] To avoid misunderstanding let me clarify that the constitution of an institution is its de facto constitution whether or not it is justified, or morally defensible. Its de facto constitution determines what it is in fact, whatever the merits of its existence in that form or any other.

Assuming that these observations remove the objection to the application of my account of authority to the relations among institutions, is it not true that my account cannot be accepted as an account of political authority, for it does not include a requirement that such authority must have a public nature? The answer may require no more than some conceptual sensitivity. My account is a general explanation of all practical authorities, not only of political or legal authorities, and therefore it cannot contain a requirement that authorities be public bodies, unless that requirement applies to all practical authorities, which it does not, nor does Waldron claim that it does. If legal and political authorities are necessarily public bodies, this should emerge when the general explanation of authority is applied to political and legal ones. With regard to legal authorities it clearly does emerge, for being a public body is in the nature of a legal authority. Again, such authorities are creatures of their constitutions, and their de facto existence is independent of their moral legitimacy. They are public even if not morally legitimate simply because they are legal.

Matters are not that simple regarding other political authorities, if there are such, for the scope of the political is controversial and far from clear. As Waldron observes, I ventured the thought that given that political authorities are unlikely to be legitimate unless they secure desirable coordination, they are unlikely to be legitimate unless they enjoy de facto authority, and that gives them a public character. Call this the argument for the public character of political authorities, derived from the need to coordinate.

It is still open for someone to claim that it should be definitional that political authorities are public institutions, which it is not in my account. Perhaps, but that is not the sort of concession that Waldron is, or should be interested in. Suppose one allows that it is analytic that if an authority is a political authority then it is a public institution. It would follow that, for all that the definition establishes, there can be authorities which are not so-called political authorities, but are indistinguishable from political authorities in all normative aspects, except that they do not meet some normatively irrelevant condition for the application of the predicate 'political'. They may deal with the same issues, use the same means to secure the same goals, etc., enjoy legitimacy for the same reasons and yet fail to be political authorities because they fail the definitional test. Perhaps this is so, but if so it is a fact without normative interest. The argument for the public character of political authorities from the need to coordinate does not warrant that all political authorities are public. But it establishes why we can expect them to be, and what normative difference that fact makes—being based on the need to secure desirable coordination as a condition for legitimacy. Perhaps it is worth mentioning an additional feature of legal authorities: they claim[8] authority to punish people, and to use coercion (partly to enforce punishment, but often for other purposes). A person or institution may enable me, should they be willing to guide me, to track reason better than I can without following their directives, but

---

[8] Though it is disputable whether it is essential to the law that they do, or merely a feature of societies known to us.

to constitute anything like a legal-political authority they need, first, to issue directives over the matters regarding which they have that advantage, and, second, to have the authority to enforce their directives and punish disobedience (and the will to do so). Otherwise, their authority will not be what we recognize as public authority. But to have that additional authority, the authority to punish and to use coercion, they need to meet the normal justification thesis regarding an additional range of issues, and over other people, those who will be required to enforce their directives, adjudicate disputes, and apply sanctions.

These considerations supplement the previous ones in suggesting that the normal justification thesis may after all succeed in capturing the normative relevance of our normal understanding of 'political authority'. All this having been said, there may still be force in at least one of Waldron's criticisms. Suppose someone actually issues directives regarding a certain area of my life (they need not apply exclusively to me) and that I would track reason better if I follow his directives. Does such a person have authority over me? I do not suggest that he has authority to punish or coerce me. That is unlikely. But does he have authority at all? I may, for example, not know of his existence. It seems plausible to add a condition for the legitimacy of an authority. Something like a requirement that people over whom it has authority should have reason to find out, and should be able to find out whether it has such authority (at a cost not disproportionate to the benefit in tracking the reason its supposed authority can bring). Perhaps it should also be a condition of the authoritative standing of any directive that those subject to it have reason to find out whether it exists and can find out its content.

III.

Hillel Steiner and **Andrei Marmor** contributed two illuminating articles on equality. I learnt much from both, and my comments here will be relatively marginal. This is particularly true regarding Steiner who admirably sets the stage for the possibility of egalitarian principles of entitlement to certain outcomes (I imagine that some additional considerations will have bearing on the value of, or requirements for equality of treatment—an aspect of egalitarian concerns whose special features I rather neglected). He and I differ regarding negative freedom, which I do not believe to be something of constant quantity, nor to be inherently valuable. Its value depends, I believe, on the value of the actions it enables (if any, for one may have negative liberty to do what one lacks capacity, and/or opportunity to do), and the value of the ability to choose whether to perform them, and of its exercise. But these are matters on which Steiner has written much, but not on this occasion. So let me confine myself to a reflection on one of Steiner's arguments which particularly intrigued me. He argues that there could be satiable and non-diminishing goods (I did not deny that, but could not think of important examples), of which, he claims, negative liberty is one. Regarding such goods, he offers several arguments for their equal distribution, one of which I find particularly intriguing. Here is Steiner's statement of the point:

For a non-diminishing entitlement principle to be valued for its own sake—for it to be an independent citizen in a pluralistic republic of entitlement principles— it *must* be regulated by a strictly egalitarian rule. And this necessity appears to dictate the nature of our valuation of that rule itself. Since that entitlement principle's being valued for its own sake entails its being regulated by that egalitarian rule, that rule must itself be valued for its own sake: the equal distribution of the entitled good is itself intrinsically valuable. Were it not so, were it valued solely for its contribution to the satisfaction of some other entitlement principles, this would imply that the very entitlement principle it regulates is itself one which is instrumentally subservient to those other principles and not one which is valued for its own sake. If changing circumstances can bring it about that the value of an unequal distribution of apples exceeds that of an equal one, we are bound to infer that persons having apples is not valued for its own sake.

It is a fascinating and instructive point. However, if Steiner is right and an egalitarian distribution is the result of the entitlement to this kind of good being valued for its own sake, then the resulting equality in distribution is what I call by-product equality. It is a case where equality in some respect is a result of valuing something other than equality. My arguments were not designed to deny that equality is often a by-product of pursuing other values. It cannot possibly be otherwise. The only question is whether equality is valuable for its own sake.

Marmor argues for equality from the importance of relativities as tests of the sufficiency of the provision of any good, when we judge how well-off people are in various respects. He convincingly argues that disparities in the level of provision of any good are among the factors determining status or class, and that independently of considerations of envy. But, one may ask, what is wrong with status, apart from envy and equality? How do we get from relativities to equality? The argument establishes nicely that accepting an advantage which is part of a package, benefiting others to a degree which changes the level of sufficiency can make one less well-off. But no conclusions about equality follow. Marmor himself mentions that what matters are not only levels of resources but also the relative numbers of people at each level. The relativity of levels of sufficiency speaks of interdependence between the level at which sufficiency is reached and the different levels of provision at which other people find themselves, as well as the number of people at each level. But that does not establish a case for equality, nor does it establish that disparities of material resources cannot be compensated for by other factors, other rewards.

IV.

Issues of pluralism, and the related difficulties of the reaction to the growing ethnic, and cultural and religious diversity of many countries are complex and difficult. **Bernhard Peters's** paper illustrates the way the actual situations confronting us can present quite distinct features, generating different problems and making very different responses appropriate. I of course agree with him that the relations between pluralism and conflict are complex. Conflict does not presuppose pluralism, nor need pluralism lead to conflict. His analysis of conditions and situations in which conflict arises in situations of de facto pluralism is instructive, and shows that traditional multicultural issues, of the kind that I, or Kymlicka discuss, should not be allowed to obscure other phenomena.

Kymlicka, in a very helpful contribution, both surveys and contributes to the debates about multiculturalism. He pays special attention to the vexed problem of the stance of liberal countries, i.e. those where the general culture is consistent with liberal ethical principles, towards illiberal groups, minority groups, among them. In this context he attributes to me the view that 'illiberal groups have no claim to support: only groups that respect and enable the autonomy of their members deserve support'. (234) I am sorry if anything I ever published conveys that impression. It is certainly inconsistent with my general view of ethical and political principles, which regards liberalism and its emphasis on the importance of autonomy as a transient historical phase, whose ethical outlook is legitimate and valuable for societies with certain forms of economic, social and cultural organization, but not for others.

In saying this I did not, and do not, support ethical relativism. There are ethical values, and principles, which apply to all, and to all human societies at all times. These include duties of respect to people, which include duties not to deny them conditions needed to enable them to lead worthwhile, fulfilling lives. As we know, these few words raise many complex questions regarding their full meaning and consequences. For present purposes, suffice it to say that in contemporary conditions they imply a duty on states to see to it that their inhabitants have the conditions for leading worthwhile and fulfilling lives, and if necessary to bring them about through direct or indirect state action. Given this background, I can object to supporting illiberal groups in liberal states only if such groups, or such support, will be inimical to states discharging that duty. (I disregard here other considerations on the assumption that they are either of lesser importance, or that they apply only occasionally). That is sometimes the case. Most commonly this is so when the illiberal groups have seriously oppressive attitudes towards some of their own members, oppression whose ill consequences cannot be avoided through exit from the group, and where there are alternative, less supportive policies which can ameliorate the conditions of the oppressed.

Most of the time, however, the illiberal cultures present in countries which aspire to be liberal, present a mixture of oppressive and non-oppressive features. So do the majority cultures of these states. Most of the time the prospect of those cultures changing in a less oppressive direction, especially when it is coupled with opportunities for exit for those of their members who suffer most from their oppressive practices, is more promising than any heavy-handed state attempt to reform them, let alone suppress them. Most of the time there are possible ameliorative policies which will encourage such desirable changes, without too many adverse side effects.

To conclude, nothing in my writing should be taken to support the view that only liberal communities deserve state support. We should be hostile to oppressive practices both in majority and in minority groups. But most of the time that would not justify withdrawing all forms of support from the oppressive groups, though it will justify a variety of measures to bring such practices to an end, and to avoid their oppressive consequences for individuals.

Kymlicka wonders to what extent he and I differ on substantive policies or whether the appearance of difference is more terminological. In one respect I think that it is partly terminological, and partly a result of focusing on different parts of the globe, and using their terminology. To Kymlicka, as to many Americans and Canadians and perhaps to Australians, and a few others as well, nation-building means creating a new American or Canadian nation out of the immigrants of varying ethnic backgrounds who inhabit their countries, and the indigenous peoples living within their boundaries. In many other countries ethnicity predates modern states, and states were created to accommodate it: Italy was created for Italians, Germany for Germans, and Serbia for Serbs, etc. In these cases there is no nation-building to be undertaken. Rather, there is nationalism, and chauvinistic exclusion of minorities to be overcome.

At other times the terminological differences between us signal moral differences. I use 'a right' much less than Kymlicka does, probably because I believe that there are many fewer rights than he does. I think that there should be opportunities of exit, but doubt that there is in general a right of exit. I believe that people, even those belonging to ethnic or religious minorities, should have opportunities to lead fulfilling lives. But I am not sure that this vindicates the existence of minority rights (though in some cases it does). Similarly I believe that we should not be indifferent to difficulties and limits of people's abilities to have fulfilling lives even when the existence of the difficulties is not a manifestation of unfairness. We should, I believe, be concerned with people's opportunities to have rewarding lives as such, and not merely with whether they are treated fairly or not.

There are other differences of outlook: Kymlicka starts from an analysis of social situations in societies he is familiar with, and aims at concluding with concrete policy recommendations. I start from what I take to be basic moral principles and aim to illustrate some possible applications, primarily in order to bring out that these principles should not be blamed for the short-sighted and unhelpful ways in which they are sometimes applied. I do not know what are the principles which, for example, lead Kymlicka to reject the desirability of ethnic neutrality, other than that it is not practically likely to be adopted. I think that I know why I reject it: because different ethnic cultures need not be ethically equally good or bad, and we should not, at the fundamental level, make ourselves blind to moral differences (= neutral between them). Therefore, like Kymlicka, I am not sure that our writings betray many important differences between us regarding concrete policies.

V.

My remarks about rights above may make you think that whatever our disagreements I have some sympathy with the views expressed by **Griffin** and **Tamir**. But that is not so. There is much in Tamir's article which I do not understand. What I seem to understand suggests that we hold different views about the nature of both rights and theory. I have similar reservations about Griffin's paper. At one point he says:

> to apply the term 'human right' we have to be able to tell what rights we have simply by virtue of being human, and we have little agreement about the relevant sense of 'human'. There are very many cases in which we have no agreed criteria for whether the term is being correctly or incorrectly used. That is why supposed human rights have proliferated with so little control. (161–2)

But is it really true that there is no agreement on the relevant sense of 'human'? Is 'human' a term with many meanings? What is needed is not helpful linguistic legislation, but arguments to establish what features of human beings are relevant to establishing rights which all humans have, if there are such rights. Griffin's own argument in this article (whether or not it is successful) is an example of the sort of argument we need. Instead of treating it in this way Griffin takes himself to be a kind of terminological hygienist, claiming that right-terms are 'useful' only if they meet certain conditions of specificity of application, precision and determinacy, and making suggestions how to change the meaning of 'human rights' to improve its usefulness.

I believe that such efforts are wasted, and not only because they are unlikely to succeed. By and large our moral terminology is sufficient for all our needs. If 'human rights' is unhelpful Griffin is free to not to use it. Not using it is not a way of refuting the substantive claims made with the use of the term. To do that one must engage with their arguments and rebut them (a task which will most likely require mentioning the offending expression, but need not require using it). But by not using the term he will avoid incurring whatever unhelpful aspects or consequences its use has. What I find mysterious is Griffin's thought that philosophers have the task of linguistic pruning:

> Of course, we can use the word 'rights' so that its domain of application coincides with the whole domain of moral obligation, but I think that we ought not to. It seems to me that an account of general moral rights should be able to pass a redundancy test. The word 'rights' should not just provide another way of talking about what we can already talk about perfectly adequately.

What puzzles me here is that Griffin ignores the simple question: what does 'a right' mean? If its meaning does not makes its domain of application coincide with the whole domain of moral obligation then clearly it is a mistake to use it as if it does, the mistake being not redundancy but incorrect use of the term. If, however, its meaning does make it redundant, in the sense that we can say whatever we say using the term equally easily without it (true of many terms), what sort of a fault is it? Griffin does not claim that there are concepts or thoughts one cannot express except by using 'rights' in a meaning it does not have. Nor would such an argument stand a chance. To the extent that Griffin's substantive arguments in his article convince, this is because they show that given the meaning of the terms, there are no group rights. They do not show that even though, using the terms in their current meaning, there are group rights, we should not talk of them as such.

A similarly suspect methodology is followed by Tamir. In a crucial passage (appearing twice in her article) she writes:

This paper is, then, a word of caution, calling upon liberal political theorists, and liberal political activists to acknowledge the fact that rights can rarely help to rebuild a community but can easily be used to strengthen dominant sub-groups, privilege conservative interpretations of culture over reforms and disadvantage all those who wish to diverge from accepted social norms and question the traditional role of social institutions. Liberals should then be aware of the price embedded in bestowing rights on groups and be more cautious in their support of such rights. (185, and see 189)

These sentences capture much that I do not understand. Does Tamir mean that those in power should not bestow legal rights on groups? But why not? Is it because groups do not have rights? That is the way many people argue for or against the existence of legal rights. That is, many take the non-existence of moral rights to be a case against the creation of legal rights. I think that such arguments are inconclusive. There can be cases where the law should create legal rights which are not merely the embodiment into law of moral rights.[9]

But that does not seem to be Tamir's meaning. The obvious price that supporters of that argument have in mind is that groups will have legal rights to which they are not entitled. Contrariwise, the supporters of that argument would concede that should groups have rights there may be a case for granting those rights legal recognition in spite of the drawbacks such recognition may have for others. After all, we all know that rights impose duties or restraints on others. That is, if you like, their point. We should not suppose that Tamir is recommending here that liberals should ignore group rights because respecting them involves an imposition.

Perhaps Tamir does indeed mean bestowing rights by 'bestowing rights', but that is not because she thinks that liberals have rights in their gift in the way that I have it in my gift to give a right in my property to other people. Rather, perhaps she thinks that my whole 'discourse' in the preceding paragraphs shows a misunderstanding of what 'rights' are. Truth is not in question when we consider group rights. The issue is not to come to understand whether

---

[9] See my 'Rights and Politics', *Indiana Law Review* 71 (1995), 27–44.

groups have rights, and what, if any, rights they have. There is here no question of truth. 'Group rights' is an expression which we use as a rhetorical weapon to achieve goals we pursue. And she warns us that the use of the term 'group rights' will not win us the goals we, fellow liberals, pursue.

This way of understanding her makes sense of the beginning of the quoted passage. What is the point of 'calling upon . . . [liberals] to acknowledge . . . that rights can rarely help to rebuild a community but can easily be used to strengthen dominant sub-groups, privilege conservative interpretations of culture over reforms and disadvantage all those who wish to diverge from accepted social norms and question the traditional role of social institutions'.(185) Does she mean that false claims of rights will strengthen the wrong party, the wrong cause? If they are taken as true they may well do so. That goes without saying. Falsehoods generally, if mistaken for truths, may lead to bad consequences. That should lead one to correct such mistakes. But that can hardly be Tamir's message here. Or, does she mean that even though groups have rights, liberals should not be free and easy in acknowledging the fact because it has consequences at odds with liberal views? If that is so, perhaps liberals should give up their political views since they are at odds with the rights groups do have. That cannot be her meaning either. What she must mean is that the whole question of whether groups do or do not have rights is misguided for there are no truths about such matters. Rights discourse is a tool, a weapon, to be used when its use helps one's own side, and as it happens, the tool of 'group rights' helps the opposition.

It has to be acknowledged that even though I was driven to this understanding of Tamir, having failed to find another which makes coherent sense of some of her statements, it is not an understanding which can be consistently attributed to everything she writes. Some of her statements seem to suppose that the existence or otherwise of rights is an objective matter. Just like Griffin's, many of her arguments do not depend on, and some are inconsistent with the methodological claims which I find puzzling.

There is one strategy of arguments for or against group rights, i.e. one assuming that their existence is an objective matter, with which I have some sympathy and which may appeal to Tamir, and be confused by her with the views I cited, which are inconsistent with the objectivity of rights. Arguably group rights exist only if their existence can be justified as instrumentally valuable. The argument I have in mind goes something as follows: group rights exist if and only if, were people to behave as they would were they to believe that such rights exist (but assuming that the rest of their beliefs are affected only in as much as is necessary to bring them into line with this belief), and did they intend to respect them, their conduct in so acting would have good consequences, meaning consequences which are good for other reasons than that they may constitute respect for these rights.[10]

---

[10] Some would endorse the argument only if augmented by another about the chances and/or the costs of the belief in the right being accepted.

Tamir's dismissive remarks about utilitarianism make clear that she does not think that that is the right way to think of individual rights. That is, she does not appear to believe that we can identify good consequences independently of respect for rights, such that the case for alleged rights can be made by whether or not respect for them will have such good, independently identified consequences. But, even if one does not accept that form of argument regarding individual rights one may accept it for group rights. One may hold that what ultimately matters, morally speaking, are human beings and how they fare in life. Individual rights may provide part of our understanding of what is intrinsically valuable about people and their lives, but collective rights cannot. They can only be justified instrumentally.

This conclusion is far from obvious. If relationships with other people, and groups of people, and their quality, are part of what matters intrinsically about people and their lives then, if enjoying individual rights contributes to what is intrinsically valuable about people's lives, it would seem not unreasonable to suppose that the same is true of group rights. This is an important and fascinating question, but not one to be explored here as Tamir never provides an argument why group rights can only be justified instrumentally, if that is indeed what she thinks.[11]

I have already remarked that my doubts about the attitude to rights, and to philosophy that Griffin and Tamir betray do not undermine all their arguments, some of which I agree with. I find it impossible, however, to engage in a thoroughgoing discussion about the case for, and the nature and significance of group rights, and nothing less will do justice to their expressed concerns. I will have to confine myself to a few remarks, hoping that they will be understood as no more than a few observations which do not settle the main issues.

Griffin says:

What is special about these supposedly strong group goods is merely that their *description* refers to several individuals together as interacting parts of a functioning whole. It is not that their *value* cannot be reduced to individual values. The value of conviviality resides in the enjoyment that each individual experiences singly. The specialness in these goods is something conceptual. The point seems to be that we do not properly describe conviviality without introducing how the enjoyment of one person works to enhance the enjoyment of another, and so on. (167)

In other words, he thinks that the group aspect of the experience is in the way it is brought about. For example, and without implying that Griffin himself regards pleasure as a sensation, I can have a sensation of pleasure caused by eating an apple and a sensation of pleasure caused by being with other people. The pleasure is the same; the difference is in the cause. Were he right on that he would have also been right that there is nothing in that to support the case for

---

[11] My remarks here allow for instrumental justifications for some rights, and for such justification to affect the stringency of rights independently established. I was addressing only the question whether this is the only way to establish group rights.

the existence of any group right. But those who rely on such premises in arguing for certain group rights understand the case very differently. For them, the experience, the pleasure, itself is different. It is a pleasure in being in convivial company: the being in company is part of the experience (just as the pleasure in playing computer chess is different from the pleasure of walking by the river—they are not the same pleasure caused in different ways). Moreover, the pleasure of conviviality is necessarily shared—it is experienced by several people if it is experienced by anyone, and that itself is part of the experience, not merely of its cause.

Addressing himself specifically to my argument for a right to self-determination which depends, among other things, on the way people's prosperity and self-respect depends on how their encompassing group is doing, Griffin observes:

This suggests that standing behind the proposed right to self-determination, in those special circumstances in which such a right arises, is a broader right that one has to the prosperity and self respect of one's encompassing group. (169)

I agree that groups have no right to their prosperity. But the 'suggestion' he found in my argument is not there. It may betray the mistake[12] of thinking that a right can be justified only by another right. Hence, if a right to self-determination is justified by consideration of the prosperity of the group there must be a right to such prosperity. Alternatively, he may think that if I believe that the group interest in self-determination is a right, i.e. sufficient to impose duties on others, then I must think that the group interest in its prosperity also justifies such a duty. But that does not follow. Both points, if cogent, will entail that either individual rights entail that individuals have a right to their prosperity, or the value of individual prosperity cannot play any role in the justification of the existence of rights. The right to self-determination justifies duties when and because, according to my argument (in the paper jointly written with A. Margalit) it is the only practical way to secure freedom of the group from oppression and humiliation, which is usually the case where there has been a history of oppression, etc. It cannot possibly follow from that that encompassing groups have a general right to their prosperity.

Tamir advances powerful objections to accounts of rights which make their existence depend on the outcome of cost-benefit analyses. (194–6) She does not explain what she understands 'cost-benefit analysis' to be, but the context suggests that it is a view which regards all good and bad aspects of reality, or consequences of all actions to be fungible and measurable. If so, then whatever the merit of her criticism of cost-benefit-analysis based accounts of rights it does not apply to my account which is not committed to the fungibility and measurability of all good and bad aspects of the world. Her supposition that it is results from thinking either that if a right exists only if the reasons for its existence are better, or that if the reasons for and against its existence relate to the

---

[12] Which I discuss in 'Rights and Politics' (n. 9 above).

quality of human life, then its existence is based on cost-benefit analysis. But while such an account of the concept of rights is consistent with a cost-benefit analysis approach (and its compatibility with a variety of views about the reasons for the existence of rights is one of the strengths of the account) it is not committed to it (and I do not in fact accept it).

Griffin thinks that human rights and group rights protect not any kind of interest but only some special human interests. This may be true of human rights. But not even Griffin thinks that it is true of all rights. Why then does he think that group rights are like human rights in this respect? In the absence of an answer one suspects that in the background lies a certain privileging of rights as matters of exceptional importance. This is a familiar view (explicitly endorsed by Tamir), but not one which I share. However, this is yet another matter which cannot be thrashed out here.

This and other of the points made by Griffin and Tamir have to be resolved if we are to have a general theory of what kinds of group rights exist, let alone detailed arguments for the existence of some specific group rights. My interest in writing about group rights was (apart from the article on 'National Self-Determination'[13]) more limited. I was merely venturing an explanation of the concept of group rights. Griffin and Tamir's aim is not entirely clear to me.[14] They may have doubts whether and if so what group rights exist, or about the benefit of employing the concept, or of the adequacy of my explanation of the concept. But sometimes they appear to doubt the cogency of the concept itself, and it is that case which I am not sure they made.

Readers will know that both Tamir's and Griffin's articles, like those of other contributors to this volume, contain a great wealth of arguments, observations and suggestions, the bulk of which I did not as much as mention in my comments here. In fact, the best of the points made in the book went unmentioned here, simply because my task was of criticism, and the unrewarding aspect of that task is that it may leave, in this case the erroneous, impression that the writer failed to appreciate the true quality of the articles he commented on.

---

[13] (with A. Margalit) *Journal of Philosophy* 87(1990), 439.

[14] Much of their, especially of Tamir's, criticism of my view takes me to have advanced a theory about what collective rights there are, rather than an explanation of the concept of collective rights, and they rightly complain that many questions such a theory should answer remain unanswered in my writings. This suggests that their target may not be the concept but specific claims about the existence of certain collective rights.

Bibliography of the Works of Joseph Raz

I. Books
II. Books of Essays in Translation
III. Books and Chapters Edited
IV. Articles

Joseph Raz's articles and chapters of his books have been translated in many languages, including Bielorussian, Bulgarian, Chinese, Czech, French, German, Georgian, Hebrew, Italian, Japanese, Latvian, Lithuanian, Polish, Spanish, and Ukranian. Also, many of his articles and chapters have been reprinted. The bibliography does not list the translations and reprints of Raz's articles. Unless they were not published in English, we list where the articles were published first in English.[1]

I. BOOKS

The Concept of a Legal System. An Introduction to the Theory of a Legal System (Oxford: Clarendon Press, 1970, 2nd ed. 1980).
The Authority of Law (Oxford: Oxford University Press, 1979).
The Morality of Freedom (Oxford: Oxford University Press, 1986).
Ethics in the Public Domain (Oxford: Oxford University Press, 1994).
Practical Reason and Norms (London: Hutchinson, 1975, 2nd ed. Princeton: Princeton University Press, 1990, 3rd ed. Oxford: Oxford University Press, 1999).
Engaging Reason. On the Theory of Value and Action (Oxford: Oxford University Press, 2000).
Value, Respect, and Attachment (Cambridge: Cambridge University Press, 2001).

II. BOOKS OF ESSAYS IN TRANSLATION

Law as Authority. Essays in Jurisprudence (in Japanese), ed. by Mitsunori Fukada (Tokyo: Keiso Shobo, 1994).
Freedom and Rights. Essays in Political Philosophy (in Japanese), ed. by Yasutomo Morigiwa (Tokyo: Keiso Shobo, 1996).

III. BOOKS AND CHAPTERS EDITED

Law, Morality, and Society. Essays in Honour of H. L. A. Hart, ed. with P. M. S. Hacker (Oxford: Oxford University Press, 1977).

---

[1] We are grateful to Brian Bix, Chaim Gans, and Mitsunori Fukada for their help in putting together the bibliography. See also Joseph Raz's regularly updated bibliography at http://users.ox.ac.uk/~raz/.

Practical Reasoning (Oxford: Oxford University Press, 1978).
Authority (Oxford: Blackwell's Publishing, 1990).
Postscript to The Concept of Law by H.L.A. Hart, edited with P. A. Bulloch, published posthumously (Oxford: Oxford University Press, 1994), 238–76, 306–7.

IV. ARTICLES

'Cassirer's and Wittgenstein's Philosophies of Language' (in Hebrew), *Iyuun* 16 (1965), 69–99.
'Austin and the Sovereign's Power' (in Hebrew), *Mishpatim* 1 (1969), 372–9.
'Legal Principles and Judicial Discretion' (in Hebrew), *Mishpatim* 2 (1970), 317–28.
'On Lawful Government', *Ethics* (1970), 296–305.
'The Identity of Legal Systems', *California Law Review* 59 (1971), 795–815.
'Prof. Ross and Some Legal Puzzles', *Mind* 81 (1972), 415–21.
'Legal Principles and the Limits of Law', *Yale Law Journal* 81 (1972), 823–54.
'Voluntary Obligations and Normative Powers', *Aristotelian Society, Supplementary Vol.* 46 (1972), 79–102.
'On the Functions of Law', *Oxford Essays in Jurisprudence* (Second Series), ed. A. W. B. Simpson (Oxford: Oxford University Press, 1973), 278–304.
'Comment: Reasons, Requirements and Practical Conflicts', *Practical Reason*, ed. Stephan Körner (New Haven: Yale University Press, 1974, and Oxford: Blackwell Publishing, 1974), 22–35.
'Kelsen's Doctrine of the Basic Norm', *American Journal of Jurisprudence* 19 (1974), 94–111.
'The Institutional Nature of Law', *Modern Law Review* 38 (1975), 489–503.
'Permission and Supererogation', *American Philosophical Quarterly* 12 (1975), 161–8.
'Reasons, Decisions and Norms', *Mind* 84 (1975), 481–99.
'Kelsen's General Theory of Norms', *Philosophia* 6 (1976), 495–504.
'The Rule of Law and its Virtue', *Law Quarterly Review* 93 (1977), 195–211.
'Promises and Obligations', *Law, Morality, and Society. Essays in Honour of H. L. A. Hart*, ed. with P. M. S. Hacker (Oxford: Clarendon Press, 1977), 210–28.
'Legal Validity', *Archiv für Rechts- und Sozialphilosophie* 53 (1977), 339–52.
'On Legitimate Authority', *Philosophical Law. Authority, Equality, Adjudication, Privacy*, ed. Richard N. Bronaugh (Westport, CT: Greenwood Press, 1978).
'Prof. Dworkin's Theory of Rights', *Political Studies* 26 (1978), 123–37.
'Principles of Equality', *Mind* 87 (1978), 321–42.
'Introduction', *Practical Reasoning*, ed. Raz (Oxford: Oxford University Press, 1978), 1–17.
'Legal Reasons, Sources and Gaps', *Archiv für Rechts- und Sozialphilosophie* Beiheft 11 (1979), 197–215.
'Sources, Normativity and Individuation', Raz, *The Concept of a Legal System* (Oxford: Oxford University Press, 2nd ed. 1980), 209–38.
'Authority and Consent', *Virginia Law Review* 67 (1981), 103–31.
'The Purity of the Pure Theory', *Revue Internationale de Philosophie* 35 (1981), 441–59.
'Promises in Morality and Law' (Review of Patrick S. Atiyah, *Promises, Morals and Law* (Oxford: Oxford University Press, 1981), *Harvard Law Review* 95 (1982), 916–38.
'Liberalism, Autonomy and the Politics of Neutral Concern', *Midwest Studies in Philosophy* 7 (1982), 89–102.
'The Claims of Reflective Equilibrium', *Inquiry* 25 (1982), 307–30.
'The Problem about the Nature of Law', *Contemporary Philosophy. A New Survey, Vol. 3: Philosophy of Action*, ed. Guttorm Floeistad (Dordrecht: Kluwer, 1983), 107–25.

'Postscript to Legal Principles and the Limits of Law', *Dworkin and Contemporary Jurisprudence*, ed. Marshall Cohen (New Jersey: Rowman & Allanheld, 1983), 73–87.

'Legal Rights', *Oxford Journal of Legal Studies* 4 (1984), 1–21.

'Hart on Moral Rights and Legal Duties', *Oxford Journal of Legal Studies* 4 (1984), 123–31.

'On the Nature of Rights', *Mind* 93 (1984), 194–214.

'Right-based Morality', *Theories of Rights*, ed. Jeremy Waldron (Oxford: Oxford University Press, 1984), 182–200.

'The Obligation to Obey. Revision and Tradition', *Notre Dame Journal of Law Ethics & Public Policy* 1 (1984), 139–55.

'The Morality of Obedience', A Review of Philip Soper, *A Theory of Law* (Cambridge, Mass.: Harvard University Press, 1984), *Michigan Law Review* 83 (1985), 732–49.

'Authority and Justification', *Philosophy & Public Affairs* 14 (1985), 3–29.

'Authority, Law and Morality', *The Monist* 68 (1985), 295–324.

'Value Incommensurability. Some Preliminaries', *Proceedings of the Aristotelian Society* 86 (1985/6), 117–34.

'The Inner Logic of the Law', *Reason & Experience in Contemporary Legal Thinking*, ed. Torstein Eckhoff, Lawrence M. Friedman and Jyrki Uusitalo, Rechtstheorie Beiheft No. 10 (Berlin: Verlag Duncker & Humblot, 1986), 101–17.

'Dworkin: A New Link in the Chain', *California Law Review* 74 (1986), 1103–19.

'Autonomy, Toleration, and the Harm Principle', *Issues in Contemporary Legal Philosophy. The Influence of H. L. A. Hart*, ed. Ruth Gavison (Oxford: Clarendon Press, 1987), 313–33.

'Government by Consent', *Authority Revisited*, ed. J. Roland Pennock and John W. Chapman (New York: New York University Press, 1987), 76–95.

'Morality as Interpretation', Review of Michael Walzer, Interpretation & Social Criticism (Cambridge, Mass.: Harvard University Press, 1987), *Ethics* 101 (1991) 392–405.

'Liberating Duties', *Law & Philosophy* 8 (1989), 3–21.

'Facing Up: A Reply', *Southern California Law Review* 62 (1989), 1153–235.

'Liberalism, Skepticism and Democracy', *Iowa Law Review* 74 (1989) 761–86.

'Facing Diversity: The Case of Epistemic Abstinence', *Philosophy & Public Affairs* 19 (1990), 3–46.

'Rethinking Exclusionary Reasons', Raz, *Practical Reason and Norms* (2nd ed. Princeton: Princeton University Press, 1990), 178–99.

(with A. Margalit), 'National Self-Determination', *Journal of Philosophy* 87 (1990), 439–61.

'Introduction', *Authority*, ed. Raz (Oxford: Blackwells 1990), 1–19.

'The Politics of the Rule of Law', *Ratio Juris* 3 (1990) 331–9.

'Mixing Values', *Aristotelian Society, Supplementary Vol.* 65 (1991) 83–100.

'Free Expression and Personal Identification', *Oxford Journal of Legal Studies* 11 (1991), 303–24.

'Formalism and the Rule of Law', *Natural Law Theory*, ed. Richard P. George (Oxford: Oxford University Press, 1992), 309–40.

'The Relevance of Coherence', *Boston University Law Review* 72 (1992), 273–321.

'Rights and Individual Well-Being', *Ratio Juris* 5 (1992), 127–42.

'H.L.A. Hart' (1907–1992), *Utilitas* 5 (1993), 145–56.

'On The Autonomy of Legal Reasoning', *Ratio Juris* 6 (1993), 1–15.

'Multiculturalism: A Liberal Perspective', *Recht in een multiculturele samenleving*, N.J.H. Huls & H.D. Stout (eds.) (Zwolle: W.E.J. Tjeenk Willink, 1993), 127–48.

'A Morality Fit for Humans', Review of Samuel Scheffler, *Human Morality* (New York: Oxford University Press, 1992), *Michigan Law Review* 91 (1993), 1297–314.

'Moral Change and Social Relativism', *Cultural Pluralism and Moral Knowledge*, eds. Ellen Fraenkel Paul, Fred D. Miller, Jeffrey Paul (Cambridge: Cambridge University Press, 1994), 139–58.

'Interpretation Without Retrieval', *Law & Interpretation*, ed. A. Marmor (Oxford: Oxford University Press, 1995), 155–75.

'Rights and Politics', *Indiana Law Review* 71 (1995), 27–44.

'On the Nature of Law' (The Kobe Lectures for Legal and Social Philosophy of 1994), *Archiv für Rechts und Sozialphilosophie* 82 (1996), 1–25.

'Intention in Interpretation', *The Autonomy of Law*, ed. Richard P. George (Oxford: Oxford University Press, 1996), 249–86.

'The Moral Point of View', *Reason, Ethics and Society. Themes from Kurt Baier, with His Responses*, ed. J. B. Schneewind (Chicago: Open Court 1996) 84–116.

'The Importance of Rights and their Limits', *Western Rights, Post-Communist Application*, ed. Andra Sajo (The Hague: Kluwer Law International 1996), ix–xviii.

'Liberty and Trust', *Natural Law, Liberalism and Morality. Contemporary Essays*, ed. Richard P. George (Oxford: Oxford University Press, 1996), 113–29.

'Why Interpret', *Ratio Juris* 9 (1996), 349–63.

'When We are Ourselves: The Active and The Passive', *Aristotelian Society, Supplementary Vol.* 71 (1997), 211–29.

'The Amoralist', *Ethics and Practical Reason*, eds. Garrett Cullity and Berys Gaut (Oxford: Oxford University Press, 1997), 369–98.

'Postema on Law's Autonomy and Public Practical Reasons. A Critical Comment', *Legal Theory* 4 (1998), 1–20.

'Incommensurability and Agency', *Incommensurability, Incomparability and Practical Reason*, ed. Ruth Chang (Cambridge, Mass.: Harvard University Press, 1998), 110–28.

'On the Authority and Interpretation of Constitutions: Some Preliminaries', *Constitutionalism. Philosophical Foundations*, ed. Larry Alexander (Cambridge University Press, 1998), 152–93.

'Two Views of the Nature of the Theory of Law: A Partial Comparison', *Legal Theory* 4 (1998), 249–82.

'Multiculturalism', *Ratio Juris* 11 (1998), 193–205.

'Disagreement in Politics', *The American Journal of Jurisprudence* 43 (1998), 25–52.

'Explaining Normativity. On Rationality and the Justification of Reason', *Ratio Juris* 12 (1999), 354–79.

'The Central Conflict: Morality and Self-Interest', *Well-Being and Morality. Essays in Honour of James Griffin*, ed. Roger Crisp and Brad Hooker (Oxford: Clarendon Press, 2000), 209–38.

'On the Socratic Maxim', *Notre Dame Law Review* 75 (2000), 1797–806.

'The Truth in Particularism', *Moral Particularism*, ed. Brad Hooker & Margaret Olivia Little (Oxford: Oxford University Press, 2000), 48–78.

'Notes on Value and Objectivity', *Objectivity in Law and Morals*, ed. Brian Leiter (Cambridge: Cambridge University Press, 2000), 194–233.

'Reasoning with Rules', *Current Legal Problems* 54 (2001), 1–18.

'The Practice of Value', *The Tanner Lectures on Human Values*, Vol. 23, ed. Grethe B. Peterson (Salt Lake City, UT: University of Utah Press, 2002), 113–50.

'On Frankfurt's Explanation of Respect for People', *Contours of Agency. Essays on Themes from Harry Frankfurt*, ed. Sarah Buss and Lee Overton (Cambridge, Mass.: MIT Press 2002), 299–315.

Index

Printed in the United Kingdom
by Lightning Source UK Ltd.
114037UKS00001B/156